TOPOTHESIA

Topothesia

PLANNING, COLONIALISM, AND PLACES IN EXCESS

Ameeth Vijay

FORDHAM UNIVERSITY PRESS NEW YORK 2023

Copyright © 2023 Fordham University Press

Fordham University Press gratefully acknowledges financial assistance and support provided for the publication of this book by The University of California, San Diego.

All rights reserved. No part of this publication may be reproduced, stored in a retrieval system, or transmitted in any form or by any means—electronic, mechanical, photocopy, recording, or any other—except for brief quotations in printed reviews, without the prior permission of the publisher.

Fordham University Press has no responsibility for the persistence or accuracy of URLs for external or third-party Internet websites referred to in this publication and does not guarantee that any content on such websites is, or will remain, accurate or appropriate.

Fordham University Press also publishes its books in a variety of electronic formats. Some content that appears in print may not be available in electronic books.

Visit us online at www.fordhampress.com.

Library of Congress Cataloging-in-Publication Data available online at https://catalog.loc.gov.

Printed in the United States of America

25 24 23   5 4 3 2 1
First edition

Contents

Introduction 1

Part I: Improving Places: Liberal Colonialism and the Speculative Imaginary of Early Planning

1. Garden Cities: The Art and Craft of Making Place in Edwardian Britain 31

2. Planning as Imperial Cultivation in the Work of Patrick Geddes 60

Part II: Diminishing Horizons: The Ambivalent Temporalities of Development

3. Capturing the City: Regeneration, Policing, and the Ghosts of Postcolonial Britain 95

4. The End of London: Temporalities of the Gentrified City 126

5. Level Up: Zadie Smith's NW and the Promise of Progression 158

6. Geographies of Discontent: Brexit and the Politics of Abandonment 185

Coda 215

ACKNOWLEDGMENTS 221

NOTES 225

BIBLIOGRAPHY 285

INDEX 308

TOPOTHESIA

Introduction: Topothesia
Planning, Colonialism, and Places in Excess

In the summer of 2013, the Southbank Centre in London hosted a series of temporary, "pop-up" installations that they called the Festival of Neighborhood. This festival vaguely recalled the Festival of Britain, held in 1951—a grand exhibition of science, technology, architecture, and design intended to reflect and reproduce sentiments of postwar and postausterity national revival.[1] If that seminal event reflected and reproduced the tenor of the incipient welfare state in a postwar (and increasingly postimperial) Britain, in its own smaller way, the Festival of Neighborhood spoke to the aesthetic and economics of contemporary urban development.

Sponsored by MasterCard, the "neighborhood" referred not only to South Bank but to neighborhoods as locations in general: "Come along and get involved in celebrating our neighbourhood, your own and neighbourhoods across the world."[2] The aesthetic of the exhibition was deeply garden-centric, playing plants and trees off the austere concrete surroundings to connote a sense of revival.[3] They encouraged visitors to "relax in one of London's best-kept secret gardens on top of the Queen Elizabeth Hall: vegetable plots mingle with wildflowers—and a rooftop cafe nestles under scented bowers. This summer, the garden extends across to the Hayward Gallery with a peaceful Woodland Garden."[4] In producing these exhibitions, artists and groups like Wayward Plants, the Edible Bus Stop, and What If: Projects blurred planning, architectural, and artistic practice (see Figure 1, Figure 2a, and Figure 2b).[5] The garden aesthetic was put in service of a spatial and social project, the revitalization of (implicitly decayed or dead) locations and, it is implied, the people in those locations.

For example, *Octavia's Orchard*, by What If: Projects, sought to revive the

Figure 1. "Roll Out the Barrows" (Mak Gilchrist for the Edible Bus Stop). An exhibition for the Southbank Centre's Festival of Neighbourhood (2013).

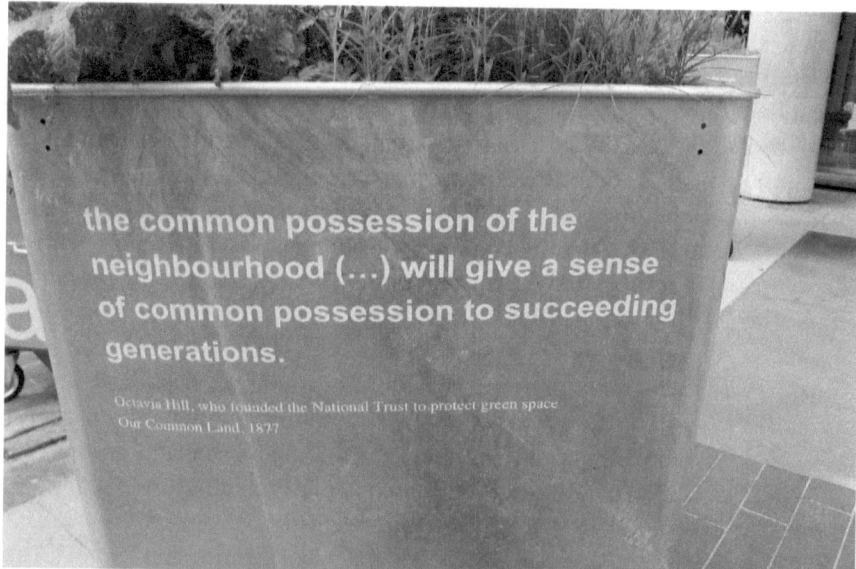

Figure 2a. "Octavia's Orchard" (What If: Projects). An exhibition for the Southbank Centre's Festival of Neighbourhood (2013).

Figure 2b. "Octavia's Orchard" (What If: Projects). An exhibition for the Southbank Centre's Festival of Neighbourhood (2013).

legacy of Octavia Hill, the relentlessly moralizing late-Victorian social philanthropist discussed, among her cohort, in Chapter 1. This installation consisted in tree saplings in concrete planters, which featured quotations from Hill, such as her 1888 remark that "there are indeed many good things in life which may be unequally apportioned and no such serious loss arise, but the need of quiet, the need of air, the need of exercise, and, I believe, the sight of sky and of things growing, seem human needs, common to all."[6] Hill refers here to the notorious inequality of Victorian London, with its mansions and slums, which at the time seemed to want to apportion unequally not only material wealth but also breathable air. However, she justifies the inequality of classes through the suggestion of an urban pastoral, which, through restoring to the working classes such things as air, views of the sky, and things growing, would satisfy human needs, beyond which there could be no further complaint.

What If: Projects further condenses this visuality into the image of a single tree set against the backdrop of a council estate. Once adopted, they write that the estates that adopt these trees would be further given "support and training from [the National Trust's] expert gardeners."[7] They continue, "Our work is focused in inner city areas and we develop ideas and strategies for more sustainable urban environments. We investigate neglected, forgotten and unloved spaces and develop opportunities these places can offer to communities and the city. Proposals for change are based on a detailed understanding of an environment and the people that inhabit it. Essential to the development and delivery of our projects is the engagement with local communities."[8] What If: Projects continues what is a long tradition of philanthropically minded designers venturing into neglected, forgotten, and unloved spaces in order to plant some trees. These trees stand in for a future council estate garden, one that, through planting and pedagogy, will also help cultivate individuals and (local) communities reconciled to, as the Hill quotation suggests, the inequality of a neoliberal London.[9]

These neo-Victorian interventions speak in the idiom of contemporary development in the "world city," a nexus of global investment, public-private initiatives, and real estate. This discourse refers to a city (once again) in *ruin*. This was recognized by Tony Blair at Aylesbury Estate in his first major speech as prime minister, where he said that there would be "no no-hope areas" and "no forgotten people in the Britain I want to build."[10] Blair used the setting—a large, working-class council estate—as a symbol not only for urban decay but for social fracture in general. That is, the massive concrete structures of the estate concretized a host of political concerns while at the same time transforming them into a generalizable affect, something that could be felt as a problem even if the solutions were hazy. This gesture was repeated thirteen years later in 2010, as David Cameron launched the ultimately successful "Broken Brit-

Figure 3. The future Battersea Power Station development.

ain" political campaign at the defunct Battersea Power Station (Figure 3), similarly making promises to forgotten people and places in a "country in need of regeneration."[11] In both cases, urban "regeneration" operated as an inarguable solution to the universally recognized problem of ruin and decay, both expressed through metonymic urban landscapes. Both politicians suggest a latent vitality exists among the city's postindustrial ruins, waiting to be revived. Developers, planners, and designers accordingly offer up speculative visions of the future city, a revitalized epicenter of culture, education, and innovation amid glass towers with green rooftops. What is undisclosed is the production of the gentrified global city: a space of information and service economies, of consumption, tourism, speculative investment, and housing insecurity.

This book tracks this constellation of ideas, ideology, practices, and aesthetics through the twentieth century to the contemporary moment. "Topothesia" is a rhetorical device referring to the vivid depiction of an often-imaginary place.[12] This book uses the term to theorize urban planning as a mode of speculative fiction, one that, even in its most mundane documents, is compelled to produce elaborate fantasies of future places. As topothesia, the imaginaries of planning and contemporary development are tightly linked to histories and practices of liberal colonialism, from the nineteenth century to the present day. I link the archive of planning theory in the late British Empire to contemporary practices of urban development in order to understand more generally the form and the stakes of their speculative worlds. Planning allows

Figure 4. An advertisement for Letchworth Garden City.

for the construction of future places that are both utopian in their ability to resolve political disagreement and at the same time tantalizingly realizable. In building these worlds, I further find that planners continually co-opted literary critiques of the present and reveries of the future, retaining that literature's aesthetics while eschewing its politics. This speculative imaginary, I argue, is only possible within the ideological framework of colonialism and the history of empire within which it developed.

I trace planning from its rise as a global profession in the early twentieth century to current practices of capitalist development in the twenty-first. Beginning with the influential garden-city movement, early planning unsurprisingly inscribed the cultural prerogatives of the late empire into its presumptions about what *place* was and what it could do. Though planning grew further into a humanistic and technocratic practice, *Topothesia* argues that these early inscriptions, assumptions, and imaginaries continue to shape contemporary development.[13] The professional infrastructure of town planning that develops in the early twentieth century (journals, conferences, university positions, government offices, etc.) emerges as a response to the problem of the slum, a figure that condenses economic inequality in a spatial form. In isolating this figure, incipient planners like Ebenezer Howard and Patrick Geddes sought to resolve and reconcile the effects of capitalism through a conception of future places whose realization could be brought about by the art of planning rather than through political agitation (see Figure 4 and Figure 5). Accordingly, I argue that both metropole and colony were subject to

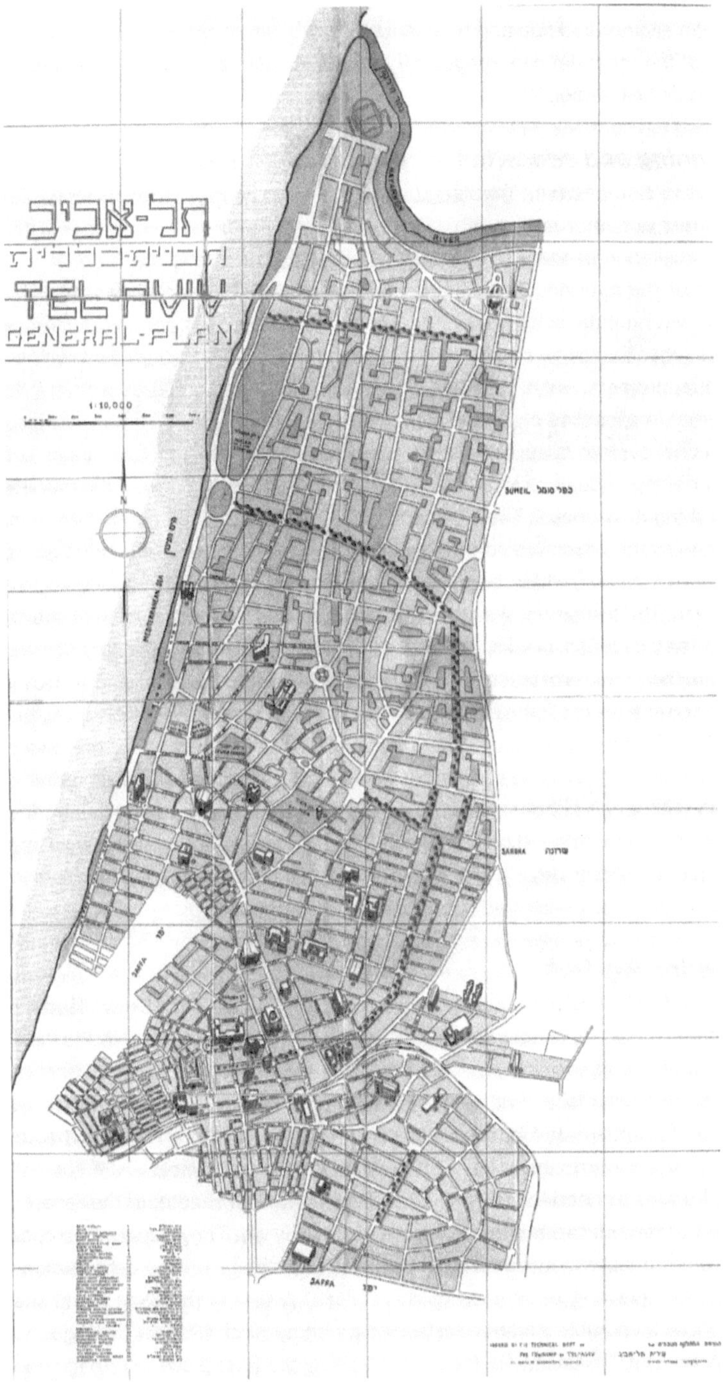

Figure 5. Patrick Geddes's plan for Tel Aviv.

the same practices of spatial formation and often for the same reason: the resolution of political tension through an apolitical imaginary of place.

Part I of the book considers these early practices, while Part II shows they inform contemporary urban development and the processes of gentrification. Analysis of contemporary urban development and gentrification discloses ongoing practices of colonialism. Throughout, imperial and postimperial Britain serves as a metonym for the enterprise of urban development more broadly. The early work of British planning was particularly influential in establishing planning as a professional discipline, one separate from other fields like architecture and necessary for the operations of the state. The colonies served as a zone where early practitioners could test theories and models and develop global professional links. At the same time, as a field and set of practices, urban planning is obviously not limited to the space and history of colonial and postcolonial Britain. Despite areas of influence and overlap, planning and development in Global North spaces clearly reflect differences in the policies of the state and particular histories. Similarly, not only do different postcolonial spaces differ in their relationships to former European empires, but patterns of contemporary development vary tremendously within each particular context. Keeping these limitations in mind, *Topothesia* situates its analysis within the field of British postcolonial studies while also considering how these dynamics relate to concerns within urban studies more broadly.

The Speculative Fictions of Place

Topothesia is not a historical account of this gap between the vivid fiction of place and its reality but rather reads this gap as a literary index of planning's governing, multiple, contradictory epistemologies. It reads the proliferation of planning theory, documents, advertising, etc. as themselves concretizations of political futurity, even when avowedly apolitical—that is, as ways of understanding what places should be, for whom they should be for, and what they should look like. Planning-as-literature, therefore, deemphasizes narrative control, including assumptions of top-down intentionality, while remaining attentive to what its speculative ideas foreclose in their pursuit of a particular future.

The speculative has many modes. Just as planning can be viewed as a kind of speculative fiction, so too have the various literary genres of the speculative framed their imaginings through reference to place. That is, planning is not just analogous to literary speculative fiction, but the two have an interwoven history and epistemology. Since Thomas More's *Utopia* and certainly from its emergence as a mass-marketed genre in the nineteenth century, fantastical, speculative, and scientific fiction have been literary modes used to imagine utopia (or dystopia). These speculations have included extrapolations of technological development and exaggerations of political ideology. They have also tracked closely with the epistemology of "discovery," that is, of colonialism.[14] The colonial epistemological mode of charting and surveying "new" worlds found its way, for example, into the pulp adventures of H. Rider Haggard, Arthur Conan Doyle, and Robert Louis Stevenson, authors who rendered imperialism into fantasies for "big and little boys" (in the words of Haggard's protagonist Allan Quatermain).[15] Others in this time period, however, used the speculative as a way of critiquing the present and/or imagining otherwise. For writers like H. G. Wells and William Morris, the fantastical and speculative become a place to foreground the brutal power dynamics of imperialism (for example, in Wells's *War of the Worlds*) or explore the potentialities of anarchocommunism (in Morris's *News from Nowhere*, as discussed further in Chapter 1).[16]

The more contemporary appellation "speculative fiction," then, gathers under its label various kinds of science fiction, fantasy, and adventure literature.[17] As capacious as the term is already, it can be productively expanded to define modes of imagining and the way in which the explicitly literary is entwined with ways of perceiving, anticipating, and relating to future places. Shelley Streeby, for example, notes that for more contemporary authors the speculative prompts a "move off the page," becoming, for example, intersectional feminist practice for writers like Octavia Butler.[18] The visionary space opened up by fiction is one that allows for world making in the present, a chance to think and imagine otherwise. As such a mode of world making, the speculative can be particularly generative for already marginalized subjects.

Given this, as a literary characterization, *speculative fiction* does more than group together and extend genres of science fiction and fantasy. Rather, it conceives of the speculative as the aesthetic means to a specific, if open-ended, political project. Thus, the fabulations and wish landscapes of speculative fiction connect to everyday attempts to imagine otherwise and conjure an *elsewhere* in the space of the here and now, as José Muñoz argues. Muñoz deploys Ernst Bloch's formulation of a concrete utopia to think about spaces of queer performance and possibility. He writes that "in our everyday life abstract utopias are akin to banal optimism," while "concrete utopias can also be daydreaming-like, but they are hopes of a collective, an emergent group, or even the solitary oddball who is the one who dreams for many."[19] Utopia, here, is not a fully realized, imaginary place but rather a gesture, one that has an everyday quality and is found in ordinary contexts (for Muñoz, the stages of Los Angeles's Spaceland, for Bloch, in fairytales, folklore, and daydreams).

Bloch's everyday "wish landscapes" simultaneously imagine and give access to an imagination of a world that is otherwise.[20] As daydreams, they are ephemeral and separated from reality in their own enclave.[21] Concrete utopias are the thought bubbles in comics, dots connecting to a wish landscape of ambiguous status, one that can vanish and return. Placeless as it seems, this wish landscape is also another place. In this sense, the concrete utopia is both similar to and different from Michel Foucault's concept of heterotopia, which he articulates as the coexistence of multiple incompatible spaces in one, real, heterogeneous space.[22] The heterotopia is marked by a *relation* to other sites and to other temporalities; similarly, concrete utopias like daydreams exist as an imaginary elsewhere in the time and space of the present. On the other hand, a heterotopia relates a heterogeneous multiplicity within a self-same space—for example, the uncanniness of a museum, or cemetery, or airport. In contrast, the concrete utopia, as utopia, concerns itself with creating totality within an enclave—even if that enclave lacks permanence, even if it is tethered to "reality" only through looking away.[23] That is, the realness and realizability of the concrete utopia is less important than the act of imagining a possible other world. The act of imagining itself indicates that there is "something missing," as Theodor Adorno says in conversation with Bloch. Where this "something missing" would ordinarily produce alienation, the concrete utopia directs the subject toward possibility.

The opacity of a liberatory future, the future of "another world" that we are told is possible yet seems hopelessly impractical, "utopian" even, can still be placed in relation to the present. It's just that, as Kara Keeling writes, this is a relation between incommensurable temporalities.[24] This is especially true for marginalized subjects. She writes, "Black futures exist 'after the future,' blossoming in spite of what presently seems destined to be the future ... as a historical production open to both Fanonian invention as well as capture, 'Black existence' anchors an opacity that invites and frustrates knowledge, transparency, and measure." This blossoming is for the sake of opening up "radical rupture within the quotidian, one that harbors presently impossible possibilities." Citing Bloch and Munoz here, she posits a "utopian project that might activate what is 'no longer conscious' in the past in interest of moving toward a 'not yet here.'"[25] Adrienne Brown ties this relationship to the future more explicitly to the architectural structures and infrastructures of modernity, specifically the skyscraper. Considering investments in the skyscraper by Black authors, artists, and thinkers, Brown notes how they "cast the skyscraper as an instrument for future-gazing, figuring it as a site for imagining if not utopia, then a more inclusive configuration of affiliation to come."[26]

The speculative temporality of the "not yet" is central to Bloch's formulation of "anticipatory illumination." Keeling understands the "not yet" not just in terms of the future but as drawing together those elements of the past that have been marginalized by the procession of a normative, straight temporality of progress. That is, the "not yet" is the possibility culled from the ruins and rubble of capitalism and colonialism.[27] Aimee Bahng cogently articulates this relationship:

> By enjambing these two formulations of the not yet—one that seeks to illuminate histories of empire and exclusion, and another that insists on futurity as an opening up rather than a closing down—I want to consider the relationship between the waiting room and the horizon. For it is precisely in the exile's relation to time—the point at which one is pushed out of what could be called straight time, settler time, or the profitable time of compound interest—that one can glimpse the horizon of the not yet, where not yet manifests itself not as a decree of foreclosure but as an embrace of the unknown.[28]

Bahng here speaks to the subaltern potential of speculative fiction—how the "not yet" of the speculative in fact illuminates that which has been left mute in what Dipesh Chakrabarty calls the "waiting room of history," projecting them into the future in messianic fashion. In that sense, speculation is a potentially provincializing gesture and as such enables queer, migrant, and subaltern temporalities.[29]

Yet these potentialities, everyday as they are, are discernable only as a silhouette against the actualities of capitalism and colonialism, which operate both as hegemonic social fact and also through their own imaginative, speculative futures.[30] Their speculation is not only about securing a realizable future but is also an intervention in the present, as a necessary orientation toward an imagined horizon. The speculative mode is politically ambivalent: Capitalist development also creates horizons for the future of the built environment in ways that constrain and discipline the "not yet" of the future. As such, not even the completion or exact realization of development projects is necessary to their efficacy.[31] Rather, through planning documents, illustrated models, advertisements, and political campaigns, they illuminate a possible near future.[32] There is thus a mutual imbrication of different kinds of not-yets that both liberate and govern the subject from the position of the future(s).[33] These futures compel both stasis (as both entrapment and stability) and movement (as both freedom and dislocation) for subjects that are "stuck in situations of ambivalence."[34] Through an analysis of urban development, this book tracks the speculative as both an opening up *and* a closing down of possibility. In fact, throughout, I am drawn to moments in texts that point to the *indiscernibility* of those gestures. The creative texts I consider, especially in Part II of the book, do not fall under the genre rubric of "speculative fiction" but rather speak to how the speculative forms ambiguous horizons for the contemporary subject. In many ways they invert the expected effects of the speculative, saturating the future with anxiety and worry and the past with disappointment and regret.

In the remainder of this Introduction, I discuss the main themes of the book along with summaries of each chapter. The individual chapters concentrate these themes and aspects of my broader argument, but these themes resonate throughout. For example, as you will see in the next section, the first chapter of the book explores the processes of an urban liberal colonialism via the particular way that a set of colonial practices and ideologies took Britain itself as an object for its interventions. However, the themes of interior colonization and liberal improvement are present throughout the book and certainly return when I consider the role of contemporary capitalist development, both in the urban center of the world city (Chapter 4) and in the reification of the rural countryside (Chapter 6). Through introducing the argument in this way, I hope to show that the structure of the book—including its temporal, geographic, and cultural scope—is an integral part of its argument. The way that the book's central themes echo throughout correspond to the hopes of development, which always projects itself doing better next time as it speculates upon and creates the profitable ruins of the future.

As I establish throughout the book, planning took a particular role in the management of *excess*. For example, in Chapters 1 and 2, I show how the figure of the slum emerges in the writing of early planners as one that is excessive in a variety of ways—a space extraneous to the workings of the circulatory city, containing subjects whose marginality positioned them outside the social order.[35] The solution to this problem—liberal colonization—aimed at either integrating these subjects or formalizing their externality (for example, in the space of the colony). Contemporary development bears the trace of this concern over excess in its *neoliberal* colonizations, as it works to further define and segment space, at times for the putative sake of reintegrating marginalized subjects and at other times formalizing their exclusion. These aspects of planning and development can certainly be productively analyzed through a Foucauldian lens, as the management and rationalization of space and the (re)production of particular biopolitical regimes that enfolded subjects within regimes of class, race, and sexuality across the empire and at "home."[36] Yet through close analysis of the aesthetics of planning, I find a parallel rhetorical and epistemological mode: topothesia, which is a description that refers not just to place but to an imagined place, in a vivid and lively way. That is, it is ironically the language of liberal-colonial planning and development that is itself *excessive* as it attempts to evoke a reconciliatory, quasi-utopic future. This produces texts that are at times irrational, contradictory, and wildly speculative even as, and in fact *because*, they seek to formalize excess. This aesthetic corresponds to an epistemology that is everywhere concerned with preserving and reproducing authentic locality, including the informality of the quotidian everyday. Thus, I argue that the aesthetic mode of the speculative and the political status of the local are far more vexed than it would seemingly appear.

At stake is the reproduction of community and identity: the way these can be managed and controlled but also how they can be imagined, formed through affect, and marked by multiple forms of relationality, some incompletely hegemonic, others haltingly gestural and directed to a not (yet) present "otherwise." Community, especially its will to plenitude and completion, has a troubled relationship to its outside: marked as excess, situated either externally or at a border, the outside both challenges and defines the homogeneity of the ideal community.[37] Yet even that which is at one time heterogeneous and marginal can be placed in relation to community; for particular subjects marked as such, this relation is fraught with ambivalence.[38] To affirm this ambivalence, somewhat, is to exist in a negative community: a community without community, relation without relation, heterogeneity without heterogeneity. The *without* is existence that jumps between the poles of excess and absence without traversing the intermediary distance.

This existence might be considered, at least partially, through formations of Blochian "hope," in the joyful, excessive ephemerality of performance or the modes of investing in the present provided by the imagining-otherwise of speculative fiction. As open-ended as these formulations are, however, they imply a resolving, at least temporarily, of an ultimately unresolvable ambivalence. As such, much of the literature and film I consider in this book does not take the form of speculative fiction's more usual genres (science fiction, utopian fiction, etc.), nor does it only register processes of anticipatory illumination in its more hopeful articulations. Rather it is work that *responds*, from the borders of community, to the not-yet of a hegemonic discourse. It exists in the shadows of the vivid, speculative imaginations and illuminations of development and planning programs. From those shadows, the not-yet of neoliberalism is a cruel optimism, one that governs the formation and relationality of subjects *without* justice.[39] This produces affects that are similarly ambivalent: ambulatory hope and pleasure but also anxiety, worry, inadequacy—not-yets whose potentiality is offered but always-already foreclosed.[40]

Cultivating Locality

Topothesia argues that planning, as a technical practice, also necessitates the imagining of other, future spaces and worlds and speculating as to future possibilities. These elements of planning draw from utopian fiction that locates the ideal society in a time and a place outside *of* and closed off *from* the deprivations of the contemporary. Planning, as it develops into a profession in the early twentieth century, instead seeks to reconcile utopia with the reality of the mundane, and in doing so it "places" its interventions in real spaces (the slum, the colony) and real times (the near future). Questions of geography, expressed in the dialogic relationship of town and country, have long been central to the concerns of cultural studies and British historiography. The relationship can be analyzed with regard to its concrete political economy (the processes of enclosure, industrial transformation, relation to empire) but also, per Raymond Williams, as a structure of feeling.[41] This structure of feeling forms a loop in which an idealized past gives way to a ruined present and becomes both identity and ideology. Within this, planning offers itself as a future-oriented reconciliation, a way to revitalize both town and country not in negative reaction to modernity but through it. As David Matless argues, planning was never opposed to the preservation of natural spaces; rather, both planning and preservation were attempts to reconcile the antinomies of modernity into a harmonious future.[42]

Topothesia understands the practice of town and country planning not only in the context of the transformation of space but as related to the uses of culture by the state. As David Lloyd and Paul Thomas have argued, culture in the Victorian era served to mediate the interests of the state and the formation of the subject.[43] Culture works as a form of *cultivation* of the individual, integrating them into civil and political society. This encapsulates the state's disposition toward both the working classes and colonial subjects as subjects in need of improvement. As Chapters 1 and 2 will discuss, in the context of colonization, "improvement" and "cultivation" first referred to land, property, and place. Brenna Bhandar writes that whereas those who improved the land-as-property "were deemed to be the proper subjects of law and history, those who did not were deemed to be in need of improvement as much as their waste lands were."[44] At the same time, this ideology of improvement was not merely repressive. As Tania Li writes, "The objective of trusteeship is not to dominate others—it is to enhance their capacity for action, and to direct it . . . their intentions are benevolent, even utopian. They desire to make the world better than it is."[45] Within this context, planning is not just the technical management of space but a framework within which to understand the cultivation of individuals and societies. Incidentally, the pathos of the garden as a verdant environment of natural abundance and harmony neatly aligns with the ideology of cultivation.

As Chapter 1 discusses, early planning grew as an extension of nineteenth-century social philanthropy movements, including the work of Octavia Hill, who took up the work of "improving" the so-called deserving poor, which quickly came to involve also improving their urban environments and their housing.[46] The garden city, first proposed in 1898, was thus a particular kind of solution: urban yet away from the metropolis, verdant and healthy, and capable of producing, through its very design, social harmony.[47] If the beginnings of professional planning in the late nineteenth century saw attempts to concretize a quasi-utopian imaginary in *real places*, it also operated according to the logic of liberal colonialism. Moreover, throughout *Topothesia* I consider the way this imaginary was presented as a reconciliation of political conflict and disagreement.[48] Whether in regards to working-class agitation in late-nineteenth-century British cities, anticolonial movements in the Raj, or the contemporary politics of space, housing, and migration, the creation of new, planned spaces continually promised to displace conflict and integrate dissatisfied subjects.

This is not just the nexus of capitalism and extractive imperialism but refers to a way of understanding social relations within this nexus. Specifically, liberal colonial endeavors are those that seek to *improve* and *develop* people and places.[49] It takes hold in the nineteenth century but evinces clear through lines to the present and encompasses a range of interventions, some more "progressive" and others more reactionary, but all self-conceptualized as a will to improve. Through imagining a future and working to create it, planning stages improvement both in the speculative models and theories on paper and in the "real" places created.

This imagination of "other" worlds, meanwhile, aligned with the colonial mode of discovery as the space of the colonies was speculatively imagined, slowly mapped, articulated in advance, and used as a social laboratory.[50] Accordingly, planning as a profession had antecedents in the many proposed and realized forms of colonization, from the planned settlements and cities of Australia to the extensive discourse on appropriate architecture in the imperial Raj.[51] Thus early-twentieth-century planners drew on more established epistemologies when they encountered supposedly blank spaces or spaces that could be both preserved and improved through their subsumption within empire and responded with surveys and speculation.

The utopian modes and colonial ethos of high-modernist planning has often been criticized as being overly top-down and too detached from on-the-ground practicalities to fully understand the implications of their grand projects.[52] High modernism was a state-led, technocratic enterprise that envisioned a "sweeping, rational engineering of all aspects of social life in order to improve the human condition."[53] As David C. Scott argues, its epistemic perspective is encoded in its documents: name registries, agricultural and forestry surveys, colonial landholding records, five-year plans, and maps. The aesthetic of those maps spoke to the abstract, repetitive logic of planning and its fixation with order, symmetry, and geometry, all grasped from a "God's-eye view, or the view of an absolute ruler," which, through reference to scientific progress, "disallow other competing sources of judgment" and "banish politics."[54] This critique of planning helpfully illustrates how the top-down, transformative perspective of state planning can be colonialist and as a practical matter fail to create spaces that fully engage with the local histories and everyday, lived experiences of residents.[55] Elleke Boehmer and Dominic Davis have recently characterized this dynamic as "planned violence," referencing the critique of colonial urban development. They share with the above critiques a sense of the "contingency of these rationalist, geometric planning regimes," emphasizing, in opposition, that "the array of informal social and economic activities that undercut and override the once-colonial city captures a different and more enabling notion of infrastructure."[56] Dipesh Chakrabarty further offers a postcolonial critique of colonial abstraction by considering affective histories—encoded in "bodily habits" and "collective practices"—of the Global South's alternative modernities.[57]

Topothesia, however, turns to planning in its more formative moments and in its contemporary instantiations to show that the "local" was and is a central concern and object of knowledge for planning and development. I argue that it was not the case that the technocratic and colonial practice of planning simply vacated the local from a lofty position and perspective. Similarly, the local cannot be characterized as simply those informal, everyday practices that remained outside the scope of the modern state; nor can it been considered as a straightforward vector of recalcitrance and resistance.[58] Rather, an analysis of the top-down, synoptic perspective of the state that aimed to produce systemized, global knowledge needs to be put into relation with an entire discourse of locality, informality, place, and particularity. Overdetermined in this way, the local becomes a way for planning to mitigate its own high-modernist tendencies, balancing the geometry of its plans with the aesthetic vibrancy and immediacy that attends to locality and place. As such, instead of sweeping away the local, planners have been continually engaged in preserving locality in its varied forms.

The combined discourse and aesthetics of urban development are a speculative mode of understanding place. Early-twentieth-century planners like Howard and Patrick Geddes (Chapter 2) used diagrammatic models, richly detailed practical-theoretical texts, and pedagogic lectures and conversations to impress the importance of town and country planning to their fellow middle-class elites, both in Britain and the wider empire. If "topothesia" refers to the vivid description of an imaginary place, the intensity and particularity of the *description* is what nourishes the aesthetic potential of the *place*. In these moments, the putatively dry, technical discourse of planning becomes excessive in its florid attention to detail, evoking a futurity that is sensuous and tangible, promising a utopia that is not distant but just over the horizon. This mode of speculation has been pluralized and carried into the contemporary practice of development. For example, as Hannah Appel writes, "the development plan is both speculative in itself (in that its execution is not possible given current investment conditions . . .) and reliant on the speculation of others, aimed to seduce speculative capital."[59]

Finally, this book does not necessarily follow the conventional (if multiple) conceptions of "space" versus "place" in critical discourse. The former is often conceived as abstract, detached from any locality, with the latter being more particular and even immediate. As Karen Tongson writes of the blurred landscape of American suburbia, "Normativity itself is no longer a stable category found in fixed spatial environments."[60] As such, a category like *place* cannot serve as a heuristic for any presumed dynamic of power and resistance. Rather, the valuation of space and place changes depending on context: Space-as-abstract might allow the deterritorialization of exclusionary identities, on the one hand, or represent the alienating, hollowing-out effects of global capital, on the other. Likewise, place might be a metonym for community and the salubrious benefits and phenomenological richness of the everyday, or it might be a straightjacket of bounded normativity. Covalent with these concerns are those of perspective: Do we approach space/place from a height, taking a global, top-down perspective, or is our position grounded, concerned with a detailed and "messy" world, that is, with something identifiable as reality?[61] I argue that this is a false distinction and instead turn to theorizations of space/place that allow for complexity, overlap, and contradiction.[62] Topothesia is the vivid description of often imaginary places. Their speculative, imaginary quality makes them abstract, hazy, and ethereal. Yet through their vivid, excessive description they operate in the affective register of particularity. In the context of planning, topothesic places are speculative and *not yet* real. They are realizable and as such emerge in the very play between abstraction and particularity.[63]

Development Temporalities and Their Others

Part II of *Topothesia* examines the connections between the ideologies of colonial planning and those of more contemporary "neoliberal" planning. From the nineteenth century, liberal colonialism not only worked to produce the "local" as an object of knowledge, but this production is a through line through midcentury modernization to the neoliberal, postcolonial present. Rather than articulating either a defense or an updated critique of high modernism, I trace a genealogy of the local as itself an object of planning and preservation. This is not, to be clear, a repudiation of the former critique but rather an attempt to understand the more complex, dynamic, and overdetermined relation between planning's global and local epistemologies.

As such, *Topothesia*'s timeline skips over the midcentury. This is not to deny the obvious importance and impact of postwar national planning on the geography of the United Kingdom. In many ways, postwar planning was a culmination of Ebenezer Howard's liberal humanism.[64] Decades of advocacy for housing, land reform, and a welfare state that protected its citizens from the vagaries of the free market culminated in a postwar consensus that drastically expanded notions of what the state could and should do for its citizens. Planning evolved into a professional enterprise in its own right and held its own consensus that there was "nothing to be gained from overcrowding," leading to the construction of new towns.[65] Indeed, postwar planning not only rebuilt areas destroyed by the war but also those slums removed through extensive clearance and rehousing programs.[66]

The postwar consensus in Britain thus combined comprehensive planning authority, a need to rebuild, a continuing belief in environmental determinism, and the demands of and faith in the ameliorative capacities of the state. This legal and social framework took a material form of large-scale construction in the decades after the war: buildings and infrastructure made of glass, concrete, and steel, in many cases exhibiting an intentional modernist architectural aesthetic. As Ashley Maher writes, this was by degrees different from the "picturesque" garden-city aesthetic, even if postwar construction bore of the imprint of Howard's ideas (for example, in the production of New Towns).[67] Together, these elements form the high-modernist paradigm of development and planning. As noted earlier, the high modernism of the midcentury nation-state, including its way of identifying social problems and providing top-down and large-scale solutions, has been the subject of thorough and extensive critique. This critique encompasses the deployment of state planning globally; indeed, it was often Euro-American planners and consultants that guided the political, economic, infrastructural, and aesthetic "modernization" of newly independent colonies.⁶⁸ Within the Anglo-American context, critique of high modernism led to New Urbanist interventions in planning, which in many ways sought to revive a particular construction of the "local" lost in the postwar, despite the continued influence of garden-city ideals.⁶⁹

When taken together, however, this periodization tends to somewhat occlude the historical through lines that together form the idiom of development. Contemporary debates around the scope and perspective of spatial plans, including the proper role of the state and "best practices" for place making and regeneration, thus tend to occur within a limited paradigm. In these debates, the welfare state, along with its programs of social housing and the heavily associated modernist aesthetic, can be easily contrasted with continuing privatization of the housing market and the advent of regeneration schemes; that is, that particular periodization frames contemporary discussions around design and development in ways that can be constraining. What is forgotten in that exchange is the longer entwinement of liberalism and colonialism and the way that particular practice of colonialism has found repetitions with difference from its advent in the nineteenth century. *Topothesia* is directed toward tracking that longer history and, more importantly, the imaginary of place that animates it and continues to direct the trajectory of development in the present. To this end, I have chosen to remove the postwar from its usual position as a historical inflection point, deemphasizing it so as to foreground the continuities of a liberalism that never quite went away. In addition, I also seek to place into question other customary temporalities. For example, the "post-" of the postcolonial refers as much to the repetition of colonial gestures as it does to the way they emerge differently in succeeding generations and through experiences of migration and displacement. Similarly, and perhaps above all, the linearity of "development" and the supposed finality of "modernization" are shown to be in actuality cyclical and recursive, especially in the way they are ideologically deployed for the sake of liberal colonialism.

The continuities from the nineteenth century to the present are multiple: liberal colonialism and its ethos of improvement and cultivation, the *slum* as problem and the *garden* as solution, the phenomenogeographic emphasis on *place* and the *local*, the deflection and resolution of social conflict through development, and, of course, the temporalities and aesthetics of the speculative. Part II asks distinct questions about the speculative enclave—that dynamic wherein the space of the "otherwise" and the time of the "not yet" unfold. In particular, I consider how the "not yet" of speculation becomes available for capture within the structures of development. Here I analyze how development produces a social consensus on what the future built environment could and should look like. Unlike in Chapter 1, in this analysis I find that the figure of the planner is disaggregated into a complex and variegated set of public-private institutions and individuals.[70]

Overall, instead of treating the collapse of the welfare state through a lens of nostalgia, I show how contemporary development is a continuation of the liberal "home" colonization of the early twentieth century. Similarly, rather than read the politics of race, identity, and community as evincing nostalgia for empire or a melancholic refusal of multicultural "progress," I show how race is *reproduced through* the ideological and ideational work of *speculation*. Like early planning, development refers not just to the technical transformation of space but to an epistemology of progress that structures horizons — what *place* looks like, what it should look like, and how it forms the condition of *possibility* for contemporary subjects. Thus, it is not necessarily the case that literature provides alternatives; rather, these chapters interrogate the postcolonial necessity to draw outlines around the contentless gaps in modernity — areas foreclosed and shunted, possibilities delimited and visible only through pastiche and recomposition, things that survive beyond the collapse of their conditions of possibility and mutely haunt the edges of what's left.

The concrete geographic context of Part II is postcolonial, neoliberal Britain. As in Part I, I treat this context as metonymic. My analysis centers on Britain's specific imperial history and contemporary politics while opening up and making available a broader lexicon and theoretical understanding of development as colonization, globally and locally. Further, the United Kingdom is postcolonial not just because of historical or demographic fact (e.g., Britain was an imperial power; postcolonial migrants inhabit the United Kingdom). Such a framework reduces analytical possibilities, such that continuing forms of colonialism, descended from the practices of formal empire but significantly mutated, appear as a type of anachronism. Thus, the reproduction of race can only be read as its lingering persistence, as a "postcolonial melancholy," in the terms of Paul Gilroy.[71] Racism and nationalism, rather than being epistemologically constitutive of the contemporary, become something of a recalcitrant and inert legacy, associated with the Little England isolation rather than the vernacular cosmopolitanism of its cities. As Chapter 6 shows, both the cosmopolitan city and the supposedly isolated country can only be understood through colonial processes of development that operate across global, regional, and local scales. The project of teasing out traces of what had been erased, of reading into the present instances of both hybridity and radical difference, and of recovering the ephemeral but alternative speculative pasts and futures should continue alongside an equally substantive analysis of continued erasure, subsumption, and speculative violence.

Topothesia is thus situated within postcolonial studies, seeking both to build upon and interrogate the main concerns of the field. Postcolonial theory has been successful in identifying how traces of the colonial linger, haunt, and return in the present. Here the "post-" of the postcolonial has less to do with a discrete historical periodization and more to do with the epistemological and temporal relationship to these traces. This is perhaps something that unifies some of the disparate strands of the field—the idea that the work of postcolonial studies has to do with recognizing gaps and absences (in the archive, for example, or in Eurocentric conceptions of modernity);[72] recovering the traces of what has been erased, or was never named in the first place, or has been lost across time and language (or, dwelling with the difficulty of what is irrecoverable or with what, having been repressed, only returns in violent and illegible ways); and in working out the myriad ways that colonial formations are inescapably hybrid and pluralized, that despite the intention of an extractive and regulating power, any colonial and postcolonial society contains perhaps ample possibility for resistances that challenge sovereignty through recalcitrance, subversion, and rewriting.[73] The relational focus of postcolonial studies has thus led it to produce theories of hybridity and simultaneously to reject forms of subsumption.[74]

Such projects of recovery and reappropriation have at times positioned postcolonial aesthetics as liberatory because they suggest that the self-promoting articulations of Euro-settler modernity are incomplete, subject to unraveling, or simply false. This disposition has been especially pronounced (if not limited to) metropolitan postcolonial studies, that is, work that considers mostly English- and French-language contexts in the Global North. The optimism of this work can leave something to be desired given the continuance of forms of colonialism. Perhaps more to the point, its methods and epistemological concerns create its own gaps and occlusions. Some have sought to reground this work more squarely in political-economic analysis, turning away from the politics of identity and representation and toward the supposedly more concrete problems of class. Others have noted the substantial differentiation within what might be considered colonial/postcolonial, including differences in historical relationships, past and current forms of governmentality, and global positioning.[75] Of particular concern here is highlighting the myriad of experiences and forms of life possible in the Global Souths, pluralized spaces that are nonetheless often neglected in Euro-American academy.[76] For literary scholars, these concerns manifest in the prompt to study and read in a plurality of languages and to pluralize the boundaries and canons of Anglo-European languages and literature.[77] Together, these positions try to understand and address the epistemic and material violences of colonialism. Indeed, they suggest the imbricatedness of these violences, such that trying to place emphasis on any one aspect closes off a fuller understanding.

As such, Part II of this book considers the way that the structures of locality and place become subject to capture and co-option. Key to this is an analysis of how "neoliberalism" repeats, with difference, the practices of liberal colonialism within the contexts of globalized finance and the postcolonial nation. Through a complex process, a consensus understanding of what space should look like and whom it should be for comes to be hegemonic. Though the city, and particularly "global" cities like London,[78] has been a focal point in geographers' efforts to understand the political economy of space, this consensus extends to the shifting economies of Britain's provincial areas. In being made available for global finance, I find that both "town and country" are subject to logics of development in postcolonial Britain in ways that reproduce both economic and racial marginalization. The result is an affective geography characterized by a sense of abandonment, less of "being behind" as much as it is one of being left behind. At the same time, the concrete social and economic impacts of this geography fall unevenly on differently marginalized subjects.

Outline of Chapters

Chapter 1, "Garden Cities: The Art and Craft of Making Place in Edwardian Britain," introduces the themes and archive of *Topothesia* through a comparative analysis of Ebenezer Howard's *Garden Cities of To-morrow* (1902) and William Morris's novel *News from Nowhere* (1890). *Garden Cities of To-morrow* is often credited with marking the beginnings of modern urban planning.[79] The professional infrastructure of town planning that develops in the early twentieth century (journals, conferences, university positions, government offices, etc.) emerges as a response to the problem of the slum, a figure that condenses economic inequality in a spatial form. In isolating this figure, incipient planners, Howard included, sought to resolve and reconcile the effects of capitalism through a conception of future places whose realization could be brought about by the art of planning rather than through political agitation. I read Howard in comparison with Morris's *News from Nowhere*, which imagines a postrevolutionary London characterized by social cooperation, collective economic production, and verdant sensuality. The incipient fields of planning and design were highly influenced by the work of Morris and the Arts and Crafts movement as a whole; at the same time, this influence amounted to a co-option of its aesthetics without its political animus.[80] Instead, I argue that planning, even within the metropole—Howard characterizes garden cities as "home colonization"—operated via a logic of liberal colonialism, whose goal was improvement and reconciliation of the working classes. Accordingly, I contend that both metropole and colony were subject to the same practices of spatial formation and often for the same reason: the resolution of political tension through an apolitical imaginary of place.

Chapter 2, "Planning as Imperial Cultivation," continues by tracking the garden-city imaginary in the work of colonial planners, in particular through the work of Patrick Geddes. Geddes is credited for inspiring the now-common phrase "act local, think global," and in this chapter I argue that both scales—the local and the global—were made possible by the infrastructure of empire and produced through colonial practice. Like many of his contemporaries, Geddes found colonial administrators to be willing to turn to planning to solve their problems, including the increasing "problem" of anticolonial political agitation, and able to offer planners more resources and latitude given the nature of colonial hierarchy. Working in India and Palestine in the interwar period, Geddes did not seek to use this authority to evacuate the local but instead sought to preserve and reproduce locality in order to further integrate it into existing imperial structures. In so attending to the local, Geddes imagined the figure of the planner as a gardener of places and cultivator of people. Indeed, much of his work in India is pedagogical in nature—rather than unidirectionally imposing his plans, he sought to educate the native populace on the importance of city planning for environmental and social renewal.[81]

Part II of this book considers how traces of a colonial ethos are reproduced and reappropriated in postcolonial contexts. It also seeks to understand the multitude of ways that speculative thinking can produce futurity, especially through the conceptions and affects of place. Rather than simply resolve "speculation" into the familiar dynamics of power and resistance, however, Part II also interrogates the way the potentiality of the "not yet" is inherently ambivalent—a horizon that closes down as much as it opens up. This is tracked through the interventions of artists and writers who similarly inquire into how the "otherwise" of the speculative can possibly acquire coherence. Chapters 3 through 6 center particular moments and spaces to this end: the urban riot as both excess and absence in its forms of community, representation, and meaning (Chapter 3); the "town" whose protean character gives way to a kind of nonromantic "lastness" (Chapters 4 and 5); the "country" that composes itself through structural and affective abandonment (Chapter 6); and throughout subjects who live with the suffocating impossibility of time, both in the ghost stories that seem to govern the present and the denial of any survivable futurity.

Chapter 3, "Capturing the City: Regeneration, Policing, and the Ghosts of Postcolonial Britain," explores the politics of the welfare state through the lens of Thatcher's Britain. Here I analyze two responses to a series of similar events, namely, the urban riots of 1981 and 1985 in neighborhoods of London, Birmingham, Liverpool, and elsewhere. Like the figure of the slum, the event of these riots concatenated the contradictions and tensions of a postcolonial and neoliberal Britain. The first response I consider is that of Michael Heseltine: Working in Thatcher's government, he proposed urban redevelopment, including increased green spaces alongside the expansion of corporate business, as a response to the riots. At the same time, the state aggressively and successfully moved to privatize social housing, with the gray concrete of the council estate figured as the aesthetic opposite to Heseltine's green vision in ways that were clearly racialized. I argue that planning and development, both public and private, borrowed heavily from the colonial imaginary detailed in Chapters 1 and 2 and, further, that the neoliberal city, even in the former metropole, cannot be understood without reference to its colonial origins. Further, I analyze the role that spatial surveillance and policing plays in shaping urban design, in particular considering Alice Coleman's critique of council estates as a form of order-maintenance policing, more popularly known as broken-windows policing. Heseltine's and Coleman's characterization of urban social "disorder" has a way of constricting the possible ways of inhabiting and representing a city. I examine how Black artists responded both to the riots and to neoliberal spatial interventions, in particular through a reading of John Akomfrah's 1986 film *Handsworth Songs*, produced by the Black Audio Film Collective. I argue that Akomfrah's film does not attempt to straightforwardly document the "local realities" of neighborhoods like Handsworth in opposition to government rhetoric but more complexly works through the difficulty of such a representation in a way that throws into relief Thatcher's neocolonial urbanism.

Chapter 4, "The End of London: Temporalities of the Gentrified City," theorizes the contradictory temporalities of contemporary London: the *contingency* and *temporariness* of "pop-up" culture and the postemployment labor market, the rhetoric of *sustainability* and *legacy* put forth by developers, and the experience of the city in a perpetual end state, producing the affect of *lastness*. Contemporary development implicitly draws on the liberal colonialism of early planning. One important shift, I argue, is that the particular planner has been subsumed within a complex social field consisting of public-private agencies, private developers, and design-consultant firms. Together they produce a vast number of texts dedicated to their "placemaking" capacity, to use their own idiom. Thus, instead of turning to one particular figure to anchor Chapter 4 (as I do in the first two chapters with Howard and Geddes), I analyze the rhetoric and aesthetics of the excessive documentation produced by this wider technocratic field in order to draw out the logics animating development in the gentrifying city. As intent as this rhetoric is in opening up possibility in the city of the near future, it also produces a sense of *lastness*, which I analyze in Chapter 4 through halted ramblings in a gentrified London by the psychogeographer Iain Sinclair. Gentrification functions not as simple economic displacement but only through the creation of an aesthetic framework, one centered, paradoxically, on locality and community. Simultaneously, the agents of these projects are both mobile and global: international financiers, planning consultants, architectural and design firms that are the descendants of the "global"—which is to say, imperial—exchange of ideas in the early twentieth century.[82] Specifically, I look at two large "regeneration" projects in London that I argue are also metonymic for the operations of development more broadly: the planning for the 2012 Olympic Games and the redevelopment of Battersea Power Station in south London. Both projects frame their intervention through the creation of place and locality, despite their global funding structure, the expansiveness of their projects, and their role in reinforcing London's position as a "global city." Discourse around Olympic planning tries to reconcile its "pop-up" temporariness with the supposed legacy it is leaving behind. Meanwhile, Battersea Power Station's developers cast the project as a remediation of a polluted, brownfield past into a more verdant, vibrant, and creative future. Both projects, I argue, evince the aesthetic character of contemporary mass-scale gentrification.

Gentrification has been a key term in analyzing this political-economic transformation of the city and its new, cultivated subjects. Contemporary gentrification is entangled with histories of empire and its practices of colonialism at several levels.[83] One, the acquisition of space and displacement of populations has been described as a form of pioneerism, including by developers. Planning for the Olympics and for Battersea Power Station describes areas of the city as "brownfield"—ruined, decayed, and putatively empty spaces to be revitalized, regenerated, and populated by waves of middle-class settlers. In speaking in the language of ecology, sustainability, and preservation, these projects also repeats a solicitude for natural spaces that require the attention and guardianship of outsiders.[84] In its imagery and rhetoric, sustainability in contemporary development is the descendent of the figure of the garden for early planners. Both encounter spaces that are in states of ruin and degradation—polluted, overcrowded, misused, and not conducive to either arboreal or human flourishing. Contemporary development extends its intervention to include a concern for global sustainability, as if, through "good" design, even urban megaprojects could solve the problem of climate change.[85] Further, taking their cue from critiques of top-down planning, developers frame their intervention as promoting informality, local identity, and *creativity*. This is an entrepreneurial creativity in which the city becomes an incubator of new ideas and connections among "creative-class" professionals.[86] This framework in turn operates well within the larger parameters of neoliberalism in disclosing how their developments will produce the disruptive creativity of individual innovators. Key to this vision is the ethos of *design*, one that mixes the technics of planning with the qualified creativity of the practical arts. If planning is still associated with a rigid and rectilinear way of imagining space, design poses itself as a creative and open-ended framework that allows for surprising but not excessive social production. This framework posits the subject as creative and innovative and as an entrepreneurial citizen whose activities help shape the city while enhancing its brand.[87]

In this way, the city is the stage not only for its own development but for the development of the self. The creative, entrepreneurial self operates as a telos of modernity to be achieved through innate creativity, planning, and design. Chapter 5, "Level Up: Zadie Smith's NW and the Promise of Progression," evaluates the parameters and methods of reproduction for the creative, entrepreneurial subject within the context of development through a close reading of Zadie Smith's 2012 novel NW. The novel tracks protagonists who contend with the normative assumptions of being gendered, neoliberal subjects. They feel coerced into seeing the self as proceeding through planned stages and are either haunted by their inability to take the "next step" in life (career, motherhood, house, etc.) or trapped by their successful performances as "model" subjects. The novel explores these affects in the context of the gentrifying immigrant neighborhood of Willesden in London, in which the politics of home ownership saturate interpersonal intimacies. I show that the aesthetics and rhetoric of urban development are mirrored in the contemporary notions of social mobility through self-improvement, which creates a frustrating and delimited horizon especially for women and people of color. Instead, the novel explores the "cruel optimism" of the planned self and the profound dislocations in contemporary identity.

Finally, Chapter 6, "Geographies of Discontent: Brexit and the Politics of Abandonment," asks how these dislocations of space and identity are formative not only in urban but also in provincial areas. I analyze this dynamic in particular through Caryl Phillips's novel *A Distant Shore* (2003), which in many ways prefigured the debate about Britain's geographic fracture in the wake of the 2016 referendum to leave the European Union. Bringing together research from geography on the effects of rural gentrification and the impact of tourist economies, I show how the prerogatives of planning have imagined futures of productive and socially cohesive knowledge economies even in nonurban spaces but ironically created conditions of economic inequality and racial hostility. In doing so, I turn to perhaps the most unlikely geography of postcolonial analysis—the provincial flashpoints of Brexit—in order to demonstrate the reach and extent of the planning imaginary and its ongoing, neocolonial mode. My aim here, as it is throughout the project, is not to flatten out the development of spaces or the experiences of differently marginalized subjects. Instead, I seek to show the capaciousness of development's speculative imaginary, in which visions of the future displace divisions in the present. Without ceasing to be a speculative opening-up, spatial development also creates "geographies of discontent," places and communities marked less by integration than by disintegration. Thus, the temporalities of speculation do not come with fixed political valences. Throughout the book, I do not try to separate those modes of speculative imagining that are necessarily reproductive of power from those that are necessarily resistant—interruption of a particular future can reveal the contingency of power just as much as the vivid imagining of an alternative future, and both contend with nonreparative failure.[88] The relational dynamics of colonialism—its creation of hierarchies and separations, its extractive capacity, its will to subsume and improve—continue to inform contemporary operations of power, and thus postcolonial analysis continues to be relevant if it can expand its methods and horizons.

PART I

Improving Places: Liberal Colonialism and the Speculative Imaginary of Early Planning

1
Garden Cities
The Art and Craft of Making Place in Edwardian Britain

Recent years have seen a revival of the garden-cities idea, a model for urban planning first laid out in Ebenezer Howard's 1902 *Garden Cities of Tomorrow* that was extremely influential if not foundational for the development of twentieth- and twenty-first-century urban planning. Recent iterations emphasize the need for more sustainable housing; for example, Nick Clegg and Eric Pickles, in a proposal entitled "Locally-Led Garden Cities," seek to "unlock up to 250,000 new homes between 2015 and 2020" in developments that will be "well-designed, and bring together high-quality homes, jobs, and green spaces in communities where people want to live raise their children."[1] The rhetorical appeals of new garden cities are many, not just because of its market-driven approach to opening up new housing for younger buyers but because of the dense imaginary of the garden itself, connoting personal and environmental health and, more latently, the possibility of a genuine connection to place and community within a sustainable modernity.

One prominent and recent example of a new garden city is Ebbsfleet, part of the postindustrial Thames Estuary (rebranded as the "Thames Gateway"). Stretching from East London to the mouth of the Thames, the area consists of many polluted "brownfield" sites and is noted for deprivation, a chronic lack of employment, and the social isolation of "overspill" estates. The new garden city, proposed by George Osborne with some £300 million of funding to incentivize private developers and speed up planning consent,[2] would turn derelict sites of cement manufacturing into "real" places, with jobs, transport, an amusement park, and, of course, gardens and greenery.[3] Patrick Barkham, however, wrote in 2014 that "there is one problem with Ebbsfleet garden city: there is already a town here, Swanscombe," whose residents "feel like they are being erased from the map."⁴ Nevertheless, the state, coordinating with developers, has pushed forward with urban "regeneration" in the Thames Estuary, with the Conservative, Liberal Democrat, and Labour parties all intent on turning what they see as empty, derelict, and economically anachronistic zones into real, environmentally sustainable places that would, through their creation, integrate willing residents into their vision of a "locally led" global economy. As Jonathan Glancey writes, "under New Labour and Coalition governments, we are supposed to have enjoyed an 'urban renaissance,' along with eco-towns, the Thames Gateway and the positively insane Pathfinder project, whereby streets of perfectly good 19th-century homes in Liverpool and Manchester have been demolished for no discernible reason."⁵ The imaginary of the garden city, first defined in an era of Edwardian new liberalism, is thus well suited to the ecomodernizing intentions of neoliberal planning.

This chapter argues that the garden city is inherently a technology of liberal colonization, an attempt to reconcile class tensions within Edwardian Britain through the creation of what Howard termed "home colonies." The garden-city movement he inspired immediately sought to deploy the idea to areas in the broader British Empire; more profoundly, the movement sparked the rise of town planning as a practice and profession, supplying conceptions of what a *place* is and what it could do to reconcile social tension and revive community within the epoch of technological modernity. I argue that latent in modern planning is the idea that the creation of *place* would, all by itself, create new social relations in ways that resolve unbearable political conflict without the need for politics as such.⁶

Within my argument, "colonization" includes a necessarily large scope. In addition to being an activity of territorial domination, settlement, and/or extraction and more broadly conceived in terms of political and cultural hegemony, colonization here refers to a speculative practice of imagination. The colony, in this sense, exists as a place that is located in a future that is also an *elsewhere*. Further, the garden-city imaginary appealed not just to the need for more housing or for social reform but to a sense of the particularity of place, one made all the more tangible by the aesthetic of the garden, which promised health, vibrancy, and a sense of immediacy. So posed, the garden city spoke to a desire for a realizable utopia, a figuration not trapped by nostalgia or romantic lament for something lost or by attempts to preserve and recreate but rather one that reconciles the green and pleasant past with the possibilities of modernity. Place creation is both a managerial optimization of society's productive forces, producing normative subjects along the way, and a practice of speculation and aesthetic construction.

The development of this aesthetic took place in a dense context of "new" imperialisms and liberalisms, inequality, social reform, and utopian thinking in the late nineteenth and early twentieth century. It involved a wide and animated range of discussions about the city, architecture, and how to change society—discussions that in turn influenced the multitude of incipient planners and designers that developed the profession in the geographical heights of the interwar empire. This chapter will focus on two figures, Ebenezer Howard and William Morris, both of whom concatenated contemporary thinking into a definite aesthetics. Howard's garden-city model, marked by the good intentions of social reform, rendered utopia as realizable by a process of (home) colonization. Morris, meanwhile, articulated a more radical politics in part through an Arts and Crafts aesthetics; these aesthetics, in fact, have been notably more influential to designers than Morris's socialist politics.

The histories and themes introduced in this chapter will resonate throughout the book—Part II will show how the practices of "home colonization" repeat, with differences, in a contemporary, postcolonial Britain. Early planning emerged through a nexus of interrelated ideologies: the paternalism of Victorian social philanthropy, the context of late imperialism, and the project of modernization as governed by an ethos of progress. Where Part I of the book examines the development of this nexus, Part II charts the way it reverberates. For example, this chapter argues that garden-city planning was in part a response to a politically tumultuous era, with place creation offered as a way to mediate social agitation and conflict. It is no coincidence that this gesture was repeated as a response to urban conflict in Thatcherite Britain (itself often associated with the resurgence of laissez-faire capitalism and nostalgia for empire), as explored in Chapter 3. Similarly, the enduring appeal of the garden remains even in the large-scale development and infrastructure projects of the last decade, like the Thames Estuary redevelopment and other "regeneration" schemes. This is in part attributable to the way the garden aesthetic works to make *place* seem local and particular, qualities that infuse Morris's utopian fiction. I contrast this with contemporary fictions that situate characters and settings in an ambiguous relationship to that utopian horizon.[7] Throughout, I show how development schemes, including early garden-city planning, adopt this imaginary while confidently promising concrete, realizable spatial "fixes"—a project of improvement, modernization, and liberal colonialism that ignores the historical debris it itself creates.

In fact, my reading of Morris's *News from Nowhere* in this chapter is the only place in the book where I analyze fiction that is explicitly utopian and thus more within the bounds of "speculative fiction" as a literary genre. The novel was an inspiration for early planning rather than a reaction to it. As such, my analysis of it here helps consider how early planning adopted the aesthetics of utopianism not as a means to the kind of anarchic socialism that Morris espoused but rather as a way of mediating and designing away political conflict as such. This selective adoption of Arts and Crafts is not only repeated in the aesthetics of contemporary development but in the individualized emphasis on *design* that repeats and adopts Morris's beloved adage: "Have nothing in your house that you do not know to be useful, or believe to be beautiful." The importance of design for utility, beauty, and improvement can thus been seen in individual practices of gentrification and consumption that focus on creative reuse, design, and aesthetic minimalism. As Chapters 4 and 5 will show, tasteful improvement of the house along these lines also reflects the improvement of the designed, considered self, one who has benefited from "the life changing magic of tidying up."[8] As with Howard's garden cities, this gentrification aesthetic takes up aspects of Arts and Crafts while both house and occupant remain within an economy of displacement and financial speculation that goes uncontested. At the same time, my analysis of *News from Nowhere* shows how the agonistic politics of *community* latently disrupt the smooth continuity of the *beautiful* in Morris's utopia. That is, in addition to being subject to capitalist capture, Morris's speculative fiction opens up space both for Blochian possibility and for ambiguous and troubling questions about the nature and limits of community, questions that linger in the contemporary ethos of design.

Garden Cities of To-morrow articulates its intervention against figures of excess: the overcrowded city, the slums of "darkest England," and the "deserving" and "undeserving" poor that inhabit those slums. Garden cities, as "home colonization," promise to manage that excess, reconciling spaces and people to the normative order of civil society. This question of excess haunts *Topothesia*. What happens to the excess that is supposedly managed and reconciled via colonization and place creation? What are the stakes of inclusion or exclusion, both ambivalent, into community imagined and constructed along these lines? And what can the specific aesthetic form of planning literature tell us about the imaginary of modernization and its lacunae? To this last point, I find that Ebenezer Howard's *Garden Cities of To-morrow* is not only a document of rational modernization but also one that channels the excess it finds in the contemporary city into a speculative horizon that is itself excessive, bursting with purple prose, grandiose promises, and an elaborate visual language. That is, planning produces its own excesses, and this not only speaks to its outsized ambitions but also to the cultural and political anxieties of modernity. The legacy of those ambitious, speculative horizons, the anxieties they contain, and the excessive subjects they unwittingly produce are what I examine in Part II, where the vivid imaginaries opened up in part by the garden-cities movement are resolved into a more ambivalent affective terrain—places marked by a temporality of *lastness* and a geography of abandonment.

Finally, there is a subtle but significant difference in how I situate planning texts like Howard's *Garden Cities of To-morrow* and the interior logic by which these texts work. Namely, my overall analysis considers these specific texts as *metonyms* through which we can understand political-economic and cultural structure. That is, the reading pertains both to the specific circumstances that gave rise to the garden-cities movement and also connects, for example, to the politics of land, housing, and development or to the garden as a persistent structure of feeling in British culture. These are the broad stakes of *Topohesia*. The texts themselves, however, avail themselves of a full and excessive array of representational language in order to articulate their speculative visions. At the same time, garden cities were to be taken, like many quasi-utopian projects, as microcosms—worlds unto themselves that were at the same time examples to be followed and replicated. The arguments in this chapter thus speak to these two registers: the multifarious representational logic of the primary texts and the way that I situate these texts as part of a broader and indeed still active epistemology of place.

Liberalism, Home Colonization, and Social Reform

Midway through *Garden Cities of To-morrow*, Ebenezer Howard makes what might be considered an odd reference. Critics and biographers have documented the many sources of inspiration for *Garden Cities*: the reform and charity work of Octavia Hill and Charles Booth (among others) in East London, the utopian thinking of Morris and Edward Bellamy, the politics of Peter Kropotkin, the City Beautiful movement in Chicago, and many others. Here, however, Howard cites Edward Gibbon Wakefield, who advocated for aggressive colonization and settlement of Australia:

> Wakefield, in his *Art of Colonization*, urged that colonies when formed—he was not thinking of home colonies—should be based on scientific principles. He said: "We send out colonies of the limbs, without the belly and the head, of needy persons, many of them mere paupers, or even criminals; colonies made up of *a single class of persons* in the community, and that the most helpless and the most unfit to perpetuate our national character, and to become the fathers of a race whose habits of thinking and feeling shall correspond to those which, in the meantime, we are cherishing at home. The ancients, on the contrary, set out *a representation of the parent State—colonists*

from all ranks. We stock the farm with creeping and climbing plants, without any trees of firmer growth for them to entwine around. A hop-ground without poles, the plants matted confusedly together, and scrambling on the ground in tangled heaps, with here and there some clinging to rank thistles and hemlock, would be an apt emblem of a modern colony."[9]

Howard offers this passage without much reference to its original context of settler colonialism, except to mention that the mass, organized migration envisioned by Wakefield is possible within England, from overcrowded slums to garden cities. Howard's aside before the passage that Wakefield "was not thinking of home colonies" does much to elide settlements in Australia with those outside of London under the same general rubric. The passage itself relies on two biological analogies: In one, colonists are likened to bodies without a torso or head; in the second, the colonists are subsidiary and humble plants lacking the support of larger trees. The latter analogy is visually dense, with the directionless, creeping plants of a surplus population growing "confusedly" in "tangled heaps" among the "rank" flora of the indigenous environment.[10] The analogy suggests cluttered disorientation, rather than an organized, planned, and maintained environment. In both cases, Wakefield laments the degraded state of a colony inhabited only by a lower class and not able to reproduce the parent state.[11]

Conversely, Wakefield thinks that the model Greek colony "consisted of a general contribution of members from all classes, and so became, on its first settlement, a mature state, with all the component parts of that which sent it forth. It was a transfer of population, therefore, which gave rise to no sense of degradation, as if the colonist were thrust out from a higher to a lower description of community."[12] To form a cohesive and coherent body politic, the confused lower classes must be joined by their more noble counterparts. In this description, the space of the colony is one of social reproduction and class reconciliation, in which component groups form a complete and unified body or ecology. That is, Wakefield is concerned not just with removing society's excess but placing them in colonies that, like children, are reproductions of the parent metropole.

What excites Howard in citing this text, seemingly, is this notion of a fresh start, a place that produces organic social harmony, community, and sense of purpose: the colony.[13] Howard advocated the garden city as a home colony not just for the *residuum* of the city but for the middle classes as well, so as to produce just the kind of social integration Wakefield imagines possible in Australia. What were the conditions of possibility that allowed Howard to pose home colonization as a practical solution to the ills of modernity? Addressing this question requires thinking through the long, entwined histories of capitalism and colonialism that produce Howard's historical moment.

A focus on Howard's articulation of home colonization shifts some of the assumed divisions within the late British Empire, particularly in terms of geographic scale. Home colonization was more than merely an incongruous metaphor; as Stoler and Cooper have argued, metropole and colony were constructed mutually through shifting practices and forms of knowledge production. Thus, the "language of class provided a template for how the colonized racial 'residuum' was conceived . . . [and] in Europe drew on a range of images and metaphors that were racialized to the core."[14] Taking home colonization more seriously puts these geographic scales into question by indicating that the putative space of the metropole could also be characterized as a space of colonization. Colonization, then, refers more directly to a mode of governmentality. Rather than operating against a backdrop of geographic division, colonization is a set of practices and ideologies through which geographic relations are constituted. As such, an analysis of home colonization productively reframes, without doing away with, the metropole/colony distinction and its attendant questions of power, identity, and difference. The aim is not so much to once again deconstruct the metropole/colony binary but rather to consider how and why a structure of relationality and iterative reproduction develops and persists (and one that, as will be shown in later chapters, outlives the formal institutions of empire).

The most proximate social context of the garden-city movement was late-Victorian social reform, through which concern for the urban poor, environmental and biological improvement, and colonization operate within the ideology of new liberalism. Liberalism has a conflicted history with colonialism, with liberal intellectuals being among both the most vocal opponents and advocates of colonization, sometimes simultaneously.[15] Yet by the late nineteenth century, liberalism and colonialism had been articulated together into a cultivated ethical disposition in which the colony and its inhabitants were projects for improvement.[16] In this way the projects of a liberalism that improves and a colonialism that civilizes could be conjoined. As Barbara Arneil writes, liberal colonialism was not only "an external process by which non-Western peoples are subjected to [a] colonial power . . . it is also the internal processes by which certain kinds of British citizens (poor, 'idle,' mentally disabled and ill) are forcibly segregated in domestic colonies at the turn of the twentieth century within Britain itself as well as in British settler states."[17] Within the context of social reform, however, colonization became a means of social integration rather than simply of segregation.

From Slum to Garden

The garden-city movement brought together technologies of power and epistemological understandings of place under the modernizing rubric of planning. Importantly, the space of the colony bears a particular relationship to the space of the slum throughout the nineteenth and into the twentieth century. The slum carried with it connotations not only of poverty but also of *excess*. It housed a "surplus" population that prompted a range of affective valences from the middle class: pity, contempt, fear, fascination. This space consistently raised the problem of "what to do" with the unemployed, which itself could be split into the deserving and undeserving poor. Working-class agitation in the 1880s, in particular, led some to view the slum as intolerable. In this view, if this surplus population was ripe for revolt, it was not because of the political economy that produced the slums but rather because of the overcrowded conditions of the slum itself; that is, political contestation was perceived as a spatial problem.[18] The proposed solution was to send this surplus to the colonies, which were a safety valve for middle-class society as a whole. The metaphor of the safety valve, in which the slum becomes a boiler, figures the industrial city as itself a kind of machine, one whose functioning could be engineered and maintained on a technical basis. The mechanistic depersonalization of class politics was a kind of displacement of affective reactions to the slum.[19] Colonialism formed a common sense, such that home-colonization schemes "were promoted by every conceivable public and private organization in the late nineteenth and early twentieth centuries," with progressive or even radical groups subscribing to dividing the poor into deserving and undeserving and conceiving of the whole problem as one that could be approached through environment and place.[20]

Nevertheless, the figure of the slum continued to be politically reactive in ways that reveal the highly differentiated social space of the putatively homogenous nation. The metropolitan slum was seen not just as a starting point for an exterior colonization but itself was a colony of the city. Often this was manifested in terms similar to William Booth's *In Darkest England*.[21] In one sense, this relationship was analogical, with the implicit or explicit suggestion that any part of England ought not to resemble the conditions of the colony or, worse, the not-yet-Christianized, "darkest" frontiers.[22] However, these sorts of reformist ethnographies were made possible by a genuine sense of otherness, for example in how the problem of the surplus population was framed in terms of unwanted migration (from the countryside).[23] Ethnography, geography, and social Darwinism together gave late Victorians a "fairly complex vocabulary of domestic racial difference ... [and] an extensive social imaginary of race that they could apply to their own working class."[24]

These discourses are deeply entwined with processes of colonization, race formation, and the discipline of sexuality across metropole and colony. The problems of London's East End thus could not be contained in political discourse through reference to the working class alone; rather, the unemployed poor, especially the undeserving, *unemployable* poor and the slum they inhabited together composed an image of alterity that prompted a mode of racialization. This coalesced into theories concerned with the relationship between the environment and population. Here, the moralistic attitude toward the slums becomes one of urban ecology, with a concern for the determining aspects of the environment, what James Winter identifies as an "interpretative framework: the proposition that crucial aspects of human life and history are determined by distinct physical settings."[25] Accordingly, improvement of the individual depended at least in part on improving the environment—or even, if possible, creating an entirely new place.[26] These ideas of environmental determinism led to the model-village movement, in which wealthy industrialists, intent on maximizing the productivity of workers, built "total social environments" in the form of model villages and company towns.[27] The focus on the determining aspects of the environment brought together discourses of sanitation, hygiene, health, and the overall "fitness" of the general population—the biopolitics of the city.[28] Urban social reform and the garden city thus involved a colonial disposition toward the slum: It responded to anxieties about health, productivity, and proximity through the creation of salubrious new environments. As the rest of this chapter and the book will show, this colonial disposition was less interested in erasure than in *cultivation*, a process of improvement by which the excessive aspects of the slum (including its inhabitants) were given form and texture; it was reliant upon, not antithetical to, the creation and cultivation of the local. Moreover, this process was thought to be sufficient to resolve social conflict and contradiction.

Social reform combined these ideologies of environment with a liberal imperialism in which notions of improvement and progress subtended the dutiful, paternalistic humanism of Victorian and Edwardian individuals like Octavia and Miranda Hill, Henrietta and Samuel Barnett, Charles Booth, William Booth, Beatrice Potter and Sidney Webb, and many others (all of whom were in direct conversation with Howard).[29] This took many forms: Octavia Hill's poor relief and housing renovation (with John Ruskin), Samuel Barnett's Toynbee Hall and East End settlements,[30] William Booth's Salvation Army, Henrietta Barnett's later Hampstead Garden Suburb, and many other interventions. Throughout, social reform often conceived of itself explicitly as a mode of colonization, advocating for both farm and labor colonies. One of the most well known of these might be William Booth's farm colony in Hadleigh, which purported to improve the young men of the slums in three steps: first, through temporary employment with the Salvation Army; second, through being sent to Hadleigh to learn practical skills in the more amenable countryside setting; and third, to be dispatched to the empire, improving the colony in turn.

One of the most notable aspects of social-reform practice and rhetoric was the mediating role of "nature," of special importance to the imaginary of the garden city. As several scholars have noted, the project of colonialism contains many etymological ties to pastoral cultivation of the land: for example, the Latin *colōnia* refers to the *colōnus* as "tiller, farmer, cultivator, planter, settler in a new country" and thus connotes "'farm,' 'landed estate,' and 'settlement.'"[31] Relatedly, Robert Home notes that the precursor to the British Colonial Office was called the Board of Plantations, *plantātiōn* suggesting both the propagation of new plants and, from the sixteenth century on, "the settling of people, usually in a conquered or dominated country; esp. the planting or establishing of a colony; colonization."[32] Liberal colonial improvement, congruous with these connotations, placed particular emphasis on the restorative effects of the countryside and practical education in agricultural colonies.[33]

Social reformists articulated the reforming capacities of the natural environment in striking terms. Henrietta Barnett, for example, thought that the "renewing and spiritualising effect . . . of the birds and flowers and trees would have a good moral influence on slum dwellers."[34] Meanwhile, prominent journals advocated greening the city as a compound solution, capable of improving the health, morality, and aesthetics of the urban environment all at once.[35] Together, these indicate the "fantasy of remedying slum chaos and slum brutality through communal aesthetic revelation" and specifically through an aestheticized nature.[36] The rhetoric of the natural world and the pastoral throughout the nineteenth century, culminating in the preservationist movement, is for some a nostalgic reaction to industrialization. However, as David Matless argues, the preservationist movement is more accurately read as an integral part of planning as social reform.[37] "Town and Country" planning sought to preserve undeveloped spaces for public consumption and as part of a more comprehensive plan that separated land uses. The garden city, with its zoned spaces and green belts, brought together these concerns into a single imaginary, one that could reconcile the imagined pastoral past with a healthy, technological modernity.

Garden Cities and the Aesthetics of Social-Spatial Integration

Howard's notion of the garden city is in active conversation with the social-reform and home-colonization movements of the late nineteenth century.[38] This is made clear from the opening pages of *Garden Cities of To-morrow*, in which Howard writes: "It is wellnigh universally agreed by men of all parties, not only in England, but all over Europe and America and our colonies, that it is deeply to be deplored that people should continue to stream into the already over-crowded cities, and should thus further deplete the country districts."[39] *Garden Cities* and the planning movement that followed are developments that occur quite squarely within the dominant paradigm of liberal colonialism, specifically an understanding of the capacities for the environment as such for cultivating productive subjects.

What does this context mean for the politics of garden cities and early planning? Howard makes clear that the project is reformist without being explicitly socialistic.[40] In studies of the garden-city movement, there is a tendency to restrict and define its political stakes: Garden cities are considered either as a technology to segregate and sanitize the city in advance of the mass-suburb projects *or* as an ideal for sustainable, communal modern living, one in conversation with the anarchic utopianism of Peter Kropotkin and William Morris and one forgotten in planning's move to high modernism.[41] However, it would be simplistic to read *Garden Cities* simply with regards to the degree to which the author explicitly conforms to dominant ideologies in the pursuit of social control.[42] For example, despite the liberal-colonial context, *Garden Cities* does not have the alarmist, chauvinistic tone that characterizes so many late-nineteenth-century texts about the slums of "outcast London," nor is it as pointedly condescending and patronizing toward slum inhabitants as the Barnetts, Hills, and Webbs.[43] I will try to leave the multiple political trajectories of the text open so as to indicate the diverse ways and means by which the garden-city idea gets taken up again throughout the twentieth and twenty-first centuries.

Further, instead of treating *Garden Cities* as only a social document, I remain attentive to the contingent form of the text: What becomes active and transportable is not just the notion of rational, sanitary urban planning for large populations but also the affects evoked by the image of the future garden city. The garden city is a fundamentally speculative endeavor. In describing the concept, Howard begins by writing, "the reader is asked to imagine an estate of 6000 acres," before describing how the city looks and feels and how it is organized and financed.[44] That is, instead of a proposal, Howard seeks to create an imaginary place for the reader, one that feels utopian yet is realizable via rational planning. It begins by establishing what Frederic Jameson terms a utopian "enclave," that is, a "space in which new wish images of the social can be elaborated and experimented on."[45]

The universality of this image is established in the opening pages of *Garden Cities*, where Howard describes the problem of the overcrowded slum as a point of political consensus that can be resolved through an apolitical solution:

> The key to the problem [of] how to restore the people to the land — that beautiful land of ours, with its canopy of sky, the air that blows upon it, the sun that warms it, the rain and dew that moisten it — the very embodiment of Divine love of man — is indeed a Master Key, for it is the key to a portal through which, even when scarce ajar, will be seen to pour a flood of light on the problems of intemperance, of excessive toil, of restless anxiety, of grinding poverty — the true limits of Governmental interference, ay, and even the relations of man to Supreme Power.[46]

This description of the land owes much to the Romantic tradition. Interrupting his technical proposal is a drama of landscape, evoking in the reader a pastoral image that is not only a lost past but a potentially "restored" and restorative future. The politics of housing, land reform, and poverty thus become background elements to the figure of the "land," characterized both by immediate sensations (the feeling of wind or sun, the visuality of an open sky or dewy surface) that are, at the same time, an "embodiment" of the transcendental. The problems enumerated are familiar, yet together, being "excessive" and "grinding," Howard attempts to give the mundane politics of housing a more theatrical affect of oppression, with this sense of excess mirrored overall in the breathless, self-interrupting, run-on sentence. The "restless anxiety" is not just of some urban mass but in a reader dissatisfied with modernity yet unable to conceive of an alternative.

Garden Cities proceeds in this manner, consisting both in detailed explanations of how the city would be financed and planned and also in descriptions that intensify the stakes and outcomes of such planning.[47] These come together in perhaps the most influential part of the text, the "special archaic charm" of quaint images that feature "elaborate hand-drawn Victorian lettering" and were originally "printed in delicate pastel colours."[48] For example, in the passage just quoted, the idiomatic use of a "key" to a problem first becomes a metaphor for Howard's proposal and then is used as the basis for an informative image (Figure 6).[49] This image is an infographic, relating different aspects Howard's solution (e.g., "Health, Recreation, Education,"

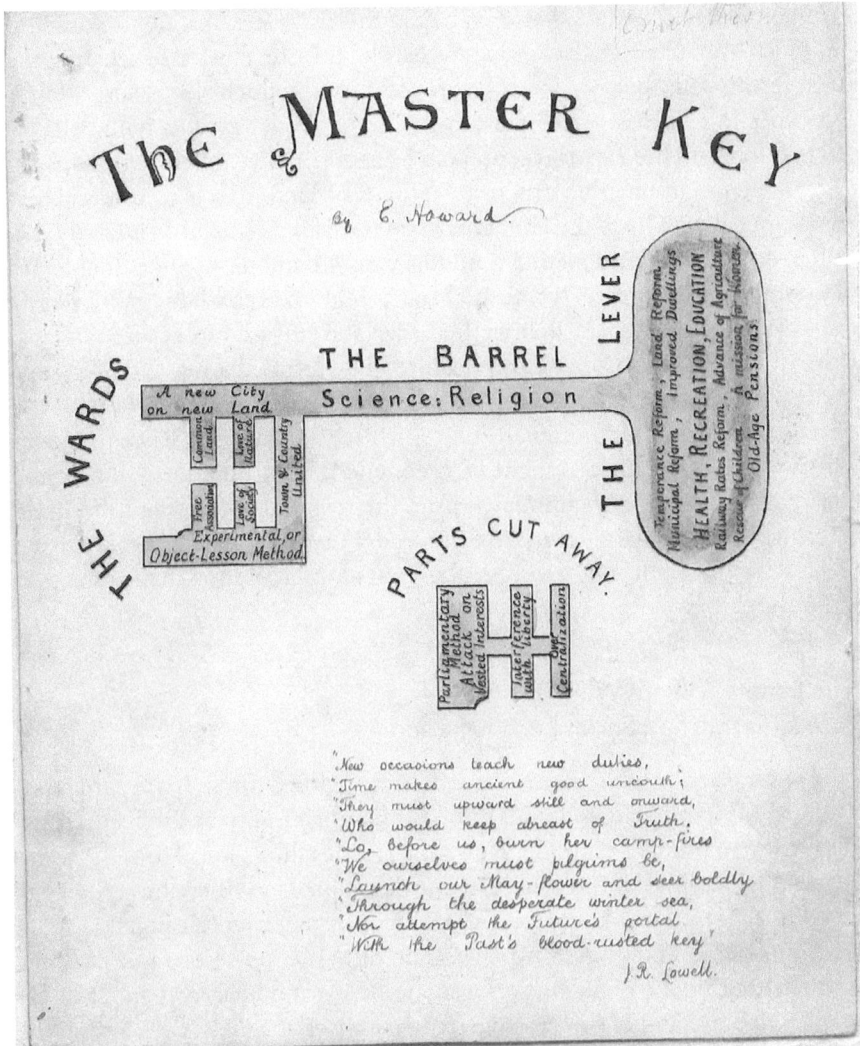

Figure 6. The Master Key, from *Garden Cities of To-morrow*.

"Science:Religion," and "a new city on new land," etc.) to one another and in opposition to conventional politics that is "cut away" (e.g., "parliamentary method," "attack on vested interests," "interference with liberty," "over centralization").[50] This image might help the reader visualize the complexity of the problem and help make sense of the possible solution.[51]

The image, however, bears a family resemblance to a calligram, where these multiple, heterogenous parts of the "key" are represented by an image of an actual key. The fact that it is shaped this way does as much to obscure the informational content as it does to clarify it. Instead, what is accentuated is the form itself, that is, Howard's proposal as a notional key. "The Master Key" does less to "convince" than to invite the reader into its bounded formal economy, as the expansive, utopian imagery of Howard's descriptions acquires a seemingly tangible structure. In this way, Howard seeks a solution that would appeal equally to the concerns of conservatives, liberals, and socialists. Rather than simply articulating a middle ground among political ideologies and opinions, he constructs a textual space that takes aesthetic particularity and immediacy ("the sun that warms" the land, for example) and places it within the structure of formal universality.[52] The former carries with it a range of affective qualities, including a nostalgia for the past, discontent with the present, and desire for a utopian future, while the latter sets the parameters within which those affects might be reconciled. Both inhere not just in the "idea" of the garden city, abstracted from the text, but within the form itself. In this way the text operates to place the reader inside its logic, a position from which the garden city might seem as the most natural solution to the problems of the slum.

"The People, Where Will They Go": Place Creation and Social Reconciliation

The "naturalness" of the garden city is doubly signified through the particularity of the garden image itself and through the universality of a self-sustaining technical scheme. For example, Howard imagines the space of town or countryside as magnets, drawing people in one direction or another; the garden city would be the strongest magnet, with "each person as a needle" such that "constructing magnets of yet greater power than our cities possess can be effective for redistributing the population in a spontaneous and healthy manner."[53] He pictures this in another informative image of three magnets, each listing the benefits and drawbacks of town, countryside, and garden city spaces, with the last of these being composed only of benefits. The figure of the magnet sets its own parameters: what counts as an appropriate solution is the creation of a stronger magnet in the form of a place. Even if there are disagreements as to how to create that kind of place, or if attempts to create that place fail in some aspect, they do so within a similar understanding. This logic is not wholly of Howard's invention; rather, one can read Howard's mediation of concepts of environmental determination through the formal qualities of the text.

The bounded, universal logic of the magnets might appear as overly mechanistic. However, in the text they are infused with *particularity*, that is, the sense that the created place will be one of intimate connection of land, town, and community. Howard writes,

> But neither the Town magnet nor the Country magnet represents the full plan and purpose of nature. Human society and the beauty of nature are meant to be enjoyed together. The two magnets must be made one. As man and woman by their varied gifts and faculties supplement each other, so should town and country. The town is the symbol of society—of mutual help and friendly co-operation, of fatherhood, motherhood, brotherhood, sisterhood, of wide relations between man and man—of broad expanding sympathies—of science, art, culture, religion. And the country! The country is the symbol of God's love and care for man. All that we are and all that we have comes from it. Our bodies are formed of it; to it they return. We are fed by it, clothed by it, and by it are we warmed and sheltered. On its bosom we rest. Its beauty is the inspiration of art, of music, of poetry. Its forces propel the wheels of industry. It is the source of all health, all wealth, all knowledge. But its fullness of joy and wisdom has not revealed itself to man. Nor can it ever, so long as this unholy, unnatural separation of society and nature endures. Town and country must be married, and out of this joyous union will spring a new hope, a new life, a new civilization.[54]

Spaces of town and country here are not just mechanistic magnets but are figured through a more emotive, gendered archetype of the family. The new city becomes a child of a masculine "culture" and a prototypically feminine "nature" and in this way is a figure of social reproduction—the way that, from the overcrowded ruin of the present, a hopeful, revitalized future may emerge. The masculine town is itself composed of the intimacy of family and/as community, one whose cohesion, as expressed through well-defined relationships, produces the "broad expanding sympathies" that are necessary for the continuation of culture. The feminine country, meanwhile, is deeply maternal, the elevated origin of all life and a source of continual comfort.[55] The exclamatory sentence in the middle of the passage—"and the country!"—introduces an extravagant set of vivid descriptions that evoke both the visceral solace and warmth of the maternal figure and the full romance of nature as *experienced* by the sensing self. The garden city is not primarily illustrated as a rational solution to contemporary problems in this passage. Rather, the "joyous union" of town and country operates as a quasi-transcendental figure, one that evokes the immediate comforts of family and natural landscape as evidence of the "full plan and purpose of nature."

What also is notable in this passage is Howard's characteristic emphasis on reconciliation. Elizabeth Outka writes that the aesthetic is able to "weave temporal fragments together, sustaining the contradiction between modern imperatives and nostalgic longing while at least temporarily satisfying both."[56] Importantly, the garden city is not the *merging* of masculine town and feminine country but rather their *"marriage."* For early-twentieth-century planners, the merging of town and country resulted in what for them was the most detestable of spaces: the suburb, an indeterminate, chaotic space that, like the slum, had no connection to the particularities of place.[57] Rather, the garden city, as a real *place*, is one characterized by distinct elements that are put into a productive relation. The relationality of town and country produces other reconciliatory relationships, for example, between modernity and tradition and between the middle and working classes.[58] Unlike some of the other home-colonization experiments, the garden city was not simply a place to house a surplus population that, as Malthusian social thinkers contended, ought not reproduce. Instead, the home colony is a site of social integration and reproduction, one that through the creation of a new place would reconcile the tensions of contemporary life.

This concern with integration and reconciliation is evident in Howard's diagram of the garden city. Aspects of the image are suggestive of all of the fears and fascinations of social reform, for example, in the "farm for epileptics" and "industrial schools" that evince liberal modes of cultivation and education for the working class and/or marginal subject. However, these are secondary to the overall effect of the image, namely, its character of self-containment, with everything a city needs in a set of concentric circles within a portion of a larger circle. The self-containment of the garden city is not realistic, causing Howard to note in the 1902 edition that the images were diagrams and not plans; the difference seems to be in the representational status of the image, where the plan supposes a more direct correspondence between image and actual city. This means, however, that the diagram is expressive of the garden city as concept.[59] The diagram seeks to organize multiple sets of relationships to create a cohesive community with no excess.

Together, the set of relations between built and "natural" environments, between occupations and classes, and between the community and its more marginal members form the basis of what counts as a place, as opposed to the nonplace of the slum, the suburb, or, indeed, the sprawling metropolis as a whole. Howard writes that it is essential

> that there should be unity of design and purpose—that the town
> should be planned as a whole and not left to grow up in a chaotic

GARDEN CITIES

> manner as has been the case with all English towns, and more or less with the towns of all countries. A town, like a flower, or a tree, or an animal, should, at each stage of its growth, possess unity, symmetry, completeness and the effect of growth should never to destroy the unity, but to give it greater purpose, nor to mar the symmetry, but to make it more symmetrical.[60]

The model, from diagram to plan to built instantiation, allows for flexibility to account for local conditions and individual will; it is not after all, as Howard takes pains to point out, a socialist imposition. What is left, and what is most important to Howard, is the formal unity as expressed in the text. Here Howard likens the city to a flower, tree, and animal, whose growth can be abundant yet contained within an overall order. In this way, Howard employs a biological analogy within which the city, at its best, resembles and recapitulates natural form.[61] Nature can and should resound within the city, but within a structure and a plan that allows for it to be cultivated along particular lines. That is, the local content must be guided into a universal form that expresses unity, completeness, and symmetry—a totality without excess. Place is itself constituted by a series of relationships and a logic of integration, within which there would be no surplus. This self-contained form gives structure to the affective dimensions of the garden city. Howard addresses what is outside the individual garden city through the concept of social cities (Figures 7 and 8). Roughly, Howard proposes to slowly replace the entirety of England with connected garden cities. The image that is included in the 1898 edition places

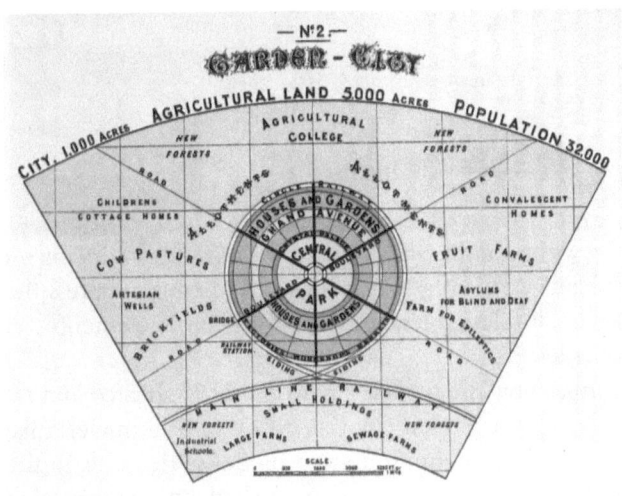

Figure 7. The Garden City, from *Garden Cities of To-morrow.*

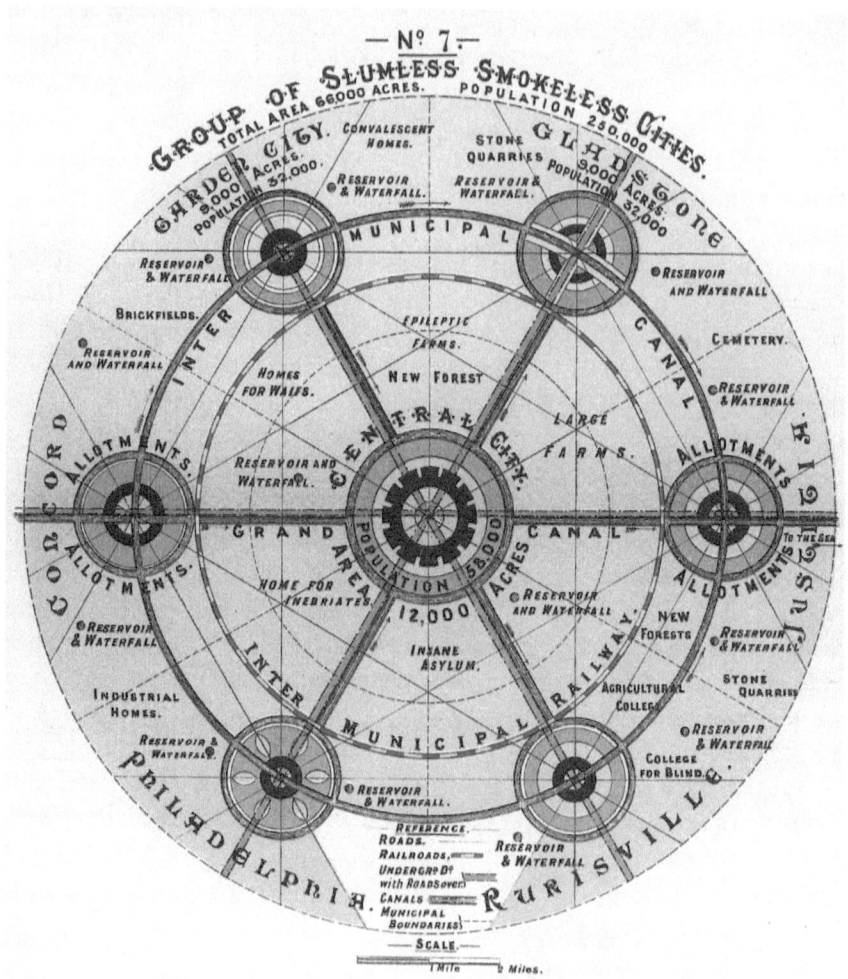

Figure 8. The Social City, from *Garden Cities of To-morrow*.

the circular garden city within more circles of increasing size, producing an image that is symmetrically divided by radial lines, all of which express the relationality between the "slumless smokeless cities" and other elements[62] in progressively larger schemes.

The social city describes how the garden city would be replicated and reproduced over time. That is, the garden city was meant to be a model. Like other "social experiments," from communitarian model settlements to the model villages of Cadbury and Lever, the garden city had a pedagogic value as an example for study and future use.⁶³ The model is a *perfect example*, a somewhat oxymoronic formulation in that it needs to be both average and exemplary, typical and prototypical. It implies that there could be imperfect examples, which contain errors yet still approximate the original model to a greater or lesser degree. The garden city as model is, in this way, not only a spatial but also a temporal concept. It is both a built, living city attentive to local conditions and a model to be replicated sometime in the future; indeed, the Letchworth garden city was as much an instructive spectacle for social reformers, architects, and future planners as it was its own city.

The *model* serves a temporal form of self-containment, in that the outside of the garden city is simply that which is not yet a garden city. Taken all together, *Garden Cities* presents a kind of representational cascade: a diagram that will become a plan, a plan that will become a self-sustaining place, this place a model for future replication in the formation of a social city. Each stage has an expressive, speculative character and is contained within this temporal progression. Thus the second garden city, at Welwyn, advertised its space through reference to the future, a temporal juxtaposition of "before" and "after." This technique was in fact widely used by Howard, Henrietta Barnett, and other garden-city proponents, as they showed audiences images of urban slums juxtaposed with those of garden cities. The aim was not simply to expose a contrast in living circumstances but to convince the audience—potential investors—of the surety of a speculatively imagined future.

On the topic of colonization and the need for "new" territory to settle the surplus population, Howard writes that

> a new planet, or even a territory not yet individually portioned out, is by no means necessary if we are but in real earnest; for it has been shown that an organized, migratory movement from over-developed, high-priced land to comparatively raw and unoccupied land, will enable all who desire it to live this life of equal freedom and opportunity; and a sense of the possibility of a life on earth and once orderly and free dawns upon the heart and mind.⁶⁴

In advocating for home colonization, Howard reveals the pretenses of liberal colonialism: first, that the colonies are a territorially blank space, much like a new planet, and second, that colonization must start with "raw" and "unoccupied" land. The settler cultivates and in turn is cultivated. That is, the reconciliatory aspects of Howard's design are throughout *Garden Cities* liberal in character, both in his suspicions of political extremes (i.e., socialism)⁶⁵ but also in his optimism that through creating a space conducive to edifying relationships among classes, the problem of an uncultivated excess could be solved. As will be shown in Chapter 2, the garden-city movement thus operated with this integrative and speculative conception of place in mind. Their replications of the garden-city idea were themselves styled as models for future replication, not just in a specific locale but throughout the empire. Therefore, far from indicating a turn inward,[66] the garden city sought to reconceptualize how and on what basis *place* could be constructed, namely, through a universal practice of colonization.

In this way, a real place is one bounded by a formal universality but also characterized through an aesthetic of particularity. The relationship between *Garden Cities* and the context of liberal colonialism can best be understood not only through the details of Howard's scheme and its many influences but through the form of the text as well—a model that contains and bounds the affects that it produces. The garden-city movement espoused different versions of a new liberalism that was universal in scope (and thus also global in many dimensions). Incipient planners were confident that political tensions of many sorts could be addressed through the creation of place, one that would be a pedagogic example ripe for replication but also powerful in producing affects of locality and community.

Uday Mehta writes that liberal colonialism aggrandized the particularity of contingent European circumstances into a universal theory that it then imposed upon the world. While not contesting the deployment of a formal university, this claim needs to be modified, as the universality of liberalism was itself dependent on continually producing particularity. In order to be reproduced, the model garden city requires not only rational boundaries but affective investment. Mehta implicitly recognizes this when he writes that "even when these stark conditions of terra nullius are acknowledged not to exist . . . from the perspective of thought, they could easily be made to exist. From the writings on India and the empire more generally, one gets the vivid sense of thought that has found a *project*, with all the grandeur of scale, implicit permanence, purposefulness."[67] It is precisely within this sense of the *project* that garden cities organize aesthetic particularity into a formal structure to create a model. The city thus emerges as a crafted, aesthetic object in which is embedded affective attachment and a commitment to a speculative future.

William Morris and the Beautiful Community

The garden-city movement from its inception was heavily influenced by William Morris and the Arts and Crafts movement he helped found. As argued earlier in this chapter, planners conceived of their practice as a tangible craft, emphasizing careful, aesthetically conscious design. Utopianism shares with architecture and planning the form of the blueprint or the *model*—"thought experiments, hypotheses, or metaphors addressing the question, 'What say the world was something like this?'"[68] They were also influenced by Morris's political ethos, which rejected the impersonality of industrial modernity in favor of genuine, harmonious social relations. Morris was socially connected to the reform movement and directly mentored planners of the later generation, notably Charles Ashbee.[69] As Volker Welter writes, "the British arts and crafts movement is among the first of a series of movements in European art and architecture insisting on the artist's comprehensive responsibility for all aspects of the human environment and life."[70] Morris's utopian socialism was likewise influential for planning and social-reform movements, despite the fact that the latter explicitly and implicitly advanced a project not of socialism but of liberal colonialism. The influence of Morris is part of what led garden-city planners to the conclusion that they were practical artists and that the city was a craft project, one that produced social reconciliation as simply one of the effects of good design. In contrast to this apolitical stance, others understand Arts and Crafts to be the expression of a humane, creative Marxism. The ways in which Morris's political aesthetics are and have been overdetermined is suggested by Michelle Weinroth in her analysis of the 1934 centenary of Morris that featured, rather astonishingly, an inaugural address by Stanley Baldwin, who "spoke of Morris exclusively as a superior artist of eminent gentility and human warmth, dispensing with any reference to Morris's political role as founder of the British socialist movement."[71] What are the forces that are capable of taking a generalized social-aesthetic structure—Arts and Crafts—in profoundly different directions?[72]

News from Nowhere was published serially in Morris's journal *The Commonweal* in 1890. It was intended as a response to Edward Bellamy's 1888 utopian novel *Looking Backward*. Morris wanted to envision a socialist utopia in which cities were in fact pastoral gardens, communities of artisans working collaboratively and in harmony with nature, but not under a singular, controlling state. The socialism of Morris's utopia was humanistic rather than scientific: It privileges individual craftsmanship over machine efficiency and personal connection over state-organized society. The popularity of these utopian novels speaks to the way that authors and readers in the late nineteenth century turned to speculative fiction to understand and mediate the political tensions of the period. As indicated in the Introduction, they indicate the potential for speculative fiction to "imagine otherwise" in the present, and in that sense they do a certain political work on their own. This chapter will explore, however, how even Morris's fairly polemical novel includes gaps and latent contradictions within his utopian vision.

In the novel, the nature of utopian English society and the historical changes necessary to achieve it are narrated by Richard Hammond in dialogue with William Guest, the novel's protagonist. He describes the once and future England:

> England was once a country of clearings amongst the woods and wastes, with a few towns interspersed, which were fortresses for the feudal army, markets for the folk, gathering places for the craftsmen. It then became a country of huge and foul workshops and fouler gambling-dens, surrounded by an ill-kept, poverty-stricken farm, pillaged by the masters of the workshops. *It is now a garden, where nothing is wasted and nothing is spoilt*, with the necessary dwellings, sheds, and workshops scattered up and down the country, all trim and neat and pretty.[73]

Utopian England is imagined as an enlarged garden, punctuated by small and quaint spaces of craft manufacturing. This future place recalls the sparse simplicity of a vague medieval time, recreating its "orderly and bright" spaces and its "sense of architectural power" but without the need for fortresses and armies.[74] Raymond Williams argues that this places a deceptive emphasis on the nineteenth century as a unique epoch of natural destruction—a "foreshortening of history" that suggests an "in-built tendency to contrast the damaging industrial order with the undamaging, natural, preindustrial order."[75]

Morris's verdant tableau draws on imaginaries provided by Romanticism, late-nineteenth-century romance, and socialist politics. In condensing these into the concrete space of the garden village, however utopian, Morris deeply influenced the incipient planning movement. Morris would always try to link his aesthetic, utopian sensibility to a necessarily intertwined politics. He was, especially as he grew older, committed to socialism and anti-imperialism. Critics, both in his time and later, were quick to point out the many, perhaps inevitable, contradictions in his work. For example, *Punch* satirized the divergence between Morris's socialist politics and the wealthy clientele for his handcrafted furniture and tapestries; later critics would call Morris the "first champagne socialist."[76] It is a further irony that Morris's romances were made popular by "mass-produced Longmans editions [that] were more responsible for fostering a sense of socialist community down the years than . . . the Kelmscott objets d'art."[77] Meanwhile, Morris and utopianism more broadly were criticized for being impractical by scientific socialists, who emphasized agonistic politics and materialist dialectics; this included Engels, who, Elizabeth Carolyn Miller writes, called Morris "a pure sentimental dreamer" and "sarcastically commented in 1887" how "as a poet [he] is above science."[78]

The garden-city movement, which was characterized by a technocratic, "apolitical" stance that was in fact subtended by new liberal ideology, bears out different aspects of both critiques. It was too easy for garden-city enthusiasts to adopt the aesthetics of Morris's vision for a holistic and organic society, where "nothing is wasted and nothing is spoilt," while dropping all but the shell of its more radical politics. At best, Arts and Crafts in this sense was merely a vehicle for bohemian circles of "champagne socialists."[79] At worst, it helped provide an aesthetic model for its opposite, namely, the new liberal colonialism of the social-reform and town-planning movements.

Morris thus leaves behind an ambiguous legacy. Certainly, his utopianism was grounded in a politicized aesthetics, even if it could not fully escape from the contradictions of capitalist production. For example, his publishing and craft endeavors were, clientele aside, attempts not only to shrink the process of production and consumption but also to reorient modern life around a conception of the beautiful. The *News from Nowhere* suggests that the path to this kind of socialist future lies through *imagining* otherwise in fiction that is speculative rather than realistic, and one that frames its narrative as a dream. Further, the community described in *News from Nowhere* is not only incidentally beautiful but one that derives ethical meaning and social cohesion through its aesthetic unity. Rather than simply being a source of pleasantness, this aesthetic unity grounds organic and genuine relations between people, and this is the core of its utopianism.

Community: Insufficiency, Excess, and Absence

Morris's writing speaks to debates around the sustainability of British capitalism and imperialism during his time, but it can also be situated within a broader frame of thinking the possibility and desirability of community. The conditions of possibility for community as such are closely tied to what remains in excess outside its borders and what finds itself absented within. That is, are imagined and realized communities self-sufficient totalities? Or is community inherently a structure of insufficiency, one that not only leaves behind but requires an outside in order to define itself? Leela Gandhi's *Affective Communities* is especially useful in establishing this frame. While she does not discuss Morris at length, she does argue that late-nineteenth-century utopianism made possible unlikely ties among those marginalized by the status quo, a true politics of friendship that produced "self consciously creative forms of anti-imperialism" and, indeed, many other kinds of opposition.[80] These affective communities were not and could not be founded on assumptions of sameness, especially in the exclusionary forms of the nation or of the "west," for example. Instead, Gandhi turns to discussions of the aporetic "community without community" found first in Georges Bataille and then in the poststructuralist thought of Jean-Luc Nancy, Jacques Derrida, and Maurice Blanchot, among others. Within this conversation, the attempt to positively articulate the utopian community responds to existing limitations in theorizing the relationship between the individual and the social. For example, the Kantian, sovereign subject supposes itself to be integral and able to interact with an "outside" (whether epistemological, ethical, or aesthetic) through a transactional and universal reason. Notions of community, meanwhile, had often been influenced by Hegel's epistemology of recognition and, more tangibly, in the attempt to produce world-historical homogeneity through the nation-state form.[81]

Thus, what is seemingly needed is a subject that can stand apart from coercive group identification while remaining continually open to even radical otherness, on the one hand, and a community that can cohere as such without seeking sameness, either as the ground for a common identity or through the violent process of subsumption. Both of these needs are impossible, and as such the resulting community is "unworkable, inoperative, negative . . . under erasure . . . perpetually deferred, 'indefinitely perfectible,' yet-to-come."[82] In every case these articulations of community are fundamentally aporetic, characterized variously by excess—the ecstatic desires that, perhaps, dislocate the sovereign subject—and absence—an insufficiency that makes the desiring subject still need the other in order constitute itself. Is the garden England of *News from Nowhere* such a community without community? Heuristically, it would have to reject a notion of individual or communal self-sufficiency in favor of an always-open hospitality to outsiders and to the marginalized—a friendship that does not demand sameness. It would have to continually risk itself to accommodate visitors, including those yet to arrive and literally to-be-determined. This community would be noncommunitarian, built on a groundless ground of in-betweenness and conjunction, an anarchist relationality not of individuals but rather between "an emerging and unpredictable assemblage of positions" or singularities.[83]

In many ways, Morris's Nowhere *is* recognizable as a community of friendship where harmonious social relations are achieved only through the absolute freedom of the creative individual. William Guest, as the name suggests, is a figure for this community's ethics of hospitality as a visitor, returning from many years in a foreign land. In fact, the more he is included in the community of nowhere, the more he becomes a figure of estrangement: Over the course of the novel, his alterity is further emphasized such that he becomes a visitor from a distant planet and from times past. This extends even to basic concepts that Guest tries to understand, like "politics," "poverty," or "school," which have no meaning for the people he meets. For example, while work is central to the operations of this community, it no longer no longer appears as "work" because it follows so naturally from singular desires, which are free to change, even from day to day, without causing any disruption.

Despite his alterity, however, Guest is not necessarily a figure that would put Nowhere at risk. Though in a dream, he is not the kind of "spectral presence," in the terms Derrida sets forth, that speaks to a fundamental "coexistence of incompatible values" and to "non-reciprocity, to dissymmetry, or to disproportion . . . to the irreducible precedence of the other."[84] This is partly because despite his supposed travels abroad, he is ultimately not a figure of racial alterity, salient because such a figure is important, at least implicitly, in the critical discourse about community discussed earlier.[85] In addition, the community that Morris imagines seems to posit a human nature, one that is fundamentally Rousseauian in character: Once the degradations of civilization, particularly those of the nineteenth century, are removed, people are capable of expressing their essential creative humanity. This contrasts with the character of absence that Blanchot finds in any structure of "community." Rejecting the community founded upon either common experience or fusion into a group interiority, Blanchot suggests that the idea of community always wrestles with the "the infiniteness of alterity, while at the same time deciding its inexorable finitude," a movement that "ruins immanence as well as the usual forms of transcendence."[86] In *News from Nowhere*, however, society appears not just as in nature but as naturalistic, as a capitalistic division of labor becomes its opposite, with needs, abilities, and desires effortlessly matching themselves to one another. In this sense there is absolute self-sufficiency.

Hammond's description of Nowhere's production, where "nothing is wasted and nothing is spoilt," seems to apply more generally to a society that does not have or need any excesses or absences, where every potential is accounted for. It is a community that takes the form of a sleepy afternoon, "the sort of afternoon that Tennyson must have been thinking about, when he said of the Lotos-Eater's land that it was a land where it was always afternoon."[87] The speculative futurity of the novel is also what denies alternative futures. It does not imagine a future but rather *the* future, when a forever-deferred utopian socialism finally arrives; having arrived, it is self-reproducing and contains no capacity (or need) for alternative futures. Similarly, the telos of the model garden city was only its replication over the entire space of England and, eventually, the world. Once created, both imaginaries suppose their own self-sufficiency, sustainability, and reproducibility. In this world, socialism is not just a principle of equality but a community without alienation, where beautiful people produce beautiful art and objects in a beautiful garden landscape.

The Aesthetics of Community

The assumptions and problems of this self-sustaining community are most apparent in the emphasis that *News from Nowhere* places on the beautiful. As mentioned earlier, Morris's most popular phrase is "Have nothing in your houses that you do not know to be useful or believe to be beautiful." In *News from Nowhere*, the space of the community is itself a house, and physical beauty is an index for Nowhere's utopian character. There is a constant emphasis not just on the beauty of the crafted objects and the natural landscape but also on the people themselves. For example, this is a society that prevents and even reverses aging, because while "one ages very quickly if one lives amongst unhappy people . . . southern England is a good place for keeping good looks."[88] Similarly, Clara says of Guest, "I think in a few months we shall make him look younger; and I should like to see what he was like with the wrinkles smoothed out of his face."[89] The authentic, artful life in Nowhere has a quasi-magical effect on aging, and the community's salubrious aesthetics produce people who are "free, happy, and energetic . . . and more commonly beautiful of body also, and surrounded by beautiful things."[90] Similarly, the green surroundings serve as an environment that is capable of producing different kinds of subjects. Together, the beautiful community is physically regenerative and creates its own aura of vitality.

The beautiful both marks and reproduces the utopian character of the community. Further, beauty is taken to be most persuasive in the novel when associated with the women, who Guest remarks are "at least as good as the gardens, the architecture, and the male men."[91] For example, he is astonished, on account of her physical beauty, to learn that Clara is forty-two years old: "I stared at her, and drew musical laughter from her again; but I might well stare, for there was not a careful line on her face; her skin was smooth as ivory, her cheeks full and round, her lips as red as the roses she had brought in; her beautiful arms, which she had bared from her work, firm and well-knit from shoulder to wrist."[92] This passage, and the novel as a whole, is not just descriptive of beauty but filled with desire. The sensual imagery is in fact cliché—musical laughter, ivory skin, rose-red lips—but as such it turns Clara into an archetypical woman, existing perhaps only in utopia. Opposed to the idealized beauty of Nowhere's women is the very real, from Guest's point of view, ugliness of nineteenth-century women: "the row of gaunt figures, lean, flat-breasted, ugly, without a grace of form or face about them; dressed in wretched skimpy print gowns, and hideous flapping sun-bonnets, moving their rakes in a listless mechanical way. How often had that marred the loveliness of the June day to me."[93] These women mark the essential ugliness of the nineteenth century and in turn the unequal, destructive quality of industrial modernity.

Work, too, becomes a matter of beauty, both in producing the beautiful but also in making labor itself "attractive." The point of work and life is pleasure, and thus the aim of any socialistic society is not to remove work but rather to "beautify our labor."[94] As Ruth Kinna argues, Morris privileges explicitly artistic work over other types of labor, while insisting, following Fourier, that all types of necessary labor would be taken up willingly in the absence of capitalist economic coercion, for example, the "most necessary and pleasantest of all work—cultivating the earth."[95] Here, not only is the end of labor to produce the beautiful (and the useful), but labor itself is aestheticized, made beautiful and "attractive."[96]

There are many potential problems in grounding community in the beautiful. For example, while the appeal of this idealized future community lies in part in its beautiful architecture, gardens, and goods, the description of Nowhere as a community only of beautiful, ageless people has subeugenic undertones. Morris did write during a period where Francis Galton's eugenics were accepted science and racial difference seen as natural fact, though there is no evidence that this particularly informed *News from Nowhere*.[97] Second, the community of beautiful people also unsettles due to the male gaze of the narration, which clearly sees the preponderance of beautiful, ageless, possibly available women as part of this future's utopian character. It might be the case that the aesthetic beauty of the community is tainted through its associations, conscious or not, with these highly racialized and gendered social constructions. At the same time, however, it should not be the case that one can simply remove these problematic elements and leave in place the rest of the beautiful community—its garden landscape, quaint architecture, and "dainty" meals. Rather, the primacy of the aesthetic works to figurally enclose the utopia of the novel. The beautiful is not only notoriously unforgiving but is almost definitionally a self-sufficient whole. An otherness beyond this whole would not be a risk only because it would not be capable of representation.

Planning and the Dream of Community

Nowhere, then, can be read as a site of sublimated desire for the beautiful. In its self-sufficiency, the way that it reproduces itself and its sustaining labor "naturally" and without political artifice, the novel's aesthetics influenced and chimed with the assumptions of planning. Similarly, the cultivated taste for beautiful things within the Arts and Crafts movement became a specific and forceful type of commodity fetishism, an amplification rather than a critique of the consumer economy. Much of the legacy of Arts and Crafts, then, was an aestheticized politics (or rather, an apolitics) instead of a politicized aesthetics. For this reason, as discussed earlier, Morris's aesthetics were often considered politically inert sentimentality (at best) by the scientific Marxists of his day. Alternatively, later figures like E. P. Thompson have rendered Morris into a heroic figure whose concern for an essential and creative humanity corresponds to the early Marx and whose focus on the natural world anticipates the environmental movements.[98]

Rather than take any of these positions, this reading tries to identify in Arts and Crafts a set of affective and aesthetic structures and the way that those structures have become embedded in planning practice. That is, instead of rendering Morris as a particularly heroic figure—either for his craft production or for his socialism—the significance of his work can be seen in the way it works through, often unsuccessfully, the social contradictions of the period. In a way, the legacy of this work is not just its polyvalent, utopian aesthetic imaginary but in fact its inability to link that imaginary to a coherent politics. For example, the fact that Arts and Crafts production needed to enter circulation as (high-priced) commodities was not particular to Kelmscott Press but rather a generalized, and rather inescapable, feature of the consumer economy.[99]

Morris's imaginary of place and the Arts and Crafts aesthetic overall has been susceptible to reification in this way; as such, however, it opens onto sets of problems and contradictions that have only intensified across recent historical eras. Morris's ethos becomes congruent with neoliberal practices of individual improvement, such as DIY, minimalism, and creative reuse. Arts and Crafts utopianism is wedged, awkwardly, between the political dream of a cooperative, communal future and the aesthetic lure of improvement through consumption in a capitalist economy. As we will see in Chapters 4 and 5, the latter is the aesthetic of gentrification, through which spaces are appropriated and tastefully improved; indeed, often this improvement takes the form of kitsch Victorianism, recalling, for example, the quaint style of Arts and Crafts or "repurposing" the relics of an industrial economy like warehouses, factories, or even power plants. Yet the utopian dream of *Nowhere* lingers in the background of these practices of spatial and self-improvement. That is, the contradictions of the beautiful, self-sufficient community are still latent and worked out in contemporary culture.[100]

Meanwhile, comparing Morris and Howard shows concrete historical linkages and a common frame to the incipient worlds of planning and design in the late nineteenth century. It also shows, however, the multivalent politics of this frame, including areas where utopian and colonial thinking found common ground. In the next chapter, I will show how garden-city designs flourished in the context of empire through the prolific (and excessive) writings of Patrick Geddes. Geddes takes up many of the concerns of Howard and other social reformists—the slum, overcrowding, industrial modernity, and the disappearance of local culture—and mediates them by expanding the spatial and temporal scales of planning. Planning, in Geddes's thought, will become a means to "act locally" while "thinking globally." That is, the role of the planner will be to reinvigorate and capture the spirit of a local place within a global-imperial context and to do so by capturing the "primitive" essence of that place and manifesting it in a utopian, but realizable, future.

2
Planning as Imperial Cultivation in the Work of Patrick Geddes

> My ambition being . . . to write in reality—here with flower and tree, and elsewhere with house and city—it is all the same.[1]

> A city is more than a place in space, it is a drama in time.[2]

In 1915, Patrick Geddes, a Scottish biologist, sociologist, and town planner, was invited to India by Madras's governor, Lord Pentland, in the hope that "Geddes would advise municipal administrators in India about the new emerging subject of town planning."[3] Geddes, who had just published his lengthy treatise *Cities in Evolution* in 1915, traveled throughout India from 1915 to 1919, consulting on planning projects and publishing reports, eventually becoming founding chair of the department of sociology and civics at Bombay University. In his initial report for the governor, he writes what could be the thesis of his entire theory of urban planning:

> Town-planning is not mere place-planning, nor even work-planning. If it is to be successful, it must be folk-planning. This means that its task is not to coerce people into new places against their associations, wishes, and interest—as we find bad schemes trying to do. Instead its task is to find the right places for each sort of people; places where they will really flourish. To give people in fact the same care that we give when transplanting flowers, instead of harsh evictions and arbitrary instructions to "move on," delivered in the manner of officious amateur policemen.[4]

Inspired by the incipient garden-city movement in Britain, Geddes articulated a humanist view of urban planning, one explicitly opposed to a top-down approach that imposed the singular view of planning authorities onto a space and people. As the quotation suggests, Geddes considered the figure of the planner less as a visionary architect of urban space and more as a gardener, not only in creating literal green spaces but in cultivating people and places. At the same time, he developed much of this theory while working in the interwar empire, in which the British imperium was both at its sprawling territorial height and being increasingly challenged by anticolonial movements.

This chapter addresses the mutual relationship between early urban planning and the late empire, arguing that the ideologies and modes of governance of the latter are embedded in the epistemologies of the former. Geddes's "work was carried out as part of a complex network of imperial connections and determined by a multiplicity of actors and local realities . . . his work throughout the Empire should be considered as one town planner of many working throughout the colonies, forming a substantial professional network sharing various traits."[5] Interwar planners, many of whom would be instrumental in creating aspects of the postwar welfare state in Britain, relied upon the hierarchical power structures and technical infrastructures of empire to develop their theories and practices. However, while critiques of urban planning have articulated it as a practice that often eliminates local character and distinction, the work of Geddes and other colonial planners suggests that power can operate as much through horizontal, bottom-up practices as through vertical, top-down ones. This contradiction cannot be simply explained as the result of cognitive dissonances and even hypocrisies of the individual planners or the governing authorities. Rather, figural *cultivation* operated as an epistemological mode that resolved these contradictions through an understanding of empire as a practice of social reproduction rather than one of social repression. Urban planning, even in an explicitly imperial setting, was thus not always concerned with the elimination of local character and distinction.

Geddes is an interesting figure for interwar planning because of the range and volume of his work, the diversity of contexts in which he worked, and his considerable, if at times muted, influence on planning (Lewis Mumford in particular). Meanwhile, he adopted an avowedly humanist, pacifist, and apolitical disposition; he was neither a stalwart defender of British imperialism, nor sympathetic to contemporary anticolonial and anticapitalist movements, nor even a political moderate. Rather, such positions were displaced by a holistic and syncretic conception of the planned place. Inspired in part by

Ebenezer Howard, Geddes held planning as the key to creating an ideal community, one functioning without disagreement or excess.

This speculative imaginary of the future city and its cultivated citizen ostensibly counteracted the racial hierarchies of empire and the economics of extraction (of both resources and labor), replacing them with a humane, urban translocality. Indeed, Geddes is credited with inspiring the popular environmentalist slogan "Act Local, Think Global." As such, the relationship between his work and its imperial context has often gone unexamined; instead, as Noah Hysler-Rubin writes, "in India, Geddes is described almost entirely as representing the opposite of the British government's aims, disregarding his imperial role and turning only to the needs and aspirations of the local population."[6] However, the interwar empire, particularly in long-established colonies like those in South Asia, was marked both by the intimacy of colonial relationships and by an increasing sense of global connectivity (through circuits of trade, production, and communication). This dynamic made it conducive to the fantasy of a postpolitical, technological, and creative global society.

This chapter focuses less on the enactment of Geddes's plans and more on the way his writings index the ideological assumptions and epistemologies of the interwar empire. What were the conditions of possibility that enabled a figure like Geddes to imagine future places and theorize social relations within them? Answering this question requires a dual approach, not only examining the concrete social context of early-twentieth-century planning and empire but also analyzing his work as an aesthetic cultural production. Geddes's work demonstrates how planning is not simply a technical enterprise but an aesthetic and literary mode of speculation.

In fact, his writing encourages such a reading. Geddes sees art and literature as perhaps the prime expressions of a city's *genius loci* (spirit of a place) and often reads literary texts as types of city surveys. For example, in *Cities in Evolution* (1915), he writes,

> We say with Shelley, "Hell is a city much like London"; we see how slow must be our journey out of its Valley of Shadow. . . . Yet less fiery presentment of the city's life-process is needed than any of these sternly mythopoetic ones. What better, then, than Blake's? A veritable town-planner's hymn:
>
> > I will not cease from mental strife,
> > Nor shall my sword fall from my hand,
> > Till I have built Jerusalem
> > Within this green and pleasant land[7]

He goes on to situate his work within "the various and vivid protests of nineteenth-century romance," most often citing the trinity of "Carlyle, Ruskin, Morris."[8] The suggested reading section that appends *Cities in Evolution* prominently recommends authors ranging from Stevenson to Dickens to Zola (under the category of "town surveys").[9] Often, *Cities* rhetorically marks itself as narrative, as when he describes the process of town expansion through the analogy of the Cinderella story. In other texts, the aesthetic form of his planning theory is more explicit. *The World Without and the World Within* stages a dialogue with his children that likens planning to gardening (as discussed in what follows). *The Masque of Learning and Its Many Meanings* is a theatrical pageant of civic history and was performed in Edinburgh in 1912. Some of his most passionate projects were not actual civic interventions but rather exhibitions that narrativized the history of cities in a variety of fora (including a museum in Edinburgh that he called the Outlook Tower). In India, Geddes sought contact with the poet Rabindranath Tagore, with whom he shared an extensive correspondence.[10]

Geddes expands upon the garden-city ethos, suggesting not just a resolution to contemporary class conflict through planning but a reconciliation that would be transhistorical and translocal, harmoniously connecting the individual spirit of each place to a replete global community in the future. This chapter treats Geddes's writings on the city as topothesia—a speculative and aesthetic imaginary of a future place. Later chapters will ask how the totalizing social ecology imagined by Geddes—places that are simultaneously local and global in perfect harmony—finds political form and literary response in the present. For example, Chapter 3 will consider moments of social conflict in Thatcherite Britain and the persistent turn to planning, development, and design to mediate this conflict; my reading of John Akomfrah's *Handsworth Songs* there will point to the absences, gaps, and ambivalences of the Geddesian imaginary. Similarly, Chapter 6 will read Caryl Phillips's *A Distant Shore* in order to study the regional geography established by the forces of development as one not of harmony but of social fracture and discontent. Thus the focus on Geddes and his cultural milieu in this chapter is not meant to exclude the literary but to show how the speculative imaginary of early planning echoes, ambiguously, into the contemporary.

Patrick Geddes and the Garden-City Movement

Patrick Geddes began his academic career as a biologist before branching out to sociology and the incipient field of town planning in his native Edinburgh. In 1911, he was hired as a planning consultant in Dublin and later invited to India and Mandatory Palestine. In this trajectory, he was not particularly unusual among his contemporaries, as "by the interwar years, colonial India was a surprising experimental ground for urban design."[11] British planners operated in several parts of the empire in the interwar period, including India, South Africa, Malaysia, Nairobi, Zanzibar, Singapore, and Palestine. Robert Home has detailed the strong connection between the interwar empire and garden-city planning, the latter of which had an "evangelical zeal."[12] There are many examples of prominent architects and designers developing an embryonic field of planning abroad: Edwin Lutyens, who went from planning Henrietta Barnett's quaint Hampstead garden suburb to designing the British government's new capital at Delhi in 1915; Herbert Baker, Lutyens's co-planner, who had already deployed garden-city ideas in South Africa;[13] Charles Ashbee, a former Toynbee Hall resident and Arts and Crafts enthusiast who went from designing handmade furniture in Chipping Camden to town planning in Palestine;[14] Henry Vaughan Lanchester, editor of *The Builder*, who co-founded the Town Planning Institute shortly after returning from New Delhi and Madras and later crafted plans for colonial Zanzibar along Geddesian lines; and Patrick Abercrombie, who joined Geddes both in Dublin and in Palestine before returning to Britain to author the post–World War II plan for London. The mutual influence between the practice of planning and colonial governance was at once "characterised by extreme exertions of power on behalf of the colonial state" and also capable of operating in a highly decentralized and heterogeneous manner as it adapted itself to local situations.[15]

These individuals and others formed a mostly male cohort of planners who tested their speculative visions of the future city in the contemporary empire. That is, the infrastructure of empire made possible the global movement and circulation of British planning ideas in a way that was intrinsically gendered. As such, the work of women in developing urban planning has often gone unacknowledged; for example, Geddes's contemporary interlocutor Jaqueline Tyrwhitt, as Ellen Shoshkes extensively documents, was in particular responsible not only for publishing an edited collection of his India reports widely but also in spreading his influence among the myriad of organizations and schools that were founded in the growing field.[16] As discussed in Chapter 1, planning grew out of the social-reform movement, one led by as many women as men and one that organized its moral imperative around a concern for domesticity.[17] City planning, on the other hand, and particularly in the empire, foregrounded the experiences and agency of men, ultimately producing the figure of the globetrotting European expert consultant. While the work of women such as Octavia Hill was deeply colonial in character, it is significant that the role of women becomes diminished as urban planning and reform achieves professional respectability. What remained prominent, however, was an understanding of the city and its inhabitants in environmental and biopolitical terms.

The "Eutopian" City of the Future and the Slum Cities of the Present

Geddes cites Howard's *Garden Cities of To-morrow* as an example of what he calls "eutopian" thought—idealistic yet concretely realizable—praising its focus on "electricity, hygiene, and art, by efficient and beautiful town planning and associated rural development, and by a corresponding rise of social co-operation and effective good-will."[18] The terms that Geddes conjoins here are indicative of his holistic approach. "Electricity, hygiene, and art" bring together technology, policy, and human creativity, while proper town planning leads unambiguously to social harmony. Rather than seeking the production of green spaces for the sake of mere sanitation or anxious control of unruly subjects, planning emerges as a supposedly conflict-free method of reimagining a sustainable social world, one whose incidental benefit would be negating politics as such. Like Howard, Geddes takes an integrative approach, aiming to include all aspects of social reproduction within the bounds of the reimagined city, a relationality of elements without excess.

Before considering Geddes's work in India and Palestine, it is important to note the way that Geddes and interwar planners continued and developed the legacy of the garden-city movement. What is generally understood as his signature work, *Cities in Evolution* (1915), takes many of the concrete practices of social reform and planning and incorporates them in a universal (if rather unwieldy) theory of the city. Like other early planners, he was less interested in a nostalgic return to the past than in looking forward to a reconciliatory future, one that would solve the problems of the industrial age (such as the existence of urban slums) while retaining its technological capacity. He terms the present age of industrial pollution, overcrowding, and social conflict the "paleotechnic" and the coming age of gardens, art, and social harmony the "neotechnic" (following the Stone Age designations paleolithic and neolithic).[19] Geddes, like other social reformers and early planners, identifies the *slum* as a site of particular concern, as it concretizes the problems of early-twentieth-century life.

Geddes universalizes the slum as *the* problem of "paleotechnic" modernity and frames garden-city planning as a globally applicable "neotechnic" solution not only in terms of spatial scale (i.e., in empire) but also as a comprehensive reimagining of social relations. For Geddes, urban spaces become species of the genus *slum*: "Ghetto-slums, Port-slums, Works-slums, Shop-slums,

Barrow-slums, Pub-slums, Trull-slums, Thief-slums, Doss-slums all the way out and back again to the Embankment."[20] The expansiveness of the slum as *type* includes the wealthiest neighborhoods as well—the "super-slum." Thus even wealthy areas reveal their fundamental slumness in their

> labyrinth of dreary drying-greens, cut up by mean walls into a web of proportionless quadrilaterals, triangles, and clumsy trapeziums. In this way whole acres lie derelict, spoilt for every vital purpose. . . . Gardening has sometimes been attempted, but with little result. At best there is a forlorn tree or two, self-sown, or planted anyhow . . . what is it but slum, impure and simple? Indeed worse; for deadly dull, its gardens childless.[21]

Geddes finds the symptoms of slum character everywhere, but its most consistent expression is in the quality of gardens and trees. These symbolize dereliction and death rather than a particular affliction of poverty. That is, it is not the inequality of city spaces that drives Geddes to action but rather a universal struggle against slum living, a social withering evinced by withering gardens—either their derelict and spoiled absence or dreary, drying, and dull half-presence. Thus, people of all classes face the common problem of "forlorn" trees and "childless" gardens, with the latter also pointing to a hopeless future, a crisis in the temporality of paleotechnic society itself. In this way, the urban slum becomes an almost metaphysical figure for the crises of modernity. Geddes makes explicit what his contemporaries only implied: that the slum is not just a "decayed" physical space within the industrial city but rather a dense figure that connected a host of problems—social, biological, technological, political, and moral.

Cultivating Environments and Subjects

In addition, Geddes continues the prerogatives of liberal colonialism, especially its concern with moral improvement, education, and cultivation. As seen in Chapter 1, the garden city responds to the problem of the slum not only through its cultivated urban greenery but more importantly through cultivating future citizens. Like Howard, Geddes thinks in terms of the *model*, linking the planning of cities to the forms in which they become available as representations. For example, once created, the garden city is not only a functioning urban space but a general model of civic engagement and an image of the future city that might be replicated elsewhere. It is both itself and a representation of itself, an example for planners and the public of how a garden city could be created and what it would look like. Geddes thus argues that the making of cities and citizens is ongoing in a continual production of models and examples:

> The general education of the public as regards better housing and garden suburbs, though slow and difficult until object-lessons were ready, is now going on rapidly, and in the easiest and most natural of ways, of direct observation and experience. Every co-operative tenant, every new garden-city or suburb occupant, is helping in this, and by example. His associations are actively propagandist.[22]

Every new garden city is a partial replication of a model and at the same time serves as a living model for other future garden cities. Each local instance can stand out in its own particularity while simultaneously adhering to a general model, and in so doing it becomes edifying to others.[23] In this way, this continual relay of exhibition and mimicry has, for Geddes, a potential amplifying effect, producing a global neotechnic age in a decentralized, organic fashion as new planners are inspired by newly created spaces.

Geddes also inherits from the garden-city movement a concern with the *local*—the idea that place must first be marked by immediacy and particularity before being integrated into a more holistic structure. In this way, Geddes was explicitly opposed to the "death-dealing Haussmannism" of top-down planning.[24] For Geddes, this takes the form of a perspective on the city that privileged experiential detail obtained through walking, observing, and experiencing. Walking through Indore, for example, Geddes sought "a view of the city from the perspective of the perambulating viewer whose sight radiated from a moving point . . . constantly changing field of vision, bringing different subjects and activities in and out of focus."[25] This perambulatory perspective acquires purchase through an emphasis on direct experiences and dynamic interactions within the city. As such, planning necessitated knowledge that was close to the ground. Robert Home writes, "Geddes was more aware of the relationship between Indian social practices and the urban landscape than British colonial officials had ever been. He wanted to encourage the revival of customs and traditions which prompted a clean environment."[26] His aim was to uncover, through walking and research, the *genius loci*—the spirit of the place.[27]

However, this position was not unique by the interwar period. In fact, his integration of the local and the global fits into a wider ideological pattern of late European empires, namely, that "Europe's power elites were now taking pains . . . to reassure each other that their coercion and brutality were no longer frank attempts at extraction but reasoned efforts to build structures capable of reproducing themselves."[28] A distinction can even be made between a coercive *mission civilisatrice* of late-nineteenth-century imperialism and an emerging ideology that was both more expansive and subtle, one premised on inculcating productive and self-regulatory environments and subjects. Thus the "focus on people working under the direction of town planners to uplift their own environments was construed as a suitable form of local self-government," with "British efforts at fostering local self-government among Indians consist[ing] of encouraging native participation in municipal organizations."[29] The practice of planning thus worked to cultivate and teach civic participation. In identifying with and caring for local environments, these newly formed citizens might also be personally and politically invested in the structures of empire.[30] Geddes's focus on the local coincided with these strands of late imperial policy. For example, Geddes favorably cites his contemporary Henry Vaughan Lanchester, who "expressed with a wise conservatism, a respect for Indian architecture, craftsmanship, and ways of life. Without entering unduly into imperial politics, it may here be recalled that city planning has ever been a part of imperial policy."[31] Similarly, invoking the local in planning was a way for Geddes to reference "imperial policy" without undue entrance into "imperial politics."

For example, referring to political agitation in India, he laments the "spirit of unrest" among imperial subjects. For this he blames the "neurasthenia" of Indian universities. He writes that "the cure lies not through repression, however inevitable this may seem or be in given cases. For this growing dissatisfaction calls for far more general treatment—nothing less than that of putting the Universities—and thus the whole of education with them—upon a fresh footing, at once new and old . . . in the continued service and ascent of man."[32] Neurasthenia, a pseudobiological state of fatigue and lack of energy, is a trope of eugenic thinking and had been used to describe a state of degeneration among the "undeserving" poor in Europe and the recalcitrant colonial subject. As seen here, educational neurasthenia could also be linked to a spirit of (political) unrest, insofar as the latter expressed the unfocused energy of the not-yet liberal subject.[33] For Geddes and others, especially in the late empire, the solution is not repression but rather renewed cultivation and the production of different kinds of subjects.

For Geddes, politics at any scale, imperial, national, or local, was a distraction, and political tension could be resolved through locally attentive planning. For example, in a letter on his way to India in 1915, he writes:

> I increasingly feel the value of our own exhibitions in India and that of my conservative yet constructive attitude and influence in cities and towns to be of direct political as well as social value . . . an unexpect-

edly direct bearing on order and stability—even of the Empire—not only by economy etc. but by tending to check the revolutionary spirit by the Eutopian one—and cast out devils by ideals, so rendering a very direct form of service even in and for these times of war.[34]

The exhibitions that Geddes refers to here consisted of pedagogical lectures and displays of good town-planning practices. His presentations intend to do more than simply engage in an ongoing debate among professionals as to the best and most efficient way to organize a city. Rather, he imagines them having a wider value in "checking" the revolutionary spirit, whether based in class or colonial tensions, and in this way "Eutopian" urban design could be a "third alternative" to the agonistic politics of war or revolution.[35] The "revolutionary spirit" is figured as devilish, but the solution is certainly not simple repression; rather, he offers a speculative vision of the future city as a way of mediating social conflict in the present. More than just a temporary, compensatory gesture, an empire of garden cities could be imagined as a self-sustaining colonialism.

Like *Garden Cities of To-morrow*, the speculative form of Geddes's writing is the key to understanding his complicated influence on the field of planning. His writing was voluminous and covered an array of topics in different disciplines, often in a meandering, disorganized, hyperbolic style that both charmed and confounded his interlocutors. It foregrounds planning's speculative and narrative aspects—the way planning needs to tell stories about potential, imagined futures. Clavel and Young write that "attempts to characterize Geddes' thought are often replete with frustration," yet within his texts is a coherent "Geddesian urban theory, promoted within a field he named 'Civics' to encompass both its intellectual content and its connection to urban action."[36]

Ironically, in attempting to articulate a holistic, syncretic, and optimistic understanding of social relations through planning, Geddes's texts become formally excessive. Chapter 1 noted this same irony in the writing of other planners, but Geddes's texts almost seem excessive on principle: They are repetitive, lengthy, and desultory affairs filled with digressions, run-on sentences, and confusingly mixed metaphors. At any point, he is liable to slip into his preferred rhetorical mode of extravagant purple prose that extolls the wonders of the "eutopian" city to come. Further, he often turns to the visual in order to communicate his ideas, producing what he called "thinking machines"—elaborate, formalistic diagrams that, in attempting to encapsulate all of his thoughts at once, become dizzyingly complex and esoteric. Despite intending to condense his ideas into a small yet comprehensive image, these diagrams are almost impossible to understand without further explanation.[37] They are indicative of a desire to contain a social theory within a stable structure and frame.

The Planner as Gardener

Planning is generally speculative, in that it is an activity that involves imagining future environments and then taking concrete steps to realize that imaginary. For garden cities, it was important that these environments be green, with varied forms of production and transportation, and not overcrowded for reasons of health and sanitation. The term "garden city," however, appeals not just because it implies gardens *in* cities but imagines cities *as* gardens. That is, the city is analogous to a garden, and for Geddes the planner tends to the city as a gardener. Influenced by his training as a biologist, he makes extensive use of various biological analogies—horticultural, ecological, evolutionary—to conceptualize the city.[38] More than simply greening and "sanitizing" polluted urban environments, garden-city planning comes to represent a "civic awakening . . . in healthy upgrowth, capable not only of survival but of fuller cultivation also, towards varied flower and fruit—flower in regional and civic literature and history, art, and science; fruit in social renewal of towns and cities, small and great."[39] The civic revitalization of the town-planning movement is one that tends toward a metaphorical cultivation; as if tending an orchard, the planner carefully sees to the growth, flowering, and eventual fruit of culture, spaces, and citizens. It takes the planner, as gardener and ecological manager, to induce this analogical urban fruit tree to not only survive but thrive.

This sentiment and metaphor is repeated throughout *Cities in Evolution*. Geddes writes in its conclusion that "the planting of future forests is already here and there beginning; among its worst slums, upon their buried filth and decay, our children are already rearing roses" and that from a "blight of disappointments," the new "civic and social order can show, beyond its first weedings and sowings, some earnest of flower or fruit."[40] The present city is rendered in metaphors of decay and blight, as in a diseased crop or forest, while the city to come is a garden or orchard whose cultivation is slow going but will eventually be fruitful. Clearly, these analogies do not operate simply in analytical or logical ways but also carry with them a distinct pathos and sensual appeal (including terms like "blight" and "renewal" that are still consistently used to negatively or positively characterize urban spaces). *Revival*, first producing only weeds—natural but uncultivated—eventually leads to flowers, fruits, future forests, and the bright roses of youth in this description. As we will see in Chapter 4, this imaginary of revival is strikingly similar to the way that contemporary development articulates its own interventions. Geddes's biological analogies, developed in the context of liberal colonialism, find resonance and redeployment in the contemporary gentrifying city.

In this way, the city is thought of as a garden, preferably one that was planned, tended to, and cultivated. The Geddesian city is, in Volker Welter's apt term, a biopolis, and the planner-gardener who took time to survey the built environment and local histories was also coming to understand processes of social evolution. To this end Geddes was inspired by the eugenics of Sir Francis Galton (like many of his contemporaries). He argues that urban revitalization is both "eugenic and educational" and that "healthy life is completeness of relation of organism, function, and environment.... Cities in Evolution and People in Evolution must thus progress together."[41] Viewed through the lens of biology, "healthy life" does not come just by way of access to gardens but rather in a "completeness of relation" between environment and organism. The city and its people are both part of larger-scale ecologies. For Geddes, the "qualities of organic life [were] determined through its interaction with the environment," and accordingly, by improving the environment, one could biologically "improve" its people.[42]

The garden as an analogy for the city and the process of improvement in general is central in another of Geddes's many works, a short book entitled *The World Without and the World Within: Sunday Talks with My Children*. Geddes stages a conversation with his children about their family garden in order to explain the general importance of planning. The text reads as a Platonic dialogue, with Geddes guiding his childish interlocutors along with questions to lead to a central moral that "one must cultivate their garden."[43] For the children, the garden is what the text calls their "out-world," where they play and work; meanwhile, their "in-world" consists of their youthful imagination, in which they dream about the garden and think about how they might improve it. Planning necessarily involves a kind of visual dreaming, with the garden as a realizable phantasmagoria. After dreaming, the children reply that they "can think about what we'll do next; and design and plan," an endeavor that applies thought to intensify the brimming vitality of the garden:

> You remember, for instance, how we looked at our garden early last spring, and saw it was very poor in bulbs, so we dreamed of it rich and bright with snowdrops, crocuses, and daffodils for another year. Then as autumn came we planned how to arrange these. Gradually the plan developed in our heads, with its patches of white and lines of gold, with its circles and groups of varied colours, its dotting over the lawns and its massing under the trees.[44]

Here plainer descriptions of actions ("how we looked," "we planned how to arrange") alternate with luxurious images of the future gardens—circles of color, patches of white, lines of gold. The gentle conjunctive ease of "rich and bright with snowdrops, crocuses, and daffodils" places the reader in a vivifying winter garden, the result of memories and dreams turned into plans and made into reality.[45] The sensuousness of the garden is reproduced in the children's nighttime imagination: "What becomes of the garden for you when we come in in the evening and pull down the blinds, or when you go to bed? 'We can still see it.' Yes, and again the sun shines, the flowers open, and the birds sing; all in some ways more beautifully than before. That is another sort of looking, is it not? The Garden has come in with you; it is in your In-world now."[46] The garden provides a visuality that is accessible and full, abounding with life and easy to reproduce and enhance in the mind's eye. It invites both immersion and cultivation—a space to be explored, analyzed, and improved.

Just like the children with their garden, the planner must first understand their local environment through direct experience, then think about this experience in both analytical and imaginative ways, before going back to the garden to care for and improve the "plants" within. The Geddesian planner emerges as a gardener, taking into account local environmental conditions in order to cultivate the local populace and make its flourishing sustainable over future generations. The appealing figure of a child dreaming of her garden, then, connects to Geddes's impulse to improve subjects into citizens through "gardening, education, and civic responsibility."[47] As Geddes writes in his plan for Indore, planners should advocate for (imperial) garden cities "no longer merely on grounds of sanitation, and economics, or reviving esthetics . . . [but] now in terms of education also . . . from that most elemental labour in which civilization began, to its highest aspects, as Gardens of Life and Youth towards their flowering; Gardens of the Sciences, Gardens of the Muses, Gardens of the Ideals."[48] In hypostasizing the garden city into the Garden of Life etc., Geddes marks planning as fundamentally a practice of education and social reproduction. This figurative mode is not directly repressive—the opposite, in fact. However, it is not neutral with respect to the operations of power that enable planning and that planning works, with intention or not, to sustain. Rather, *cultivation* was an epistemologically and rhetorically available mode for planners because of the prior existence of British imperial hegemony. Cultivation conjoins the imaginary of the garden city, with its attendant discourses of health, sanitation, and urban improvement, to the power structures of the liberal, imperial state.

Producing the Educated Citizen

Philip Boardman relates an anecdote from Geddes's work in India that is suggestive of how *cultivation* conjoined urban improvement and civic engagement, all while taking for granted the power structures of empire. In 1917, Geddes was made "Maharajah for a day" of the city of Indore. The authority granted by this declaration actually lasted for six weeks, during which Geddes attempted to undertake a survey of the city. However, "as he tramped through crowded lanes and along dirty river-fronts, marking on a map the most serious menaces to public health, the Indorians displayed signs of open hostility."[49] In response, Geddes reimagined the festival of Diwali, turning the annual celebration into an analogy about the importance of civic revitalization and hygiene. Geddes produced a dramatic parade through the city that staged the harmful effects of the slum and the benefits of the garden city in a way that he thought would register with the native population. In his planning report, he described a part of procession that would display

> the worst evils from which the City at present suffers. Indian musicians follow, with mournful music. The Tigers of ill omen appear, and figures representing diseases and scattering germs. Then upon a dirty cart with buffalos uncleansed, a dirty house, with rats therein; then the gigantic Rat of Plague, with its fleas; and upon its back the huge and hideous Narakasur, the antagonist of Rama, and now Giant of Dirt, with his destructive distribution of germs. These are courageously attacked by the spirits of cleanliness and of health, though with incomplete success. For Dirt can never be destroyed, yet the warfare with it must never cease. The City begins thus its hopeful and reconstructive presentment.[50]

This parade, which came to fruition in 1918, epitomizes the idea of the colonial cultivator-planner. It begins with Geddes wandering through Indore in order to truly understand not only its topography but its history, culture, and essential spirit—a survey that previous colonial authorities did not think necessary. He is met with a suspicion and hostility symptomatic of imperial relations; in response, Geddes repurposes an ancient festival that he saw as the equivalent of Western "spring-housecleaning."[51] As such, the parade itself appropriates the narrative of Diwali, turning it into an allegory for the importance of city planning. The result is a transformed community, with the slums uplifted rather than demolished. Notably, Geddes becomes the one that charms the plague away; such is the magic of town planning.

As noted earlier, a key component of early planning was its pedagogic function. New garden cities and suburbs were not only places to live and work but functioned as models for the planner to demonstrate their interventions. The diagrams and plans for a city are at once a self-contained expression of design prerogatives and a speculative representation of a future place; similarly, the created city itself becomes a model for its own reproduction. Geddes's work accentuates this aspect of planning, incorporating pedagogic elements not only into every stage of urban development but also centering his notion of the city as such on institutions of exhibition and education.[52] The process of planning, then, required a series of mediations through which the city would become knowable and legible. Those mediations were largely visual in character; as Ola Söderström writes, "For one of the principal pioneers of modern urban planning, Patrick Geddes, the trained eye was the best instrument of scientific knowledge, whilst graphic representation remained the most efficient vector for its diffusion."[53] As such, these representations have a "performative character" and "are not the passive repository of an exterior planning process, but one of the key sites of urbanism in the making."[54] In addition to the putatively neutral task of uncovering underlying structures to the city so as to improve them, Geddes sought to make the city visually available in particular ways.

Geddes's work in India and Palestine was centrally concerned with civic pedagogy and the creation of urban spaces as a means to create and cultivate the citizen. Both the mode of planning and the final planned place operated by way of visualizing knowledge of the city with an aim to its future (and continual) reproduction. This visuality took several forms:

- the **survey**: the first step of planning, wherein the planner comprehensively studies the geography, environment, history, and culture of a particular region in order to uncover its *genius loci*. A key part of the survey involved extensive walking through existing spaces, so that the planner had more than just an abstract or top-down understanding.
- **exhibitions and panoramas**: these gathered together examples of successful cities in the form of drawings, photographs, and maps accompanied by historical context. Geddes would often travel with these exhibitions, to expose new publics to the history of cities, the problems of industrial modernity, and the proposed solution of garden cities.
- the **Outlook Tower** and the **camera obscura**: The Outlook Tower was a museum in Geddes's native Edinburgh, the top floor of which

had a camera obscura rendering Edinburgh's surroundings for visitors. Each floor corresponded to a different spatial scale, moving from Edinburgh on the top floor and then descending to floors covering Scotland, the Anglophone world, Europe, and finally "Oriental civilisations and . . . the general study of Man."[55]
- **parades, masques, drama**: these modes of displaying and narrativizing urban change were particularly effective (for Geddes) in creating citizens knowledgeable of and invested in the process of planning and improvement.
- **universities, museums, galleries, libraries, civic centers**: civic education was not only part of the planning process but a fundamental component to the final urban fabric. These institutions were necessary to preserve the knowledge collected during the survey and would serve as focal points for the reproduction of civic engagement and improvement.

What draws these forms and practices together is a focus on visual education as a central aspect of both planning and the future city. These various modes of modeling and display are continuations of the colonial aspects of Victorian-era exhibitions, world fairs, and museum culture more generally. These various fora were crucial not only to the formation of citizen-subjects but also in mediating the colonial encounter via the controlled visuality of display.[56] *Seeing* allowed for the individual to orient themselves historically and spatially—often simultaneously, as with the many primitivist colonial exhibitions that dramatized both the expanse of colonial possessions and the time of "civilization," often figured in pseudoevolutionary terms. As Thomas Metcalf writes, museums and exhibitions were ways to "transform [a] heterogeneous mass of objects into systematically organized collections" and in doing so narrate a social and historical relationship between the British visitor (as "modern") and the colonial object (as "traditional").[57] For interwar planners, the display of "traditional" craft was also a way of narrating a space, thereby recovering and preserving ancient history. This interest in preservation can be seen in Jerusalem, for example, in which the Mandate administration was initially welcoming to C. R. Ashbee's Arts and Crafts disposition.[58]

Exhibitions aimed to showcase technological prowess while providing visitors with both edification and vicarious thrills, often derived from European colonial adventures. These interventions include panoramas, first presented by Robert Barker in 1788, and dioramas, created in 1822 by Louis-Jacques-Mandé Daguerre, of the famous daguerreotype process that he later invented.[59] By the time Geddes collaborated with his friend Elisée Reclus for the 1900 Paris exhibition, European publics were familiar with many large-scale exhibitions and extensive museum collections cataloguing the material culture of the colonies within the framework of the human sciences.[60] Further, planners, and especially Geddes, conceived of the city itself as an exhibition, displaying its essential spirit and character in preserving its history, while also being oriented to future directions.[61]

The Collection and Display of Colonial Knowledge

As James Clifford argues, in the West, "collecting has long been a strategy for the deployment of a possessive self, culture, and authenticity."[62] For Geddes, collection and display were continual processes for the production of the citizen (See Figures 9a, 9b, and 9c). For example, the survey is not only a planner's tool but something necessary to recover the geographic/environmental particularity and the ancient history of a place. Thus he writes that "for each and every city we need a systematic survey, of its development and origins, its history and its present. This survey is required not merely for material buildings, but also for the city's life and its institutions, for of these the built city is but the external shell."[63] This is an urban version of an older colonial practice; Bernard Cohn writes that "the British appear in the nineteenth century to have felt most comfortable surveying India from above and at a distance . . . they were uncomfortable in the narrow confines of a city street, a bazaar, a mela—anywhere they were surrounded by Indian subjects."[64]

By contrast, however, Geddes sought to extend the survey to include exactly this mode of engagement. Martin Beattie writes of the plan for Barra Bazaar (in Calcutta) that "Geddes acknowledged the huge part played by the

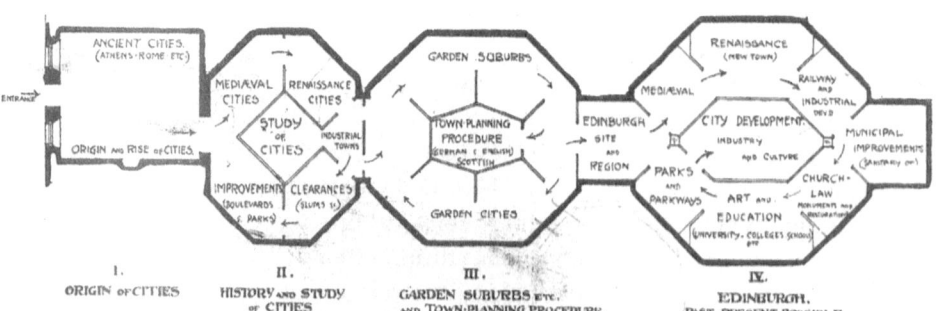

Figure 9a. Cities and Town Planning Exhibition, Edinburgh 1911. (Credit: Sir Patrick Geddes Memorial Trust.)

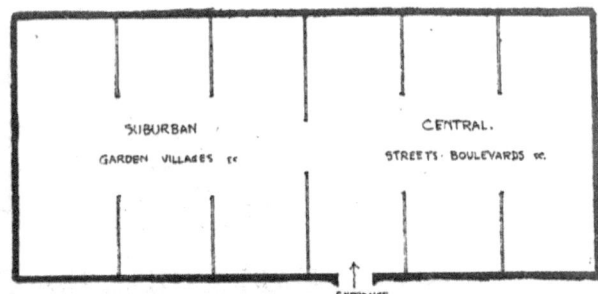

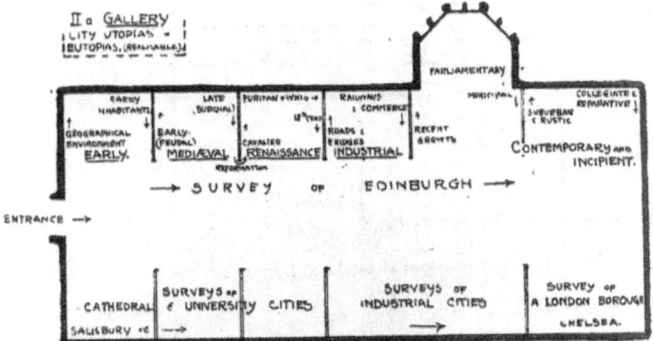

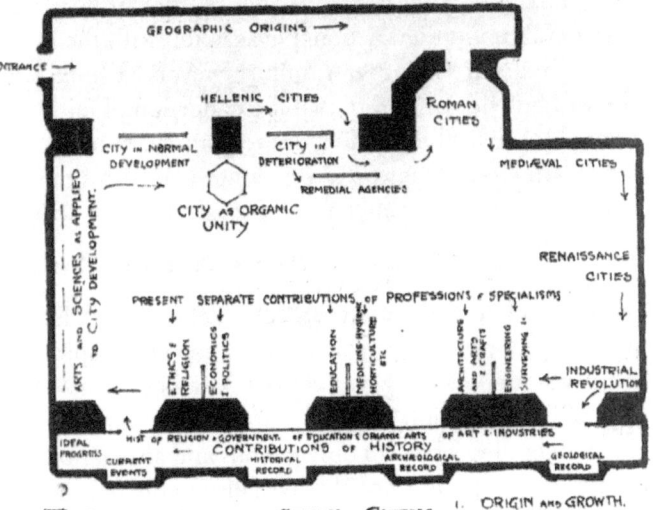

Figure 9b. Cities and Town Planning Exhibitions, Chelsea 1911. (Credit: Sir Patrick Geddes Memorial Trust.)

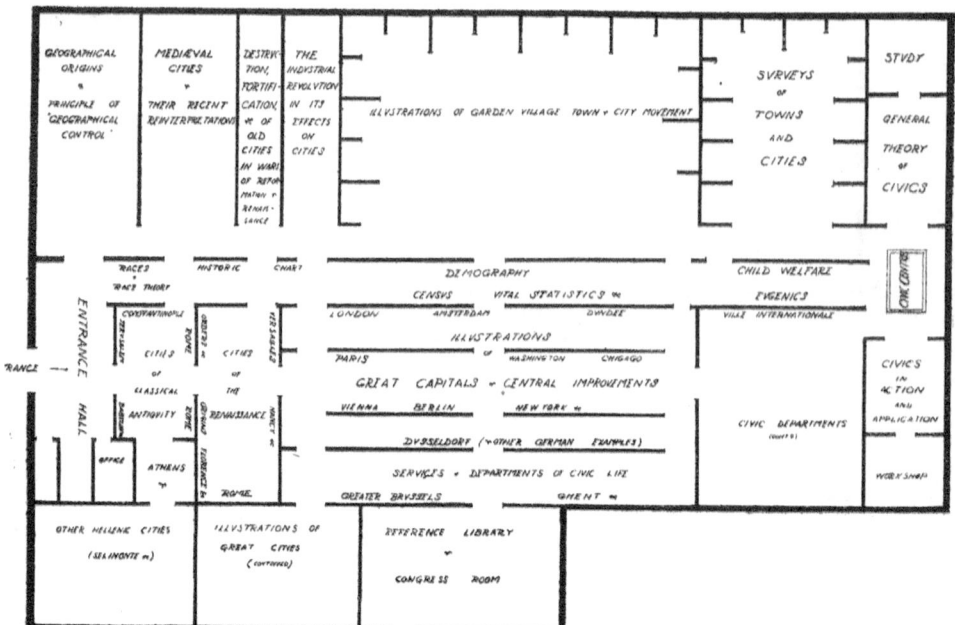

Figure 9c. Cities and Town Planning Exhibitions, Ghent 1913. (Credit: Sir Patrick Geddes Memorial Trust.)

indigenous population in shaping cities in India. For Geddes, meeting and interviewing the people of Barra Bazaar was essential so that a mental picture could be formed, 'of the daily life and working of the district in its various branches of activity and of these in their action and reaction with the city as a whole.'"[65] Thus by the interwar era, at least some surveyors of India were not only comfortable with but viewed as essential the collection of local data and experience mediated through the intellect of the planner. Geddes does not give up the distanced and global viewpoint but rather makes this outlook even more total through the constant generation of local, detailed perspective. Michiel Dehaene writes that the

> survey was for Geddes more than the mere collection of facts and data. It involved the arrangement of these data as a stimulating and inspiring panorama for the planner and citizen alike. This arrangement could take the form of the collection of displays and objects in an exhibition, or that of an endless chain of observations and associations as rendered in his planning reports, or could crystallise in the perma-

nent installation of an urban centre of study and observatory as in his Edinburgh Outlook Tower.[66]

Dehaene identifies this as an empricotranscendental structure of knowledge, following Foucault; as such, it is in exhibition and display that the particularity of the local is placed into relation to more universal understandings of environment and history. Similarly, Hysler-Rubin writes that the Geddesian planner sought to "know the landscape by means of visualisation, ordering, comparison, and display . . . through geography, Geddes linked places sentimentally, creating a common citizen responsibility and planning in the name of imperial citizenship."[67] These visualizations rearticulate existing power structures and governance practices through a humanist idiom of particularity and locality, one that creates the conditions of possibility for a planning epistemology.

There is an aspect to this epistemology that is "positivistic, technocentric, and rationalistic"—qualities that David Harvey associates with high modernism in planning and architecture.[68] "High" modernism in this sense not only refers to a particularly intense quality but to a top-down *perspective*, from which a "particularly sweeping vision of how the benefits of technical and scientific progress might be applied."[69] However, Geddes's approach is a modernism that emphasizes a *multiplicity of perspectives* that can be brought together and harmonized without being homogenized. For example, Geddes's most established model exhibition was a structure he called the "Outlook Tower" in Edinburgh (Figure 10). The Outlook Tower (intentionally) condenses everything that is most important about Geddes's thought into a physical space. The top exhibition of the tower, where the visitor starts, represents the scale of the local, not despite but because of its views of the surrounding city of Edinburgh. As the visitor descends the tower, the exhibitions move outward in space, through Scotland, the Anglophone world, Europe, then finally to the scale of the global. Thus it is "local details . . . in contact with the larger world" that make the model both based in the singularity of place yet "applicable to any city."[70] The scale of language, in this case English, is particularly interesting, as it is the only one that is not properly spatial: It does not quite fit among the geographic concentric circles otherwise established. Where, between Scotland and Europe, one would expect "Britain" or the "British Isles," instead we have the stretched and distorted space of language— specifically, English, through which the metropole is connected to both past and present colonies in a dominion that is quasi-naturalized as "social unity" and "bond." Geddes finally notes that "the ground floor is allocated to the

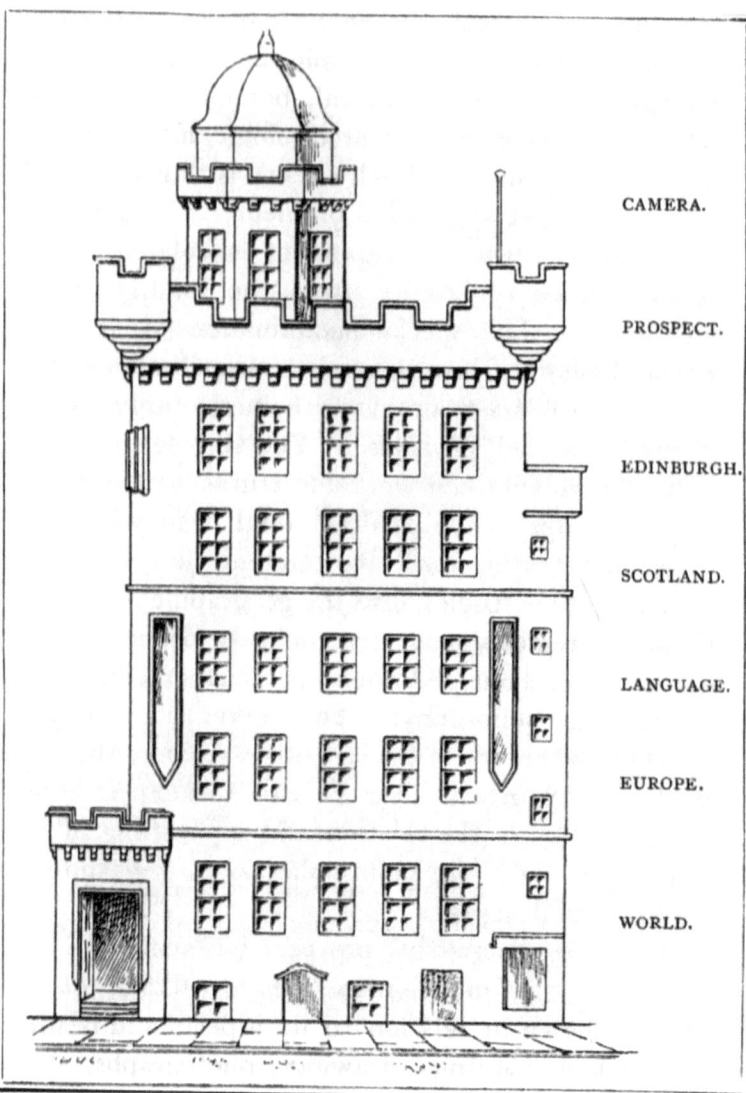

Figure 10. The Outlook Tower. (Credit: Sir Patrick Geddes Memorial Trust.)

Oriental civilisations and to the general study of Man, departments naturally as yet least developed."[71] In the space marked "World," we have the most general and the most "primitive"—the building's real foundation that marks the yet-undeveloped origin of Man as such. That the non-Occidental is a plain metonym for both "Man" and the "World" is, of course, completely taken for granted in this schema.

The turret upon the roof of the building contains a camera obscura, the roof itself offering a panoramic view of its surroundings, one that "harmonises the striking landscape, near and far, and this with no small element of the characteristic qualities of the best modern painting," according to Geddes.[72] The purpose of this visuality is not simply to lay out a topographic terrain in an accessible and appealing form but also to demonstrate Geddes's principles of social evolution, which are all present in the region of any given city as its "valley section" (Figure 11). What is important here is that the visual display is both spatial and temporal and as such points the way to a future city that would be harmonized and synchronized with its past. Thus the Outlook Tower, along with other such displays, work to give the particularity of any locale (Edinburgh, for example) a universal context, such that he could write in his reports for Indian cities that "our Tower will be the best of places for vivifying these models to the scholars upon their visits, and for stirring them to yet more fully visualise the world."[73] It should be emphasized that the purpose of the Outlook Tower, as a site of civic pedagogy, was not just atavistic recovery of a forgotten essence; rather, the fundamental objective was for that recovered *genius loci* to be transposed into a "eutopic" future. In fact, future social harmony could be articulated as primarily the result of the recovery of this ancient identity by the people. It was the planner's role to cultivate this sensibility through the myriad of forms available to them.

The forms included exhibition spaces like the Outlook Tower, which were capable of narrativizing the space and time of the city for visitors for the purposes of civic education. Beyond this, however, theater held a special appeal for Geddes, as witnessed by his Diwali parade in Indore. In *The Masque of Learning and Its Many Meanings: A Pageant of Education through the Ages*, performed in Edinburgh in 1912, Geddes more explicitly intertwines education and civic history.[74] While there are sparse stage directions, and while the masque was accompanied by music, most of the text is in the typical Geddesian style of long, ambulatory prose. The masque ostensibly expresses the "essential genius of [each] race" and details the "main achievements of an epoch of civilization"; as such, it moves from "primitive" peoples through the standard roster of "great civilizations."[75] What is notable and characteristic is the amnestic nature of the drama—the way that, as the main narrator says, past societies are "called forth in turn to live again, by the magic of its rightly read book," so that "the pageant of learning opens as new for each fresh student, not because he is ignorant, but because it is immortal."[76] This is an understanding of history and indeed of time that is derived from Plato's *Meno*. Here, education and learning operate through a metaphysical recollection, in which historical pasts can be, layer by layer, uncovered and revealed. The "eutopian" future to come, then, is based solidly on an ancient past that has only been forgotten. Geddes weds this understanding of time to notions of biological evolution and environmental determinism.

The result is a philosophy—of cities, history, and education—that can be characterized as *vitalist*, as "Geddes saw all organic life having a sort of life-force which made the organism an active participant in its own evolution . . . [this] gives a rationale for active participation by citizens in society . . . and the role for education, literature, art, architecture and planning in improving the cultural and physical environment to nurture society's further beneficial evolution."[77] Indeed, Geddes himself was deeply influenced by Henri Bergson, whom he met in 1913, and in particular referenced Bergson's *Creative Evolution*.[78] As Donna Jones argues, vitalism as a modernist philosophy and aesthetic was one that relied, fundamentally if not always explicitly, on the concept of race. She writes that biological time and social Darwinism "made it possible to speculate on the memories of racial groups," which could be preserved and recovered in collective *duration*.[79] For Geddes, this manifests as a primitivism not just as a label for the time before actual history but as a strategy for identifying universal, transcultural archetypes that survive, in changed and obfuscated ways, into modernity. For example, Geddes was attracted to the idea of caste because it grounded the notion of archetype in an ethnographically identifiable form. Caste delineated *types* of individuals and their contributions to society in a way that could be abstracted and transposed onto other cultures.[80] Similarly, he reads in Greek mythology repeating, universal structures of social relations, ones not only aesthetic or spiritual but that can be revealed to be biological and properly social. As such, the nine Muses, for example, "will be again to-morrow fully recovered—not this time by scholarship but by evolutionary sciences, psychological and social."[81]

Masque closes by linking the amnestic function specifically to universities as institutions that can hold and produce libraries, museums, exhibitions, theater, and the like. As a form of deep, evolutionary recollection, education serves to mature the child into the adult. In fact, the central importance of the masque, as art, is to help produce this kind of maturity; as Geddes writes, "Art alone supremely generalises, and all generalisation is a form of art."[82] Unlike some of his modernist contemporaries, Geddes's primitivism operates not just as a reaction to industrial modernity but as a means to create a technological and socially harmonious future. Thus, both the exhibition and the masque serve an anamnestic function for visitors/viewers, who, in engaging with the narrative model, also recover their own history. History is imagined in both metaphysical and evolutionary terms, and in particular the city is

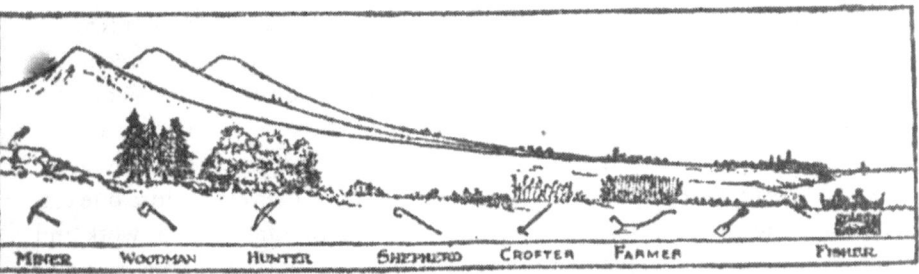

THE NATURE OCCUPATIONS (cf. p. 182)

Figure 11. The Valley Section and its natural occupations. (Credit: Sir Patrick Geddes Memorial Trust.)

seen to contain a kind of fossil record of its past, which, though buried and fragmented, could be recovered by the planner. At the same time, the city included subtle recapitulations of its previous stages.[83] Geddes used Edinburgh and its surroundings to ground this spatial theory of human history in a complex image-idea called the "valley section" (Figure 11). The valley section is a kind of ur-geography for human settlements worldwide and in any period of history. Geddes argues that the geography of the prototypical valley, from hill to sea, provides the fundamental elements of human society. This primeval history may be obscured by "paleotechnic" modernity, but its fundamental forms still exist.

Geddes suggests that the geography of the valley section corresponds to different stages in social evolution, such that "by descending from source to sea we follow the development of civilisation from its simple origins to its complex resultants . . . it takes the whole region to make the city. As the river carries down contributions from its whole course, so each complex community, as we descend, is modified by its predecessors."[84] Similarly, in every culture one can locate ancient archetypes corresponding to fundamental types of work and forms of political governance: miner, woodman, hunter, shepherd, peasant, and fisher. For example, in the valley section the hunter stands for an earlier, more tribal form of political rule, while the pastoral farmer and shepherd correspond to an equally direct spiritual purity—both elements that are still at play in the contemporary but in different forms. As such, the city and its region contain within it the memory of its entire development. The goal of the exhibition is to uncover this long, layered history and thus show that the city contains "traces of all the past phases of evolution" in the form of "fossils [or] survivals."[85]

The way that Geddes would derive a city plan from such an abstract and metaphysical concept can be seen in his 1925 plan for Tel Aviv (Figure 5). His plan was intended as a syncretic reconciliation between a Jewish past and a Zionist future; the former references the universal archetypes and ur-geography of the valley section, while the latter speaks to ability of the "eutopian" future city to resolve the contradictions of modernity. Geddes was invited to Palestine by the Zionist commission, a choice that reflected their interest in modern, garden-city planning.[86] Miki Zaidman and Ruth Kark document the extensive influence of Howard's *Garden Cities of To-morrow* on interwar settlement in Palestine, not only because of the presence of British planners but among Zionist movements themselves. Garden-city planning connoted and connected to a particular image of European modernity—green, hygienic, technological, rational. These settlers deployed this image in a speculative image of a future nation. In the creation of Tel Aviv, settlers were "aware of the fact that they were building an urban model for a new nation."[87] There, the garden-city model represented both a return to communal, agrarian roots and the possibility of a future state. As Neal Payton writes, "The garden city was a Zionist's dream come true. It reconciled both the biblical admonishment to 'sit under one's vine and fig tree' . . . with the modern Zionist's aspirations for a nation of farmers with the necessity for some form of urban settlement, supporting agricultural trade and subsidiary industries."[88] It was through this temporal reconciliation that the "immaculate image of Tel-Aviv as the White City of Modernism created ex nihilo" emerged.[89]

Planning the Eutopian University

However, all these forms of visual, performative education would be lost without preservation and future reproduction. This being the case, the university plays a key and ongoing role in the recovery of the past and construction of the future.[90] Geddes writes that "the current renewal of higher education" turns to ancient cultures and

> seeks not only to exhume their material ruins, but imaginatively to reconstruct their cities. And with these their life and thought; even their mythology, with its symbolic rituals and philosophic initiations . . . the Citizen and City Design which gave these historic cities their impulse and their unity, are for us not larger past memories merely, but working inspirations . . . the University may thus be more than a simple union of existing Colleges and Institutes. The true University blossoms from its Culture-City.[91]

This passage is characteristically exhaustive (and only a portion of a much longer paragraph). He gives history a metaphysical gloss, with the recovery of an ancient past as both archeology and spiritual reconnection. The planner, with their tools of collection and exhibition, is thus responsible for the future evolution of the city, through which the problems of the contemporary can be resolved. The city here is an evolutionary "biopolis," but one that can respond to its environment and direct its progression in various ways; hence the importance of *culture* in the "culture city."[92]

Geddes's views on education prompted correspondence with the poet Rabindranath Tagore. Like Geddes, Tagore's politics were framed within universal, humanistic values of love and sympathy within and across national boundaries; as Poulomi Saha writes, "Tagore actively espoused an alternative model of attachment, what I will call a locally-rooted globalism, which sought to balance the affective commitment with humanist ideals."[93] Similarly, Samir Dayal argues that Tagore's writing and ideas articulate what postcolonial criticism would identify as an alternative modernity, writing that "Tagore was political enough to envision an alternative modernity for India, yet his vision has been marginalized—partly because of its constitutive fragility as the embodiment of a utopic literary sensibility and partly because of the anemic (especially when compared to the muscular nationalism then ascendant) and seemingly sentimental discourse of love in which it was couched."[94] This "reaffirmation of love as an ethicopolitical category" was an aesthetic expression of a nationalism that would be both modern and Indian, cosmopolitan and local.⁹⁵ Tagore sought a polity that rejected the exclusionary, "hypermasculinist discourse of nationalism" while also reclaiming Indian identities from their colonialist characterization as traditional, static, effeminate, and dependent.⁹⁶

Tagore's general sensibility is in many ways quite similar to Geddes's, even though their speculative imaginaries came from culturally different perspectives. Like Geddes, this reconciliation for Tagore was spatial, in that there was a cultural specificity to localities, regions, and even "India" as a whole, but all operating within a synoptic global humanness. As Geddes writes in a letter to Tagore on May 5, 1921, the "scheme of an International University in India [has] the object of paving a path to a future when both the East and West will work together for the general cause of human welfare . . . bringing about international good feelings and fellowship [to] facilitate the communication of sympathy between these Continents which for various causes remain mutually alienated."⁹⁷ Geddes frequently dismisses and laments the pettiness, intensity, and violence of political positions and debates. Likewise, Tagore sought to turn away from the passionate, hypermasculine nationalism of the Swadeshi movement, symbolized by the charismatic yet self-centered character of Sandip in his 1907 novel *The Home and the World (Ghare-Baire)*. Both Tagore and Geddes place many contrasting and internally complex abstractions in play, such that their reconciliation seems to prompt the creation of universal models.

The most central connection between these two figures, however, was in their views on education, which were for Tagore made concrete in his school at Shantiniketan. Shantiniketan emphasized the importance of a holistic, creative, and spiritual education. Elise Coquereau writes that Shantiniketan "symbolizes precisely this communion between nature, Art, and human beings. Tagore conceived it as a gathering of all religions and cultures . . . where education is a celebration of nature, for which Art constitutes a fundamental model."⁹⁸ Shantiniketan appeals, perhaps, because it contains the promise of a future, unalienated life. Free from the constraints of utilitarian rationality and emphasizing other, particularly non-Western modes of knowledge, including those in a more harmonious relationship to nature, Shantiniketan suggests the possibility of a "eutopian," "neotechnic" future, to use Geddesian terms. Coquereau identifies an early-twentieth-century Indian appropriation of aesthetic primitivism, arguing that "Tagore's primitivism and valuing of nature are internally addressed, while European primitivism is an external quest for something 'beyond' and 'other' than its own location."⁹⁹ This may be, and in any case primitivism can in general be read as a dialectical response, and thus possibly a critique, of European modernity; nevertheless, this connection speaks to Tagore's own way of constructing a universal temporal framework, one that self-essentializes Indian identity, though differently from the nationalists. Here, too, Tagore's outlook squares nicely with Geddes's vitalist conception of history, in which the planner (rather than the poet) uncovers the evolutionary, cultural, and aesthetic *genius loci* of a given place.

Tagore, Geddes, and their likeminded contemporaries register the affects of the interwar period. Their ideas suggest a structure of desire, one seeking reconciliation: perspectives from above and outside that are also grounded in an ambulatory, everyday, transnational cosmopolitanism rooted in the affective and spiritual particularities of place and thought that is global in scope but local and specific in its activation. Figured as flowers in a garden, people and place acquire the immediacy of nature while being produced through mediated processes of cultivation, for example in the form of civic institutions like universities and educational-social experiments like Shantiniketan.

Geddes imagines institutions like universities, theaters, and general civic centers and agoras occupying a "modern day cultural acropolis" within the city.[100] This was evinced in his plans for Hebrew University in Jerusalem (Figure 12). Geddes was characteristically sanguine about the potential of his university in Jerusalem, writing that "the fears of unending strife between Jew, Arab and Christian over Palestine do not exist for me. There is never any permanent need for people to kill each other."[101] Similarly, in a letter asking Tagore to join the University Committee, he says that communities in Palestine "are not consumed by the mutual hatreds which are as exaggerated by the press, but open to your (and India's) message of mutual tolerance, and even goodwill."[102]

The Zionist project in Mandatory Palestine was deeply structured by the colonial ideology of improvement. Brenna Bhandar characterizes early Zionist thought as a form of "utopian colonialism" in its imagination of a future polity in a separate place: "The rationales devised to justify colonization, and, specifically, an idea of cultivation that was heavily inflected with a racial discourse of superiority, bear great similarity to European colonial models."[103] The racial discourse refers to the primitivist logic of type, the same logic guiding Geddes's theory of the valley section, that sought to fit people to place while improving both via a practice of cultivation. We see in the Zionist project the liberal ideology of improvement as somewhat detached from a narrowly defined profit incentive, as the motivation to colonize Palestine came from the imaginary of the place as a spiritual homeland.[104] We might say that the topothesic aspect of colonization was particularly pronounced in the case of Mandatory Palestine. The Zionist imaginary was not merely agrarian but instead took town planning as a central form of improvement and modernization, in particular the garden-city idea, combining as it did town and country, modernity and tradition. As Alexander Levy, the founder of the Palestine Building Society, wrote at the time: "Palestine: a garden—of God if you want, neither town nor village is suitable for us Jews and for the New Man at all. The city is too much inherent in us, the village too little."[105] Sonder details the many Zionist figures who were influenced by garden-city planning and articulated it in relation to Palestine in speculative and quasi-literary forms. These include Levy, Theodor Herzl, Davis Trietsch, Wilhelm Sitassny, Franz Oppenheimer, and Alex Baerwald. For example, Baerwald writes an essay in which a fictive city clerk in the proposed "Nordau Garden City" explains the principles of town planning while guiding a German Jewish family through the future city.[106]

This fantasy of town planning was realized in part through the Mawat Land Ordinance, a property law that, ironically, made it both an offense to cultivate certain lands while also reverting those lands to government control if left uncultivated. Mark Levine writes:

> The new understanding of mawat land as being "waste" or "barren" instead of the traditional emphasis on its unclaimed status and distance from built-up areas created the perfect tabula rasa on which to build a modern European city such as envisioned by the founders of Tel Aviv, for whom the legend of Tel Aviv's "birth out of the sands" attained the level of Ur-myth. The fact that under the new legislation, such "vacant land . . . cannot be possessed except by allocation from the State" made it all the easier to transfer it to those thought capable of "developing" it.[107]

A place like Tel Aviv was figured as both an ancient heritage and a place created from scratch along "modern" garden-city lines. This allowed it to be, both in its anticipatory imaginary and built reality, contrasted with the dramatic characterization of the "squalor, neglect, foulness, and 'levantinism' of the Palestinian cities, especially Jaffa and Jerusalem," for example in the writing of Herzl.[108] The twinned imaginary of a degraded, uncultivated, barren, slumlike present and a reconciliatory, verdant, modern future speaks to the multiple vectors of improvement: agrarian cultivation, new town planning, and the "cleaning up" of urban spaces, especially Jerusalem. Together, these would reestablish the inherent spirit of the place while simultaneously occupying it with its supposed ancestral owners.

Unsurprisingly, British architects and planners keyed into this aspect of the Zionist imaginary in proposing their own interventions: "One characteristic common to the work of all British architects who designed in Palestine during the Mandate period was a deep concern with the spirit of the place.

PLANNING AS IMPERIAL CULTIVATION

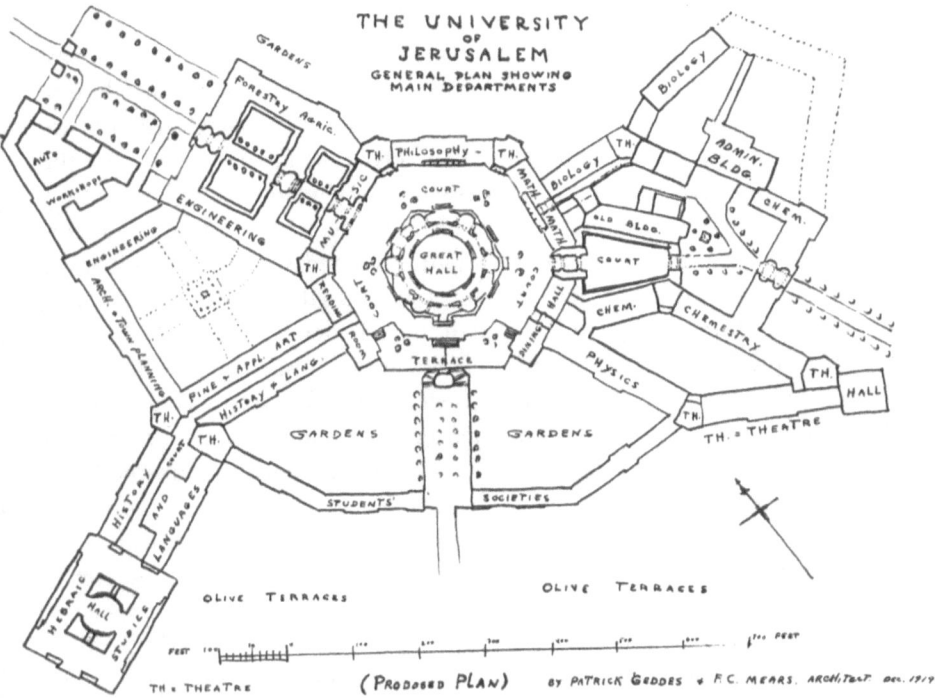

Figure 12. Plan for Hebrew University. (Credit: Sir Patrick Geddes Memorial Trust.)

Even buildings representing British authority were conceived as architectural portraits of Palestine rather than obvious symbols of British dominance."[109] As I demonstrate, planning involved a reconciliation between tradition and modernity ("the old new land"), preservation of the past and imagining the future. In Palestine, the British projected this reconciliation onto the space of the city itself. As Nicholas Roberts argues, the strict division between Jerusalem's new and old city was one imposed through British governance and planning regulations, one that cast the former as modern, green, and suitable for Jewish settlers and the latter as a site of preserved tradition for the "non-Jewish." He writes that "British urban planning was therefore built around what appeared to be two contradictory goals: (1) to make the city more modern and orderly, in a word more 'European'; and (2) to return it to its religio-historical roots. . . . The first goal entailed constructing a city that 'made sense' . . . the second objective meant peeling back layers of recent local development to uncover and preserve the city's glorious past."[110] Thus the old city was made to correspond to a "romantic and ahistorical" Jerusalem conjured from a pastiche of "travel accounts, historical and fictional texts, Orientalist paintings, and scriptural readings" and turned into a "living museum" of the city.[111]

This sensibility of the city as a visual repository and *model* for its own past and future suited Geddesian theory perfectly. Indeed, Palestine, and Jerusalem in particular, had long played a central role in his social evolutionary mythos, being a particularly important archetype, along with Athens, for the development of cities in general and as such one the best examples of a fully realized "culture-city." Thus, one of his main interests in Palestine was uncovering, displaying, and propagating its particular and particularly influential *genius loci*, accomplished both through rendering the old city into a living museum and through the creation of a future-oriented new city. For the latter, Geddes reproduced his cities exhibition and was commissioned by the Zionist Organization to create a plan for the new Hebrew University (Figure 12).[112] The university, then, was critical in uncovering Jerusalem's pasts and bringing them to bear on its "neotechnic" future—an endeavor equally concerned with the city's "spiritual" heritage as with being a place of knowledge production. As Welter notes, "Geddes's search for a new spiritual and metaphysical center for a city, which begins with his outlook tower . . . ends two decades later in the chanting of psalms around the Great Hall of Hebrew University conceived as an institute of synthesis."[113] Though not completely realized, Geddes's plan for the university shows a relational spatialization of knowledge, meticulously arranging faculties so as, he supposed, to promote collaboration and synthesis.

Conclusion: Cultivating the Slum and the Garden in the City

In sum, the garden-cities movement and town planning in the early twentieth century presented itself as a spatial, technological, and aesthetic fix to the perceived problems of modernity, as concretized by the figure of the slum. Along these lines, it conceived of itself as a humanistic endeavor transcending politics. Yet, at the same time, it was deeply shaped by the contexts of liberalism and colonialism, manifested by a concern for *cultivation*—of gardens, places, and people. Cultivation along these lines was not a process of top-down control of recalcitrant populations, and planners like Howard and Geddes did not avowedly align themselves with the institutions of capitalism or imperialism, even if those institutions helped enable their speculative imaginaries. Their interventions were preoccupied with recovering and reproducing the local particularity of place, not with suppressing it. Still, colonialism was the condition of possibility for urban planning in the way the latter sought to construct an imaginary relationship to a future elsewhere. The various texts of early planners like Geddes include their theories, manifestos, diagrams, photographs, exhibitions, museums, and the built environment of the model cities themselves; together, these narrate a path to a (e)utopian future as if that future were a place to be colonized, first in these speculative fictions and aesthetic figures and then as material instantiations, green and beautiful and full of unalienated, harmonious subjects within a nonagonistic society.

What lingering or latent influence does the colonial narrative have within contemporary urban planning? There were a number of particularly influential figures like Howard or Geddes in the development of planning as a profession. In Britain, social-reform movements continued apace, now also taking the form of Housing and Town Planning acts (in 1909, 1919, 1925, and 1932), the "Homes for Heroes" program after World War I, and the work of the London County Council architects, who began the work of slum clearance and building new housing well before World War II. The students of this first "wave" of planners would go on to design Britain's social-housing system and plan its postwar cities, including the new towns. To what degree did prerogatives of the postwar state derive from its liberal and colonial history, and to what end? At the same time, decolonization signaled the triumph of anticolonial nationalists throughout the Global South and was a chance for figures like Jawaharlal Nehru, long involved in city politics, to reimagine the space of the colony. It is notable, then, that Nehru immediately turned to the American planner Albert Mayor, who suggested creating hygienic model villages throughout India and assisted in planning Chandigarh with Le Corbusier, Jane Drew, and Maxwell Fry.[114] Fry, meanwhile, went from declaring in 1943 that "the new Britain must be planned" to working in newly postcolonial India and soon-to-be postcolonial Ghana. Did planning in the decolonized nation-state replicate aspects of colonial thinking?

The above suggests continuity across assumed historical markers and periods. While not depreciating the changing power structures of the midcentury, it is still possible to detect distinct through lines from Howard's "home colonization" to modes of contemporary, global-and-yet-local urban planning. The Geddesian planner as cultivator will find resonance in the succeeding chapters—contemporary developers, too, articulate their interventions as a desire for spatial and social integration, a concern with the specificity of place and the local, and a "eutopian" vision of flourishing cities. And, like Geddes, they downplay both the context of liberal-colonialist appropriation that enables their developments and the social conflict those developments generate, instead posing themselves as universal solutions to a host of political and ecological harms. Part II of this book will also consider a speculative, topothesic imaginary, one full of vivid detail and quasi-literary flourish, put forth by the forces of contemporary development in a postcolonial Britain. However, Part II will also audit the gaps and absences in this smooth, expansive, and overfull imaginary. These are sites where modes of social conflict or simple acknowledgment of a state of violence and fracture become marked and worked through, at least temporarily. If these first two chapters have concerned themselves with the stories of planning and its speculative narrative mode, the remaining chapters turn toward what John Akomfrah's *Handsworth Songs* calls the "ghosts" of those stories. To this end, I will query texts, subjects, and affects whose formation is haunted by topothesia, not just of planning but of the entire enterprise of liberal colonialism; its ideologies of improvement, progress, and cultivation; and its multiple, entangled, ongoing histories across empire.

PART II
*Diminishing Horizons:
The Ambivalent Temporalities
of Development*

3

Capturing the City

Regeneration, Policing, and the Ghosts of Postcolonial Britain

Nothing visible has been done. All we see are trees. We haven't been consulted about trees. We didn't ask for trees. It's as if they were waiting for these damn buildings to burn down so they could put in trees.
   —OTTO JOB, LIVERPUDLIAN, QUOTED IN THE *Wall Street Journal*[1]

If they have a house with a front and back garden, people learn to look after their house, they learn a sense of responsibility . . . and the children can help, perhaps they have a little plot of garden. And as they walk along the road, they learn that they keep outside other people's front fences. They don't go up the common greens and look up through the window and plot how they can break in.
   —ALICE COLEMAN, INTERVIEW IN *Utopia London*[2]

In the aftermath of the 1981 Toxteth riots, Liverpool was visited by Michael Heseltine, Margaret Thatcher's secretary of state for the environment. Heseltine was to formulate a plan as to how to address the riots and the conditions that made them possible. One year later, Barry Newman summed up this scheme in the *Wall Street Journal*: "The centerpiece is a plan to spruce up 865 acres of decrepit dockland for a huge international garden festival in 1984. Millions will flock to Liverpool to look at the flowers, it is hoped . . . [Liverpool] will get a jobs center, a training center, six small factory units, and trees." As Jacqueline Nassy Brown writes, "The most absurd outcome of the riots was that the British government, after carefully studying their root causes, decided that what Black people really needed was a more uplifting environment."³ Heseltine established development corporations, state institutions that became responsible for urban planning and automatically superseded local planning authorities. In addition to planting trees and other greenery in Liverpool, Heseltine established a series of national garden festivals to aesthetically and spiritually combat urban decay and late industrialization.⁴ Heseltine predicted that "after the [garden] festival has gone, houses will be built here, jobs and industry will develop, and a very large part of it will be kept for the people of Liverpool as open parkland."⁵ What Heseltine took for granted was a direct association between the problems of social alienation and community conflict and something called the "environment."⁶ By restoring the ruined, derelict environment, perhaps by planting trees, one could restore and regenerate individuals who were also seen as ruined and derelict. Groundwork UK, a charity enlisted by Heseltine to help with this regeneration, succinctly expressed this ethos: "changing places, changing lives."⁷

This chapter asks: What conditions of possibility allowed the planting of trees and gardens to be offered as solutions to the complex social problems that had developed in postwar Britain? More generally, how can changing places change lives, as Groundwork would have had it? The lines of continuity between the liberal colonialism of the early twentieth century and the postcolonial urbanism of the 1980s were apparent in the government's response to urban riots in 1981 and 1985. These events were sparked mostly by incidents of police brutality, often against Black and Asian youth already the frequent subject of increased "stop and search" policing. The riots—especially the images of them disseminated in the news media—seemed to bring together and concretize an array of issues and themes: class inequality, race and racism, police and the rhetoric of law and order, urban "decay" and the postindustrial city, among others. Accordingly, responses to these images entangle political ideologies and structures of feelings in ways that resonate far beyond the events themselves. For example, the Scarman report, a well-known government inquiry, first into the Brixton and later into the Liverpool riots, called for the state to assimilate race and class minorities in urban spaces via "community redevelopment and planning."⁸ As such, the "disturbances" shaped many aspects of Thatcherite urban policy, forming a still-current template as to how UK cities are governed and made available to capitalist processes of speculation and consumption.

The revival of liberalism in the 1970s and 1980s is notable as a break with the postwar consensus, especially given the fact that architects of the neoliberal order often took the institutions of this consensus, most notably those of the welfare state, as their antagonists. For example, starting from the 1970s especially, it became axiomatic among the Conservative and then New Labour parties that council estates were fundamentally antisocial problems whose solution was the privatization of social housing in the form of right-to-buy policies. This ideological shift away from the welfare state was most easily put into practice in areas that were of uneven interest to the public: Council housing was widespread but at the same time was not universal (like the NHS or schools), and even a section of the working class could profit from its privatization.[9] Furthermore, housing was an area in which the politics of immigration and their attendant resentments could be fully leveraged to alter the political balance. In these ways, the 1980s could be identified as properly *neo*liberal—a new version of the ideology of the 1880s and 1890s, in which the role of the state was to protect businesses over workers and, crucially, in which social philanthropy could be directed toward the improvement of conditions for the "deserving" working class. Through privatization of the welfare state through polices like the "Right to Buy" legislation of the 1980 Housing Act,[10] cities became a key site of the political struggles that have often been seen as emblematic of the Thatcher period. These politics, whether pertaining to individual housing estates or entire neighborhoods, were also defined by divisions and coalitions across class positions and ethnic identities. They referred not only to housing but to the increasingly unequal conditions within cities and the way that marginalized communities were governed and policed.

Enmeshed in these politics of urban governance, especially in the wake of urban riots, was the role of policing. This included the many hostile interactions between local police and Black, working-class communities. However, "policing" also includes the way the built environment was shaped for the purposes of increasing social control. On this point, this chapter examines how a version of "order-maintenance policing," popularly known as "broken-windows" policing in the United States, was present Britain. Specifically, I analyze Alice Coleman's *Utopia on Trial*, a critique of the postwar council estate and high-modernist architecture on the grounds that it is not "defensible," that is, available for continual surveillance and self-policing. Coleman focuses her critique on signs of "disorder" (e.g., graffiti, litter, loiterers, etc.) and suggests that policing the built environment would produce subjects less amenable to crime.

Together, figures like Heseltine and Coleman produce readings of urban "disorder" grounded in specific imagery: the dark tower-block elevator, the ominous council estate, and the riotous street, cars ablaze and windows broken. This imagery not only elicits fear but ties the production of subjectivity to the aesthetics of *place*. Black artists of the 1980s responded to this particular regime of representation in a multitude of ways in attempts to open up a more nuanced discourse on the relationship between place and identity. This chapter thus closes by turning to those artists who interrogate the politics of representation, specifically considering John Akomfrah's 1985 documentary *Handsworth Songs*. Part of the work of the Black Audio Film Collective, *Handsworth Songs* attends to issues of race, identity, and belonging in postcolonial Britain through an engagement with the 1985 riots in Handsworth, Birmingham. The film queries both the necessity and difficulty in "capturing" the riots in an authoritative documentary critique. Instead of only focusing on what is made conspicuously visible in the riots, the film also seeks to document the absences that haunt urban space. These ghosts are historical without being completely recoverable, imagined without necessarily being animated. As such, *Handsworth Songs* presents the ghosts that haunt the scene of the riots in a film that is both interrogative and speculative, questioning the way they are made to appear and thinking if and how it could be otherwise.

"It Took a Riot": Michael Heseltine and the Improvement of Place

Throughout the 1980s, incidents of police brutality sparked reactions from minority communities across the United Kingdom, especially in "inner-city" areas of Brixton, Tottenham, Handsworth, Merseyside. The political dynamic of these events seem to conform to a well-worn template, and for the purposes of this chapter I will analyze the contours of this template.[11] This entails an analysis of the range of possible reactions to these events, how they were shaped and intensified by the media, and what this dynamic says about political representation more generally. For example, there is the initial problem in how to name these "events"—are they "riots," "rebellions," "protests," or "disturbances"? How are the proximate causes—police brutality and surveillance (both particular incidents and experiences over a longer term), unemployment and deprivation, the supposed boredom of young people, etc.—related to one another and given priority? If mediated scenes of violence concretize something about this historical moment, they do so while remaining contested in meaning and producing an assortment of reactions, explanations, and political arguments. Thus, we may ask how riots, involving only a small number of people in a relatively constrained geographic space and for a limited time, come to have such an outsized importance in the cultural memory.

For the standard Conservative, the riots were straightforward evidence of the inherent criminality of the underclass, specifically the racialized "undeserving" poor. Media images communicated this idea of chaos and of a spectacular, seemingly spontaneous violence emerging from the shell of everyday life. The young individuals involved in the riots were simple metonyms for entire places and communities. This viewpoint largely dismissed the notion that the riots could be considered protests, as the violence was characterized either as "looting" or as spontaneous, aimless destruction. At its most extreme, the conservative reaction defaulted to a (racialized) Hobbesian essentialism, revealing human nature absent the ordering force of law. This was and often still is aided by a sensationalist media presentation of the events. As Jeff Rodrigues, already in October 1981, wrote, "Media treatment of 'the inner city problem,' however, tends to deal with the inner city as a phenomenon without causes, without development and without a history. Whereas in fact the opposite is true, 'the inner city problem' being the specific consequence of a number of shortsighted and ineffective planning policies, as well as structural changes in the economy."[12] Analyzing the rhetoric of the *Daily Telegraph*, Rodrigues finds in media discourse a Burkean characterization of the people involved as a "mob" or "rabble" "prompted by motives of loot, lucre, free drinks, bloodlust or merely the need to satisfy some lurking criminal instinct."[13] This gesture brings to the front the immediacy of violence to form a caricature of people and places. Against this reading, Rodrigues and others situate the inner city and its inhabitants within a more nuanced social context. As such, the left response noted the obvert racism and authoritarianism of this rhetoric and spoke instead in the language of social determination, *structure*, and long history.[14] Within this view, the cause of the riots can be located both in discrete episodes of police brutality and in *structural* racism, the long-term effects of poverty and unemployment, and histories of colonialism and migration.[15] Accordingly, solutions to these underlying causes are often expressed in reforming existing police and juridical practices and providing state-sponsored employment and benefits, including better public spaces and housing.

However understood, the riots have served as a cultural mnemonic for the Thatcherite 1980s. Thatcher herself, almost instinctually, turned to individual pathology to explain the riots. She would later write about Toxteth:

> I observed that for all that was said about deprivation, the housing there was by no means the worst in the city. I had been told that some of the young people involved got into trouble through boredom and not having enough to do. But you had only to look at the grounds around those houses with the grass untended, some of it almost waist high, and the litter, to see that this was a false analysis. They had plenty of constructive things to do if they wanted. . . . Instead, I asked myself how people could live in such circumstances without trying to

clear up the mess and improve their surroundings. What was clearly lacking was a sense of pride and personal responsibility—something which the state can easily remove but almost never give back.[16]

Thatcher was reluctant to consider issues of police brutality and systemic deprivation as causes for the riots; indeed, she instead rejects the very premise of deprivation. Thatcher uses the overwhelming "mess" of waist-high grass and litter as metonyms for individuals who lack personal responsibility and pride.[17] As Parker and Atkinson write: "Eschewing a sociological or structural reading of the sources of discontent, discrimination and a setting of profound urban decline, her view inclined towards the Treasury view that Merseyside's economy could not ever have been rescued through a further 'pouring-in' of ever more resources to no purpose."[18] This is a rejection of the idea that there are structural forces, like systemic racism or economic injustice, that condition and shape the daily lives of individuals. Among other things, this means that the welfare state serves only as a distortion and limitation of both market forces and individual will.

Thatcher's reaction to the riots resonated with many Conservatives. It is not, however, descriptive of the actual state response to the riots in the area of urban policy in Thatcher's government. Instead, Conservatives were ultimately won over by the views of cabinet member Michael Heseltine. Though not a planner, Heseltine was able to use the apparatus of the state to define the riots in spatial terms, thus requiring particular kinds of interventions. He was no less contemptuous of the system of the welfare state and local Labour governance than Thatcher and other Conservatives; however, he was also influenced by American-style public-private partnerships as a means for the state to amplify private investment. His report on the riots based on his visit to Liverpool, entitled "It Took a Riot," reflects this. Fully declassified in 2011, "It Took a Riot" focuses on the structural causes of the riots, viewing them in fact as an epiphenomenon of those systemic causes. He writes: "I cannot stress too strongly that my conclusions and proposals are not based on my fear of further riots. They are based on my belief that the conditions and prospects in the cities are not compatible with the traditions of social justice and national evenhandedness on which our Party prides itself. We must get the strengths of the community pulling in the same direction; and free the spirit of enterprise which is latent. This will not happen on *its own* or without leadership."[19] His concern is not the riots themselves but rather, somewhat astonishingly, with making cities "compatible with the traditions of social justice." Moreover, the state has a key role to play, here defined not simply as contributing funding but as leading the way in creating different conditions in the inner cities. Where a Conservative like Thatcher defaulted to individual pathology to explain the riots, Heseltine, also a Conservative, saw the riots as a symptom with structural causes and a solution based in state intervention.

Thus the standard left response to the riots—that they must be seen in the context of society's underlying structures—is in fact very similar to the actual response by Thatcher's government.[20] Certainly, Heseltine also includes normative judgments in his reports, most notably criticizing the "unemployed parents—many of them single" of the disaffected youth.[21] However, the majority of the report examines the structural causes of urban discontent and proposes state-led solutions. The causes are various: high unemployment, the effects of deindustrialization, environmental damage, inadequate housing, police-community relations, and the ineffectiveness of "hard left" local governments.[22] His solutions, broadly, are for the state to lead a "revival" of urban neighborhoods and economies by creating incentives for private investment.[23] As the report indicates, "the Americans long since took the decision to let people make a profit out of public job creation."[24] These solutions are by now familiar: The state leads reclamation of derelict "brownfield" sites and creates "enterprise zones" to lure private investment and create spaces for consumption and recreation, in other words, state-led gentrification. Heseltine would later note that "today such policies by and large command all-party support . . . but it was to be a Conservative government over the next few years that forced through the necessary changes."[25]

Heseltine has been a long-standing figure in Conservative politics across multiple eras and has produced several books arguing for specific policies (he is a vocal supporter of the European Union, for example). One of those is his autobiography, *Life in the Jungle* (2000), in which Heseltine writes about the riots and his approach to providing solutions. The "jungle" in question here is the agonism and drama of Whitehall politics and the associated thickets of bureaucracy and public opinion that Heseltine navigated in this career. Yet the title also implicitly and unconsciously leverages the loaded trope of the jungle as a space of difficulty, confusion, danger, and a certain amount of chaos—a trope that we will see repeated in response to the "inner-city problem" of 1980s Britain. In any case, Heseltine strikes what might be called, in light of *Topothesia*'s earlier chapters, a Geddesian pose in relation to the modern "slums" of 1980s Britain; that is, his perspective is one of an on-the-ground surveyor, able to take stock of the systemic causes of social dislocation while evincing humanistic concern for the improvement of the local. For example, in recounting the Toxteth riots, he writes that "now scores of youths had taken to the streets. Petrol bombs had been thrown and buildings burnt. Yet this was no mass uprising. The vast majority of people of all colours and races stayed at home and shuddered. . . . I was unwilling to accept the all-too-easy assertions that saw such outbreaks either in stark terms of disgruntled troublemakers on the one hand or police intolerance on the other."[26] Heseltine in this section correctly observes that the media representation of the riots made them seem like a far more widespread phenomenon. In this passage, Heseltine initially repeats those images before claiming a position above the more common right-left discourse. He downplays the importance of the riots and in doing so seeks to recontextualize the debate surrounding them.

Specifically, he writes that at the time the "race issue . . . was perceived to be the root cause of Liverpool's problems." However, for Heseltine, race "was a violent and dramatic symptom, not the problem itself, which stemmed from the long-term structural and economic decline of the city under a local leadership quite unable to rise to the challenge of events."[27] Even while casually dismissing the experiences of Black communities, Heseltine's argument that the riots are a "symptom" with complex origins has more in common with Thatcher's critics than with Thatcher. This division is important to mark because it also speaks to how Heseltine's program of state-led urban regeneration is what was new to "neoliberalism" compared to Thatcher's reactionary Victorianism.[28] Indeed, the former is what ended up capturing the establishment left in the United Kingdom and resulting in the very similar policy platforms of New Labour.

In this way a consensus was established for what cities should look like and whom they should be for.[29] Where the policy of the state after World War II lay in rehousing the population and building new towns, now the prerogative was on using the planning authority and finances of the state for the (often ill-defined) sake of urban "regeneration." This was effectively a state-led gentrification that leveraged the resources of the state to spur construction and development, enrich private developers, and increase private tenancy and urban home ownership.[30] Ironically, this was accomplished using many of the same tools of state planning used by Labour after the war, including the Town and Country Planning Acts and the concept of development corporations—entities that conveniently superseded local authorities' planning jurisdiction.

Together, Heseltine's tenure catalyzes a form of late capitalist spatial governance that involved privatization as one of its many techniques and practices. Heseltine chose two locations in which to experiment with state-led regeneration: the London Docklands and Liverpool's Merseyside. By choosing two distinct locations, Heseltine was able to turn regeneration into a national project and thus supersede the local Labour councils. While nominally at odds with prevailing Conservative sensibilities, Heseltine sought to deploy the planning authority of the state, as established by postwar Labour governments, to neutralize local opposition. In *Jungle*, he sums up the argument he made to Thatcher's cabinet: "If we don't act as I propose, nothing will happen. The land is in public ownership, much of it is polluted and the whole place is in thrall to extreme left-wing councils that Reg Prentice tells me are almost certainly controlled by the communists."[31] Heseltine sees spaces that are static because they are in public ownership and managed by local councils. While local, they are here described as "extreme" and "communists"—not the kind of English place-based particularity that Heseltine has in mind with his investment-attracting garden festivals.

At the same time, these sites appealed to Heseltine because they were "brownfields"—areas that had been rendered economically unproductive in the postindustrial era. Regeneration along these lines was not only a possible role for the state under Conservative governance but was a transformation that could only be feasibly catalyzed by state authority and investment so as to minimize risk for corporations. He writes:

> We turned our attention to the redevelopment of unused, often derelict—brownfield—sites. The cost of clearing the detritus of history was often too high to allow any profit on redevelopment, and certainly was far more expensive than new building on the green fields. We made public money available to pay for this negative value. Today public policy remains much as we created it. It may not be possible to avoid all greenfield development, but every effort should be made to contain it.[32]

The "detritus of history" rhetorically characterizes these areas as anachronisms and ruins. Detritus refers variously and ambiguously to environmental harm, economic redundancy, and deterioration of the built environment. Similarly, it renders not only the spaces but the people in these spaces as societal brownfields, in "thrall" to desultory leftist councils, sapped of their inherent entrepreneurial agency by the welfare state.[33] In all these ways, it continues the history of planning from the nineteenth century, which took as its object the "slum" and proposed as its solution the imaginary of a new place and along with it new people.[34]

In addition, it is certainly no accident of history that some of the most visible urban brownfields were the docks in postindustrial London and Liverpool. As Sal Nicolazzo notes, it was in fact private capital that created and securitized these spaces in the eighteenth century. For example, in London's docklands, "the Committee of West India Merchants and Planters did not only finance the Thames River Police; they were also the major force behind the construction of the new West India Docks on the Isle of Dogs—one of the major infrastructural projects that transformed London's docks at the turn of the nineteenth century."[35] These were key infrastructural sites to British capitalism and colonialism, a "transnational space where people, goods, and ships converge between journeys that shape the globe in the image of the British Empire [and] a metonym for the reach of imperial power."[36] Meanwhile, in Liverpool the docks were integral to the local economy but increasingly irrelevant, especially after World War II, a dynamic that "set in motion a cycle of decline which, by the 1980s, was manifest in increasing vacant land and buildings, population loss, decreasing personal income and spending, loss of local authority revenue, declining taxation and increasing social-security spending."[37] In retrospect, it is not surprising that a place like Canary Wharf might be reimagined as an epicenter for now-frictionless global capital.

Heseltine turned to the practice of property-led regeneration in response to the riots. This theory of urban development holds that the state should create incentives for the private market to invest in derelict and impoverished areas. As Neil Smith theorized at the time, gentrification was not simply a process of "improvement" of derelict urban properties; rather, properties were neglected until there was a sizable enough "gap" between actual and potential value.[38] While gentrification theory often focused on the individual political-economic relations of landlords and bourgeois gentrifiers to urban property and displaced tenants, this dynamic has also been conceptually scaled up to include wider and more complex processes of urban change.[39] Along these lines, Heseltine's "push for regeneration" in Toxteth "brought physical change; unsettling, unmaking and remaking the diasporic space again. . . . It was deemed so disruptive that it was talked about as a 'displacement,' and even as a stealth bordering practice."[40] To accomplish this, Heseltine enlisted the help of major British corporations, appealing to their national pride to help regenerate the inner cities.

Structurally, this took the form of the Urban Development Corporations (UDCs), in which the national government was able to gather together business executives, consultants, policy experts, and others.[41] UDCs could be given the resources and authority to supersede local authorities. Through this mechanism, the state sold council properties at a discount, established reduced-tax enterprise zones, and did the work of environmental reclamation. Ironically, the development corporation structure is what enabled Labour to construct the New Towns in the postwar era.[42] Having been identified by the state as existing in a state of dereliction, these areas found themselves replanned by private entities, with funding from the government.

As Heseltine writes, "The housebuilders moved into alien, Labour-controlled political territory with considerable courage and thus began its transformation from the desolate open spaces and dreary council estates into the balanced and vibrant community that has now emerged."[43] This passage recalls the aesthetic of regeneration, as the gray desolation and concrete dreariness of the postwar settlement is replaced by *vibrancy* and *community* in the form of garden festivals and high streets decorated with corporate logos. As will be discussed in more detail in Chapter 4, through this process cities like London or Liverpool become oriented less toward their own residents (and labor) and toward national and international financial interests.[44] Despite Heseltine's self-hagiographic account of UDCs, their problems were noted at the time. Writing in 1988, Michael Jacob took note of the "luxury apartments, with their Porsches behind security gates, stand[ing] right next to decaying council tower blocks and flats, into which no money at all has been put. The sense of community built up over years is being almost tangibly destroyed."[45] This has colonial undertones, with private capital seizing territory for the sake of its improvement.[46]

Heseltine's thoughts on urban regeneration are framed by nostalgia for once-great cities and a sense that these spaces had become ruined and lost to history. As *Topothesia* documents, this trope of urban development keeps repeating. It serves as a necessary adjunct to acts of speculation, both imaginative and economic, a way of adding pathos and gravity to the *not-yet* gestures of urban development. Heseltine creates the following scene, having been sent to Liverpool to address the riots in 1981:

> Alone, every night, when the meetings were over and the pressure was off, I would stand with a glass of wine, looking out at the magnificent view over the river and ask myself what had gone wrong for this great English city. The Mersey, its lifeblood, flowed as majestically as ever down from the hills. Its monumental Georgian and Victorian buildings, created with such pride and at such cost by the city fathers of a century and more earlier, still dominated the skyline. The Liver Building itself, the epicentre of a trading system that had reached out to the four corners of the earth, stood defiant and from my perspective very alone. The port had serviced an empire and sourced a world trade. From Liverpool's docks its ships had plied the seven seas. The quays had been the last stopping place for thousands of fellow countrymen and women and for Europeans of all nations heading for the New World and the gateway for millions of Irish labourers attracted by work

on the railways and canals of England. . . . In truth, everything had gone wrong. . . . Toxteth, a tiny microcosm in terms of location and population, became a very misleading symbol, though still a symptom of a spreading disease.[47]

The tone of this passage is melancholic and contemplative. The reader is given an image of the protagonist of urban regeneration surveying the city beset both by apathetic decay and violence. The loneliness of this image is paralleled in the city environment, both in the "majestic" river that connects Britain to the sea and in the monumental and "defiant" Royal Liver Building. Liverpool's now derelict docks used to connect the country to the "seven seas," a metonym not only for the city's industrial history but also for Britain's colonial and settler-colonial projects. In contrast, the current state of the city, Liverpool 8 included, is likened to the symptoms of a contagious disease.[48]

As such, property-led regeneration was not only about tax benefits and below-rate sale of state-owned buildings. It was and is, in a fundamental way, an aesthetic and moral enterprise. This approach is exemplified in the creation of the international garden festival in Liverpool as a response to the riots. Heseltine explained the concept: "Use public money to eliminate dereliction, and green the area to produce a high-quality environment. Stage a festival of attractions for six months and then sell the much improved site for redevelopment. We organised a national competition, offering public money for the reclamation of significant derelict sites."[49] The garden festival was held in 1984, the result of a 250-acre riverside reclamation project of the Otterspool refuse tip, in which "250,000 trees and shrubs, with some trees as high as 30 feet, were planted."[50] These trees and shrubs, alongside sixty themed gardens and some new structures, were a kind of showcase of urban regeneration, signaling the vibrancy of a community to come. Moreover, this message was not primarily for the residents of nearby Toxteth but for tourists and corporate partners; as Loftman and Nevin write, cities are increasingly captivated by such "prestige projects" in order to "compete" with other cities for investment, affluent residents, and tourists on a national or international scale.[51]

As I argue continually throughout this book, the garden serves as a metonym for renewal and regeneration. Aesthetically, it stands in contrast to the imposing and crumbling tower block and to the riotous spectacle of burning buildings. As such, it does the cultural and ideological work of imagining a green, healthy, vibrant future at odds with a ruined present. For example, Heseltine notes of the charity Groundwork UK that "it was first conceived to bring together volunteers to tackle that awful urban fringe of post-industrial blight—litter-strewn streets, neglected fields despoiled by overuse, a general seediness—which so often characterises the frontier between town and country."⁵² This passage evokes a general sense of dereliction by conflating long-term environmental damage, petty litter, and an alarmist and coded "general seediness." Set against these figures of ruin, blight, and decay is the aesthetic imaginary of the garden-neighborhood. The garden festivals were "intended to be catalysts for improvement of the image of run-down British cities suffering from derelict land, manufacturing decline and high unemployment [and] a way of attracting private sector funding for environmental improvement."⁵³ Having transformed an "unsightly . . . derelict area," the image of the garden does the work of drawing capital to the city. Thus, the neighborhood of the riots—dangerous, derelict, without recreation—is juxtaposed with the city as a magnet for investment. Here, the aesthetics of the city, rather than its politics, are what determine its capacity for revival.⁵⁴

On its face, Heseltine's project of bringing trees to Toxteth has an air of absurdity to it—a lack of proportion between the seriousness of deprivation, police violence, and anti-immigrant nationalism and a somewhat effervescent horticultural solution. However, if we inquire as to the *conditions of possibility* that make that particular solution available to address the "problem spaces" of the city, we find a repetition with difference of some rather entrenched histories: new liberalism's ethos of improvement, the facilitating role of the colonial state, the entwinement of space with many different modes of speculation, and the juxtaposed aesthetics of ruin, decay, dereliction, and pollution, on the one hand, and, on the other, an arboreal and horticultural vitality. Together they produced—or rather, reproduced—a speculative image of the city after the end of all conflict, free of disturbance.

Anticipatory Policing: From Social Norms to Quality of Life

Central to the response and longer cultural memory of the riots have been the issues and images of policing and police brutality in inner-city areas.⁵⁵ In this section, I explore how policing became embedded in the urban built environment. Specifically, Britain sees developments that parallel the US invention of "order-maintenance" policing, also known as "broken-windows" policing. Coined by James Q. Wilson and George L. Kelling and popularized by New York Police Commissioner William Bratton, this theory held that the policing of minor forms of disorder, such as graffiti, litter, panhandling, and group loitering, could work to establish social norms and reduce more serious crimes. "Disorder" for broken-windows theory consists of *visual* and *environmental* cues—all those things that for some planners and developers are indicative of the slum, the inner city, or the derelict neighborhood. These cues are signs that can be read hermeneutically to uncover a deeper social decay; as signs, however, they also produce social meaning and norms in urban environments. As such, removing the signs of disorder through policing and establishing "order" can have the effect of ameliorating social decay and reducing the instance of violent crime.

Bernard Harcourt writes that broken-windows theory "leads to an uncritical dichotomy between disorderly people and law abiders—or, more generally, between order and disorder," with the result that the "theory has transformed conduct that was once merely offensive or annoying into positively harmful conduct—conduct that causes serious crime."[56] Broken windows' emphasis on the production of social norms is actually not interested in considering how poverty, unemployment, or race might affect social spaces, instead choosing to turn to an *aesthetics* of location in which, for example, "loitering" young men become a sign of disorder. Because the latter have a "propensity" to crime and inherently produce disorder, they must be engaged through policing tactics that maximize social control. Harcourt notes that Wilson and Kelling thus consistently make a hard distinction between "families who care for their homes, mind each other's children, and confidently frown on unwanted intruders" and "disreputable or obstreperous or unpredictable people: panhandlers, drunks, addicts, rowdy teenagers, prostitutes, loiterers, the mentally disturbed."[57] An unwillingness to police the latter turns a "stable neighborhood" into an "inhospitable and frightening jungle."[58] Familiarly, the metaphor of the jungle is used to connote chaos and disorder and is implicitly racialized.

Though broken-windows policing has a US-centric history, there are parallel developments to use policing to maintain social control in the United Kingdom, particularly through the institution of antisocial-behavior initiatives.[59] The authors of *Policing the Crisis*, for example, note how Anti-Mugging Squads engaged in a kind of "anticipatory policing" that, by increasing surveillance and interactions between police and civilians (for example, on the London Underground), played a role in increasing the overall crime rate and extending the purview and impact of legal institutions on everyday life.[60] Risk management—the anticipation and prevention of crime—is a core part of the genealogy of police. As articulated in Patrick Colquhoun's 1796 *Treatise on the Police in the Metropolis*, the role of the police was not only anticipatory, but its proper object was the poor and specifically the indigent, the latter of which were supposedly more susceptible to crime.[61] Police, per Colquhoun, includes not just criminal policing but is also a form of social policy. Further, together this interrelation between crime and control indicates that "deviance is a social and historical, not a 'natural,' phenomenon [and] for acts to be 'deviant' they must be recognized, labeled, and responded to as 'crimes.'"[62]

In particular, policing in the 1970s and 1980s was geared toward order maintenance, for example in policing that "targeted Black cultural forms such as music, dress, and speech, specifically performed by Black youth in public spaces."[63] In fact, one of the more blatant examples of "anticipatory policing" was "Operation Swamp 81" in Brixton just before the 1981 riots. Named, in astonishing honesty, after the infamous anti-immigrant remarks of Margaret Thatcher, this operation saw an increase in police in Brixton. Swamp 81 and the policing of Black communities more generally made use of provisions in the 1824 Vagrancy Act, which made "suspicious behavior" (shortened by the law as the designation "sus") "an arrestable offence without any other crime having to be committed, any witnesses other than two police officers, or even a victim."[64] The extensive use of police stops, disproportionately targeting Black youth as "sus," exacerbated tensions with police in the weeks before the riots. News images of the riots then became the ultimate sign of disorder and social decay, a way of capturing and presenting "crime" without disclosing its conditions of possibility.

Alice Coleman: Design as Surveillance

Practices of police surveillance and the neoliberal of improvement came together in the work of Alice Coleman, particularly her study on modernist housing estates, *Utopia on Trial* (1985). A geographer and later housing advisor to Thatcher, Coleman criticized council housing as the "scene of many kinds of social malaise."[65] Following Jane Jacobs, *Utopia on Trial* argues against the large scale of "utopian," high-modernist architecture and its capacity to afford community life.[66] She argues that these spaces themselves produce crime and disorder, and her solution is to design space so as to maximize surveillance, which for her means an emphasis on individual ownership of property and single-family housing. For Coleman, this critique of statism had ends that were in line with Thatcher's interest in dismantling the welfare state in particular, in that the design of the postwar estate could itself be faulted as producing "social malaise," without reference to the dynamics of poverty, employment, class, race, or policing, while the owner-occupied single-family home provided a solution through essential features of its design.

Utopia on Trial shares several features with anticipatory, order-maintenance policing. Coleman is centrally concerned with violent crime, yet instead of studying crime directly she turns to surface-level environmental cues, writing that "as we could not afford time to lie in wait for incidents to happen, we chose types of malaise that leave behind visible traces: litter, graffiti, vandal damage, and excrement."[67] The analysis of these broken windows–style signs of "disorder" is the main focus of her study, and she takes for granted their determinative effect on social norms. That is, these "visible traces" (and others, like loitering) both serve as evidence for a deeper, amorphous social decay and are also assumed to *reproduce* the conditions for that decay. Citing Oscar Newman, she criticizes design that does not allow for "defensible space" or the ability for not only police but for the community as a whole to surveil itself at all moments. It is precisely the shared, communal spaces of postwar council states that lead to this lack of surveillance. They are a "confused space, shared by too many people to permit natural, unconscious self-policing," a situation where "criminals feel safely anonymous while inhabitants feel vulnerable [and thus] it is difficult or impossible to develop a social structure based upon mutual trust or responsibility."[68]

Indeed, the preoccupation with criminality is present in the form of the book as well, with the titular analogy of the "trial" carried throughout each of the book's chapters ("Utopia Accused," "The Evidence," "Cross-examination," etc.). That the critique of "utopia" takes the form of a legal trial belies the claim from Coleman and her associates that they generally "do not intend to ascribe blame."[69] Similar to how broken-windows advocates render victimless crimes into acts of serious harm to the community and social order, Coleman seeks to render the built environment into a criminal mastermind. Personifying the design elements of modernist estates as "suspects lined up for identification," she asks, "What are their descriptions? Are they of good character? Do they keep bad company? Do they have alibis? Are they ringleaders, or accomplices, or innocent parties?"[70] Having established the scene, the text parses the transcripts of resident interviews for references to specific architectural features (the "suspects") and notes whether residents were "for" or "against" said features.[71] Here, elements of architectural design themselves become "sus," elements of a resident's complex interactions with a built environment that can be individually isolated and captured. From here, a "suspect" is evaluated with regard to whether its "spatial organization [will] encourage or discourage their control and maintenance" through communal surveillance and self-policing.[72]

Despite collecting statistics for litter, graffiti, etc. on several London housing estates, *Utopia* is many places written in a speculative style. Coleman jumps from observations of design features—common greens, for example, or first-floor garages—and invents whole-cloth stories about how they invariably lead to crime and social deterioration. Such speculative thinking attends to every ostensibly empirical metric of malaise: Signs of urine are attributed wholesale to alcoholics in the community, tolerance of whom in turn attracts not only more alcoholics but also methamphetamine users, while litter as a categorization extends from "any chance piece of rubbish" to "concealed murdered bodies," as if per an inevitable progression from one to the other.[73] Like advocates of order-maintenance policing, she marries a rational-choice criminological model, in which design elements either incentivize or discourage criminal activity, with the assumption that some subset of the population has a "propensity" for crime: "There are a few who will always rise above adversity, no matter how appalling their environment," she writes, "while at the other end there are a few who will always be sluts or criminals, even in ideal conditions."[74] Designing for surveillance and social norms minimizes the deleterious effects (both racialized and gendered) of the latter.

Similarly, she not only dismisses the role that unemployment and poverty might play in "social malaise" but speculates that the design of housing estates might itself *produce* individuals less interested in employment: "We can envisage a chain reaction in which badly-designed blocks of flats make children less easy to bring up and more likely to become anti-social and uncontrollable. When they go to school, they may well resist educative control and be unwilling to learn, giving the school a reputation of a blackboard jungle."[75] Despite the constant rhetoric of basing design in empirical study, this imagined "chain reaction" is purely speculative and topothesic in the way it invokes the scene of childhood within the confines of the badly designed block of the home and the (again racialized) "blackboard jungle" of the school.

In fact, Coleman continually stresses the influence of housing design on children. For her, housing should be built to clearly separate public and private spaces and should be individually owned and maintained. The immediate benefit to this kind of suburban-style housing is to maximize surveillance and defensible space, since everyone will be clear as to their area of jurisdiction.[76] There are secondary benefits, however. Fences, walls, and garden hedges all serve to clearly demarcate between private and public in a way that the common spaces of the estate do not and as such encourage the social norm of respecting private property, *especially* for children:

> In houses with gardens children can spend their formative pre-school years under close parental supervision. The garden is a safe place where toddlers can gain the self-confidence that comes of venturing out alone while knowing that help is immediately at hand if needed. They learn to care for the home territory, partly through the natural impulse to imitate parents, and partly by being taught, until litter abstention and litter clearance become engrained habits.[77]

Whereas the common green of the council estate has a "confused" sense of ownership and thus encourages antisocial activity, the space of the private garden is one of liminal experimentation for the child. The garden mediates the relation between home and world and between the supervising parent and the venturesome but increasingly self-policing child.[78] The garden is presented in this text as a scene of *cultivation*. In Chapter 2, I analyze Patrick Geddes's use of the garden as a staging ground for the development of his children's speculative abilities: Through planning, playing, and growing, the garden works as both a cultivated space and one that cultivates the social imagination of children. For him this dynamic, applied more generally, results in the production of community. Coleman picks up on many of those same tropes, with a Lockean supplement that any sense of community is dependent on security, and security is dependent on private property. Similarly, where Geddes bases his planning theory on a primitivist schema of human social development, Coleman establishes her design priorities in the biological need to "produce shelter with an adjoining piece of territory, and to impress it with distinctive marks of identity" where "the decoration, the garden layout, the boundary fence . . . proclaim the residence of a unique family rather than a faceless unit among the masses."[79] Thus we see a throughline between Geddes, the humanistic and optimistic colonial planner, and Coleman, the urban geographer of the neoliberal project. Whereas Geddes's influence found voice in the cohort of postwar British planners, Coleman became a leading voice in criticizing the work of that same cohort. That is, against the ostensible periodizations of the twentieth century and against the surface-level "political" divisions of the postwar period, we see deep epistemological continuities.

Capturing Black Britain: *Handsworth Songs* and the Politics of Representation

In *Shades of Black*, Stuart Hall writes that "Thatcherism and free market neoliberalism were the forces that successfully hegemonized this crisis in the postwar settlement."[80] The preceding analysis of Heseltine's use of UDCs and Coleman's order-maintenance architectural critique indicates some ways in which the crisis, concretized through the images of what Hall calls the "racial upheavals of 1980–81 and 1985," gave way to a consensus on how urban space and its layered sociality should be visibly ordered. That this ordering made partnerships with global capital and deployed the figure of the garden to aestheticize political disagreement shows how neoliberalism echoed the political-economic orientations and structures of feelings of liberal colonialism. This dynamic was one of capture and assignation, of reading the "confused" spaces of the council estate and the mediated images of riot as both evidence and cause of social "disorder," moves that in fact ran parallel to more leftist attempts to see in the riots structure, meaning, and voice.

This dynamic turns the built environment and urban landscape into a high-stakes regime of representation, all the more so for Black British artists.[81] *Handsworth Songs* was produced by the Black Audio Film Collective (BAFC) and funded by BBC Channel Four.[82] The catalyst for this funding was the riots themselves.[83] The film is an experimental documentary, mixing Akomfrah's live footage from Handsworth and elsewhere, interviews with local residents, newsreel clips, and archival footage. Rather than simply "documenting" the riots as event or the stories of locals, however, the juxtaposition of these scenes interrogates how the riots connect to and generate narratives in excess of themselves. That is, the film is not an attempt to locate and explain the "causes" of the riots but rather explores how the immediacy of temporary events carry with them opaque historical undercurrents.

To understand the impetus for producing such a film and the debates it prompted in its reception, it will be helpful to place the BAFC within the context of Black British art. My use of the term "Black" here refers to migrant and minority culture in Britain, a "political Blackness" that includes Asian minority art and culture.[84] As Sophie Orlando writes, in the context of twentieth-century Black British culture, the "term 'Black' does not define an identity or an ethnicity . . . it is rather a political space for artists belonging to minority groups in Britain within which art and art history can be discussed."[85] This formation has its own history within the reception of Black arts in Britain, and it is a political one. For example, Eddie Chambers notes that "Black British art" is a construction of the 1980s and a reaction to the way that minority art in Britain had been both particularized by ethnicity and as a result excluded from being considered "British."[86] As opposed to this particularization, political Blackness articulated identity through political resistance. Artists like Chambers and Keith Piper, collaborating in Birmingham in the early 1980s, used collage and mixed media to interrogate racism in history and popular media, juxtaposing primary-source material with ironic and provocative text in order to produce a "tool to assist us in our struggle for liberation," as Chambers wrote in the statement for the 1981 exhibition "Black Art an' done" at Wolverhampton Art Gallery.[87] Similarly, Lubaina Himid, Sonia Boyce, and others turned to satire and feminist positionality in order to claim space for Black cultural production.[88] Protests against the National Front and police brutality, as well the riots themselves, catalyzed these cultural-aesthetic formations, which together were attempting to work through *how* and *on what basis* identity could be articulated and represented given the occlusions of British society and the increasing violence of the British state.

It was in this context that the BAFC was situated as an "intersection of multiple avant-gardes."[89] They interrogated the production and reception of Black British art by disclaiming what Kobena Mercer calls the "burden of representation."[90] Their work emerges—necessarily—from their distinct cultural and ethnic locations without providing a particularized "voice" that could be reified by the British art establishment. However, they questioned how such a minoritized identity could be leveraged into political resistance. As Kodwo Eshun writes,

> the "Black" in Black Audio Film Collective was not informed by the kinds of identification with post-war Pan-Africanism and the 1960s Black Arts Movement favoured by the BLK Art Group; the Collective distanced itself from the ancestralist imperative . . . [and] remained unconvinced and skeptical of the leftist faith in working-class black youth as a potential agent of revolution. Nonetheless, it would not be accurate to say that BAFC prefigured the artistic belief in post-blackness articulated by Thelma Golden. Instead, the condition of raciality invoked by their name might be profitably understood as a question of the unthought, as a dimension of possibility.[91]

I would like to figure this suggestion—that the BAFC explored the unthought of raciality—as a silhouette against the brightly lit background of planning, police surveillance, and place making explored earlier in this chapter. What both contend with regards to the riots are the problematics of *capture*, as various parties seek to understand and explain the root causes of the riots, turning to journalistic and ethnographic detail, systemic critique, and racialist tropes in turn. Against this oversaturated background, the articulation of Black identity is constantly subject to capture, appropriation, and particularization, or else an articulation that can only be perceived as noise.[92] For Akomfrah to use film, and not only film but documentary, to explore the subject of the riots thus immediately throws up a host of problems associated with the possibility of political representation.[93] As such, the aesthetics of the BAFC questions the place-making assumptions of planning that assumed a "harmony between people and their location" such that creating or transforming the local would necessarily result in changed people and changed social relations.[94]

BAFC wanted to challenge both the images of Black people produced by mainstream cinema and challenge the notion that Black creators and filmmakers had to work in a realist mode. In some ways the latter would prove to be the more controversial aim, as the BAFC produced "avant-garde" films that dealt with their subjects in unexpected (and nonpolemical) ways. Josh Romphf writes that "directly opposed to the didactic forms of documentary representation found in the newsreels, *Handsworth Songs* undermines the aims of such footage by creating a sense of ambiguity as opposed to clarity . . . television news and documentaries strive for closure; they attempt to find the most obvious cause of a given problem."[95] In this way the film counters the ethnographic response to the riots—the will to collect and analyze stories. Michael Heseltine, for example, approached urban regeneration through an ethnographic disposition: He was the government minister who visited the local community to gather and understand their stories. Conversely, *Handsworth Songs* not only considers issues of unemployment, inequality, and police violence as social facts but also reflects on how places and people are represented and what that representation is capable of disclosing. Rather than "tell the story" of the riots, Handsworth Songs speaks to the "construction of an oblique and partial history of the formation of black communities in postwar Britain."[96]

For example, in one scene, we see Handsworth the day after some riots. As debris is cleared, the viewers hear the following narration:

> On the 10th of September 1985 a journalist is pestering a middle-aged Black woman on the road, he wants her opinion on the disturbances: "Did you have a relative involved? Could we talk to one of them?" He is writing a story. She says to him calmly: "There are no stories in the riots. Only the ghosts of other stories. If you look there you can see Enoch Powell telling us in 1969 that we don't belong, you can see Malcolm X visiting us in 1965 and a Conservative said: 'If you want a n—— for your neighbour, vote Labour.'" She remembered Malcolm strolling through Smethwick saying: "If this is the centre of imperialism then we have a common struggle." For a moment the voice of Malcolm swooned over the ashes of decline.[97]

Whereas the reporter seeks to interview—"pester"—those involved and produce a vignette of Handsworth for an outside audience, the middle-aged woman suggests that the "story" of the riots involves a much longer history. As John Solomos writes, Birmingham is where "Enoch Powell made his famous 'rivers of blood' speech in 1968, which represents a major symbolic stage in the politicization of immigration and race in British political culture."[98] Moreover, could a journalistic interview grasp the abstracted relationship of imperialism to the scene of the riots? The tone of the voiceover suggests that the journalist, in his naiveté, does not understand that he is unable to *represent* the situation in full. Instead, he produces a superficial mediation of the riots for an impatient readership.

The question of voice dominated the film's immediate reception. Most notable was an exchange between Salman Rushdie and Stuart Hall. Rushdie criticized the film for focusing on images of violence and police—similar to images circulating in the media—rather than exploring the vibrant, multicultural everyday life of Handsworth. Referring to the scene just excerpted, he writes, "The trouble is, we aren't told the other stories. What we get is what we know from TV." Instead of "telling those ghost stories," he contends that BAFC is too busy "describing a living world in the dead language of race-industry professionals."[99] Rushdie wanted a more ethnographic approach, one that would productively complicate the pejorative, one-dimensional images found in popular media, redolent as they were with racist and classist stereotypes. This would yield an understanding of Britain's complex, hybrid, multicultural "fabric."

Handsworth Songs is certainly not such a project, even if it also reacts against mainstream representation. Though the film contains both ethnographic detail and polemical interviews, when these and other images and sounds are juxtaposed, the overall effect is to interrogate the aesthetic regimes through which one can understand race and society. The "ghosts of other stories" in *Handsworth Songs* are not an attempt to chronicle the histories of immigration and colonialism as only social facts. These are ghosts that cannot be recovered by a mass-observation-style deep ethnography of Britain or through a Rushdian literary production of (urban) Britain's dizzying multiplicity.[100] As Nina Power writes, "The film is a significant example of counter-media in the sense that it radically slows down the demand for instant explanations, a demand that always amounts to more or less overt condemnation."[101]

The BAFC artist Reece Auguiste remarks that *Handsworth Songs* grappled with the problem of "how best to dramatise the past which is, for a few minutes, encapsulated and imprisoned by time" and finally "allowed" to speak by a news media that claimed the right to "articulate your emotions [and] define your sense of belonging or displacement."[102] Simone Sessolo argues that *Handsworth Songs*, against this appropriation of voice by media and political discourse, creates a fuller and more accurate representation of the voices of the rioters. Referencing Gayatri Spivak's "Can the Subaltern Speak?" he writes, "The immigrant rioters, who were in a subaltern position because they had no political representation, performed acts of violence to be heard, but the media dismissed them as hateful and immature . . . *Handsworth Songs* attempts to give voice to this silenced minority."[103] This echoes the famous and oft-cited observation by Martin Luther King Jr. that riots are the "language of the unheard." This omnipresent quotation simultaneously contains and glosses over the nuances of subaltern representation and the *presence* of political sound making: "Language" suggests communication that is meaningful, potentially translatable, and therefore commensurate with the dominant order. The figure of the "unheard," on the other hand, suggests sound that is inaudible by that very same dominant order. Or, if audible, that appears as ambiguous noise—strange, unexpected, and dangerous. Further, their ghostly character suggests that they are marked as much by absence as presence—by an inability to perceive and account for their relationship to concrete events.

Handsworth Songs explores these problematics of capture and voice in multifarious ways. For example, the film repeats a particular scene, once near the beginning of the film and then again near the end, of a Black man evading and running away from the police (Figure 13).[104] In the first instance, we hear foreboding ambient music[105] and see images of Handsworth streets occupied by police and covered in scattered trash and rubble, some of it smoking. Bystanders watch the police from corners and front doorways, even though said police appear to be standing around, waiting; even without the extradiegetic sound, one can imagine that space where there is tension in the air. The scene of the man running begins mid chase, as he is hemmed in by police that he tries to avoid. We see him careening down a street. He moves to his left to avoid the baton of an officer, pushes against a wall to keep his balance, tries to split two other officers and almost succeeds before being tripped and falling to the ground. Still flailing and trying to get away, several police officers converge with their riot shields to constrain the man. The camera has to move out of the way of the officers as they pin him against the wall; it then moves around to get a better view, also capturing several women sitting on the wall a few feet away. The second time this scene appears, closer to the end of the film, it is shown at half speed, with the same music. The speed accentuates each movement and contortion of his body, containing the same visual "information" but saturating the affects of the scene.

This scene dramatizes the processes and stakes of "capture"—the police trying to capture this particular man; politicians, journalists, and academics trying to capture the causes and social contours of the riots; and, self-reflexively, a documentary that has the ostensible aim at capturing some quality of poetic truth of its subject. When edited together, the proximate social context and the histories of imperialism it contains become ghostly, haunting the scene, evasive and eluding. The police conducting the arrest, the politicians

Figure 13a. Still from *Handsworth Songs*.

Figure 13b. Still from *Handsworth Songs*.

conducting the inquiries, the community prompted to produce a voice, and the film bearing the burden of representation can only have an opaque and incommensurable relationship to that which they seek to capture.

Handsworth Songs throughout reflects on the problematics of representation in this way, placing into question the *documentary* as neutral knowledge creation. The film's opening shows archival footage of a Black man in a museum of industry, with the spinning wheels of industrial machines themselves resembling a film projector. Parts of this footage recur twice later in the film; in one instance, he says that "it is still good for a West Indian to come here and taste the mature atmosphere of ages of civilization. England is so rich with the culture of the past that nothing the living can do can destroy the vast wealth of accumulated tradition over the years. Anyone can come in and take no notice of the living. We can elevate ourselves learning from the dead."[106] There's a classic postcolonial irony in the appreciation for the British technology and culture that was so dependent upon and deeply tied to its empire, but then that is the optimism of immigrants.[107] This individual takes comfort in that romanticized relationship as a way of ignoring the present, taking no notice of the living. Far from not seeing the ghosts of the past, he dwells exclusively among them. This is a further irony, as it mimics both a melancholic attitude among British nationalists and the way in which they take no notice of the living, in Handsworth for example, until they can no longer be ignored.

One of these scenes is followed by shots of the press, cameras in hand and grouped together, as they record a memorial for Cynthia Jarrett, whose infamous death at home at the hands of intruding police set off protests and the Broadwater Farm riots in Tottenham in 1985. In this scene, Akomfrah focuses on the abundance of cameras documenting the scene in addition to his own: CCTV cameras overlooking the space, the all-white press crowding the memorial, one photographer who intently engages the zoom on his camera (Figure 14), another who strains to capture the perfect "representative" image of the flower wreaths atop the lead car in the funeral procession. Similarly, when Akomfrah visits a public, televised meeting in Handsworth about the riots, he chooses to focus on the intense mediation of the event. The close shots of news cameras are accompanied by the sound of a producer who is concerned about the lighting, suggesting that it is too dark, "a bit down in the front." As the film shifts to extreme close-ups of the faces of the audience, we hear a response from a second producer that the "problem" is the "color of their skins." This technical discussion of lighting unwittingly reveals the racial history encoded into the technology of representation; thus film, as a socially produced technology and practice, becomes haunted by that history despite its pretentions toward mere documentation.

Figure 14. Still from *Handsworth Songs*.

Together, these edits disclose a scene of panoptic mourning, attempts to account in mediated representation that which would remain unaccountable by the law. They stage both excess and absence; as David Marriott writes, "it is around that invisibility—of racial hegemony and capital—and the excessive visibility of the socially undesirable, that the political and commercial legitimacy of CCTV coheres."[108] These scenes and screens entwine the forces of the public-private state (CCTV) and those of the news media, which respectively work to maintain social control and form a consensus on how instances of disorder ought to be read and interpreted. As Roy Coleman writes, this entwinement finds expression in the neoliberal idioms of "regeneration" and "quality of life," where "camera surveillance merges 'crime control' with a broader strategy that seeks to manage a notion of 'quality of life' that in turn reflects the re-imaging of 'place.' At the local level, this has been accompanied by a move towards 'public order,' 'zero tolerance' or 'quality of life' policing that has formed a strand in urban regeneration."[109] Indeed, this project of defining "disorder" by making it visible was not only instituted by the state but in "partnership" with businesses who helped fund the extensive CCTV networks in British cities.

Against this, *Handsworth Songs* dwells on what is not (or not quite, no longer, and not yet) visible. For example, the film makes extensive use of archival footage to conjure the overlapping and at times contradictory ghosts of the present. In part, the contradiction is between official and unofficial histories, yet the film is not a project of simple recovery of the latter.[110] Rather, BAFC "films underscore an irreconcilable agonism, for gaps, absences, distortions, fabrications and contradictions arise on all sides," both in the intimate and unacknowledged time of family memory as well as in the homogenous time of the nationalist and imperialist imaginations.[111] In that way the film meditates on the reproduction of such gaps, absences, distortions, and contradictions. For example, much of the archival footage and photographs evokes the optimism of the Windrush era. We see images of people arriving by boat, singing calypso and dancing. One set of images is accompanied by a nostalgic narration: "Remember the nights of coruba cocktails and coruba sour, their secret pregnancies, your wet nursing and me nappy washing . . . that night, I moved from an idea to a possibility. I was born in a moment of innocence."[112] The black-and-white images and this narration are saturated with nostalgia. The time of the present (the 1980s), in ruin, is contrasted with the era of ostensible arrival, as Black people are greeted and welcomed to Britain. Placing themselves in relation to a past, these individuals can imagine a future for their children.

Patrick Williams remarks that "the brief and fragmentary nature of many of the images is matched by the absence of commentary and explanation, while the most extensive voice-overs are poetic, allusive, meditative or incantatory, not obviously or necessarily related to the images on the screen at that moment. From these fragments and refusals stories do emerge, however, though they may be as dislocated as the individuals and communities to whom they relate."[113] Further, the dislocated archival imagery is matched not only to reflective voiceover but to the disparate sounds of the film in general, which are "spread out over a vast sonic landscape of peaks and trenches, creating a new map of time, telescoping one promise into another, one time traversing another."[114] Together, the inherently fragmentary montage effects become the occasion to reimagine the past and create a counterfactual history. This gesture is what evokes the move from idea to possibility, the chance to materialize one's dreams. That is, this alternate history does not straightforwardly document the experiences of the 1950s migrant generation. Rather, it recreates the phantasmagorical Britain that populated the imaginations of colonial subjects. The sense of "possibility" evoked by this speculative past is juxtaposed with the dead ends of the contemporary city without further comment.

In another montage, young women step off of ocean liners with their bags,

Figure 15. Still from *Handsworth Songs*.

packages, and children (Figure 15). We see color footage of people gathering at the port, showing documentation to officials.[115] This is followed by a black-and-white montage of rainy English streets and the interior of a home with a Black family. Together, the film narrates the migrant's experience of arrival:

> I walk with my back to the sea, horizon straight ahead.
> Wave the sea away and
> back it comes.
> Step,
> and I slip on it.
> Sit, and it's underneath,
> seeping and shaming me,
> crawling in my journey's footsteps.
> When I stand, it fills my bones.
> Daytime, it drags me to the moon.
> Even with feet of solid ground,
> and with prospects ahead,
> it is there,

under the paving stones,
on the horizon.
And then, I slip through the cracks,
I think,
to be shamed by the sea.
Nighttime, I am the sea,
and if I walk from shoreline to coast,
it will fill my shoes,
washing my journey away.[116]

The narration is contemplative and mournful. To invoke Derek Walcott, the sea is history, omnipresent and controlling even while distant. Similarly, it is articulated here as a kind of "sea-oriented unconscious," and as an unconscious, latent and not fully knowable.[117] The narrator is positioned as helpless, almost on the verge of drowning. For example, with a tidal gesture, she "waves the sea away and back it comes," the dismissal of her "wave" ineffectual against the relentless and overwhelming waves of the sea. These waves are figured as an inescapable and disproportionate force, as even in daytime, "it drags me to the moon." Here the moon loses its gravitational pull, becoming merely an occult destination on the other side of the tides.

The sea, of course, is central to the identity of "Black Atlantic" subjects, being the geographical terrain of imperialism and slavery and as such a site of formative loss, of both history and alternate histories.[118] For postcolonial migrants to Britain, it also symbolized a journey and a sense of arrival, the optimism and anguish of being Black British. This contradiction is suggested by the montaged archival footage, most polemically at the end of this sequence in images of racist graffiti. In fact, Sessolo argues that the last line of this narration, "washing the journey away," represents the "social and political integration" of Black subjects against the prerogatives of the state and English nationalism. Somewhat similarly, Eshun writes that

> *Handsworth Songs* suggests it is possible to resurrect the memory of past lives. By invoking those absences, a ghost narrative might emerge, one charged with the fleeting moment of anticipation when colonial subjects believed their mother country would welcome them into a new future. The film marshals all its formal qualities to recover this fragile utopianism, not only to indict the present and to protect the memory of the dead from amnesia but also to come to the assistance of the living at a moment of social breakdown. The result was a postidentitarian space that imbued the pessimism of the intellect with the poetics of the elegiac.[119]

The elegiac account of an alternative history of "welcoming" and "integration," however, repeats the ideology of the British "mother country" that always projected itself as an ideal, if not at times utopian, space. Postcolonial theory, especially during the 1980s and 1990s, certainly worked tirelessly to show that Britain's colonial encounters were constitutive rather than incidental to its identity, thus suggesting that English parochialism be replaced by a more inclusive vernacular cosmopolitan ethic.

However, this proposed "inclusive Englishness" is more adjacent to the project of multiculturalism than to a decolonizing ethos. If the film speaks to multiple audiences, it does so through these montage effects, which recreate the elegiac-utopian story of arrival using mixed archival footage, poetic voiceovers, and music. For others, the artifice of these montages points to the overdetermination of their elements. We see the process of representation as both enigma and violence. As Stoffel Debuysere suggests, "What is felt is a melancholic agency which cannot know its history as the past, cannot capture its history through chronology, and does not know what it is except as the persistence of a certain unavailability and unavowability that keeps haunting the present."[120]

Indeed, the sea is a much more slippery and historically vexed figure. Its operation is suggested in the previously referenced scene through the alliteration of its effects and actions—it seeps and shames as the narrator steps, slips, and sits. Figured as such, one can imagine that the sedimentation of the sea, instead of being separated into buried geological layers, washes onto the shore without distinction—suggesting the process of ruination through an "absence of ruins."[121] The ambivalence of the sea is suggested by the end of the narration: Having become overtaken once again, having it fill her bones and shoes, the narrator becomes the sea. Ironically, in doing so she is not submerged and drowned in history. Rather, the journey is washed away, leaving what might be an outline of freedom.

The politics of representation and capture are also a part of the legacy of BAFC and other artists who came to prominence during the 1980s, especially as they started to receive official recognition.[122] Eddie Chambers writes that it seems "impossible now for an artist to make work which the state cannot warm to or manipulate for its own ends, co-opting it as reflecting its own agendas of justice, pluralism, inclusivity, and equity, coupled with its self-image of dynamism and creativity."[123] This speaks both to the pressures of minority artists to "represent" in particular ways and to address a politics of location without being rendered "motionless" by it.[124] There is a way in which *Handsworth Songs*—in its critique of regimes of documentary, ethnography, and representation; its use of fragmentary archival footage; and its staging of the scene of capture—suggests that "something is missing," to repeat Bloch's observation of the speculative. While Akomfrah would consider how the "something missing" could have utopian implications in later films, notably *The Last Angel of History* (1996), *Handsworth Songs* is "defined by [an] impossible gesture, a desire to cease and entrap the ghost . . . [of] history and myth."[125] As discussed at the beginning of this chapter, riots are a phenomenon marked by excess, not just as a scene of violence but in the forms of representation and types of discourse that it produces. The conditions of possibility that give rise to these phenomena are not merely subterranean but aqueous and ghostly, history as obscured, ethereal, and only visible through political and/or aesthetic fabrications. In this context, Heseltine's fascination with tree planting as a "solution" to the riots and to the space of the inner city is an attempt at grounding that excess, giving it tangibility and particularity. This gesture is as absurd on its face as it is foundational for the interventions of twentieth-century planning, and before that the colonial logics of cultivation and planation, and perhaps even a mythical sense of place through which locations and people can be made British.[126] It was also a gesture unmistakably tied to the ideology and economics of urban development and a neoliberal understanding of "progress," such that the means to changing and "improving" urban places (and thus, ostensibly, urban people) has become a kind of common sense.

Chapter 4 will pick up this story in the aftermath of the 2011 riots in London. The disturbances were again touched off by the police's shooting of an unarmed Black man, Mark Duggan, in Tottenham, which led to protests and riots. Also recurring was a certain discourse, in which Theresa May, then home secretary, could imitate Thatcherite talk of the inherent "criminality" of the events, LSE sociologists could propose to "Read the Riots," and the (reconstituted) Greater London Authority could echo Heseltine in producing a report entitled "It Took Another Riot."[127] In this case, however, the Heseltinian solution was already well underway, with public-private entities like the London Thames Gateway Development Corporation picking up and extending the "regeneration" of the city with massive new schemes, notably including the 2012 Olympics. Kodwo Eshun remarks that *Handsworth Songs* still resonated in 2002 when it was shown at *Documenta 11*; by that same token, it also resonates in 2012 and 2022, its histories returning in familiar guises, as ghosts are known to do.[128]

4

The End of London

Temporalities of the Gentrified City

Each story of regeneration begins with poetry and ends with real estate.

—KLAUS KUNZMANN[1]

Chapter 1 discussed the utopian roots of planning, specifically in its conception of the *local*, explored in William Morris's utopian novel *News from Nowhere*. *Nowhere*'s protagonist, William Guest, explores a postrevolutionary London by sailing along the Thames, which had been cleared of pollution and returned to a seminatural state, full of gardens; among the trees, artisans work in a peaceful and equal community. Today, Morris's narrator would not be able to make such a journey along the Thames, which the *Guardian* reporter Jack Shenker observes largely resembles a "high-security prison corridor than a public right of way."[2] This is attributable to the proliferation of securitized glassy luxury apartments and office spaces, all part of numerous, developer-led "regeneration" schemes that have transformed and gentrified many areas of London over the last four decades. The exclusivity of these developments, along with the lack of affordable housing in London and the more general decline of social housing in the United Kingdom, epitomize the opposite of Morris's vision of a verdant, creative city: a London symbolic, as it was in 1890, of economic inequity.

Morris's concern for economic equality has been pushed to the background in the lustrous imaginary of private development. This chapter explores, however, how development offers a putative compensation for this state of affairs, namely, an aesthetic landscape that promises to restore futurity and community to the city. That is, even large-scale capitalist development, in the form of regeneration projects, produces a vision aesthetically similar to Morris's utopia through the creation of a new, revitalized *place*: Emerging from the ruin of industry is a city of rooftop gardens, "creative" workers, spontaneous pop-up spaces, and peaceful views of the river. To analyze this legacy of urban utopianism, I turn later in this chapter to a discourse of "development," a term that captures the interlinked processes of investment, planning, and design that characterize contemporary London. This includes the eclectic mix of real estate firms, construction companies, architecture groups, and semipublic entities who all produce an extravagant amount of planning documents, surveys, extended advertisements, and detailed proposals for the city to come. Together, this literature works beyond the mere technics of planning to provide speculative visions of the future city.

Thus, more than simply a smokescreen for real estate cash grabs, I consider the discourse of contemporary development—in marketing, planning proposals, and the inherent signification of the built environment—as necessary to its economic transactions. Here financial and narrative speculations are conjoined as an aesthetics of development that imagines and articulates future places as realizable utopias. The chapter focuses on two particular projects along a central riverine corridor of development within the city: the London 2012 Olympic project centered in Stratford and the redevelopment of the Battersea Power Station. The Battersea Power Station (BPS) development is part of a larger redevelopment of south London but also seeks to further draw financial investment to areas along the Thames. The Olympics, meanwhile, was a project dreamed up by Ken Livingstone and Tony Blair under a Labour government and brought to fruition under the equally enthusiastic Conservative governance of Boris Johnson and David Cameron. Following the pattern of state intervention and public-private partnerships set by Michael Heseltine (as discussed in Chapter 3), it was part of a larger "Thames Gateway" project, which aimed to transform the "brownfield," working-class expanses of east London into more active, less neglected, "greenfield" sites. Both projects are metonymically illustrative of the dynamics of urban "regeneration," suggesting the stakes of urban "place making" in the world city and the tremendous aesthetic production that is development's condition of possibility. They speak to a common sense in urban policy, dominant in London but ascendant globally, in how and for whom cities should function.

Ecologies of Excess: Lastness as Affect and Aesthetic in Iain Sinclair's *The Last London*

My analysis of contemporary development aesthetics begins with Iain Sinclair's 2017 work *The Last London*, which negotiates the "unreal" space between the transience of the present and the temporal promises of an endlessly capitalist future. As the title suggests, the text marks an endpoint both for the city and Sinclair's prolific psychogeographic writing about it. "Psychogeography," a term coined by the situationist Guy Debord, attempts to provide alternative cartographies of the city, reading urban environments through individual experiences that accrete over time into a dense material archive.[3] Sinclair is in fact heavily influenced by a genealogy of continental thought about the city: He cites Baudelaire, Benjamin, Rimbaud, Bréton, Debord, and other surrealists and situationists.[4] A self-styled flâneur, he accordingly engages with the city through endless walking and in doing so seeks to excavate layers of history embedded in the urban geography.

A number of other Anglo writers and filmmakers have been similarly influenced by this continental genealogy. This work includes Patrick Wright's *A Journey through Ruins: The Last Days of London* (1991); Patrick Keiller's trilogy of *London* (1994), *Robinson in Space* (1997), and *Robinson in Ruins* (2010); Owen Hatherley's *A Guide to the New Ruins of Great Britain* (2010) and *A New Kind of Bleak* (2012); and, somewhat more distantly, the work of Will Self and John Berger.[5] A notable motif running through all this work is various figurations of ruin. For Sinclair, the figure of London's ruination par excellence is the redevelopment of the Lea valley for the 2012 Olympics. Olympic sites invite an association with ruins, partly because of the ancient history of the Olympics but also because of the many underused facilities populating the world's former Olympic cities.[6] The ruination of the Olympics is ambiguous for Sinclair, referring both to the corporate redevelopment, regeneration, and gentrification of east London and at the same time operating as a means for him to uncover lost or buried histories in the same spaces.[7]

For the latter, Sinclair takes up Walter Benjamin's notion of the ruin. Benjamin famously writes that the ruin produces an "appreciation of the transience of things, and the concern to redeem them for eternity" in the form of allegory, narration, history.[8] Even while criticizing the ruination of Olympic development, Sinclair also references Benjamin's angel of history (via reference to a 1978 interview of Jean-Luc Godard) to frame his interest in the "debris" of London—the discarded objects and meandering stories that he finds on his many walks. This debris includes the literal refuse and remnants of the built city, even those that are underground or underwater, but also refers to Benjamin's "pile of debris," that is, the lives of the past forgotten in the relentless calls for progress.[9] Critics have made extensive use of the Benjaminian concept of the ruin in a variety of historical, cultural, and theoretical contexts, while also adding nuance to the different ways ruin can be narrated. As scholars from Ann Laura Stoler to Gastón R. Gordillo have written, the ruin can be a site of ossified history that works to obfuscate ongoing violence and ruination or to potentially offer alternative ways of understanding history as social process rather than simply social fact.[10] In contextualizing Sinclair's work, this exhaustive critical discourse can be kept in mind, especially given Sinclair's direct references to Benjamin. At the same time, and apart from this critical discourse, ruination can be identified as a particular structure of feeling in contemporary Britain. That is, a sense of ruination and figures of ruin have been appearing in British politics and media, as well as in the work of the abovementioned writers who take up this theme. Its ambiguous sense of bleakness allows it to be tendentiously deployed in the service of a dominant ideological consensus or, conversely, to more critically characterize the destruction wrought by development and financial speculation. Considered in this way, ruination covers a range of associated phenomena, such that cultural critiques of very different political persuasions turn to similar affective valences.[11]

The Last London is a book that specifically encounters the experience of the gentrified city, both the way gentrification manifests itself in the aesthetics of urban landscapes and what it seeks to erase. Gentrification has greatly expanded its conceptual purview since Ruth Glass's seminal *London: Aspects of Change*, becoming a privileged term to discuss contemporary spatial relations, both in academic discourse and popular culture.[12] Initially referring to the political economy of urban real estate and the specific practices of middle-class urban colonizers in the so-called inner city, it's now a term used more generally to refer to embourgeoisement of space within a global economy marked by increasing inequality. This expansion has included a number of debates: whether the process is driven by a "rent gap" in property values, state initiatives, consumer preference or some combination thereof; how to define its various "stages"; whether "new-build" developments gentrify; whether it can describe urban spaces globally or just in the Global North; its relation to tourism; whether rural spaces can be gentrified; and the ways in which it relates to neoliberal transformation more generally.[13]

Further, real estate speculation has become increasingly and dizzyingly complex, dependent on international investment groups and complex financial transactions, such that defining and accounting for gentrification involves much more than tracking housing prices. This being the case, *The*

Last London apprehends gentrification through its *aesthetic*. The "third-wave" coffee shop, for example, signals to passersby that the neighborhood is changing, has changed. Not only the expense of the coffee but the preciousness with which it is prepared and the clientele—casually but sophistically attired, illuminated by MacBook—demarcate boundaries of class. These boundaries are implicit and can be crossed through the right combination of youth, attractiveness, and debt—"coffee is the new gold," as Sinclair writes.[14]

It seems that the only logical counter to the global homogeneity of urban redevelopment is the local heterogeneity of communities and places, and for this reason Sinclair, like in much writing about gentrification, renders urban change as the "strategic destruction of the local."[15] Through this process of destruction, cities come to resemble one another: "London as a suburb of everywhere: Mexico City, Istanbul, Athens. The same malls. The same managed alienation."[16] These types of pronouncements struggle to name something not yet namable. This situation, to borrow from Lauren Berlant, is a "genre of social time and practice in which a relation of persons and worlds is sensed to be changing but the rules for habitation and the genres of storytelling about it are unstable, in chaos."[17] The evocation of disappearance, loss, and a corporate sameness grapples with a heterochronic, emerging affect—a disappearance that is somehow both imperceptibly and palatably different. Instead of late capitalism, this is a *last* capitalism, one that is endlessly repetitious of its earlier enclosures and predations; it is final in the sense that it has no foreseeable end other than the end of the world. Sinclair writes of the end of the city: "I had walked here—and I would soon walk on, I'm not sure where—because my sense was that London, my home for fifty years, was being centrifugally challenged to the point of obliteration; of being unable to say just where, and why, it began and ended."[18] London becomes an Anthropocenic city marked by an incomprehensible lastness.

Perhaps for this reason, Sinclair's attempts at dérives seem consistently to fail as he confronts the "excesses of boosterism and regeneration" in the city.[19] Like his other books, *The Last London* is loosely structured as a series of very long walks replete with references to Euro-American literature, outsider artists and fellow flâneurs, and minor, mostly forgotten historical events. Yet this time the city seems to resist this kind of cultural excavation of the local. As a result, the text becomes in places sardonic, filled with a defensive, deadpan irony. Instead of lament for what has been lost and its partial recovery through narration, images of the gentrified landscape come in exasperated, descriptive fragments, as if criticism of its development is both self-evident and impossible to communicate. For example, he writes of "the din those improvers make. The decibels of patronising signs. The notices that appear in advance of demolition. The defining political requirement of our era is the art of getting your apology in first. And often. Letting the world know that you are sorry about being sorry. . . . Ecology of excess."[20] This is followed by a sarcastically quoted list of phrases from these signs: "TRANSFORMING WASTE . . . CREATING SPACE TO INSPIRE . . . PUTTING PEOPLE FIRST . . . DELIVERING GOOD DECISIONS . . . INVESTING IN COMPETITIVENESS."[21] Simple quotation serves to mock these gerund-phrases and render the language of public works and private development ridiculous and meaningless. The "din" of the "improvers" derisively conflates the noise of construction with the rhetorical noise of development-as-improvement, the way its slogans fill urban space to capacity and block out views of the sky. The litany of these slogans in capital letters seems to mirror development's "ecology of excess" with its own excesses, direct quotation becoming the best available mode of critical reflection. It is the faux-innocence of these phrases, which anticipate their own criticism and apologize in advance, that necessitate this approach. Even so, more earnest city dwellers might not understand what could be wrong with, for example, "putting people first."

In this way, Sinclair alternates between mourning and irony in attempting to capture the absent spirit of London, settling on the concept of lastness: "The last London," he writes, "is a lost London, a city of fracture and disappearance."[22] This is both new and not new: The modern city has been consistently characterized by a sense of transience, by appearances and disappearances.[23] In this sense lastness, if it means anything, cannot be understood in relation to linear time. Lastness must refer instead to a structure of feeling that emerges from a hollowed-out global economy, with its inequality, debt, precarious labor, and gentrified spaces. It connotes both the end of the city and its final form, disappearance and permanence all at once. Neil Smith has argued that gentrification operates at the "urban frontier," continually pushing at new boundaries, new places for investment and speculation.[24] Yet while these practices undoubtedly continue spatially and economically, lastness corresponds to the ambient sense of irrevocable change, the city having become something else, without yet naming or being able to name what this is.

However, this speculative affect too easily universalizes itself into a general political unconscious. That is, while lastness may describe gentrified London for Sinclair, this may not be a shared affect, or it becomes shareable only by absorbing and subsuming difference. In this case, the distanced flâneur attempts to speak for the displaced urban subaltern whose condition of possibility was always disappearance. Sinclair makes reference to his complicity, reflecting the disposition of both middle-class gentrifiers and the developers who apologize in advance, who are "sorry about being sorry."[25] Sinclair is himself a media fixture chronicling the disappearances of London, which by his own account compromises his outsider perspective: "As the publication of books, which would once have been called a literary career, became little more than the excuse for presentations and themed 'Edgelands' readings in universities, galleries, shops and hospitals that looked just the same, generically neutral, faintly paranoid, with background hum of white noise, so my grip on the city that provoked and sustained my fictions faded."[26] The tone is self-referential and sharp, with Sinclair uneasily placing himself within the repetitive sameness he otherwise observes at a distance. Speaking in part from personal experience, I can say that it is likely these readings were attended by artists funded by development projects or through corporate sponsorship of the Olympics, academics like myself who write dissertations and books on the topic from third-wave coffee shops, and architects and designers, well-read in the critical literature, who hope to do better next time. If, in this setting, disappearance is a generalizable contemporary affect, then Sinclair and the audience are its agents and its objects, unevenly.

Similarly, Sinclair presents his chapter on the photographer Effie Paleologou as a way acknowledging and mitigating—apologizing in advance—criticism that his flâneurie is exclusively male. He paraphrases this criticism: "No women, no validity to your report. Prejudiced, misogynist, inconsequential: nailed. There is no defence. It's not worth trying, though I sometimes do . . . and then, from a certain perspective, it does look decadent. Indulgent. Colonialising the environment and the lives of others."[27] In the very gesture of acknowledging this potential limitation, Sinclair drops into a free-indirect discourse to speak in the assumed voice of his interlocutors, who operate from "a certain perspective." The acceptance of this criticism is almost painfully reluctant, exhibiting the mix of defensiveness, embarrassment, condescension, and guilt characteristic of contemporary conversations around identity and representation. The relative absence of women speaks in part to a myopic occlusion but also to a "grip" that he is losing on the fading city. Similarly, whereas in previous works Sinclair would posit disappearance and absence as the occasion to search for Benjaminian allegories of the city, now lastness seems to challenge such projects of recuperation. For example, much of *The Last London* is structured around the seeming permanence and then disappearance of a rough sleeper on a bench in Haggerston Park whom Sinclair names a "vegetative buddha."[28] Sinclair fixates on this man, homeless and yet always present on this bench, seemingly impassive in response to his changing surroundings. Eventually, Sinclair finds that he is no longer on the bench. The nameless, voiceless homeless man on the bench becomes a figure for lastness, the fixity of his transient state itself subject to disappearance. Sinclair attempts to transform this individual into an allegory for the ruin of urban capitalism, but this yields no insights into what has been lost and how. Rather, Sinclair's figuration is at best opaque or, worse, stereotyped and sentimental. In these failures of representation, the subjects of *The Last London*—the homeless man, the city—disappear, but without producing meaning for the witnessing flâneur.

The text contains many more figures of problematic otherness, at times marked in passing. He seems bothered, but only slightly, at his inability to accurately identify these others. For example, he writes that he used to periodically see a "Vietnamese couple, or Cambodian perhaps . . . they disappeared right after the 2012 Olympic moment," or he refers to "the Romanian (or Armenian or Kurdish) women—my shameful ignorance of the Babel languages of the city hurts."[29] Elsewhere he locates a "wooden tribal fetish, a mask" set out for recycling: "African, Melanesian? I can't be sure."[30] In this last case, even while knowingly comparing this gesture to the "cultural appropriations of Picasso's mask-heads of the Cubist period," he fails to escape primitivist cliché: "With my fingers I could feel the strokes of the chisel or blade, the force of the original maker."[31] Similarly, outside the closed Brompton Cemetery, a "tall elegant black woman, a lamia from a superior class of sepulchre, appears at my shoulder. She gestures with an open hand . . . I can hear her high heels ringing on the pavement, but she is not there."[32] It is not that the text should or can include a fuller and therefore complete representation of the city's voices but rather that Sinclair, in evoking his experiences and perceptions, simultaneous claims and undermines the "outsider" perspective of the flâneur. That is, the possible position of critique, of disclosing and uncovering allegories of ruin through endless walking, reveals itself to be also entrapped in the production of the city. Rather than identifying a shared affect or reclaiming the authenticity of the local, *The Last London* can only mutely point to what it cannot quite represent. The homeless "vegetative Buddha," the possibly "Vietnamese couple," and the "elegant black woman" are figures of absence and incommensurability and at the same time are indicative of a city that has exceeded the ambit of the flâneur.

The city, delimited spatially by the London orbital and the greenbelt, becomes for Sinclair a representational circle with no outside.[33] The city's built environment becomes cluttered not just with advertisements, which had been there before, but also with constant advertisements of itself. As consumers of the city, inhabitants both buy into the self-image of development and improvement and feel alienated and entrapped by its omnipresent demands. This manifests in any number of ways: nostalgia for the anachronistic "local" that is always on the verge of its own reification, anxiety about the inherent complicity of consumption, uncanny bewilderment as "home" becomes unrecognizable, or the suffocating anger of displacement. The hegemony of development, here, is not just the extent of its official power structure but the way it creates a common sense, either preventing the possibility of thinking otherwise or continually co-opting oppositional practices. In fact, the two form such a closed circuit as to be indistinguishable, with such oppositional practices and resistances having already become another bourgeois cliché. In this way, these urban, late-capitalist structures of feeling themselves circulate back through the process of planning and development, which accordingly promises to offer a resolution through the creation of new places.

Temporalities of Urban Development: The London 2012 Olympics and Battersea Power Station

One of those "new places" is Queen Elizabeth Olympic Park, whose ongoing development was of course prompted by the London 2012 Olympics (Figure 16). As a "mega-event," each Olympics requires a large and increasing amount of public and corporate funding in order to stage a short, two-week sporting festival. Planning for the Olympics, given the need for (oftentimes new) arenas, venues, and housing, has the ability to rapidly change significant portions of a city. As they have made increased demands of cities, Olympic officials, city planners, and private developers have all taken care to stress that, beyond the temporary spectacle of the event, the games would provide a city with a meaningfully positive *legacy* in the form of infrastructure, built environment, and community feeling. As Tony Blair remarked early in London's bid, "As well as being a wonderful sporting and cultural festival, the Games would drive the environmentally friendly regeneration and rejuvenation of East London."[34] Similarly, in 2006 Sebastian Coe emphasized the importance of the Olympic legacy, which was "absolutely epicentral to the plans for 2012. . . . Legacy is probably nine-tenths of what this process is about, not just 16 days of Olympic sport."[35] Legacy was the aspirational horizon of the games, the mere idea that they would not be temporary but lead to an unambiguously positive reformation of the city. For Iain Sinclair, the Olympics are most representative of the last London, what he calls an "Olympicopolis" that is "a city divided into two hemispheres, two Westfield supermalls. A city of pop-ups, naming rights, committee-bodged artworks, cash-cow academies, post-truth blogs, and charity runs."[36] In the planning for the Olympic games, the prerogatives of the neoliberal city were on full display not only in the construction of massive new-build residential and commercial districts (all within a foreshortened planning process) but also their relentless advertisement as an indisputable

Figure 16. Post-Olympic Construction at Queen Elizabeth Olympic Park.

public good. Per their official motto, the Olympics would "inspire a generation."[37]

These were the conspicuous contradictions of the London 2012 Games: a costly, temporary, and exclusive event that had, at the same time, to produce a vision of an equitable inclusive future, or, in the parlance of the International Olympic Committee (IOC), a "sustainable" "legacy" of economic and social improvement for all. The Olympics presented an image of a secure and harmonious future London at odds with an insecure and fractious present, whose insecurity was only exacerbated, ironically, by the planning and development that accompanied the Olympics itself. The stark contradiction between the temporary nature of the games and the supposed permanence of their effects discloses a more general and fundamental temporal dialectic inherent in neoliberal economies, which seek to mitigate and absorb the temporariness of the present through the creation of speculative futures. Understanding the nuances of this dialectic—how its terms are constructed, reconciled, and undone and to what ends—is critical in determining how contemporary finance capitalism reproduces urban space in its own image, particularly in the "world city" of London. The Olympics exaggerate both the production of the temporary and claims to futurity.

This is perhaps appropriate for a city taken with the notion of the pop-up: with pop-up restaurants, pop-up cinemas, pop-up museums, and pop-up gardens spreading throughout the city.[38] The aesthetic of the temporary, in planning and culture, found its economic equivalent in the short-term employment boost in the lead-up to the games, which included work for migrant workers hired to maintain the facilities, themselves sleeping ten to a room in portable cabins.[39] At the time of the games, over 1 million British workers were on zero-hour contracts—a vast reserve of contingent labor who have no certainty in work or income.[40] Contingent labor for the Olympics also included seventy thousand unpaid volunteers who, as Blair approvingly noted, came from "all sorts of different walks of life."[41] LOCOG was not alone in suggesting the primary beneficiaries were the volunteers themselves:

> The recruitment of a large volunteer workforce provided first-time experience of a working environment for many young people, at a time when work was hard to come by. Thanks to their Games training and the example set by the Event Services team on the ground, volunteers learned the importance of punctuality, smart appearance and personality, among other characteristics, and a level of crowd safety training that they will be able to take forward after the Games.[42]

This army of volunteers, including those who participated in the celebration of the opening ceremonies, is a caricature of the pop-up labor market.[43] The temporary is thus neoliberal temporality in practice, produced by demands for flexible labor, without rights, guaranteed benefits, or even citizenship. In this context, contingency acquires a more general cultural value as that which is open and unconstrained, so that the insecurity of the temporary can actually be repurposed as producing secure futures.

Thus, the top-down ethos and concrete modernism of postwar planning has, like the welfare state it accompanied, partially given way to something else in the latest of late capitalism. Understanding the problems with outdated top-down management, urban planners increasingly emphasize openness and contingency, plans sensitive to the possibilities of "everyday" life. Yet in the current moment, contingency and open, uncertain futures are not lacking but instead seem omnipresent. Contingency—in the form of migrant laborers, guest workers, interns, temps, freelance everything, adjunct teaching, crowdsourcing, service work—is the current temporality of labor, the quality of its newness, in the postemployment finance economy. In these conditions, the utopian horizon for labor—and it is in these conditions that planners enthusiastically and good-naturedly work—is legacy, certainty, a semblance of permanence that exists past the appearance of transience, time itself. That is, legacy claims to mitigate, via futurity, what it relies upon and reproduces.

The speculative vision of the future articulated in the London candidate file and in the countless planning documents and mission statements of public, private, and public-private entities chimed easily with the already popular temporal rhetoric of regeneration.[44] As Graeme Evans remarks, regeneration, by definition, "is a response to a sustained decline (or de-generation) and regeneration therefore seeks to transform a community or place that has displayed symptoms of environmental, physical, social or economic decline."[45] The very real deprivation of the host boroughs was rhetorically mobilized by planners and politicians, who generally did not speak to the historical reasons for the existence of such inequality but nevertheless suggested planning, and specifically the Olympics, as a solution.[46] The site was thus characterized as a "polluted and derelict post-industrial landscape" containing "300 hectares of centuries-old industrial contamination and blight in the heart of East London."[47] Regeneration thus poses itself as the only available response to a city in physical, and thus economic, ruin, such that David Cameron could say that he would ensure that the "Olympics legacy lifts East London from being one of the poorest parts of the country to one that shares fully in the capital's growth and prosperity."[48] Further, planning for the Olympics had to clear a figurative ground, establishing the site as beyond any redemption save that provided by the games and its attendant urban planning. The alliterative phrasing of an early ODA planning report referred to processes that were as much ideological as material: "Demolish, Dig, Design."[49] The Olympics were thus sold through a discourse of ruination that propelled calls for regeneration, as a way of opening up the amorphous, unusable spaces of the city to revived life and distinct purpose. For this reason Graeme Hayes and John Horne, referring to Naomi Klein's *The Shock Doctrine*, call London 2012 disaster capitalism's "apparently benign twin."[50]

Doreen Massey notes that London's geography of inequality is created in a shift away from what might be called industrial landownership (where land is owned essentially as a condition of other production) toward financial ownership, of land as itself the means of extracting a profit.[51] For this reason, it is this half-empty space of dereliction, these ruined and degenerate brownfield sites, that are taken as objects by planners seeking to regenerate and revitalize.[52] Regeneration is part of an ideological consensus with regards to how cities function in a global economic geography, in which megaevents serve as advertisements for tourists and are thought to catalyze urban transformation. The world city is a place that exists not just or not even primarily for residents but rather to market itself to "potential investors, tourists, visitors . . . providing new gentrified work, leisure and housing spaces for the creative classes."[53] However, as a nonprofit report on the Olympics notes,

> rather than "harmonious development and the preservation of human dignity," we face a scenario of a massive public sector investment, mainly from UK and London taxpayers, resulting chiefly in corporate benefit, gentrification and the potential displacement of the most disadvantaged local residents, as the Government and Olympic bodies scramble to recover the debts created by the Games.[54]

For this reason, the legacy discourse of the Olympics was an attempt to reconcile the temporariness of the present—its contingency and uncertainty—with the fullness of the future. Planning the games was a working through of the essential temporariness of the games themselves, a practice that continually reckoned with its own impossibility.

The rapid timetable of the Olympics, along with the inherent contradictions of megaevents and their "legacy," lay bare the ideological foundations of the development consensus, which can be found in other sites of urban regeneration. One of the largest of these is the "Vauxhall Nine Elms Battersea Opportunity Area" extending from Battersea Park to Lambeth Bridge along the south side of the Thames. This development centers around the restoration of Battersea Power Station (henceforth BPS)[55] and the construction of several new buildings into a cluster of corporate headquarters, luxury apartments, and flashy retail spaces, with Apple as the first confirmed corporate tenant.[56] Like much of the private development for the Olympics (including a mall, luxury housing, and corporate offices), BPS is what Davidson and Lees refer to as new-build gentrification, arguing "that despite the different character of new-build developments there are striking parallels between those developments and previous waves of London's riverside renaissance of gentrification, such that new-build developments can, and should, be identified as landscapes or as forms of gentrification."[57]

However, BPS does not explicitly frame its development primarily by advertising the luxuriousness and exclusivity of its offerings but rather conceives of itself as integrated with the local, focused on community, open to creativity, and deeply concerned with sustainability—a verdant, immediate, creative city (Figures 17a, 17b, and 17c). BPS is design conscious and on brand, with almost an absurd number of architectural firms, design groups, and "placemaking" consultants involved in the project, including "starchitectual" firms like Fos-

Figure 17a. Development image for the Battersea Power Station Regeneration Project.

ter + Partners and Gehry Partners, both of which are currently placing their eclectic imprint all over the city.[58] The cultural work of these designers takes the form of a proliferation of documentation: lengthy corporate manifestos, expansive narratives for each building and aspect of the scheme, a regular magazine with interviews and opinion pieces, an extensive web presence, and other design and planning documents that amount to thousands of pages of material. These documents are filled with images of the appealing, green urban landscapes that will be constructed, photographs of stylish architects and designers, and bright, twee illustrations accompanying terms like "community" or "place." In fact, *Place* is a fundamental concern of the designers, who call themselves "placemakers," wrote a 230-page master document called the *Placebook*, and continually articulate their desire to "create a genuine sense of place."[59] All these texts read as a kind of (acritical) theorization of the city: They are replete with references to urbanists and geographers and self-aware of the history and cultural connotations of urban planning. The financial speculation[60] of BPS is based in a kind of cultural speculation through the creation of these narrative and aesthetic futures. The concern for *place* in contemporary development thus reveals an anxiety about insecure futures.

BPS developers fetishize contingency while laying claim to a stable futurity. Here, openness in planning and architecture is a form of "future-proofing," in which transience is a mark of adaptability to future conditions. Thus they frame their practice as one that attends to the local by creating the formal conditions for urban spontaneity and creativity. For example, disavowing the top-down, bird's-eye-view perspective of postwar architecture and planning,

Figure 17b. Development image for the Battersea Power Station Regeneration Project.

Figure 17c. Development image for the Battersea Power Station Regeneration Project.

David Rockwell states that while "it seems counterintuitive to think about architecture in terms of agile structures or impermanent spaces ... cities are more about the shifting, messy vitality and surging energy of the streets and less about the heroic view from above."[61] This "messy vitality" counterpoises any perception of sterility that might be associated with large-scale development.

This flourishing of the momentary and the temporary occurs within a larger scheme that promises a permanent revitalization. BPS developers specifically divide their planning into four phases: "Meanwhile," "Pioneer," "Emerging," and "Mature" (Figure 18).[62] The stages reconcile the immediacy designers seek from urban life—its fleeting, temporary, Baudelairean character—with the need to cast their intervention as a permanent and sustainable urban good. This "Staged Placemaking" is a kind of theater of gentrification, "a subtle art that seeks the highest returns for a site, by focusing on what it takes to make somewhere special every step of the way."[63] The first "meanwhile" stage continues the trend of the pop-up evinced in the planning for the Olympics, implicitly taking inspiration from the many ad-hoc "cultural" events sponsored by the games' financiers. BPS planners aim to produce "idiosyncratic, thrilling, catch-it-while-you-can experiences," for example, "temporary cultural events taking place in unusual settings such as abandoned buildings, museum galleries and railway stations," which will have "a scarcity value and [that] come imbued not only with a strong sense of authenticity, but also exclusivity."[64] These "unusual spaces" aspire to give the development an up-and-coming character while at the same time insuring the capital investment. Likewise, the "meanwhile" is especially designed to attract artists, or "those special early individuals, with a hunger for newness and an eye for the next big thing."[65] This is accomplished by "giving away space to people with creative energy, offering low rents to quirky shops so they can sit alongside luxury brands, putting on spectacular free events, providing temporary facilities in early phases."[66] Ironically, they consider the gentrification that is produced by artistically minded middle-class individuals to be more authentic than new-build corporate design, with the former leading to a "transformation [that] tends to produce more enduring places with greater cultural cachet" in trendy neighborhoods.[67]

The designers almost seem to be imagining younger versions of themselves inhabiting these spaces, with the "Pioneer" phase designed for young "creatives."[68] Thirty years ago, Neil Smith argued that gentrification operated through a frontier spatialization, with gentrifiers occupying the position of pioneers venturing into an "empty" territory.[69] Now, developers enthusiastically adopt settler-colonial rhetoric, arguing that in the latter phases, "even

Strategic thinking: Living

HABITAT

A mature community in nature comprises all the species that can happily co-exist without fighting for the supply of food, water or a place to build a nest, den, lair or burrow.

Only when there is an abundant and lush habitat available with many different kinds of trees and plants, is biodiversity achieved and the most sophisticated creatures thrive.

HABITAT CHART

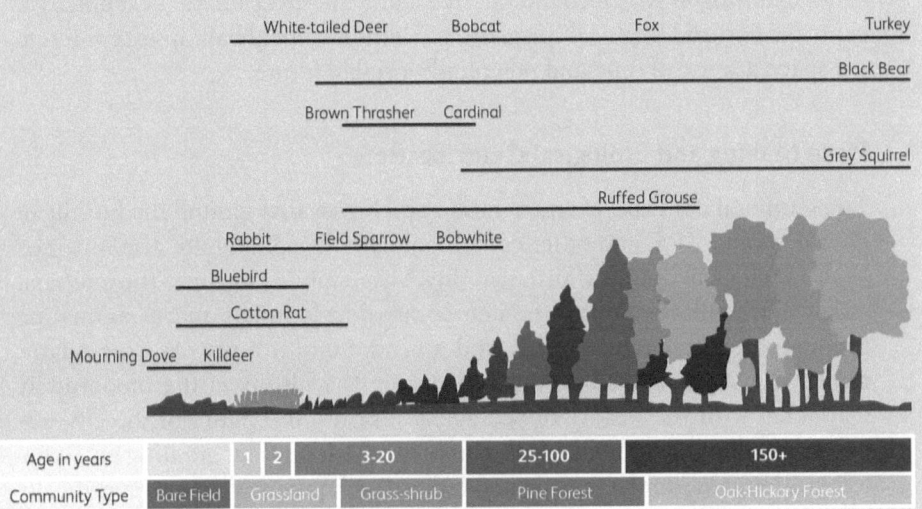

Figure 18. Ecological succession as a metaphor for place making, in the *Placebook* for Battersea Power Station.

though some of the early pioneers will have moved on, ready for a clean slate, a fresh challenge," it is important that "the vibrancy and creativity of the early phases remains and is not snuffed out in the manner of so many areas entering late gentrification."[70] If this is ensured, the "late adopters know that, having waited so long, prices will be at a premium, but then there is comfort in this, knowing it represents a good investment for the future—reassuringly established."[71] Phased development is thus a kind of spatial risk management, one that balances the speculative aesthetics of the meanwhile with the desire for both financially secure investments and a permanent, sustainable, revitalized community.

BPS continues the trend to make the Thames and Thames Gateway a focal point for regeneration, one that uses neutral terms such as "sustainability" and "community" but that in fact "constitute[s] . . . nothing more than state-led, private-developer-built, gentrification."[72] A disused coal plant is not just an industrial ruin but also stands for the ruination of industrialization, a metaphor that allows development to present itself as "transforming what was essentially an urban backwater into a central component of the capital's social and cultural landscape."[73] The aesthetics of a postindustrial ruin that was "decommissioned, in disrepair and down-at-heel" in an "under-used part of London" make it the perfect site to sound the historical echoes implied by regeneration's prefix: revitalization of a dead and polluted structure, restoring and reclaiming its Art Deco interior, recycling the space for the next phases of gentrification and financial speculation.[74] This historical palimpsest confers to the space a sense of time and potentially a stable future.

Place Making and Ecological Gentrification

The temporal concepts of regeneration and legacy that ground the futurity of the Olympics, BPS, and other contemporary development are accompanied by the ecological notion of sustainability. Sustainability captures the temporal stakes and contradictions of contemporary development and its animating promises of a restoration of life and an indefinite futurity. As Ross Adams remarks, "When it was becoming clear that the history of the modern city coincided with the history of ecological disaster, the figure of the city was transfigured into a technological structure of redemption, granting an eschatological urgency for large-scale real-estate development."[75] This is specifically accomplished through natural metaphors for the city, itself a legacy of early planners like Ebenezer Howard and Patrick Geddes. Adams identifies the late nineteenth century as the moment when "planners had fully reformulated the city as a 'biological organism,' whose naturally 'functional parts' were enabled through strategies of infrastructural connectivity . . . the focus of city planners and politicians turned towards optimizing systems of circulation."[76] BPS is accordingly envisioned as a "new lung of public space," to make the city breathe again.[77]

The temporal progression of development, which BPS designers seek to reproduce through "staged placemaking" (Meanwhile, Pioneer, Emerging, Mature), becomes an ecological analogy:

> To reimagine "phased development" in this way it is useful to look beyond the property world for inspiration. In nature, such a process is known as serial progression—the successive ecological stages that see barren landscapes evolve over time into lush forests, providing habitats for abundant life (the final climax community).... In this way, each successive stage of ecological development paves the way for the next, bare ground becomes grassland, grassland gives way to shrubs, shrubs to woodland and forest—more and more diverse landscape environments that support larger and more demanding forms of life.[78]

Through the imaginary of ecological succession, the developers figure the postindustrial city as a barren and lifeless area to be repopulated, as though in the aftermath of some devastating natural disaster. Ecological succession is an example of what Matthew Gandy calls the "ecological imaginary" of the city: the naturalization of urban change as a "cyclical dynamic alterable through technological modifications rather than by political contestation."[79] In solving an ecological problem, "sustainable" development and environmental gentrification appear as incontestable goods. As Melissa Checker writes, "Operating under the seemingly a-political rubric of sustainability, environmental gentrification builds on the material and discursive successes of the urban environmental justice movement and appropriates them to serve high-end redevelopment that displaces low income residents."[80] This naturalization makes development's final intervention appear inevitable and permanent.

Sustainability is concretized through the aestheticized image of the garden: "Like gardens, great places can take a lifetime to evolve and mature. Few are created from scratch and most are carefully planned, nurtured and tended over the years, until they blossom. Although The Power Station is a well loved landmark on the London skyline, we need to start planting the seeds for it to continue to stay that way."[81] This figuration tempers the masculinist, planned intentionality of modernist design, adding notions of nurturing and tending in producing, supporting, and sustaining lively places. The garden encodes a quasi-mythological temporality in an accessible, seemingly immediate, verdant presence: modern laments for a lost nature and Anthropocenic worries over a rapidly collapsing future are reconciled in and calmed by these green rooftops.[82]

Ironically, while the space as a whole is metaphorized as a slowly evolving garden, many of the initial actual gardens will be temporary: The "Meanwhile" spaces include a plant nursery and pop-up parks (in addition to the usual galleries and cinemas). The nursery offers both literal and figurative cultivation:

> Physically, temporary landscapes will help create a green and friendly atmosphere and later the same planting may be reused elsewhere on the site. We will bring Battersea Power Station back to life and the natural landscape will play a critical role in this transformative process. If we start early, we can "hothouse" The Power Station as a place where things spring to life by literally growing things on-site. That's even before we get the first buildings open. In the early days, we will get the site up and running with our plant nursery, which will be able to contribute to our series of "meanwhile uses"—a canopy of trees, a temporary pond, gardens to rival the very best the UK has to offer or an art installation that sits as one with nature—will help to cultivate our site.[83]

These references to cultivation, hothousing, a green and friendly atmosphere, of bringing the site "back to life," and of it being a place where "things spring to life" casually slip between literal and figurative and in this way conflate development with organic processes. The literal, aesthetic greenness does the figurative work of bringing the city "back to life," with a plant nursery being somehow the best way to get this large-scale development "up and running." The slow, meditative temporality of London's disappearing allotments,[84] gardens that people spend years if not decades cultivating, is reversed in these "temporary" landscapes. Still, if one can assent to the cultural imaginary represented here—the peaceful vista of a (temporary) pond, in the shade of some London plane trees, next to an apparently unnoticeable art installation, Grasmere diaries in hand—then redevelopment is perhaps not so objectionable. This narrative presents urban redevelopment as an unmitigated environmental good, a temporal mediation of past environmental ruin and future sustainability, of temporary, "meanwhile" experience and revitalized permanence.

Through this ecological analogy, gentrification as urban colonialism itself becomes naturalized: "At the outset it will be a fledgling place—with limited local facilities, immature planting and new neighbors."[85] This is because "only when there is an abundant and lush habitat available with many different kinds of trees and plants, is biodiversity achieved and the most sophisticated creatures thrive."[86] Pioneer colonization acquires an appealing gloss of abundance and vitality when the settlers are metaphorical wildflowers and bees.[87] "Diversity" is here rendered as metaphorical biodiversity, the benefits being not so much about equality but rather "sophistication." Continuing the metaphor, the designers state that the final stage of development will be "a mature community [that] in nature comprises all the species that can happily co-exist without fighting for the supply of food, water or a place to build a nest, den, lair or burrow."[88] The arcadian imaginary eliminates conflict and disagreement not through repression but through the creation of an environment that, like an ecosystem, is balanced by its own natural laws.

This happy, replete coexistence defers concerns of environmental gentrification by presenting itself as beneficial to the public. However, developers take definitional control of what counts as "public," recasting it as a "meanwhile" gift rather than as a right to the city.[89] The parks, squares, and green spaces of new developments are intentionally ambiguous in this regard: These spaces are often contiguous with the surrounding fabric of the city and connected to existing infrastructure yet ultimately under private jurisdiction. BPS thus claims that its rooftop garden is a "democratic gesture" and that the site's affordable housing is a "principled step" because it is "indistinguishable from the private" units.[90] That is, having outsourced the creation of public urban space to a private developer, the latter is now free to make "democratic gestures" and offer nonstigmatized "affordable" housing.[91]

This reflects changes in the city more broadly, as more ostensibly public, green space is given over to private developers who are then able to regulate and control these areas, for example by harassing and excluding the homeless.[92] For many cities there is a "strong correlation . . . between urban land cleanup, investment in park or open space creation or rehabilitation, waterfront redevelopment, or ecological restoration, and changes in demographic trends and neighborhood property values."[93] That is, people actually affected by environmental toxins are also removed in the process of cleanup, a green gentrification.[94] The representation of these spaces in this way contains an "ideological notion of what constitutes legitimate use of public green space," which privileges a "revived and restored" nature that mitigates the "negative [environmental] impacts of urbanization."[95] That is, BPS's supposed placemaking qualities of public riverside relaxation along the Thames—including the strategies for extending "dwell time in parks and public spaces" to increase "sociability"—contain the utopian assumption that everyone would have somewhere else to sleep in private.[96]

The developers suture the gap between private and public environmental goods through consumer sustainability—private, everyday lifestyles imagined as incrementally decreasing global environmental harm. Here the prefix of regeneration, revitalization, and restoration aligns perfectly with the consumer ethics of "reduce, reuse, recycle." Urban redevelopment is necessary because "the future is inevitably about urban living," which means a "greatly reduced carbon footprint."[97] As such, the importance of sustainability is rendered as individual, moral, and psychological. As the BPS *Placebook* acknowledges, "whatever the scientific arguments, we all feel we could do more to tread a bit lighter on this fair earth. But the problem is, when we try to be more sustainable, things seem to conspire against us, and even with the best intentions we feel guilty."[98] Placing what they term "scientific arguments" to one side, the main problem facing consumers, guilt, can be addressed. The solution unsurprisingly lies in design: "But you know it isn't always your fault," the developers tell us, "the problem is that most of us live in places that just weren't designed to make being sustainable in any way convenient."[99] Design ostensibly targets the inconvenience of sustainability, but its real aim is the guilt of contemporary living, the feeling that "we," living in poorly designed, unsustainable nonplaces, are not doing enough as individuals to slow climate change.

Sustainability can then be marketed as a consumer lifestyle that is both privately and publicly beneficial. BPS is thus advertised as a "complete eco-neighbourhood," in which one's "home would be [metaphorically] powered by the world's largest carbon neutral building."[100] The rhetorical economy at work here provides the future resident with figurative carbon credits, offsets that passively accrue from the time of purchase, along with equity. Aware of the "hackneyed," "clichéd" inauthenticity of "lifestyle" marketing, developers rebrand their offerings in terms of "the emerging notion of liveability," which is

> pragmatic and everyday and deals with urban lives in their complexity, rather than trying to reduce them down to a few glossy images. Liveability allows a neighbourhood to be thought of as a series of interconnected systems and spaces, that organised well can enhance enjoyment and ease of living, from growing food on the rooftops right down to waste disposal and underground drainage.[101]

These "interconnected systems" metaphorize the city as a natural ecology, which is again paired with the literal environmental goods of rooftop allotments and the seemingly novel technology of waste disposal. Liveability serves to "negotiate the demands of the urban growth machine, anxieties about environmental change, and the desires of elite consumers."[102]

The figure of urban circulation also presents the healthy city as a bodily analogy, one that in turn reproduces healthy bodies. As such, sustainable liveability frames individual "health and wellbeing," from organic food to pop-up gyms to relaxing winter gardens, as a collective good.[103] Leslie Kern argues that environmental gentrification is explicitly embodied and gendered in its emphasis on "notions of detoxifying, cleansing, balancing, aligning, beautifying, and purifying [that] are applied to bodies that seek to be transformed, inside and out. Simultaneously, these bodies are actively consuming environmental gentrification in the new neighbourhood spaces."[104] Just as attention is paid to the tropologically feminine, nurturing qualities of place, imagined as continually reproducing creative, spontaneous, innovative activity, "healthy(-looking) women's bodies signify the health of the neighbourhood."[105]

Similarly, the physicality of urban experience, rendered through activities such as cycling, walking, and exercise (in parks), takes its familiar role in grounding the ethical subject: "Considering the number of people with obesity in the UK has more than trebled over the last 25 years," the developers write, "we all need to take a bit better care of the body we've been given."[106] Aside from the promise of a kind of moral superiority for pop-up yoga practitioners, the atoning "we all" connects the healthy future tenant to the health of the urban, national, or even global community. If lifestyle was too vapidly individualistic, livability provides space for doing good and the presumption that the everyday habits of the individual can additively produce global sustainability. With the concept of "revitalization," dissent is relegated to a perverse desire for dead cities; here, "livability" occludes the "for whom" of environmental goods by turning winter-garden relaxation into a quasi-moral activity.[107] As if intuiting that wrong life cannot be lived rightly, contemporary developers imagine a future city where collective and individual goods are fully reconciled in ecological balance.

Creative Reuse, Innovation, and the Ethical Subject of Late Capitalism

Through regeneration, legacy, staged place making, and sustainability, both the Olympics and BPS development projects lay claim to a future that is both permanent and adaptable, global in impact yet attentive to the local community. The rhetoric of contemporary development addresses the instability of the urban present—instability these projects in part cause—by creating an imaginary, future-proofed future. Its urban-colonizing gestures are naturalized as a sustainable public good. Key to this process is not only an imaginary of the future but a reconciliation of a past marked by pollution, decay, and ruination. This occurs by way of a temporal prefix: the re- in revitalization, regeneration, renewal.

BPS invokes this prefix not only in relation to environmental repair but in cultural and creative reuse. Notions of reuse and "upcycling" have been closely linked to processes of gentrification in earlier theorizations. The aesthetic of reuse makes a cultural virtue of creative salvage, visualizing the process of rent capitalization in a way that makes displacement appear as rescue.

For example, the developments in Battersea are rhetorically organized around the restoration of the power station, which is "set to become a gigantic exemplar of creative re-use."[108] The power station—"iconic, unique, raw and authentic" and "every brand manager's dream"—is particularly important because it gives the designers an opportunity not just to build but to restore.[109] The ambition of this quasi-new-build architecture is not in a master plan but in a master recycle, one that revives what was best and most authentic about the past. It is the "industrial magic" of BPS that connotes both a "rawness and atmosphere [that] are its authenticity" and a development "built to last on a heroic scale."[110] Restoring the power station recalls the "sweat equity" that early individual gentrifiers put into renovating deteriorating homes, but on a massive scale and with the sweat outsourced to working-class laborers.[111]

Restoration operates rhetorically through creating a stark juxtaposition, as in "before" and "after" photos of a home renovation. The temporality of this restoration—its before and after aspects—legitimizes gentrification by narrating it as progress and improvement. BPS is an extension at a much larger scale of what David Ley calls the "aesthetic disposition" of gentrification. Using a Bordieuian frame, Ley argues that creative reuse "establishes symbolic value through a claim to difference and authenticity, the authenticity of craft production in a setting seemingly detached from modern production and marketing."[112] In this way, the artist "deliberately presses the borders of conventional middle-class life, while at the same time representing its advancing, colonising arm."[113] Similarly, BPS designers are tasked with restoring an industrial structure much as they might a worn, charity-shop table, so as to put "the heart and soul back into the building."[114]

Michael Jager has argued that architectural reuse allows for the creation of class distinction through a selective recuperation of the past. The middle class "does not buy simply a deteriorated house when it takes over a slum, nor does it just buy into future 'equity'; it buys into the past."[115] At the same time, "the effacing of an industrial past and a working class presence, the whitewashing of former social stain, was achieved through extensive remodeling . . . the restoration of an anterior history was virtually the only manner in which the recent stigma of the inner areas could be removed or redefined."[116] For example, the BPS *Icon Book* pairs industrial-chic images of an empty interior with black-and-white photographs of the coal-fired power plant's workers.[117] In this way, design aesthetics mutes a history of class struggle and active politics. The neoliberal transition can then be described in passive-voice detachment: "As economies entered their post-industrial period and employment underwent a painful but inevitable shift away from heavy manufacturing towards the service industry."[118] Creative salvage reclaims what it deems useful or beautiful from the debris of history and mistakes this gesture as reparative. In the case of BPS, the aesthetic disposition of reuse appeals to "aspiring owners of a chunk of Britain's industrial history."[119] Accordingly, the £11 million task of restoring the chimneys was a combination of, one, the "historical research and detective work"[120] necessary to dismantle and rebuild the original designs and, two, careful craftsmanship, in which damaged material from the chimneys "will be used elsewhere on site, perhaps in artwork."[121] What was left "in such a bad condition that they represent a major safety hazard" can be turned into an industrial-kitsch tower topped with a modern, glass viewing platform for tourists.[122] The constant emphasis on the bad condition (of buildings or neighborhoods) saturates the visuality of restoration and reuse with a temporal horizon and moral virtue.

The supposed urban revitalization is also an aesthetic revival indicating, as Sharon Zukin observes, a "deeper preoccupation with space and time.... A sense that the great industrial age has ended creates melancholy over the machines and the factories of the past. Certainly such sentiments are aroused only at the end of an era, or with a loss of function."[123] This romantic nostalgia "is a way of coping with the continuous past" and as such seeks to aesthetically restore not only nature without the dirt but also industry without the pollution—and both without the labor.[124] This impulse is reflected throughout the development documents: The architects needed eight million new bricks, which had to be "painstakingly matched in size and complexion with those already in place," and for this the "original supplier was miraculously tracked down and turned out to be a small village brickworks in the Midlands."[125] The cranes that used to unload coal, and which were only built in the 1950s, currently contain "asbestos, oil contaminants, lead paint and vermin waste."[126] They will be restored with the aid of "original photos, drawings, paint samples and archive materials" and returned to the site as decorations.[127] Similarly metaphorized is the boiler house, which is being turned into a lobby surrounded by office buildings; once a source of literal power, this lobby is imagined as "the spark, the moment where an idea happens" for creative-class workers.[128] Employees from Apple and other corporations will be greeted in this lobby by "pieces of coal vacuum-sealed in illuminated glass panels, echoing its origins," and "the atrium floor will be anchored by a heroic circular fireplace at each end ... a reminder of the building's past and also a catalyst for its future use."[129] In sum, "wandering around the empty and brooding Power Station you don't need to think—you can feel its authenticity—in the exposed structure, the heroic scale of the brickwork and the unexpected delights of the Art Deco Control Room."[130] The latent industrial authenticity in these now contaminated, derelict structures makes possible a restorative aesthetic, one that selectively borrows from the cultural imaginary of the past and reassembles those pieces to construct the city's future. Safely behind glass, coal will no longer poison workers and the planet, nor will it fuel empire, but merely tell a story whose redemptive narrative arc concludes with an information economy in a gleaming and green city (with Apple's electricity-devouring data centers as comfortably out of sight as the coal mines were previously).

Restoration also confers attributes of character and authenticity not only to the space of the development but to the inhabitants. This, the designers state, "only works because we all think it's quite normal to dream of making a dream home in a disused agricultural building."[131] The hazy, intangible status of this desire—not even a dream home but the dream of a dream home—allows for it to be positioned as shared and universal and thus perhaps the aesthetic basis for an equally restorative community. In this way, the particular taste for "refurbished buildings or even older properties in general" is universalized and made culturally hegemonic.[132] BPS is figured as the "kind of accommodation that might appeal to creative occupiers, or indeed any that might appreciate state of the art facilities set against the industrial, rough, exposed existing fabric of the space."[133] As the architect for the BPS office space, Sebastian Ricard of Wilkinson Eyre, suggests, to attract these creative people one needs to provide "exposed brickwork, steelwork and services ensuring that everywhere in the scheme people are connected to the existing fabric," thus creating a "dialogue . . . between contemporary modern and the history."[134] It might be curious that the trick for corporations to attract creative employees is the very particular kind of materiality that is exposed brick, but it's because this particular material opens up to a universal temporal framework, one that links and reconciles past and future.

Here, the sprawling, optimistic, well-intentioned collection of city planners and local council members, global investment firms, designers, consultants, architects, architectural consultants, survey designers, interior specialists, etc.—what might in less critical terms be called a "creative class"—form a stratum of bourgeois organic intellectuals that simultaneously occlude and naturalize the depredations and exclusivity of the London property market through active aesthetic taste making. That is, the appeal of restoration is not just simply a consumer preference for exposed brick or distressed wood or some other trend. Rather, culture works as a narrative mode for the production of ethical subjects that operate within a universalizing, hegemonic consensus. In the case of contemporary urban development, this consensus relates to normative ideas of what counts as a place and what places, once properly made (or remade), can do to remake individuals and communities.

The importance and uses of "culture, culture, culture," as the developers

Figure 19. Items from the Battersea Power Station "Manifesto."

phrase it, is explicitly reiterated throughout the "placemaking" documents and associated with "innovation and creativity" (see Figure 19).[135] For example, the *Placebook* writes that for "most people culture is not just some pleasant diversion—it's something that can inspire them to reflect on life and help define who they are and it's this ability of culture and the arts to raise us out of the everyday that makes them so compelling."[136] Culture—here elided with "the arts"—is important for place because it is what forms and situates identity and an individual's disposition toward that place. It is what transmutes the rawness of the "everyday" into the ethos of the creative, innovative subject.

As David Lloyd and Paul Thomas write, culture was crucial to the formation of a liberal common sense organized around the naturalness of the free market and the ethos of the representative state. A paradox for the state is how to reconcile group interests with the supposedly universal institutions of the nation-state. It is culture that "resolves that paradox, not by dissolving it but by displacing it onto a temporal schema in which the subject is defined in terms of the development of its full human capacity."[137] Central to this interpellation of the individual into citizenship was the aesthetic, which they argue is an "an ethical training devoted to the 'educing' of the citizen from the human being . . . aesthetic culture represents, therefore, the very form of bourgeois ideology."[138] Human development is a progressive temporal schema that transforms while selectively retaining the authentic, ephemeral rawness of the particular into a collective "culture" that is above petty political fragmentation and has, accordingly, a boundless temporal horizon. This in turn allows "politics to take place as if material conditions were a matter of indifference" and instead establishes a hegemony that is a "disseminated form of self-evidence or 'common sense' that regulates subjects across the differentiated domains of modern society."[139]

The aesthetic cultivation and development of the citizen recurs in property development as well. "Culture" is not just what BPSDC offers to future residents in the way of art exhibitions and concerts but more substantially speaks to the desire for place to creatively transform identity:

> The term "self-actualisation" is often used to describe a category of individuals seeking to transcend the everyday and create a more meaningful life. Not content with passive consumption of mainstream media (TV, film, theatre) these people are interested in "transformational" leisure experiences, driving demand for evening classes (music, languages, craft), workshops, lectures, talks, book clubs, appreciation of art and culture and increased connoisseurship of food and drink.[140]

The developers make a distinction between passive and active consumers, the latter imagined as creative, sophisticated, quasi-artists. BPS will help individuals find a "meaningful life" that "transcend[s] the everyday," and therefore become self-actualized (this being opposed to the implicitly meaningless, mundane life of passive consumers). Self-actualization refers to a creative, entrepreneurial subjectivity in which continuous consumption and (self-)production enter into a mediation that is both daily and transcendent. "Everyone," the developers write, "wants to fulfill their true potential in life.

They want to experience that feeling that comes from starting something from scratch."[141] In this way, the ethos of the creative middle classes universalizes itself and becomes hegemonic; it doesn't matter what set of activities constitutes fulfilling one's true potential, because having the opposite goal is absurd and unthinkable.[142] Development becomes the common-sense solution to the problems of place and identity.

Such conceptualizations both delineate and reproduce class. The creative subject contains an ethics of active consumption, meaning not just sustainable grocery shopping but a disposition of creativity for the purposes of self-actualization and representation. This is distinct from those who approach the everyday, including everyday consumption, not just unsustainably but passively. The latter live in "clone towns," nonplaces dominated by chain stores.[143] The former, meanwhile, are self-contained entrepreneurial seeds of revitalization, place makers. The developers observe that Battersea is a site of "extreme potential right now, with acres of vacant space, ripe with untold opportunities," and that they "want to explore what happens when you create the sort of place where grass roots activities are the norm.[144] Like the late-capitalist obsession with technology companies formed specifically in garages, BPS developers fetishize "old warehouses on the edge of every town, crammed between and under railway lines and such" that are a "breeding ground for all kinds of companies."[145] In other articulations, these supposedly vacant, empty spaces are a sign of disinvestment and as such are characterized as dismal, abandoned, and bleak. Here, however, that emptiness carries a latent potential for creative reuse (and rent capitalization).

In Battersea, developers seek to capture and endlessly reproduce this otherwise fleeting moment of urban creativity by creating a space "more edgy and vital than the more corporate city and West End locations" while linking this rough edge with the concept of "innovation" and the economics of new capital investment.[146] The developers reproduce what was already the case among artists, namely, that they had become adept at "adopting entrepreneurial strategies" in order to "package themselves as exciting and alternative . . . against more traditional, conservative art centres in London such as the West End," specifically through the use of an "urban pastoral" aesthetic.[147] To do this, the garish corporate ethos of the city or Canary Wharf is rejected in favor of a focus on arts, pioneering creativity, innovation, and mature neighborhood community, in that specific developmental order. The master architect, having lost his halo, becomes the place director:

> Looking around London, it's obvious there are not nearly enough of those talented individuals who know how to turn a group of interesting

buildings and spaces into a living, breathing place—full of the joys of life and with a few surprises thrown in for good measure. Our place director will have a master's degree in authenticity, or at least they would if such a thing existed. Instead, we'll settle for someone that has a passion for real urban experiences and a healthy disdain for corporate precincts and disneyfication.[148]

This figure takes raw materials of everyday urban life, including its disused materiality (exposed brick, etc.), and transforms it into breathing, joyful, surprising, authentic, healthy, real place. Development becomes concerned with "capturing the spirit of the place and staying true to our principles—putting culture and the arts first, championing design quality and encouraging personal creativity."[149] Place in this idiom is a structure of capacity, everywhere actualizing potential while reproducing spontaneous potentiality. In the cultural discourse of development, the spirit of place is a latent, ghostly "authenticity" that half exists in what are otherwise spaces of ruin, neglect, and decay. The task of architecture, design, and planning is to revive the dead.

All together, London's narrative of development manifests a latent anxiety about the time of capitalism. If the goal of property speculation, as with investment in general, is to predict and manage uncertain, risky futures, the narrative of urban revitalization constructs a temporality that reconciles environmental and political tension into a vision of a healthy, cohesive, sustainable, creative community. In doing so, it renders the aesthetics of planning and architectural design and the habitus of consumption into moral conditions for neoliberal subjectivity. The a-politics of this utopian endpoint marshals a beguiling cultural imaginary in order to render political disagreement absurd and unthinkable.

The Dead Ends of Development

This chapter has considered the temporalities of development, including how the transformation of urban space is continually cast as "progress" and thus as an inarguable good. To make this claim, however, development necessitates and throws up contradictory temporalities through a variety of spatial figures, from the always-decaying slum to the spontaneous pop-up. As suggested in my reading of Sinclair, the continual leveraging of these spatial figures and the way they dominate political discourse makes the city, especially London as a "world" city, something of a cipher, unreadable and opaque. Here, the ephemerality of everyday life and the allegories of ruin that characterized the city for the likes of Baudelaire and Benjamin themselves become subject to capture and redeployment to the ends of "progress." As such, the violently changing pop-up city becomes characterized, ironically, by an effect of *lastness*, which is not a sense of permanence or deep history but rather one of finality and dead ends.

The next chapter continues many of these themes through a more detailed exploration of the types of subject formations available to those situated in the temporalities of the city. The translucent figures who populate planning images do not, of course, experience the temporal contradictions of the city. They are speculative people, and as such the restorative powers of the development-to-come serve to ameliorate the anxieties and alienation of modern life and reconcile the conflictual politics of the city. In this imaginary, the creation of *place* is what enables these subjects to become actual. That is, central to the speculative project of globally financed development is a narrative about individuals fully reconciled to the place they inhabit and that, in utopian fashion, allows them to achieve their creative and economic potential. The production of these subjects not only involves the political economy of the state or the epistemic conditions of possibility but requires the creation of an aesthetic enclave that promises actualization.

5
Level Up
Zadie Smith's NW and the Promise of Progression

The UK government is currently obsessed with the idea of "leveling up" the country. The phrase refers to a discrete geotemporal process by which those regions that are "behind" the norm will "catch up" to the rest of the country. While Britain's north/south divide is the most explicit target of this "leveling up," a 2021 Centre for Cities report noted that geographic inequity was a feature of London itself, and that the world city was even at risk of "leveling down" as a result of the COVID-19 pandemic.[1] Chapter 4 explored the temporal contradictions at work in urban development, in particular how a rhetoric of progress and images of futurity could be experienced as the opposite—as a precarious kind of *lastness*. This chapter extends that critique through a reading of Zadie Smith's 2012 novel NW. Published in the same year as the London Olympics, NW faces up to the reality of a mass-gentrified London—a city of speculation, guided by an ideology of development and progress—and "registers the psychic and material shocks of those left behind in Northwest London," as David Marcus writes.[2]

The novel tracks the relationship of two characters, Leah Hanwell and Keisha/Natalie Blake, best friends grown apart because of differences in class, race, identity, and all of the smaller, more contingent variations of personality and disposition.[3] On the whole, NW can be considered a modernist novel, especially in how it makes use of multiple perspectives (split across five sections), varying typography, montaging effects, and free-indirect discourse, all against an urban setting with all the hallmarks of "modernity," especially in its invocation of the experience of the city and way that character paths intersect (recalling, in particular, Virginia Woolf's *Mrs. Dalloway*). It asks questions about how people become distinct selves even when they all start from something like the same place, in this case the fictional Caldwell council estate in Kilburn, northwest London. However, "place," Lauren Elkin writes, "even in London, especially in today's London, is not a leveler . . . local does not mean equal."[4] The growing apart of Leah and Keisha is a means for the novel to think through the political economy of contemporary London and its inhabitants: locked in relations of anonymous intimacy, distanced through structural inequality and personal happenstance, encountering and engaging in performances of the self-made self.

This ethos is perhaps most succinctly expressed by a separate character, Felix, whose story is the focus of the novel's second section, "Guest." In discussing his ambitions to marry his girlfriend Grace, Felix says he has been living life at "a level with a lot of demons" but now claims, "I've killed them. And it was hard, and now they're dead and I've completed the level, and it's time to move to the next level . . . I'm moving up in the game. And I'm ready for it."[5] Felix renders the progression to adulthood with a colloquialism derived, somewhat ironically, from video games.[6] Moving to the "next level" of life is also a process of "leveling up," in which more experience leads to new abilities, higher resilience, and material wealth. The fantasy bildungsroman never ends but rather promises endless linear progression, without setbacks, detours, narrative bathos, or postsuccess deflation.

The thematics explored in the previous chapter—the temporalities of development, the ideology of progress, and the production of inequity and precarity—do not only exist in the overblown rhetoric of regeneration projects but also tangibly govern the lifeworlds of the city's residents. Though confronting a landscape that is increasingly not made for them, the characters in NW yet attempt to fit themselves, with enthusiasm, fitfulness, or despondency, to a hypercapitalist mold. In this chapter, I'd like to use NW as the occasion to think through urban development and gentrification not just as abstractions or macrolevel economic transformations but as ways of knowing that concretely affect the production of subjectivity, interacting, along the way, with the complex and often contradictory vectors of race, immigration, gender, and class. Starting from the "same" place, Smith's characters view their lives through the prism of steady, even progress. This sense of progress proceeds along stereotypical middle-class lines—marriage, home ownership, children—that increasingly mark the horizon of a banal cosmopolitanism. In the novel, London's gentrification can be found not just in astounding house prices and the failed dream of collective ownership but in the intimate relationships between people, friendship and relationships framed by bourgeois aspiration and fractured by its individualizing ethos.

The temporal contradictions outlined in Chapter 4 come to bear forcefully upon Keisha/Natalie. One the one hand, Natalie's story is one of relentless improvement and progress, expressed through professionalization and class mobility alongside the heteronormative achievements of marriage and children. In so many ways, Natalie is a *planned self*, one who manages the time of her being so as to progress in an orderly fashion through her life. The alienation this produces, as a crisis of authenticity in herself and her relationships, is not merely existential but rather sharply composed from the pressures of patriarchy, histories of imperialism and migration, and experiences of class on the edge of precarity in the council estate. These mirror and reproduce the violences effected through urban development and gentrification.

For example, in the climax of the novel, Natalie leaves her house to go on a long, meandering walk through London. The novel tells us that "walking was what she did now, walking was what she was. She was nothing more or less than the phenomenon of walking."[7] She seems to form an ideal flâneuse, recalling Iain Sinclair's claim that "walkers became the walk, the place."[8] Natalie, daughter of working-class immigrants from Jamaica, walks from her home to nearby Kilburn, where she grew up, before making her way to and past the restorative green fields of Hampstead Heath, unexpectedly meeting and doing drugs with old friends along the way. The walk is an urban sensorium: Natalie "couldn't resist this display of the textures of the world; white stone, green turf, red rust, gray slate, brown shit. It was almost pleasant, strolling to nowhere."[9] This is an experience of the city unavailable from the cartographical bird's-eye view and one very different from the tourist gaze, which falls only on monuments, museums, and scenes of London's official history. Like the flâneur, Natalie strolls through the city rather than walking with a particular destination in mind, an anonymous woman in the crowd.

Except this remapping of the city through the wandering subject is more of an unmapping, both of the city and of Natalie. Rather than indicating a subject that wanders to observe and find poetic engagement with the city, she is more a subject undone by the city—its ideology of self, its ensnaring hierarchies, its relentlessly threatening aesthetics—and finds herself on Hornsey Lane Bridge, literally at the precipice of death. Natalie's "flâneurie," such as it is, and *NW* as a whole form a response to the political economy and aesthetics of contemporary London. What Sinclair identifies, for him, as the lastness of London the novel suggests was a nullity that was always there, lurking amid the ruinous intimacy of gender, enclosed within the unresolved violence of race. The characters stumble upon these hunched violences as they attempt to engage with the ethos of development and progress.

The characters struggle with their attachments to and alienation from normative life, what Lauren Berlant calls the cruel optimism of a good-life fantasy, which includes the assumptions of what "success" looks like and how it should feel. Ironically, the more distant this vision becomes, the more it both enthralls individuals in cycles of desire and alienation. Berlant asks:

> Why do people stay attached to conventional good-life fantasies—say, of enduring reciprocity in couples, families, political systems, institutions, markets, and at work—when evidence of their instability, fragility, and dear cost abounds? . . . The fantasies that are fraying include, particularly, upward mobility, job security, political and social equality, and lively, durable intimacy. The set of dissolving assurances also includes meritocracy, the sense that liberal-capitalist society will reliably provide opportunities for individuals.[10]

Home ownership can easily be inserted into this series, forming an imaginary to which individuals attach and within which they stall.[11] The post-1980s housing market, with its housing associations, middle-class "improvers," and private development companies, has increasingly fractured the city into haves and have-nots; this division is sutured not only through the force of law-preserving state violence (in the form of housing law, evictions, street profiling, etc.) but also through a late-capitalist imaginary that encourages individuals to consent to and actively seek the norms of the good life.

These violences are the "ghosts of other stories" reappearing again in the neoliberal city. In its focus on London, and on the temporal contradictions of the city, this chapter should be read as an extension of Chapter 4. At the same time, the affects and structures of feeling presented throughout *Topothesia* find spectral resonances here, from the utopian alternative timeline for London imagined by William Morris to its dissolution, once again, through repeated practices of colonial cultivation and supposed improvement. Engaging deeply with literature helps draw out these resonances, especially in a highly allusive novel like NW that, through juxtaposing and overlapping narrative, renders quite concretely what contingency, lastness, and dead-ends might mean for the subject. The analysis in this chapter broadly follows the narrative arcs of the novel. First, I consider the effects of disappointment and shame through the character of Leah, who feels herself to be improperly and insufficiently adult, while obliquely registering the potential benefits of being an insufficient and nonsovereign subject.[12] Second, I analyze Natalie as a *planned self*, an ambiguously hollow creation that takes shape through the forms of heteronormative capitalism, especially through the figure and material fact of the gentrified *home*. Finally, I read her flâneurie as simultaneously an ecstatic movement of escape and as a death drive, one ultimately made possible and predicated on figures even more transient and contingent than her.

"It's the Next Thing": Unreachable Womanhood, Unbearable Liminality, and the Dream of Friendship

The first section of NW, focusing on Leah, presents the above dynamics through the figure of the apple tree, notably in a (tree-shaped) concrete poem that renders a soliloquy by Leah's husband, Michel, into verse.[13] The poem is suggestive of the entangled connotations of the "so symbolic" tree: "New branches. New blossom./New apples. Same tree?/Born and bred. Same street/Appletreeapple/Trunk, bark./Alice, dreaming/Eve, eating/Under which nice girls make mistakes."[14] "Born and bred. Same streets," a stock phrase that repeats several times in the text, refers to the dichotomy of "nature and nurture," the question of whether character and morality are innate or the result of upbringing and good works. This is a Christian dichotomy of moral value that is easily transformed into a capitalist pair explaining class difference and social "evolution." "Born and bred" refers to quasi-transcendental structures ("nature," "culture") but makes them personal; here, Leah and others question how those who grew up on the "same streets" could have diverged so far from one another and at the same time not that far from those streets. As Felix, also from the "towers of Caldwell," is told later in the novel, "Apple ain't fallen far from the tree, bruv, for real."[15] The apple tree is thus a figure for both continuity and change: Societies and individuals reproduce themselves, but a repetition with (some) difference.

Leah in particular confronts the fact that she has not fallen far from the tree and in fact is able to see Caldwell from her current flat in a nearby estate, where she muses, "Maybe it doesn't matter that life never blossomed into something larger than itself. Moored to the shore she set out from, as almost all women were, once."[16] Rootedness, here figured first as a stunted tree in temporal development, then as a spatially anchored ship, is experienced as a limitation and a disappointment. The question of reproduction is concrete for Leah, who is briefly, unhappily pregnant before getting a secret abortion. Her body becomes a familiarly gendered site of overdetermination, signifying not only a reproductive capacity but also Leah's meditations on temporality, which are of both the inherited past and the compelled futurity of children: "Which way is forward? Tick, tock."[17] The pressure to have children comes from her husband, Michel, who hopes to continue the progression of marriage and cohabitation to parenthood, and her mother, Pauline, who remarks to her on the bus, "You should get on with it. Council's set you up very nicely really, you've got a little car, you've both got jobs. It's the next thing."[18] The third-person narration slips into Leah's thoughts: "You're next. It's the next thing. Next stop Kilburn Station."[19] Leah maps the progression of the individual in life to the linear spatial path of the bus, suggesting both the inexorability and banality of movement "forward" in life.

Leah seeks to escape not only into herself but to an earlier self, where futurity was open-ended and ignored. The novel opens with a stranger, Shar, deceiving Leah for a small amount of money. For this Leah earns the censure of those around her for her childlike naivety. Even after realizing she had been taken advantage of, however, Leah is fascinated with Shar, who "is something beautiful in the sunshine, something between a boy and a girl, reminding Leah of a time in her own life when she had not yet been called upon to make a final decision about all that."[20] This desire is not a rejection of futurity but rather of progress, the even development of life from childhood to adulthood, instead seeking the confusing and pleasurable liminality of her generation's so-called extended adolescence. Here the present can stay still and not move forward, while being itself characterized by movement: "I want to stay still and to keep moving. I want this life and another," Leah thinks while fantasizing about running away with Shar.[21]

This liminal temporality is one that forgets that material conditions and pressures provide a universal template for normative adulthood. The shifting perspective renders Leah as both the "sole author" of her story and as object within the narrations of Michel, Pauline, and others.[22] Leah, we are told, "does not want to arrive . . . Why must love 'move forward'? Which way is forward. No one can say she had not been warned. No one can say that. A thirty-five-year-old woman married to a man she loves has most certainly been warned, should be paying attention, should be listening."[23] It is unclear if the question of why love must move forward is one that Leah asks herself or that the novel asks the reader, the "no one" being Leah's rebuttal to her own protests at not being warned. Meanwhile, everyone else in their life desires for Leah and Michel to have a baby and join onset-middle-age adult society. Together, these pressures form a background hum accompanying Leah's adulthood, increasingly compelling Leah's attention.[24] Shar, as a romanticized stand-in for an alternative life, catalyzes Leah's reluctance to take the "next step" in womanhood.

The characters in NW have all fallen, some closer to the tree than others, and figuratively wonder if this was because of the tree or their own individual qualities as good or bad apples. In fact, even in "failing," Leah conforms to a type: "Eve, eating/Under which nice girls make mistakes."[25] The figure of the apple tree alludes to the novel's epigraph: "When Adam delved and Eve span, who was then the gentleman."[26] This comes from a sermon by the radical priest John Ball in 1381, who in imagining an original equality in the human community, said that "from the beginning all men by nature were created alike, and our bondage or servitude came in by the unjust oppression of naughty men." This phrase was later revived by William Morris in his story "A Dream of John Ball," originally appearing in the *Commonweal* in 1888 and accompanied by an Arts and Crafts–style drawing by Edward Burne-Jones (Figure 20). Smith's use of this phrase as the epigraph thus recalls a long history of English radicalism through different figures who twinned a particular reading of a mythical past with a utopian hope for a classless future. Yet this citation must be read ironically against the reality of late capitalism and the specters of patriarchy and colonialism.

As such, the apple tree in the novel becomes a figure for the problematics of social reproduction but also of London's contemporary political economy and its neo-Victorian inequality. Leah's current estate has a communal garden with an apple tree, around which she scattered the ashes of her late father.[27] For Michel, this represents failure, or at least stalled progress:

> Brent Housing Partnership. I don't want to have this written on the front of a place where I am living. I walk past it I feel like oof—it's humiliating to me. If we ever have a little boy I want him to live somewhere—to live proud—somewhere we have the freehold. Right! This grass it's not my grass! This tree is not my tree! We scattered your father round this tree we don't own even.[28]

This monologue is a reproduction of a Thatcherite affect: not just a neoliberal economics in which the atomized individual advances but the sense that to not advance in this prescribed way is shameful, that, as Leah says earlier to her distracted mother, "Anyone over the age of thirty catching a bus can consider himself a failure."[29] Ownership, conversely, signals a proud success, figured by Michel as a potential son, a "little boy" who takes on his father's pride in home ownership.

Property ownership and an ascending professional career become, like marriage and parenthood, so many forms of progression; Leah is surprised and bewildered that these practices of "adulting" could, all of a sudden, reveal themselves to be nonironic. In one scene, Leah and Natalie discover the Our Lady of Willesden church, containing a priest who is the same as he "would have been in 1920 or 1880 or 1660 . . . but his congregation is different" and a black Madonna figure made of jet, with the power of "serendipity, restoring

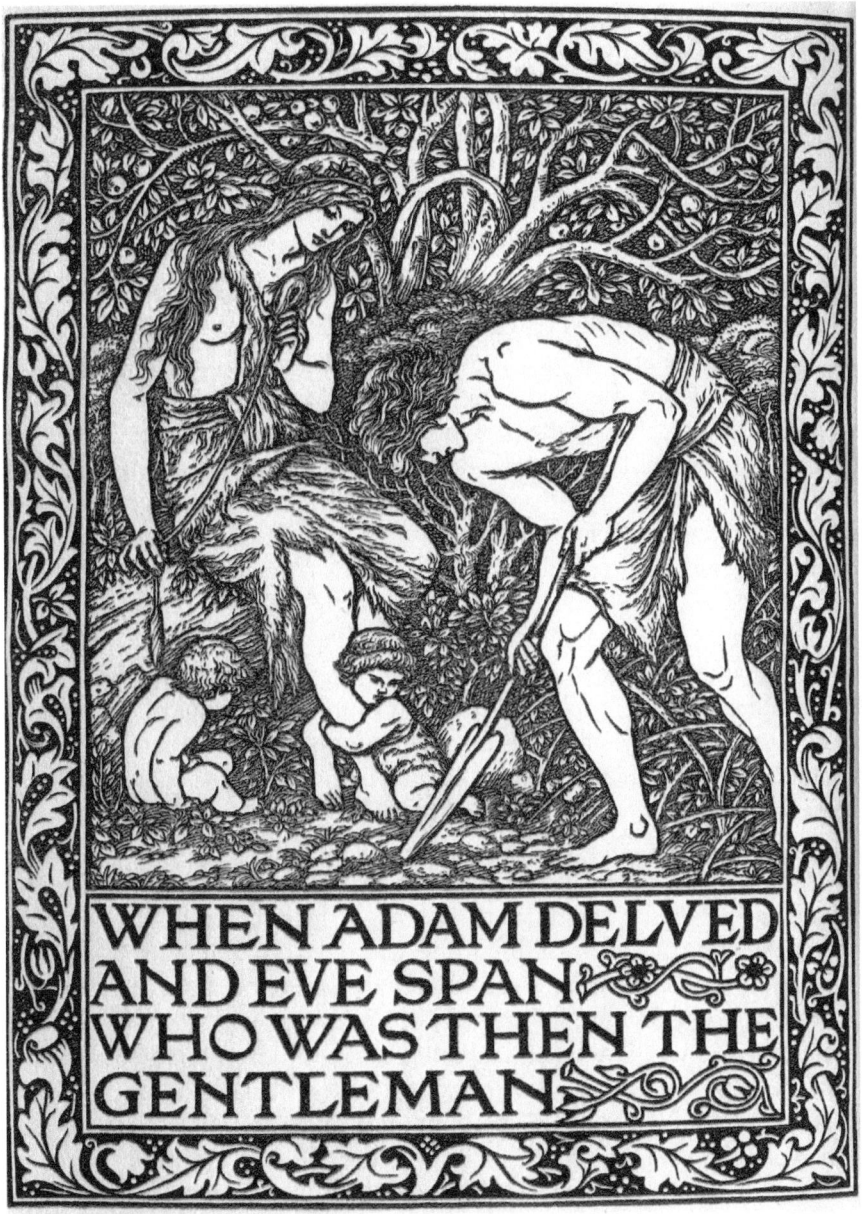

Figure 20. Edward Burne-Jones, *A Dream of John Ball*, soft-ground etching, 1888, from William Morris, *A Dream of John Ball*, 1888, frontispiece.

lost memories, resuscitating dead babies," all very relevant to Leah's predicaments.[30] Leah faints in the face of this figure, who then speaks directly to her:

> I am older than this place! Older even than the faith that takes my name in vain. Spirit of these beech woods and phone boxes, hedgerows and lampposts, freshwater springs and tube stations, ancient yews and one-stop-shops, grazing land and 3D multiplexes. Unruly England of the real life, the animal life![31]

This place and this figure are both ancient and modern; the latter, placed in contrast to the imaginary of a Celtic connection to nature, seems especially quotidian and ephemeral with its one-stop shops and multiplexes. Perhaps, as Molly Slavin writes, this "map [that] the Black Madonna assembles, and the way she forces Leah to participate in creating the map, confronts dominant geographies and builds, instead, one of many possible cartographies of elsewhere and resistance."[32] These hidden geographies function as alternative histories: Even as paths not taken, they are a testament to the notion that things could have, and might still be, otherwise. Thus, Wendy Knepper writes, the Black Madonna "reveals a concealed presence of difference and otherness to the hegemonic order, which has been there all along."[33]

At the same time, this figure is overwhelming for Leah. Rather than seeing a spiritual truth, Leah finds the continuity of the eternal into the ephemeral to be a sudden, disorienting burden. The Madonna poses a series of unanswerable questions: "What made you think you were exempt? . . . Did you hope for something else? Were you misinformed? Could things have been differently arranged, in a different order, in a different place?"[34] These questions, both rhetorical and sincere, form a demand that Leah inhabit a maternal archetype—that the insouciant, seemingly random events that led to her present should have been, all the while, adding up to something. This sense of a path not taken, of arriving at a different place (in the city or in one's life), is brought to the fore not only in Leah's nonrelationship with Shar but also in her ostensibly close relationship with Natalie. From a position of seeming equality, Leah and Natalie have evolved from interlocked childhood friends to estranged adults. This difference is also socioeconomic: Leah still lives near Caldwell and works for the council, while Natalie is a successful lawyer in the gentrifying neighborhood of Willesden.

Natalie has a picture-perfect bourgeois life: children, a sophisticated investment-banker husband, a beautiful house, and a cosmopolitan circle of friends. Leah finds Natalie's home to be an oppressive reminder of the good life that she does not have, a life that she, ironically, does not even want. Compared to this, Michel's sincere desire to have this life only further alienates

Leah: Michel is drunk "not only on the Prosecco in his hand" but also "on the grandeur of this Victorian house, the length of the garden, that he should know a barrister and a banker, that he should find funny the things they find funny . . . [Leah] looks up at her best friend, Natalie Blake, and hates her."[35] "Best friend" and "hates her" balance on either side of the name Natalie Blake, together evoking Leah's bluntly visceral reaction. Michel's earnestness in engaging Natalie and Frank on their own terms, asking Frank for investing advice, for example, strikes Leah as naive, as he does not understand that the scene of this friendship is also one of intimate class hostility. Michel can only sense that they have something that he wants but does not have and thus is unable to understand Leah's exasperation with her friend when she later says, "Who is she? Who is this person? This bourgeois existence!"[36]

Leah resents this space, which Michel desires. The real space of the house is simultaneously an image of the good life, a bourgeois habitus marked equally by its spacious garden as it is by the comportment of Natalie and Frank. The house "makes [Leah] feel like a child. Cake ingredients and fancy rugs and throw cushions and upholstered chairs in chosen fabrics. Not a futon in sight. Overnight everyone has grown up. While she was becoming, everyone grew up and became."[37] The house exhibits a gentrification aesthetic: a charming Victorian home with a large garden that expresses the creative, cosmopolitan taste of its current inhabitants. Natalie represents the finality, the lastness, of the up-and-coming neighborhood, wherein the development of the child into the adult is analogous to the development of property and neighborhoods. This home and its cliché sophistication alienates Leah as it presents an image of a different, objectively better life, one that has rendered her childhood friend into an adult and Leah, an adult, back into a child. Leah, in actuality, wants to hold on to a becoming-adult and endlessly defer adulthood's being, yet she experiences the shame of not yet being a proper adult; moreover, even if she wanted the life of prosecco, cake ingredients, and throw cushions, it seems impossible for her at this late stage. She simultaneously rejects and desires this fantastical good life and is caught needing to escape from an existence that she does not have.

Natalie is the perfect frenemy: a childhood companion who passes off condescension as simple familiarity, who performs the perpetually distracted mother in order to avoid conversation with her boring friend, "this old obligation."[38] For Leah, the image of Natalie's life speaks to the alienated desire of the Instagrammable:

> Leah watches Natalie stride over to her beautiful kitchen with her beautiful child. Everything behind those French doors is full and

meaningful. The gestures, the glances, the conversation that can't be heard. How do you get to be so full? And so full of only meaningful things? Everything else Nat has somehow managed to cast off. She is an adult. How do you do that?[39]

This aesthetic of gentrification exists without explicit reference to urban displacement and class inequality but rather offers itself as an idealized, aspirational image and in doing so remakes society along its imaginary lines. Here, gentrification is not just about the market value of the kitchen or even the beauty that helps create that value but in gestures, in glances, in the seeming existence of a unmoored, free adult.[40] The French doors of Natalie's house function as a cinematic frame, capturing a mise-en-scène both mundane and overstylized, mysterious in its banal reproduction of family life. Leah is transfixed by what is as much her own ideal ego as Natalie's performance of casual fullness; through her gaze from the garden, the image becomes complete. It is also replete with desire, if not for the good life objectively then for something, a sense of fullness, of meaning, or just the desire for desire.

Leah and Michel have not quite learned the social scripts of middle-class life, which becomes clear through Smith's description of the dinner party, a staple genre of cosmopolitan life. This begins with the "chain supermarket" that "pays slave wages" that the couple patronize, which is not explicitly named in the novel even if franchises like Sainsburys—or even Tesco—come to mind. Given the morality of consumption, Leah and Michel begin with the knowledge that "they are not good people. They do not even have the integrity to be the sort of people who don't worry about being good people."[41] They know that "broccoli from Kenya and tomatoes from Chile and unfair coffee and sugary crap and the wrong newspaper" are moral offenses to the planet, to the workers of the world, and to the personal, which is, of course, also the political.[42] This description evokes the directionless guilt that accompanies global capitalism along with the sense that the only solution is through more, slightly different consumption, and which itself is often too much to manage.

This being the case, they are unprepared to perform as anything but their already prescribed roles as "local color" and instead are outclassed by Natalie's circle of friends, a diverse and highly educated group, yet one in which "everyone says the same things in the same way."[43] Smith renders the dinner party through clipped sentences and fragments: "pass the buttered carrots," "the thing about Islam," "pass the crème fraîche," "those were the days," "pass the whiskey."[44] From the tipsy conversation, which might otherwise appear as informal and original, the novel abstracts its repetitive conventionality, the sense that this scene is overly familiar, happening all over London and beyond with only slight variations. The form of the novel, here, is also an acknowledgment of complicity with the reader, as one can only extend the fragments and compose the full image through an understanding of the clichéd scene that is the object of Smith's ironic portrayal. As Leah and Michel become aware, this is not a genre for everyone.

The Speculative Time of the Planned Self

In Leah's gaze Natalie lives an idealized life—pretentious but also nonchalantly wealthy, curated, effortless. This is a fantasy of development, of the insecure child becoming the confident, happy adult, and even as Leah questions the need to progress, to move forward, to level up, and to do so in the most conventional ways, she feels the weight of her own inadequacy. The novel at its core gives the lie to this fantasy: Natalie's performances of self give her currency in the world as a Black woman, daughter of working-class immigrants, yet "Natalie's well-planned life, her achievement of a certain image of female desirability, has led to feelings of alienation and inauthenticity."[45] Natalie, unlike Leah, excels at moving forward yet also feels compelled to keep moving, away from Caldwell, family, friends, and ultimately herself. Born Keisha Blake, she transforms into Natalie to escape some part of herself; in a section entitled "Contempt," the novel tells us that she "had become a person unsuited to self-reflection. Left to her own mental devices she quickly spiraled into self-contempt. . . . She could only justify herself to herself when she worked."[46] Contempt is something worse than the jealous hatred she passively receives from Leah; it is a hatred mixed with disgust, offending by its mere existence.[47] Work is a distraction that also gives her the economic, social, and moral capital to keep the performance going and contempt at bay.

"Contempt" mirrors the earlier dinner-party scene in style, this time narrating brunch. It is a section in which "it occurred to Natalie Blake that she was not very happily married."[48] Not finding any particular fault with her husband, Frank, Natalie thinks, "Happiness is not an absolute value. It is a state of comparison. Were they any unhappier than Imran and Ameeta? Those people over there? You?"[49] Here the third-person narration initially transitions to Natalie's interior monologue and then suddenly addresses the reader directly. In this way the reader is, potentially, involved and made complicit in this scene, a languid, expensive brunch among friends who share an unexpressed sense of competition and comparison. That is, the novel distances itself from the pretentions of this group through a derisive irony and at the same time undermines this potentially critical distance. Framed in this way, the boilerplate brunch scene reads not only as a critique (or at least a winking mockery) of bourgeois habitus but a moment for Natalie in which continual self-performance—"was it possible to feel oneself on a war footing, constantly, even at brunch?"—is exhausted and becomes contempt for herself, her husband and friends, her life.[50]

Naturally, given the setting, the conversation of these professionals eventually turns to rising real estate prices and the changing neighborhood, and to an anxious defense of their role in this process:

> Global consciousness. Local consciousness. Consciousness. And lo they saw their nakedness and were not ashamed. "You're fooling yourself," said Frank. "You can't get anything on the park for less than a million." The mistake was to think that money precisely signified—or was equivalent to—a particular arrangement of bricks and mortar. The money was not for these poky terraced houses with their short back gardens. The money was for the distance the house put between you and Caldwell.... After decades of disappointment, the coffee was finally real coffee. Wouldn't it be cruel to leave, now, when they'd come this far? They were all four of them providing a service for the rest of the people in the café, simply by being here. They were the "local vibrancy" to which the estate agents referred. For this reason, too, they needn't concern themselves too much with politics. They simply were political facts, in their very persons.[51]

Like happiness, value is not figured here as absolute. The value of a house only exists in a relative context, a formula that must account for square footage, the number of bedrooms, distance to the park, the aspirations and anxieties of a Black woman wanting to escape from her childhood, and long histories of violence that form subjects and places along these lines. As with any commodity, the labor that created and maintains a house congeals into its physical form, which can then be exchanged. However, its value in relation to other similar "arrangements of bricks and mortar" must also take into account the work of investment and speculation and, further, the way a house becomes part of an individual's own speculative practices of self-ideation.

Here, property development advertises the multicultural features of a neighborhood to rebrand displacement as selective inclusion. Fetishized for the combination of their professional careers and skin color, they add a cultivated diversity to the neighborhood as a value, affirming to themselves and others a contribution to the politics of inclusivity. This leaves these four individuals in an ambiguous position, as their professional "success" is leveraged against the existence of their communities. "Consciousness," both global and local, is ironically rendered as a loss of innocence and the awareness of sin.[52]

Like Leah, Natalie knows enough to worry about being a "good person." In a conventional sense, she has overcome her postcolonial status to achieve a position of relative power, but this is primarily expressed in terms that not only reproduce economic inequality but reinforce the bootstraps ideology of the free market. Her politics are, and perhaps can only be, a politics of inclusion, representation, and multiculturalism. That is, politics, or "being political," becomes naturalized as mere presence. Thus, as both children of immigrants and urban gentrifiers, Natalie and the others have "colonized in reverse."

From the outside, Natalie successfully performs gender. Gender, as genre, intersects with pressures for class mobility that attend to her child-of-immigrants racial status. Gender also structures her relationship to *value*, as figured in her relationship to her career, her property, and (therefore) her self. Here the home, already at the core of liberal subjectivity, is a figure both for Natalie the career professional and Natalie the mother. Thus, when Natalie encourages her mother, Marcia, and Leah to "stand in front of the bay window and admire the view of the park" in her new home, she wants them to admire and envy her by proxy.[53] In this way she and Frank were "an advert for themselves. Let me show you round this advert for myself. Here is the window, here is the door. And repeat, and repeat."[54] The couple become a product, reliant here on Marcia and Leah's willingness to buy in and show approval of the house, of Natalie's career, or of her decision to have or not have children. This sense of performance and advertisement becomes what sustains her marriage as well: She and Frank "only truly came together at weekends, in front of friends, for whom they appeared fresh and vibrant . . . and full of the old good humor, like a double act that only speaks to each other when they are on stage."[55] Natalie performs herself as natural and genuine without effort, yet it is this performance, which needs the recognition and mediation of others, to create the self. The result of this dialectic, however, is not a rich, contextualized intersubjectivity that deconstructs the sovereign self; the result is absence.

Similarly, the objects in the house become merely part of the genre of home ownership: "Natalie liked to think they told a story about their lives, in which the reality of the house was incidental . . . [but] it was also of course quite possible that it was the house that was the unimpeachable reality, and [the family] . . . just a lot of human shadow-play on the wall," and that "her own shadow was identical to all the rest . . . to the house next door, and the house next door to that."[56] Natalie's worry is not just that her taste in home decor is not so unique but that, as the house is an expression of self, that in fact she lacked substance, was only a shadow of something more real. She sees herself mirrored when meeting an "unmistakeably African" couple for sex in "charming Primrose Hill."[57] While Frank manages a kitchen renovation at home, Natalie ponders infidelity with a couple and in a house that is a replication of her own, more or less: "Farrow and Ball Utopia Green (matte) in the hall. African wall sculpture. Modern minimalist pieces. A gold record framed. A picture of Marley framed. Front page of a newspaper framed. A sort of horrible 'good taste' everywhere."[58] The name of the wallpaper ironically recalls John Ball's utopian vision of the Garden of Eden. Natalie seeks escape from the confines her life but here only finds the worst: confirmation of her own emptiness in the overly recognizable interior design.

She in fact forms herself through a slow realization that value can be arbitrary, produced out of nothing, for instance like the "air, free for the taking" that becomes an "obscure object of desire . . . defined, extracted, rendered visible" in a shoe.[59] Her burgeoning personality holds a particular kind of value in such an arbitrary fashion:

> If she climbed the boundary wall of Caldwell she was compelled to walk the entire wall, no matter obstructions in her path (beer cans, branches). This compulsion, applied to other fields, manifested itself as "intelligence." Every unknown word sent her to a dictionary—in search of something like "completion"—and every book led to another book . . . that she should receive any praise for such reflective habits baffled the girl, for she knew herself to be fantastically stupid about many things . . . in the child's mind a breach now appeared: between what she believed she knew of herself, essentially, and her essence as others seemed to understand it. She began to exist for other people.[60]

Keisha, as a child, walks along the boundary wall with a mixture of playfulness and determination, the two not necessarily being set in opposition or associated with qualities of immaturity or maturity at her early age. The boundary seems to indicate an unconscious balancing between the inside and outside of Caldwell, between her spatial and familial origins and the possibility of at least a partial escape. Meanwhile, the specificity of this trait is also its arbitrariness: She is not compelled toward the familiar virtues of reading and knowledge per se but rather to completion as an end in itself. Later, in a state of crisis and semiconsciously trying to return to her past, she repeats this gesture, walking "along the wall from one end to the other and back again . . . retracing the same area."[61] Formerly play, the wall becomes a site of anxious repetition as she seeks an escape not from Caldwell to the outside world but the reverse.

This discrepancy between inner and external valuation manifests in both an implacable arrogance and a crippling imposter-syndrome insecurity. In a church scene entitled "Surplus value, schizophrenia, adolescence," Keisha writes a song with another girl, Layla. Keisha is adept at musical notation;

Layla can sing. Keisha muses, "If these are 'talents'—the ability to sing, or to quickly comprehend and reproduce musical notation—what kind of a thing is 'talent?' A commodity? A gift? A prize? A reward?"[62] The open abstraction of this thought gives way to dread as she gazes at Layla and herself in the mirror, where she sees two girls, "one singing and the other transforming music into its own shadow, musical notation. That's you. That's her. She is real. You are a forgery. Look closer. Look away. She is consistent. You are making it up as you go along."[63] The short sentences mimic Keisha's flickering eyes as she compares herself with Layla. Where Keisha should see an autonomous self in the mirror, she sees a shadow.[64] In this image, Layla has real ability and is consistent, genuine, and authentic, whereas Keisha is pretending, passing off incidental personality traits as talent. Layla's voice suggests fullness, presence, and thus value; Keisha's notation, and by extension Keisha, is a shadow, an outline of Layla's luminosity. For Keisha, the gaze into the mirror initiates an intolerable splitting: Layla, value in excess, Keisha, absent of value.[65]

Natalie succeeds in progressing to adulthood, with a stable professional career, house, husband, and children, approaching these milestones as if they were graded assignments valid because of their external value. Keisha's development into Natalie involves, and perhaps necessitates, the partial internalization of the contingent value that others give to her. She later summarizes these in a speech at a "young black women's collective," invited by Leah: "time management, identifying goals, working hard, respecting oneself and one's partner, and the importance of a good education."[66] Natalie's personality, at least as outwardly perceived, happens to match perfectly the idiom of neoliberal self-improvement. Improvement requires that one first imagines the future self and then creates it by setting realizable goals, working hard toward those daily, monthly, and yearly objectives, all while successfully managing one's limited time; that is, the self is a result of idealistically figured and pragmatically realized planning. Natalie improves herself into existence, becoming a model of time management and hard work for others, here individuals identified as young, Black, female, and gifted.

The self develops and is structured by time. Like Leah, however, she both desires and is alienated by this structure of development, of the need to move forward in one particular way and, having done so, perform one's happiness. It is a structure, however, dependent on women—as Natalie notes at one point, "Women come bearing time."[67] Unlike Leah, Natalie is unable to rebel against this structure. Though she resents, along with her friend, the pressure to have children, "she had no intention of being made ridiculous by failing to do whatever was expected of her. For her, it was only a question of timing."[68] Natalie becomes an adult woman by conforming to type, by bearing time, that is, children. Here, too, Natalie is able to conjoin her arbitrary but externally validated talents to convincingly perform the role of mother: As she learns from reading the "Women" section of the paper, "the key to it all was the management of time. Fortunately, time management was Natalie's gift."[69] Children are another object of planning, not of the family, per se, but of the self as advertised through the happy family.

In fact, it is the mediated image of children that Natalie needs to reproduce: She finds that "pregnancy brought Natalie only more broken images from the great mass of cultural detritus she took in every day on a number of different devices . . . to behave in accordance with these images bored her. To deviate from them filled her with the old anxiety. She grew anxious that she was not anxious about the things you were meant to be anxious about."[70] Gender, here, is found in and formed through pregnancy-advice columns and message boards, social media, texts, and email.[71] Natalie resents, or at least is able to roll her eyes at, this "image system at work in the world," while falsely thinking that the actuality of giving birth would be an "experience large or brutal enough to disturb it or break it open."[72] Even though Leah looks at her "as if she had passed over a chasm into another land" after she gives birth, they share a common ambivalence.[73] They simultaneously resent the conventionality of progression and moving forward and inwardly feel the need to conform; Leah feels inadequate for not successfully becoming an adult woman by these standards, while Natalie is alienated by her performance of self, by her "daughter drag. Sister drag. Mother drag. Wife drag."[74] As Beatriz Pérez Zapata writes of this section, rather than leading to a "postmodern and poststructuralist conception of subjectivity," the "selfless subject results from the influence of political, patriarchal, and neocolonial discourses."[75] As a result, "Natalie's drag is not the result of a subversive agenda, but rather of camouflage."[76]

Similarly, both Leah and Natalie imagine a utopia that avoids the problem of progression, one characterized by endless liminality and possibility. This too is figured as a house, one with a

> long corridor, off which came many rooms—each with a friend in it—a communal kitchen, a single gigantic bed in which all would sleep and screw, a world governed by the principles of friendship . . . in this simple way—without marches and slogans, without politics, without any of the mess you get ripping paving stones out of the ground—the revolution had arrived.[77]

To build this house is to create a world of friendship only—solidarity without struggle or conflict. Politics, as in the later brunch scene, is something that, ideally, one does not have to think about. The communality of the house and its bed provides a friendship without politics. Imagined while in university, this utopia of community and pleasure is produced equally through a hazy speculative imagination of the future and in the haze of ecstasy, of "hugging strangers on dance floors . . . what could go wrong, now we were all friends. . . . Friends are friendly to each other, friends help each other out."[78] The hospitality of and to the stranger, as expressed by the hug, is infinite. In this ecstatic vision one comes out of oneself and is determined in conjunction with friends, as opposed through performances in front of them. This is of course unsustainable after the three-hour mark, as utopia rapidly comes down. Natalie later finds something like this idealized society when visiting her brother Jayden and the queer community around him—"precisely the fluid and friendly living arrangements she herself had dreamed of so many years earlier."[79] However this "arrangement was timeless" because "no women were included within the schema."[80] Natalie brings time, immediately the need to "respect" her partner and return home, but also the need to manage time, to remember herself, and to plan and cultivate the near and distant future.

Natalie's alienation with herself, with Natalie, resolves itself in the form of infidelity. All but one of her actual attempts at infidelity fail, such that her "acting out" consists mainly in checking dating websites and communicating through the character, fictional but real, of "KeishaNW@gmail.com."[81] The relatively prosaic nature of her infidelity has a deflationary effect; within the dramatic and vexed collapse of a relationship, the novel figures extramarital sex as mostly just wasting time online. That is, Natalie's dissatisfaction with herself, her marriage, and her life expresses itself as a rebellion against time management.[82]

In addition, the fictional self that Natalie creates online is barely more fictional than her real self: Both Natalie and KeishaNW are personal advertisements, selling the idea of self and seeking validation through figurative "purchase."[83] As the idea of her life increasingly clashes with her experience of it, Natalie slowly creates a new life online as a form of escape. That this escape, from Natalie back to Keisha, fails to manifest itself as such could be prefigured in her initial development into Natalie. Her courtship of Frank is itself figured as a form of personal advertisement:

> Female individual seeks male individual for loving relationship. And vice versa. Low-status person with intellectual capital but no surplus wealth seeks high-status person of substantial surplus wealth for enjoyment of mutual advantages, including longer life-expectancy . . . human animal in need of food and shelter seeks human animal of

opposite gender to provide her with offspring and remain with her until the independent survival of aforementioned offspring is probable. Some genes, seeking their own survival, pursue whatever will most likely result in their replication.[84]

Romance, here, is already an algorithm, with genetic and cultural determinants working themselves out to their rational conclusion. The loving relationship is first rendered into a strategic class arrangement, then to the evolutionary paradigm of the "human animal," and finally into a collection of selfish genes pushing themselves and their host to self-reproduction. Here the childish naivety of "love" becomes the optimization of match percentages, a process that, in fact, happens outside of Natalie's conscious will. It is not so much that she chooses to marry up into Frank's biracial, crazy-rich world; rather, the relationship, like the career, the house, the family, has an aura of destiny.

Escape to the Garden: Utopia's Others

I would like to read NW's penultimate chapter, "Crossing," as staging the temporal contradictions of both the planned city and the planned self through Natalie's (anti)flâneurie. In this section, the novel shifts form once again; though still from the third-person-limited perspective of Natalie, this part of the novel is divided by sections that track a series of place names as Natalie traverses London, moving from Kilburn through Hampstead and finally to Hornsey Lane Bridge in Highgate. Ostensibly, this walk is an ascent from concrete council estate to green heath, yet the latter, instead of coalescing the subject through its utopian immediacy, serves as the background for Natalie's dissolution. As Chapter 1 details, Hampstead Garden Suburb was planned by the social philanthropist Henrietta Barnett and designed by the garden-city planners Barry Parker and Raymond Unwin with help from the architect Edwin Lutyens, who would go on to design the new capital of the British Raj in Delhi. That Natalie turns to this space suggests both the promises of the verdant, garden-city imaginary and its ambiguous legacy as a project intertwined with liberal colonialism. Indeed, it is the same imaginary that developers of regeneration projects and real estate brokers in gentrifying neighborhoods everage and deploy when presenting their reconciliatory-but-profitable schemes.

Through her walk, Natalie seeks to reverse the linear, upward temporality of development—individual, spatial, and social. This walk is prompted by Frank's discovery of Natalie's online self. Ignoring Natalie's pleas to have the resulting conversation in private (in their extra room with a "charming Moroccan theme"), Frank says, "You're meant to be a fucking adult. Who are you?"[85] Natalie walks out of the house without any belongings, dressed in "a big t-shirt, leggings, and a pair of filthy red slippers," while informing Frank that she is going "nowhere."[86] Dressed informally, like "a junkie," or perhaps simply like a teenager, she serendipitously encounters her old friend Nathan Bogle.[87] Natalie, in a state of personal crisis, travels back with Nathan to Caldwell and to their various pasts.

Her antiflâneurie corresponds to the dissolution of the self and lies somewhere between a metaphysical collapse of identity and a panic attack; as Nathan says to her, "You don't look like you got no real problems."[88] Still, she becomes "nothing more or less than the phenomenon of walking," and thus "she had no name, no biography, no characteristics. They had all fled into paradox."[89] She is characterized by absence, of being nothing but movement going nowhere. Nathan proves useful here, as it becomes increasingly clear that he is anxious to leave Caldwell and a crime scene that has formed near there; escaping the police, he helps Natalie escape from her life. Not completely recognizing herself or the space around her, she continues forward in a daze:

> He started walking. Natalie followed. Walking was what she did now. As she walked she tried to place the people back there, in the house, into the present current of her thought. But her relation with each person was now unrecognizable to her, and her imagination—due to a long process of neglect, almost as long as her life—did not have the generative power to muster an alternative future for itself. All she could envision was suburban shame, choking everything. She thought to the left and thought to the right but there was no exit. Though, perhaps, Jayden? Again she stalled. Though perhaps Jayden what?
> What time is it Keisha
> I don't know[90]

She finds it impossible either to remember a past self or to create an idea of a future self, one outside the structure of development and the image of the good life that she feels she has ruined. The past, perhaps like Caldwell, has been neglected, while the present—her bourgeois life with Frank—is figured as the shame of suburbia, the city's other. She further tries and fails to reconfigure a sense of time and futurity within her imaginary of Jayden's queer utopia. This walk, on one hand, could be figured as an ecstatic disassociation of self, as Natalie becomes-movement and follows a line of flight.[91] She does find, for example, that her recurrent existential "dread was the hardest emotion in the world to hold on to for more than a moment."[92] She does move out of herself and into the world.⁹³ Ultimately, however, it is a movement that brings her back to a deathly stasis. The disassociation of self, rather being a different, potentially resistant, relationship with the world, is figured as a closing down of the imagination, as stagnation and suffocation, as death. Natalie, as a woman who has lost track of time, also loses track of herself.

Led by Nathan away from Kilburn and uphill toward Hampstead Heath, the walk stages the urban landscape through Natalie's state of crisis. As they leave Kilburn, walking to Fortune Green, they

> kept climbing, past the narrow red mansion flats, up into money. The world of council flats lay far behind them, at the bottom of the hill. Victorian houses began to appear, only a few at first, then multiplying. Fresh gravel in the drives, white wooden blinds in the windows. Estate agent's hoarding strapped to the front gate.
>
> [Natalie:] Some of these houses are worth twenty times what they were a decade ago. Thirty Times.
>
> [Nathan:] Is it.⁹⁴

Natalie, almost as "second nature," notices the property: the astonishing rise in value (always twinged with regret, as if imagining a past self capable of purchasing such a home and thus of imagining a different future self), the type of architecture, the color and material of the blinds, the "freshness" of the gravel. Nathan, meanwhile, is uninterested. He is seeing a different city.

The attachments that Leah and Natalie have to an idea of self and the good life have been described here as a kind of cruel optimism, an attachment—both internally produced and externally imposed, the difference being indiscernible—that prevents what it purports to achieve. Berlant is confident that "in the impasse induced by crisis, being treads water; mainly, it does not drown. Even those whom you would think of as defeated are living beings figuring out how to stay attached to life from within it, and to protect what optimism they have for that, at least."⁹⁵ There is a universality to this approach, in that Berlant speaks for both a "you" that assumes defeat in an other, and for that other, whose form of attachment falls within scope of a cruel optimism. Yet if "the present is what makes itself present to us before it becomes anything else, such as an orchestrated collective event or an epoch on which we can look back," it seems worth asking: Who is the "us" of the present and the "we" that looks back?⁹⁶ As with Sinclair's evocation of lastness, Berlant's pluralization of affect too easily becomes a making-equivalent, one that forgets that the possibility for drowning and defeat is spread unevenly, and consequently "being," if such a category is worthwhile, might include modes of nonattachment and nonidentity, of looking away.⁹⁷

Natalie, losing herself to this walk, is a being treading water, but it is not clear that she will have the energy to avoid drowning. Nathan, meanwhile, has in so many ways already drowned. While they have moments of communication, the section as a whole is marked by moments of incomprehension, especially by Natalie. These suggest the limits of perceived affect, the boundaries beyond which something becomes incommensurable and unknowable, part of a different atmosphere all together. On the different kinds of existences that nonrelation produces, Asma Abbas asks us to "hold off saying that these departures, whether spurred by one's own disgust with one's own desire, or collateral damage in the act of extinguishing it, are merely asking for some way back in."[98] Instead, perhaps other types of communities are formed through the gestures of exit: Here Natalie stumbles in trying to form an ad hoc community with Nathan, who expresses a position of incommensurability: "Truthfully Keisha I don't remember. I've burned that whole business out of my brain. Different life . . . And you go home to your green and your life and where's my green and my life. Sit on your bench. Talking out your neck about me. 'How does it feel to be a problem?' What do you know about it? What do you know about me? Nothing."[99] Nathan, not needing to manage time, to have time on his side, ends up not with endless time but with no time. The conviviality of their walking relationship falters here. A bit later in their walk, however, Natalie questions whether Nathan is involved in something criminal, assailing him with a different, lawyerly voice: "Answer the question! Be responsible for yourself! You're free! . . . We're all free!" Here Natalie affirms the philosophy of free choice, a Lockean stance perhaps corresponding to her house within Caldwell. That she does so in such an exclamatory fashion, however, similarly suggests crisis, as if these were both her deepest beliefs and at the same time dependent on the force of her exclamation. As before, she is the ideal figure through which this ideology can be expressed, especially in comparison with Nathan: two Black estate kids who ended up blocks away from each other but in very different places.

The stakes of the landscape change, however, when they reach Hampstead Heath. As mentioned, the heath has been the ideal image of the urban pastoral since Henrietta Barnett's garden city–inspired interventions in the early twentieth century. In contemporary London, the garden aesthetic, from garden cities to the Olympics, is deployed in speculative visions of the future city.[100] The neoliberal imaginary of the garden juxtaposes it with the gray concrete of places like Caldwell, with their bridges, basins, and unusable lifts—all the elements of the built environment castigated by Alice Coleman in 1985.[101] At the same time, as Phil tells Felix when the latter revisits Caldwell: "A bit of green is very powerful, Felix. Very powerful. 'Specially in England. Even us Londoners born and bred, we need it, we go up the Heath, don't we, we crave it. Even our little park here is important. Bit of green."[102] Repeating the born-and/versus-bred motif of the novel, Phil naturalizes himself as a Londoner and Englishman and, as such, articulates the reconciliatory function of a bit of green. The "bit of green," recalling not just the recent history of urban planning but also a "green and pleasant land," the English pastoral, and in turn the biblical garden, is perhaps the most worked through image in British literature and culture.[103] As a trope, it easily suggests community without the need of politics, something that, in being universal, can ground an imaginary of the future.[104]

However, that this imaginary, of trees, fields, and greenness, can also be a site of alienation becomes clear as Nathan and Natalie continue up the hill. This is initially clear as they see an "optimistic line of plane trees" planted along the road," of which "one had already been pulled up at the roots and another snapped in half."[105] Even the two walkers, however, disagree on the universal character of the green environment. Whereas Natalie remembers picnics on the heath, Nathan claims to have never visited, having not seen the point: "Why would I come up here? . . . Weren't my scene."[106] Natalie responds with an exasperation: "I don't know, because it's free, because it's beautiful. Trees, fresh air, ponds, grass. . . . What do you mean it wasn't your scene? It's everybody's scene! It's nature!"[107] In Natalie's view, the heath is free, open to all to enjoy, so free that she is offended that Nathan does not share in her enthusiastic nostalgia for childhood picnics. Nathan perhaps feels more acutely the way that the supposed freedom of public space only exists in the context of unfree, private space, that the space in which he moves is the analogue to his self: "I ain't free. Ain't never been free."[108] This is only exacerbated by the garden rooftops and riverside cafes of the regeneration projects; with trees come surveillance, police, violence.

Conclusion: Police and Trees in the Streets

The ambivalence of freedom of and in the city become more starkly juxtaposed as Natalie stands on Hornsey Lane Bridge, fortified by iron spikes, that "stopped people going nowhere" off the bridge.[109] London has continually sought to advertise itself through its skyline, consisting of historic sites and increasingly eclectic contemporary architecture.[110] Natalie's view of this advertisement is fragmented: "St. Paul in one box. The gherkin in another . . . the tower blocks were the only thing she could see that made any sense, separated from each other, yet communicating."[111] As Molly Slavin writes, "Natalie's center [the tower blocks] intermixes with myths of what London, England,

Britain is or has been or should be."[112] By the end of this walk, the aesthetic freedom of the heath, or the distanced view of the skyline, or, for that matter, the supposed freedom of walking itself resolves for Natalie only into the freedom of death: "Here nothing less than a break—a sudden and total rupture—would do. She could see the act perfectly clearly, it appeared before her like an object in her hand—and then the wind shook the trees once more and her feet touched the pavement. The act remained just that, an act, a prospect, always possible."[113] The rupture she hoped would occur with childbirth—the rupture with and against the dominant image system of the world—here is only possible by stepping (or climbing and jumping) off the bridge. This death is not figured as an act of decisive will but rather as an object in her hand; equally, her retention into life indicates a lack of the subjective self.[114]

Natalie is saved by herself, or perhaps her lack of self. But she is also saved, more than once, by Nathan, who entreats her to get off the bridge, perhaps intuiting her intentions. This is not the first time Natalie, in crises, relies on Nathan during this walk. At the Caldwell boundary wall: "You don't look too good, Keisha. Reach for me. Natalie crossed her wrists. Nathan looked at her shaking hands. He pulled her up."[115] A minute later: "It would be something to replace this absence of sensation, this nothing. She placed a hand on his shoulder. The fabric of his hoodie was stiff, unclean."[116] Later still: "For the second time tonight she crossed her wrists and felt herself lifted up as if she were barely there, almost nothing."[117] It is only after he confronts her about her assumptions of sympathy that she resists his help, even as he ultimately encourages her to leave the bridge. In fact, Natalie responds to this confrontation—the possibility that she can't relate to Nathan's experience just because they grew up on the same estate—with fear, transforming her walking partner into a potential predator. This indicates an instinctual fear of being a woman walking at night and at the same time is a gesture in which Natalie places the burden of their collective Blackness solely onto Nathan, because it was already there.

Throughout this entire section, it is strongly hinted that Nathan has been involved with the stabbing of Felix, hence his desire to escape from Kilburn; that said, his constant evasions from the flashing lights of police cars might be simple instinct by this point.[118] Felix's murder occurs after a confrontation with two men on the Tube, one of whom may be Nathan. Wearing hoodies and headphones, these two men take up more than two seats with their bodies, thus preventing a pregnant woman from sitting down. This woman, white, mistakes Felix as their friend and requests him to speak to them; this leads to a verbal confrontation, and eventually Felix gives up his own seat. For doing this he "felt a great wave of approval, smothering and unwanted, directed toward him, and just as surely, contempt and disgust enveloping the two men and separating them, from Felix, from the rest of the carriage, from humanity."[119] Both Felix, in defending the comfort of a pregnant (white) woman, and the men, in spreading themselves across multiple seats and not backing down, perform their masculinity. They are compelled to act for a largely passive audience, who, in watching, attach meaning to the interaction, silently expelling the uncivil men from humanity while tentatively including Felix. Tammy Houser reads this scene as exposing the limits of empathy, as the "passengers are all carried away by a fellow-feeling that separates the two black men as objects of disgust."[120] Felix, meanwhile, is trapped between this unwanted inclusion and the focused contempt of the expelled. For him, this exchange results in death; for the men, possibly, a life in prison.[121]

Natalie steps away from this premise and into her old life. She does this, the novel suggests, with some renewed "clarity," both that "freedom was absolute and everywhere, constantly moving location" and with regards to her children, "not something to be merely managed any longer."[122] The freeness of freedom, its essential character, is defined both as absolute and its ability to be unmoored, to move. At the same time, even a moment of potential emotional honesty with Leah becomes constrained by Natalie's defensiveness of her "success" and need to perform self. Eventually she retreats into cliché, telling Leah that divergence in life is "because we worked harder . . . we were smarter and we didn't want to end up begging on other people's doorsteps. We wanted to get out. People like Bogle—they didn't want it enough . . . people generally get what they deserve."[123] James Arnett points to the way Smith ironizes the structure of the realist novel, writing that Natalie "brandishes the meritocratic-bootstraps rhetoric of desire and self-fashioning, playing into the expectations of the realist novel as form, a form that fetishizes the individual and individual development," but that this supposed development is shown to be a self-serving pretense.[124]

The novel ends with perhaps its bleakest irony. Leah and Natalie, best friends at times, hostile enemies at others, are able to once again bond as they report Nathan to the police:

> Natalie dialed it. It was Keisha who did the talking. Apart from the fact she drew the phone from her pocket, the whole process reminded her of nothing so much as those calls the two good friends used to make to boys they liked, back in the day . . . two heads pressed together over a handset. "I've got something to tell you," said Keisha Blake, disguising her voice with her voice.[125]

Natalie is able to have an authentic relationship with Leah, herself, and her childhood through this act of disguising. Where as child she might have called Nathan to tell him of Leah's "love" for him, now she calls the police to mark him as a person of interest. Leah and Natalie, whatever the differences between them, bond over their shared divergence from Nathan, who "didn't want it enough," who gets what he deserves.

The range of readings of this scene is suggestive of its ambiguity. Lourdes López-Ropero sees it as a scene of "female solidarity, loyalty and understanding" and "affirmation of civil society," and Lynn Wells writes that "Natalie creates the possibility that the truth of Felix's death will be known, and that, in the process, he will be transformed from another statistically unimportant black man to an individual worthy of his own history."[126] Jesse van Amelsvoort is perhaps most optimistic, writing that "Leah/Natalie/Keisha makes a call for justice . . . In NW's closing pages, Forster's ethical humanism meets Gilroy's postcolonial humanism; connecting is a socioethical responsibility."[127] On the other hand, Tammy Houser notes that the solidarity between the women is created by "uniting against an out-group whose inner perspective is totally ignored or misinterpreted," and David Marcus calls the scene "sinister" in that "Leah and Natalie are not calling a junior high crush but, in fact, possibly putting a former one in jail: a man of acute danger but who also has never been given a chance."[128]

For Leah and Natalie to call the police if they suspect Nathan has information or was involved with a murder is on the one hand the most rational and expected reaction, and if by itself it does not rise to the heights of "socioethical responsibility," it seems like the best available option. On the other hand, a call to the police is an act of faith: that the system of justice will arrive at the correct conclusions, objectively and without prejudice, that its disciplinary and punitive measures construct an equitable society. It is the faith that the police themselves are something more and better than simply agents of the state's law-preserving violence, that they will arrest Nathan and people who look like Nathan without brutality and, indeed, avoid murdering them in the process. Nathan may be a person of interest, but even so, what is striking about this closing scene is that it figures the inescapability of social reproduction, of being born and bred, as seeming choices in freedom conform to type, both in the "successes" and "failures" of progression. In calling the police on her childhood friend, someone who potentially just saved her life, Natalie affirms her position within this structure and its ideology of freedom and development.

Nathan's attenuated presence in the novel, even while accompanying

Natalie up to the heath, is reminiscent of the spectral quality that John Akomfrah ascribes to history in *Handsworth Songs*. Indeed, Vanessa Guignery ascribes to Nathan a "ghostly existence" in the novel as "an outcast who appears furtively in each section," while both Lynn Wells and Annalisa Pes note that Nathan's last name, Bogle, is also a term for a ghost.[129] This history is also one of violence and surveillance; thus we see Natalie transmuting her crisis of identity into the social crisis of mugging and knife crime.[130] Over the course of her free, aimless walk, she becomes convinced that Nathan is "sus" and reconstitutes her identity through the antagonism of that category.[131] As will be evident in the next chapter, the categories through and against which "progress" is defined reproduce a geography of violence.

6
Geographies of Discontent
Brexit and the Politics of Abandonment

> Mahmood runs a modest newsagent's in a small town in the north of England that boasts neither a cathedral nor a university. Mahmood lives in a place where if, on a Saturday afternoon, one happens to turn on the television set as the football results are being read out, towns of unquestionable insignificance will be freely mentioned, but Mahmood's small English town will simply not exist.
> —CARYL PHILLIPS, *A Distant Shore*

This book has tracked the way ideologies of progress and improvement have been articulated and realized in vivid descriptions of imaginary places, specifically in the rhetoric of development. "Development" is part of the legacy established by early-twentieth-century planners and includes the entire apparatus of public and private investment in planning, architecture, design, and construction. The preceding chapters have shown how development takes as its objects neglected, "unloved" urban spaces and promises to improve them and their inhabitants, bringing out the latent characteristics of particular places for the sake of a sustainable, socially reconciled future. I have argued that this relationship between the technological modernity of the development apparatus and the "unloved" spaces it seeks to improve is properly understood as a colonial relationship. This is not only because it shares a history with the explicit practices of empire, and not only because the neglected spaces of urban Britain coincide with patterns of postcolonial migration, but because "colonization" best describes the relation of power active in the present.[1]

This chapter continues these themes but turns away from the urban in order to explore the geography and figuration of English provinciality, specifically through an analysis of Caryl Phillips's 2003 novel *A Distant Shore*. English provinciality has not typically been considered an appropriate object for postcolonial studies; indeed, if anything it is an antiobject. It has likewise not prominently featured in British literatures of mobility and migration, the work of Phillips included, and is in fact associated with the opposite of mobility. However, my analysis in this chapter shows the necessity of extending postcolonial critique to unlikely places in order to consider the contingency of place itself and the way it is formed by colonial practices. In doing so, I recall elements of planning introduced in Chapter 1, namely, that in the British context spatial planning was not "urban" but rather figured as "town and country" planning. Indeed, garden cities promised a reconciliation between town and country spaces in the same way that they promised a reconciliation between tradition and modernity or between social classes. Patrick Geddes (Chapter 2) took this holistic approach further by concentrating not on the city but on the region. To this end he coined the now widely used term "conurbation" to discuss integrated town and country relationships. He also sought to reconcile the particularity of all these local regions with the scale of the universal and the global—a humanist dream of world peace through planning that implicitly took for granted the context of actually existing empire.

This chapter analyzes how these concerns for town and country relationships find expression in contemporary development. I argue that spaces marked as provincial and "insignificant" are not underdeveloped remnants but in fact are produced and reproduced through processes of spatial planning, regeneration, and development. In doing so, I seek to parse and reframe the way that regional distinctions are made and maintained and thus also to reconsider politics of identity that emerge from those distinctions. That is, I view the race and class politics of contemporary Britain not as merely a legacy of colonialism, residing latently in place. Rather, those politics are reproduced through the ongoing practices of development and regeneration, which, like London's megaprojects (Chapter 4), stake a claim to improving the neglected spaces of the present while creating the conditions for the future's ruination. If, in the contemporary moment, there are geographies and peoples who have been abandoned or left behind, we can ask if it is because processes of modernization have been unequally extended across different spaces and demographics or because modernization itself is the cause of geographical discontent.

Brexit and a Geography of Discontent

Boris Johnson spent the summer of 2020 promising to "level up" the country, which involved not only finally leaving the European Union but also dealing with regional inequality and the aftermath of the COVID-19 pandemic. He said his goal was to "unite and level up, and to that end we will build, build, build, build back better build back greener build back faster, and to do that at the pace that this moment requires."[2] In his first full speech as prime minister, he added, "that means uniting our country, answering at last the plea of the forgotten people and the left-behind towns by physically and literally renewing the ties that bind us together."[3] Like Blair and Cameron before him (see the Introduction), and like his American contemporary Donald Trump, Johnson invokes the plight of the forgotten people and their "left-behind" towns and proposes as the vague solution of building (including "building back better," referencing the slogan of his other American contemporary, Joe Biden). Chapter 5 discussed the implicit ideology of "leveling up," a videogame metaphor yoked to the liberal colonial logic of progress and development that patterns both urban space and the subjects of capitalism. Johnson, unlike Blair and Cameron, did not deploy this rhetoric in front of a site of London's urban decay but rather in reference to the United Kingdom's larger geographies, not neighborhoods but entire regions "left behind" and thus implicitly in need of "catching up." This focus, from London's former mayor no less, suggests that the eye of development gazes beyond the "brownfield" sites of the city to the entire "brownfield" regions that could, with enough building, be leveled up.

Johnson's rhetoric suggests an understanding of how Britain's geographies govern its political formations. In 2019, the London School of Economics published a report entitled "Understanding Brexit at the Local Level: Causes of Discontent and Asymmetric Impacts." The report views the 2016 EU referendum through the lens of geography and affect in describing what is by now a familiar postindustrial scene:

> Local economic features have contributed to create a "geography of discontent," especially in zones where regeneration policies have failed. Areas such as Mansfield and Pendle suffered a difficult industrial restructuring process after the collapse of the mining and textile industries. They have become increasingly dependent on an economic model based on low-skill and low-paid jobs, as well as on controversial business practices which instilled precariousness in the labour market and limited social mobility. In turn, these local dynamics have been

stimulated and reinforced by the fact that these areas are geographically insulated from the main economic hubs. These towns are struggling to compete with bigger cities to attract talent and investment.[4]

This report details changes in the economy that have produced individuals that feel "abandoned" or "left behind," namely, a shift to knowledge and service economies that was accompanied by increased inequality. Thus the report concludes that "while at the ideational level the Leave vote can be interpreted as a defensive reaction that seeks to preserve identity and culture, from a material socio-economic point of view, this vote means the opposite: a disruptive force aiming to truncate the current path of economic development and promote change."[5]

A "geography of discontent" summarizes the way that economic transformations translate into affective geographies, that is, a sense that the political complexity of Brexit should be a reference not just to regional inequality in resources, jobs, and infrastructure but also to the forms of recognition that accompany geography.[6] It is also the case that the effects of this uneven geography of discontent might not be able to be simply split between urban and nonurban[7] or between remain and leave; rather, it seems that Brexit concretized without necessarily resolving a set of constituent political tensions whose historicity was not even capable of being fully disclosed. As such, the commentary that has followed the 2016 vote and that dominated UK politics and political news until 2020 has been marked by confusion. The LSE's conclusion that Brexit would exacerbate the problems it supposes to solve is not only attributable to the mendacity of the leave campaign and misrecognition on behalf of voters but also because "Brexit" has become for the moment a privileged empty signifier of British political economy for those on both the now reified leave and remain sides.

There have been innumerable attempts to locate the proximate and ultimate causes of the EU referendum vote in June 2016. Especially given the worldwide political context of rising xenophobia, commentators have mainly focused on how much of the vote can be attributed to concerns about immigration. More conservative commentators argued these concerns were rational fears about globalization and the supposed stresses that immigration placed upon the culture, economies, and government resources of host states since the formation of the European Union in 1992 and especially since many Eastern European countries joined in 2004.[8] Others pointed out that these claims could not be substantiated economically and that fears over immigration have a long precedent, have remained steady over time, and cannot be attributed to EU membership.[9] Thus, perhaps, the Brexit vote might be indicative of a nostalgia for empire and/or the lingering racial attitudes of particular segments of the UK population.[10] Along these lines, still others noted some distinctive features of leave and remain voters, with the former being described, charitably or not, as a "white working class" that was on balance older, less educated, and exhibited a distinct culture.[11] For example, David Goodhart's *The Road to Somewhere* contrasts the culture and economic outlook of a cosmopolitan elite of "Anywheres" with the more traditional culture- and place-based affiliations of "Somewheres," with the latter having been neglected by the former.[12] He suggests that the decline of the welfare state can be primarily explained not by a shifting economic model but by the cultural dislocation of the somewheres.[13]

There is other criticism, however, that perhaps more productively considers geographical fragmentation in the context of economic and planning policies, especially over the last forty years. For example, just after the EU referendum Torsten Bell argued that while the vote could not be explained by recent decreases in wages or increases in levels of immigration, it could be described by longer-term trends in living standards and equality. He wrote:

> It's not the unequal impact of the recent recession driving voting patterns—or indeed as some argue the impact of migration driving down wages in some areas. Instead, in so far as economics drove voters' behaviour last night, it is areas that are, and have been for some time, poorer. Or to put it another way, it's the shape of our long lasting and deeply entrenched national geographical inequality that drove differences in voting patterns. The legacy of increased national inequality in the 1980s, the heavy concentration of those costs in certain areas, and our collective failure to address it has more to say about what happened last night than shorter term considerations from the financial crisis or changed migration flows.[14]

This geographical inequality does not neatly map onto rural and urban areas but rather speaks to a geography at the margins, one that projects affective dislocation. If there are places that have been "left behind," it is important to consider what "catching up" to the rest of Britain would look like. Boris Johnson's plan to provide billions of pounds of new funding for deprived towns is the analogue (warped by his careerism) of the regeneration projects, including the Olympic site and Battersea Power Station, that he oversaw in London.[15] That is, it casts marginal spaces within the temporality of ruin whose solution is not simply nostalgia for the past but in an imagined future space.

Regeneration has been the primary mode and idiom of planning not just in urban areas but nationally, while at the same time marking a neoliberal shift from more central planning to a myriad of public-private entities with overlapping jurisdictions.[16] The leave campaign made much of the lack of local sovereignty caused by EU regulations and standards, but these standards have been accompanied by a shift toward devolution of state planning and a shift to "localism" since 1997. At the same time, planning has not become more democratic: The reforming of spatial scales from hierarchal government to relational public-private "governance" is in practice (even) more opaque and unreachable than what was ostensibly a more top-down approach, as residents have been recast to "users" and "stakeholders."[17] The result is instead an "increasingly complex and tangled" hierarchy of the scales and purposes of governance, all of which are brought together in the idiom of "place-making."[18] Together, this idiom seeks to manage abandonment, distributing the varied results of regeneration unevenly.[19]

Moreover, regeneration seeks to reimagine and revitalize spaces of postindustrial "decay" and in doing so produces a consensus of what proper places should look like and what they should do. Namely, regenerated places are those that face outward, making themselves available for knowledge-economy investment, with the assumption that this investment will trickle down in the form of job opportunities for residents. This imaginary is fueled by the creation of local enterprise zones, retraining schemes, and the attempt to turn former spaces of production into spaces of consumption. Here, towns and regions are valued by their ability to advertise themselves as "places" and attract tourists. As Abigail Gilmore notes, local "culture" has become a privileged category in measuring global appeal:

> The policy gaze on participation in the arts has grown [as has] culture's utility to a range of policy goals—including regeneration, economic development, social inclusion and health . . . cultural tourism methodologies for spectacular creative agency—mega-events, flagship cultural institutions, blockbuster shows and public art works—have become part of the armoury of place-based strategies based on visitor economies. They aim to attract arts participants as tourists and improve place image, regional competitiveness and differentiation.[20]

Creative cultural production, especially that which draws tourists, indexes whether a place has been left behind or sufficiently regenerated and modernized.[21] These strategies seek to use "place image" as a way to reconcile the particularity of the local (through the reification of cultural forms and local participation in the arts) with the appeal of the global (through megaevents and public artworks). Place image in this context has a topothesic function: It produces an imaginary enclave in which place and inhabitants are reconciled to each other and integrated into a national culture and global economy.

In this way, the idiom of place making in development suggests that all villages, towns, and regions ought to face outward to a "creative" economy of science, technology, and arts. Within this framework, any given area in southern Wales or northern England is a few steps away from becoming another Silicon Valley, if only it could attract the right mix of corporate investment and tourist consumption. Even, and perhaps especially in local consultations, the place-imaginary of regeneration comes to displace any alternative visions of an economy or culture. That is, "users" are asked their opinion as to how to modernize and progress, without the consideration that it is in fact these processes of modernization that reproduce the effect of those who feel "left behind" and "abandoned." The contradiction of areas that benefit from EU funds but that voted leave might at least partially relate not to the funds themselves but to the imaginary of the future that they compel.[22] In sum, instead of considering the geographies indexed by "Brexit" as anachronistic—either because they are marked by nostalgia for a Great British past or because they've been economically left behind—we might examine the ways those geographies and their politics are productions of the present. As will be clear in the ensuing reading of *A Distant Shore*, whether in town or country, modernization and regeneration produces its own others.

"Towns of Unquestionable Insignificance"

Unlike many of Caryl Phillips's novels, *A Distant Shore* not only features England as a setting but specifically a provincial England. The novel's protagonists—Dorothy, a retired schoolteacher, and Gabriel/Solomon, a former soldier and asylum seeker from an African country resembling Liberia or Sierra Leone—both live in the new suburban development of Stoneleigh at the top of a hill near the (fictional) village of Weston (Gabriel changes his name to Solomon). This village is itself near a larger unnamed town/city in northern England where Dorothy was born. The vibrancy and commotion of the city is nowhere to be found in these places; rather they are characterized by a stagnant stillness matched by Phillips's turn to a more understated prose style. Other towns in the novel, like the one inhabited by Dorothy's ex-lover Mahmood, are similarly isolated; like the other characters, he lives in a "place where if, on a Saturday afternoon, one happens to turn on the television set as the football results are being read out, towns of unquestionable insignificance will be freely mentioned, but Mahmood's small English town will simply not exist."²³ English places like these can be thought of as "small places," using Jamaica Kincaid's term; they are marginal to national culture as the result of active political and historical processes.²⁴ In *A Distant Shore*, narrative elements are "meticulously shrunk, suburbanized, and rid . . . of any lingering mythic quality," with the "body of postcolonial theory with which [Phillips's writing] is associated seeming entirely too sophisticated for the brutish drunken 'strangers'—as opposed to 'survivors'—who litter the unhappy village."²⁵ For a writer like Phillips to use a narrative of migration to focus on English provinciality shows how the operation of power inheres in the very split between global and local, province and metropole, or roots and routes, through which places acquire particularity.

Postcolonial criticism has added considerably to debates about contemporary identity by linking the literal mobility of the postcolonial migrant to the mutability in identity, both in ways that challenge putatively stable national identities. Some of this criticism has been challenged as inattentive to material conditions and local differences and, ironically, as universalizing the postcolonial subject as one constructed through subversive routes rather than normative roots. In turn, there have been several attempts to reconcile the affirming, open characteristics of mobile identity with attentiveness to concrete local struggles and resistances. These discussions replace the acritical aspects of cosmopolitanism with concepts that are more attenuated yet still propose to challenge the homogeneity and fixed aspects of identity. For example, referencing recent work by Bill Ashcroft, Paola Della Valle argues that *A Distant Shore* shows how the "transnation begins in these quotidian exchanges and interactions between individuals of different cultures and races within the state boundaries."²⁶ Such an articulation reads an otherwise bleak novel in terms adjacent to Paul Gilroy's notion of conviviality, which tempers the blind optimism of humanist cosmopolitanism through a focus on the transformative capacity of everyday interaction, even in spaces of contestation and racism.²⁷

Other critics of *A Distant Shore* are by degrees less optimistic about the possibility of intercultural communication in the novel. For example, Petra Tournay-Theodotou reads the geography of Weston/Stoneleigh as "miniature spatial allegories of the nation at large" that "encapsulate[s] the tension between a conservative, essentialist Britain with its inability to accommodate change . . . and the demands of a society in flux."²⁸ In this reading, the nonurban Weston comes to represent the continued hostility of English nationalism. Likewise, Allesandra Di Maio argues that Weston "stands metonymically for England" and the community is "symbolic of the nation."²⁹ These critics and others emphasize the challenge that a globalized modernity, which they find particularly in the figure of Solomon, presents to a localized and essentialized nationality, which in turn strikes back at the former with hostility and violence.[30]

However, villages like Weston are not places untouched by time, indicative of a stable rural much less national identity, but in fact have continually changed as the result of various planning policies and political-economic shifts. Much like colonial spaces, towns like Weston have been produced as the other of Britain's supposed progress, and this active and ongoing production of marginality is naturalized and absorbed by place itself in national discourse. That is, just as a subversive mutability of identity has been associated with the literal mobility of the migrant, an exclusive, nationalistic identity is associated with a literal stasis of provincial subjects. These associations, however, prevent a complete historicism of present conditions, naturalizing nativism into the seemingly unchanging countryside landscape instead of working through how normative structures have been and are continually produced. Instead, constructions of subjectivity become naturalized into geography: urban and in flux, therefore pluralistic, on the one hand, immobile, stagnant, and thus essentialist, on the other.

As opposed to this reading, this chapter argues that the novel uses the provincial setting to explore how political conflict seems to follow from place (instead of the reverse) and also how different individuals and groups can be both marginal and actively marginalize others. The character of Weston's marginality lies in its "unquestionable insignificance." Phillips's exploration of insignificance is in striking contrast to the scope and stakes of novels like *Crossing the River* (1993) and *The Nature of Blood* (1997), which take up themes of genocide and deep historical trauma. Indeed, the insignificance of Weston is dramatized even within *A Distant Shore* when Phillips describes the horrors of war that Gabriel experiences before he immigrates as an asylum seeker, where he later changes his name to Solomon. By contrast, in the provincial spaces of the novel, violence is etiolated and faded, as the northern English countryside becomes the end of the world. What is instead produced is a deadening stillness and banality in a novel where the climatic event (Solomon's murder) is revealed in its opening section, similar to how Dorothy states that the "policeman and policewoman came to tell me about Solomon as though they were enquiring about an unpaid parking ticket."[31] Weston is a place that requires one to respatialize the geographies of imperialism and neoimperialism without flattening them. Place is produced relationally, and its character of distinction and naturalness is acquired through that variegated production.

These relationships of power are complex and many times contradictory. For example, the working-class residents of Weston exhibit a virulent racism but are also stigmatized as postindustrial remnants with no function in the contemporary economy. Without denying the racism of this town, Dorothy's unstable and problematic narration also allows Phillips to hint at the historical and political processes that created economically and geographically marginal villages like Weston in the first place. These figurations of the rural community and its youth are not to be taken as literal at every point but are rather the projections of a character (Dorothy) with a collapsing psyche that has been steeped in the (many and conflicting) stereotypes of English working-class rurality. On the other hand, the same is true of the collapsing community of Weston, which projects its violence on the racialized and gendered bodies of Solomon and Dorothy. Through this ironic juxtaposition at the level of narrative, Phillips provokes a consideration of the structural and historical aspects of communal violence in all its multivalent complexity. In doing so, the novel illustrates contemporary forms of ongoing violence and oppression that characterize neoliberal Britain.

Marginal Geographies

A Distant Shore begins in the first-person voice of Dorothy, expressing a somewhat commonplace sentiment: "England has changed. These days it's difficult to tell who's from around here and who's not. Who belongs and who's a stranger. It's disturbing. It doesn't feel right."[32] Many critics of the novel have read this opening statement as one suggesting the disappearance of a stable, homogenous English identity in the face of postcolonial, transnational migration and thus the context for the racism and xenophobia directed against Solomon by the village. For John McLeod, this racism is certainly not new, and "actually not a lot has changed in England," while for Di Maio, Weston represents "an England that has yet to come to terms with the fact that its million non-whites have contributed to the shaping of its national identity, and which is a part of a larger Europe."[33] The status of both "England" and "changed" in this reading is straightforward: "England" is a stable, national topos, and "changed" refers to immigration.[34] "England has changed" would thus seem to be an echo of Margaret Thatcher's infamous concern that Britain should "finally see an end to immigration lest [the British people] feel rather swamped by people with an alien culture."[35]

In this novel, however, this statement has a more ambiguous and complicated geography. Dorothy continues:

> Three months ago, in early June, I moved out here to this new development of Stoneleigh. None of the old villagers seem comfortable with the term "new development." They simply call Stoneleigh the

"new houses on the hill." After all, our houses are set on the edge of Weston, a village that is hardly going to give up its name and identity because some developer has seen a way to make a quick buck by throwing up some semi-detached bungalows, slapping a carriage lamp in front of them and calling them "Stoneleigh."[36]

Dorothy's opening in fact contains no reference to transnational migration. Instead, despite the fact that she is from the unnamed larger town closest to Weston, Dorothy is herself the newcomer to this provincial northern English village, moving out to spend her retirement in an Old England–themed cul-de-sac. In this context the middle-class residents of Stoneleigh are the agents of change, the strangers who do not belong, yet it is Dorothy who is "disturbed" by a vague, unspoken, residual change in England. Dorothy is troubled by the ambiguity of her position: She cannot tell who belongs and who is a stranger, because she herself belongs and is a stranger.

What is produced instead is a geography in which, as Phillips has indicated, no one feels at home. However, this includes the residents of Weston, who, rather than representing the majoritarian essence of Old Englishness, are in fact economically, geographically, and culturally marginal, particularly in the North.[37] Cindy Gabrielle argues that Weston's "attempts to preserve a 'pure' English/working-class identity and traditional identification patterns at all costs are certainly at odds with the image of England as a nation of progress."[38] However, it is important to interrogate this notion of progress, which has more often been used to marginalize and oppress individuals and reinscribe the temporalities of colonialism, race, and class. Rather than existing since time immemorial, provincial identity has indeed been created as the "other" of capitalist progress, and as Doreen Massey shows, the unevenness of the British economy has only increased since the 1980s.[39]

Villages like Weston have been continually "giving up" their identities and recreating them; correspondingly, rural social identity is not undifferentiated and static but heterogeneous and always subject to change. In reading this passage, Josiane Ranguin recognizes that the "faultline here is not race, but class," arguing that "Stoneleigh is an allegory of England, class barriers acting as social frontiers."[40] However, if the residents of Weston are less than welcoming to outsiders, this might in part be because they are also in a marginal position with regards to Stoneleigh, unable to stop the building of a new suburban development that seeks to dissociate itself from the supposedly less sophisticated working-class village. Together, these readings of "England has changed" naturalize the city-country dynamics presented in the novel, where cities like London represent flux and progressive change and small country towns represent only anachronism and xenophobia. That is, they assume that place produces politics, when the reverse is true: Politics and history produce place.

Postindustrial Provinciality and the Speculation of Rural Development

The geography of Weston is specifically postindustrial: Dorothy refers to "Mrs. Thatcher closing the pits" when discussing Weston, and indeed coal mining and its demise under the Conservative Party policies are critical to understanding social change.[41] Northern England in particular suffered drastically not only from agricultural competition but from the collapse of energy prices and many lost battles with the state. Weston does not straightforwardly represent "old England, with its old ways" and "well-established identities."[42] Rather, as part of the coal-mining community, Weston is a part of what Margaret Thatcher called an "industry [that] had come to symbolize everything that was wrong with Britain."[43] At the same time that the state was responding to riots in cities over structural racial prejudice and unemployment, Thatcher and her cabinet were referring to northern miners—who were and are a strong Labour constituency—as "the mob" and the "enemy within."[44] The interests of places like Weston and the British state were never fully aligned, and they diverged further during the erosion of the welfare state and the deregulation of energy markets, and after the 1984 strike, mining communities were and are viciously split between those who went on strike and those who did not.[45]

Decades after the strike, Weston shows the way in which marginalized people can easily latch onto essentialist and essentializing identities. As Tom Nairn has indicated, it is the contemporary politics of Britain that has produced "two Englands: New Labour's 'Roseland,' versus an England not merely 'little' but marginalised, where the defeated turn to the political Right, like Duncan Smith's Conservativism or even Nicholas Griffin's British National Party."[46] On the other hand, it was also less than thirty years ago that Doreen Massey and Hilary Wainwright could report on the solidarity between racially diverse urban groups and provincial mining communities during the strike.[47] If such solidarity is no longer possible, it is important to ask what historical processes broke apart these previous alliances. Such an inquiry of course does not deny the very real and extreme racism present in northern England.[48] Rather, I argue that reading Weston as a spatial allegory for the nation naturalizes a xenophobia and racism that has more complex and dynamic historical causes.

Weston in fact evinces the colonial nature of the nationalist project itself and its continual production of local provincialities; in this sense, Stoneleigh is a new imperial front of speculative capital that is making the countryside an object of consumption rather than of production. The rural economy today looks much like the economy overall: dominated by finance and service industries and increasingly unequal.[49] It is also more focused on consumption, with even the Cortonwood colliery in Yorkshire, where the 1984 strike began (Figures 21a and 21b), having been developed into a shopping center.[50] Increased ease of transportation has meant that many newcomers are able to travel to larger towns for work, leisure, or other services; in the novel, Weston is only five miles from the "main town."[51] By 2000, the majority of the population in English villages worked outside the village, including incoming residents who bought a country home but kept work elsewhere.[52] As a bartender tells Dorothy, implicitly criticizing the new arrivals for not spending time in the village pub, "I expect they need to make some brass to pay off their fancy mortgages."[53] Indeed, aside from Dorothy and Solomon, the residents of Stoneleigh are largely absent from the novel, indicating their disinterest in village life.

Longtime rural residents are not just marginalized "passively" by structural changes in the economy but actively by incoming residents and government

Figure 21a. Cortonwood miner's strike, 1984.

Figure 21b. Cortonwood miner's strike, 1984.

policy. There is a shortage of housing, in particular.[54] Howard Newby remarks that "resentment among local people has grown at their inability to find housing for themselves and their children. Yet they have also found that the newcomers have frequently opposed the construction of new housing, especially council housing, on the grounds that it is 'detrimental to the character of the village' and detracts from the rural environment."[55] Thus "posh" developments like Stoneleigh drive class resentment and social alienation. The middle-class residents of Stoneleigh would have not only financial resources but also experience with bureaucratic power structures, enabling them to exert an outsized influence on local politics and development.[56] They might not only see the countryside as an amenity but have a specific, highly idealized notion of the countryside, one that does not include the realities of contemporary poverty.[57] For example, Sue Glyptis comments that "in many villages long-established residents aspire to provide better community facilities for their youngsters, but this has been resolutely opposed by incomers who want to preserve their new-found rural paradise exactly as they found it, or at least how they imagined it."[58] Meanwhile, the newcomers cast "the indigenous population into the role of rustic showpieces."⁵⁹ Government policy tends to yield to these demands and those of finance capital more generally. This includes areas where the government has withdrawn support, with the approval of wealthier residents, who are willing to trade state resources for lower taxes, which affects services such as public transportation that the wealthy do not use. As Newby states, "The affluent majority of the rural population has been able to overcome any problems which arise by stepping into their cars and driving to the nearest town, whereas the poor, the elderly and the disabled have been particularly vulnerable to any decrease in the provision of local services, and especially of public transport."⁶⁰ Furthermore, the fact that services have been concentrated in towns has the consequence of disadvantaging those who were already the most disadvantaged—the poor and the elderly who lack access to transport.⁶¹

Seen in this historical context, a more complicated reading of Weston develops. Its geographical development has produced an "alarming degree of social polarization . . . between those who had chosen to live in the countryside . . . and those who had been stranded in rural areas by social and economic forces over which they had no control and which were frequently reinforced by public indifference to their plight."⁶² Aware of their own poverty given its juxtaposition with extreme wealth, socially alienated, and without a future, the youths of Weston come to more closely resemble their counterparts in urban council estates. These are also the ideal political conditions for the kind of racism and xenophobia that Solomon in particular faces.⁶³ This racism is, importantly, not the result of an unchanged, quintessential English provinciality encountering difference for the first time but the result of only the most recent political-economic shifts in a long and variegated history of rural change. Obviously, racism in Britain is neither new nor confined to provincial areas but is also situational, as the parameters of its expression and conditions of its possibility change over time in relation to political economy and culture.

Naturalizing Place in "A New Development"

Weston includes traces of all the elements just indicated, including closed mines, derelict commercial-rail infrastructure, and a nearby town as a center of shopping and employment; it also contains fields and more pastoral areas. Yet, in the text, these places do not appear to be the result of the above-described political history but instead inhere in the place itself. That is, the figuration that the text gives us mimics the operative dynamics of place in national discourse insofar as their overtly historical aspects are concealed. Place absorbs ideology, history, and politics into its apparent primary naturalness, which conceals how the class and race dynamics of Weston have evolved from state policies and structural economic changes.

Stoneleigh, with its gaudy suburban cul-de-sac and "plenty of satellite dishes," attempts at the same time to resemble a supposedly quintessential English village for middle-class retirees, who seem to show little interest in understanding the actual history and circumstances of Weston.[64] In fact, history appears, when it does, as the result of changes that took place long ago and that have little relation to the contemporary period. Dorothy notes that "the only history around these parts is probably in the architecture," especially the "typical miners' houses" that face the noisy main road and "now look almost quaint."[65] These museumlike traces of history bear no direct relation on the present but are instead reified as objects for consumption, as in the "estate agents' bumf about 'Stoneleigh,'" where, referring to Weston's twinned towns elsewhere in Europe,

> it says that during the Second World War the German town was bombed flat by the RAF, and the French village used to be full of Jews who were all rounded up and sent to the camps. I can't help feeling that it makes Weston seem a bit tame by comparison. Apparently, the biggest thing that had ever happened in Weston was Mrs. Thatcher closing the pits, and that was over twenty years ago.[66]

The initial presentation of the town's history here is filtered through an advertisement for the new development with the invented name "Stoneleigh." With a flat affect, violent histories become commodified, exciting events that lend drama and character to place as it might be conceived for tourists. Here, too, Weston falls short, being only able to claim an economic injustice that also seems part of its distant history, despite being a product of Thatcher's relatively recent reign. The novel alludes, along these lines, to various derelict structures of this advertised ruined history, from the village architecture to old railways, which Dorothy describes as "some kind of monument now."[67] All of this history, as history, thus seems barely relevant to the contemporary time of the novel. Change, in a phrase such as "England has changed," becomes spatialized, producing an opacity that also restricts some of Phillips's characteristic anamnestic impulses. Nevertheless, using a discontinuous narrative, place is imbued with its violent material conditions of possibility.

Specifically, Weston is mediated through the unreliable narration of Dorothy, a character who is both a producer and victim of gendered social marginalization. It is in fact through the narrative of a collapsing psyche that Phillips is able to present not only the contradictions of her personality but also the contradictions of a working-class town that can be simultaneously a

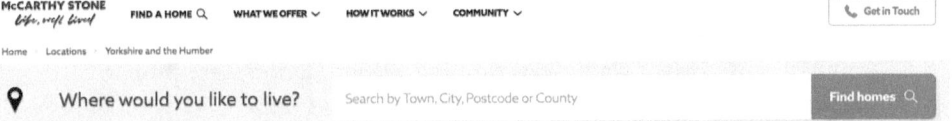

Figure 22. Advertisement for retirement homes in Yorkshire.

victim of internal colonization (and the attendant class condescension from figures like Dorothy) and at the same time ruthlessly and murderously racist. After being forced to retire, Dorothy "saw a drawing of Stoneleigh in the local paper and she bought her bungalow over the phone. Somehow the phrase 'a new development' sounded comforting."[68] Stoneleigh could easily be a development produced by a company such as McCarthy Stone, whose website offers middle-class buyers a choice of properties spread throughout Yorkshire, including the town of Market Weighton (Figure 22). McCarthy Stone advertises the many amenities available to transplants: "Yorkshire is home to numerous attractions, comprising of [sic] ancient castles, World Heritage Sites, mining museums and galleries," and, additionally, "tranquil gardens and innovative breweries."[69] Similarly, Stoneleigh is conceptually "a distant shore" for Dorothy, an escape, despite the fact that she finds herself in a "bungalow at the top of the hill in this village that is five miles outside her home town."[70] The bungalows of the new development offer themselves as a resolution, a place to spend a relaxing retirement.[71]

This is a bleak place, however, incapable of providing such a resolution. The text introduces itself by way of its setting in Weston/Stoneleigh, as just after Dorothy declares that "England has changed" she notes that "our village is divided into two."[72] Descending into Weston, she notes:

> I was surprised by how busy the main road was, with big lorries thundering by in both directions. It took a good while before there was a

break in the traffic and I was able to dash across. As it turned out there was not much to see, except housewives sitting on the front steps sunning themselves, or young kids running around. Doors were propped wide open, presumably because of the heat, but I didn't get the impression that the open doors were indicative of friendliness. People stared at me like I had the mark of Cain on my forehead, so I pressed on and discovered the canal. It's a murky strip of stagnant water, but because I was away from the noise of traffic, and the blank gawping stares of villagers, it looked almost tolerable. The skeletal remains of a few barges were tied up by the shoreline, and it soon became clear that the main activity in these parts appeared to be walking the dog. In the fields, the cows and sheep moved with an ease which left me in no doubt, that, despite the public footpath that snaked across the farmer's land, this was their territory.[73]

A contrast is drawn here between the busyness of the main road and the stillness of the town. Weston is a place that most people move through and from which some people never move. It is sonically elaborated through the noise of the traffic passing through, perhaps in part from the other middle-class residents exiting the town in their cars. On the other hand, the main road that facilitates this traffic hinders Dorothy's own movement, and the town itself is marked mostly by slight, banal activity such as walking dogs and sitting, a stillness connotative of the villagers' isolation and one that continues into the canal, which will later be the site of Solomon's murder. Like the locals' "blank" opacity, this pastoral landscape, with its stagnant water and skeletal boats, is also uninviting to Dorothy, preventing her from entering and exploring. Instead, she must retreat to her home, even though this landscape, animals and all, is supposed to be an object of consumption and peace for people like Dorothy (hence the public path).[74]

Dorothy's experience with Weston is continually blocked, mediated by conflicting desires of association and segregation. This division is partially a class division; as Dorothy's says, "we're the newcomers, or posh so-and-sos, as I heard a vulgar woman in the post office call us."[75] As is typical of Dorothy, she notes, on the one hand, a justified class resentment felt by the villagers for the people on the hill that negates any attempt she may have for association while, on the other hand, seeking to disassociate herself from the common vulgarity of the villager. The dynamics of this local geography are such that they seem to place incompatible, distant elements in an unbearably claustrophobic space producing both connection through proximity and extreme disconnection through conflict.[76] This is repeated formally in a narrative that evokes Dorothy's increasing subjective retreat from reality as well as that reality's objective hostility, thus producing ambiguity as to whether the people of Weston really are so uniformly hostile or if Dorothy is projecting a stereotype onto them. As Newby observes, "For those newcomers who moved to the countryside in order to seek the social intimacy of a happy and integrated community life, the reserve (and worse) of the local inhabitants may have been a disappointment."[77] In fact, it becomes clear that, for Solomon and Dorothy, these are not places of safety, let alone hospitality.

The deep, historical violence that haunts Phillips's other novels is present here through the landscape, for example in several bus scenes where Dorothy "sits passively, soporifically watching the world barrel past."[78] Dorothy turns to the landscape outside the bus because of her sociophobia, but these landscapes offer little escape and do more to signal a growing tension or crisis for Dorothy herself. Before Dorothy knows that Solomon has been murdered, she thinks:

> I was standing on the bus going home when I felt it in my blood that something was wrong. It wasn't just the sight of burly, unemployed men sitting in the seats reserved for the handicapped and the elderly that was disturbing me, there was something else. I stared out of the window at the town's terraced houses, great stripes of them arranged in narrow, ramrod-straight streets which, as we made our way into the countryside, finally gave way to a desolate landscape of empty fields over which the sun now hung ominously low.[79]

Typically for Dorothy, the bus offends her, specifically the unemployed men not respecting the rules of mannered society. It is, in fact, their disrespect for the space of the bus that makes Dorothy turn away. Her disdain for her fellow passengers recalls Margaret Thatcher's (most likely apocryphal) statement that "a man who, beyond the age of twenty-six, finds himself on a bus can count himself as a failure."[80] It also recalls Thatcher's not-apocryphal privatization of bus systems: The communal, public space of the bus is one also of public withdrawal and privatization. For example, Peter Ambrose remarks that "government policy has been very much to reward 'successful' regions . . . by increased infrastructural investment, and not to spend money on incentives to attract new industry to those less-successful parts of the country, the parts where old traditional industries are in decline. By its pattern of support, or rather non-support, for public transport it has shown that it has very little interest in the more isolated rural areas."[81] Thus, if the rural seems static and still, we can point to the politics of its modernization under neoliberal governance, including the decline in state resources and the political influence of newcomers whose interest is consuming an ossified rurality.

Unbelonging and the Collapse of Social and Psychic Reality

All of these scenes are mediated by Dorothy and increasingly indicate social phobia verging on paranoia. At the same time, these particular instances point to the general, material conditions of social and psychic violence. Dorothy's narration reinscribes the marginalization of Weston even as she suffers from Weston's marginalization of her. As Stephen Clingman writes, this split is repeated in the form of the novel and its "disjointed spaciotemporalities . . . in which versions of migrancy and internal exile co-exist but do not fully align, in which nation and narration are far from cohesive, horizontally unified, or identical."[82] The disjunctive time of the national, however, does not signal its demise but rather its transformation in the age of neoliberalism. In the novel, these temporal gaps give Dorothy's narrative its sense of incommensurability, as if the possibility of her existing in Weston was foreclosed from the beginning. Instead, what are explored are processes of social and psychic collapse, in which the postcolonial experience elides into continuing neocolonial operations of power.

This split is perhaps appropriate for the *Daily Mail*–reading Dorothy. Maurizio Calbi observes that the novel "is packed with issues that appear in British daily newspapers."[83] Calbi, mobilizing Kristeva and Butler, argues that Dorothy's denigration of others is in fact a projection of her own abjection and that, furthermore, this illustrates "the social and psychic process of displacement whereby those who are cast out to the margins acquire a limited amount of power by actively marginalising."[84]

These projections are amplified by papers like the *Daily Mail* and Rupert Murdoch's *The Sun*, which peddle in dramatized stereotypes about what David Cameron termed "broken Britain," defined as "the slow-motion moral collapse that has taken place in parts of our country these past few generations," caused by what he termed "moral neutrality."[85] The latter he summarized in a series of pithy phrases: "Irresponsibility. Selfishness. Behaving as if your choices have no consequences. Children without fathers. Schools without discipline. Reward without effort."[86] Dorothy's characterizations of the working-class masses in the novel are as sensationalist and subjective as a *Daily Mail* headline or Cameron speech. For example, in the town where she is a teacher, at 10:30 p.m. there will be a sudden rush of people from the twin-cinema complex, some making their way home, but most dashing to the city-centre pubs for a final drink. Of course, these new pubs with their security staff, and sawdust on the floor and loud thumping music bear no resemblance to what she recognises as a pub, but mercifully she is under no obligation to enter such hovels. At 11 p.m., when the places finally close, the unwashed rabble will slouch out into the streets, full of drink and spoiling for trouble, but she will be safely tucked up in bed.[87]

This caricature is the culture industry's unthinking mob, blindly seeking entertainment that is not that entertaining and in the meantime making all together too much noise. They represent actual cultural violence and potential physical violence and inspire Dorothy's further retreat to an interior, a home or a mind. Moreover, as a collective subject, they also exist in the text as figuration. In the text, this group of working-class subjects is a heterogeneous element, both an overly known cliché but at the same time unknown and opaque; in this way, the novel enacts a fragmentation between incommensurable entities. This violence is undeniably directed toward racial minorities. For example, the patrons of Mahmood's restaurant are

fat-bellied Englishmen and their slatterns rolling into The Khyber Pass after the pubs had closed, calling him Ranjit or Baboo or Swamp Boy, and using pappadoms as Frisbees, and demanding lager, and vomiting in his sinks, and threatening him with his own knives and their beery breath, and bellowing for mini-cabs and food that they were too drunk to see had already arrived on the table in front of them.[88]

This overwhelming anaphoric litany evokes the putrid physicality and drunken, racist stupidity of an endless English hooligan mob. It is a masculine violence in whose wake follows an untidy femininity.[89] They are a collective subject that is aggressive, noisy, messy, ill-tempered, and ill-mannered as they demand, vomit, threaten, and bellow, and they suggest the presence of an unmediated violence in alarming proximity.

When Dorothy finally is forced to retire as a teacher and decides to leave this uncouth town, she witnesses an argument between a man with a bicycle and the driver of her bus to her new home in Stoneleigh. The bicycle will not fit on the bus, and "soon the young man is shouting at the driver, then cursing him in foul language . . . she [Dorothy] looks away, ashamed and puzzled. It is one thing to be frustrated by rules, but it is another thing to flout authority in such a vulgar manner. These are not happy times for anybody."⁹⁰ The "young man" in this scene turns what should be a merely personal reaction to a generality into a noisy public affair. Dorothy, meanwhile, immediately ascribes general meaning to her particular reaction to this commonplace argument. It is succulently final: The "rules" (wherever those come from) are under vulgar attack, which signals brokenness for both societies and individuals, herself included. As she does elsewhere, she turns away from this scene on the bus, and also from a man noisily and offensively eating an apple and boiled egg, to gaze at the landscape through the window. This is an attempt at "looking away" from the perceived social disjuncture and conflict on the bus to the archetypically compensatory English landscape.⁹¹ However, she "finds herself peering out at the bleak scene of unappetising fast-food places, an RAC stand, rows of unused telephones and neon-lit petrol pumps."⁹² Her gaze is thus pulled back to the monotony and homogeneity of cheap consumer culture and to an infrastructure that belies the fantasy place-image of regeneration schemes.

That this scene features an impolite "young" man is not insignificant. Dorothy's disdain for young people may stem, perhaps ironically, from her profession as a school teacher (but only perhaps). She teaches music and over the years faced the ruination of music itself, namely, "the possibility that the pleasures of the classical world are in danger of becoming extinct."⁹³ Her teaching also marks a boundary between Dorothy's Tory sensibilities and her working-class background, as the introduction of comprehensive schools challenges her pedagogical philosophy: "I've spent most of my life banging on about how it would be better if kids of all levels and backgrounds could be educated together and learn from each other. . . . And then four years ago, the education authority scrapped grammar schools, turned us comprehensive, and they put me to the test. . . . Difficult kids I don't mind, but I draw the line at yobs."⁹⁴ The difference between "difficult kids" and "yobs" is obviously a class distinction but also a place where the working-class subject of her memory (for example, her father) and of the present is split, with the latter becoming savage and unruly. The split in the child subject, as either "difficult" or "yob," reflects one of many splits within Dorothy herself, her simultaneous positions as a member of a dominant, educated class but also not, adherent to an ideology that itself suggests her own marginalization and "victimhood," for which she is certainly not responsible.

This unruliness of children, however, becomes excessive when these children grow older; in fact, the group most often figured as ill-mannered and verging on unmediated violence is the teenage youth. Their excess is in fact not symptomatic of some deeper meaningfulness but simply marks a structural gap in the wholeness of community. In this text, that youth is not the rioting urban youth but rather the bored, provincial teenagers of Weston, some of who eventually do prove to be racist and murderous when they kidnap and kill Solomon. They are introduced with the scene of this later crime in the background:

> I [Dorothy] sat on a low wall underneath some drooping willow branches and looked around. The soft back-lap of the canal was soothing, although the jerky flight of a dragonfly buzzing about my head seemed out of place. This wall belonged to the village pub, The Waterman's Arms, whose garden gave out onto the canal. In the garden some young louts and their girlfriends were braying and chasing about the place. I watched them as they began to toss beer at each other, and then shriek with the phlegmy laughter of hardened smokers . . . I could now feel eyes upon me, and for a few moments I wondered if some of these slovenly youngsters, with their barrack-room language, weren't pupils that I'd recently had the rare pleasure of teaching. However, I thought it best not to turn and look them full in the face.[95]

Dorothy's focus on the briefly relaxing canal is interrupted by the animalistic presence of the teenagers; their shrieks and ("phlegmy") laughter indicates not the joyful promise of children playing but rather degenerate, unkempt beings, already ruined by alcohol, cigarettes, and expletives. In this way, the text takes the caricature of "Broken Britain's" youth seriously, recreating them as the violent, subhuman collectivity they are supposed to be. When Dorothy feels eyes, it is all of them who are turning to her, and she tries to escape their notice as if they were violent dogs spoiling for a fight with a passerby. She does not look them in the face, and in a sense they are faceless; in the novel, they are, with one exception, given no voice or subjectivity but rather exist as objects of Dorothy's fear and disgust. Through her narration, the relative incommensurability that constitutes the heterogeneous, "broken" society is not so much represented as staged—textual presences set into motion. Here the caricature, the cliché, is both untrue and true, imaginary productions of prejudice and real producers of violence.

Even as caricature, the youth are physical presence in its most visceral forms, a sensuality as vibrant as it is beastly. Later in the text, Dorothy sees another common scene: "Across the road in the pub car park, some louts, who are all tattoos and bared teeth, are now pushing and shoving each other and making the loud braying noises that suggest they are having a good time. She notices that two among them are brazenly advertising the contents of their bladders in triumphal watery arches, and then to her horror she realises that their performances are competitive."[96] The viscera here is somewhat literal and accompanied by primal sounds. The indication of enjoyment is signaled not even by "phlegmy" laughter but by "braying," seemingly unthinking animal noises. The enjoyment itself, lacking decorum, acquires undertones of violence—the bared teeth, the shoving—which all seem to justify Dorothy's horror. Dorothy, Solomon, and the residents of Weston are all elements that are subject to and selectively reproduce this diffuse ideological machine, and thus they are all partially minoritarian relative to one other. As a resident of the new speculative development, Dorothy is an unwitting bearer of "progress" and "regeneration," which requires the identification of ruined, "backward" places. As on the bus, Dorothy repeatedly makes this identification and then turns away; here progress produces regression, which it then cannot countenance. In *A Distant Shore*, the more that Dorothy retreats into herself out of a false prejudice and fear of an exterior, collective barbarity, the more that violent collectivity becomes real.

Abandoned Communities

When Dorothy moves to Stoneleigh, she has already been abandoned by several people: Mahmood; Geoff; her ex-husband Brian; by her school, which forces her to retire; and by her parents and sister, who have died. These abandonments, several coming in rapid succession, lead Dorothy to a physical and mental withdrawal in Stoneleigh. Many of the men to whom she is attached had primary attachments elsewhere, a pattern introduced by her father, whose primary attachment was to her younger sister Sheila, "daddy's little pet," whom he sexually abused in the family's garden allotments during their childhood.[97] Because Dorothy's psychic condition is represented as the result of a series of successive abandonments by male objects of attachment, her identity is continually defined as dependence. For example, in Dorothy's vexed, loveless relationship with Mahmood, she focuses her attention on his stories, while deferring her own: "Dorothy says very little about her own life, being concerned to make sure that the dominant narrative is male. After all, his story involves passion, betrayal, migration, sacrifice and ultimately triumph. Mahmood is a success. Her story contains the single word, abandonment."[98] She later asks him, "Are you really interested in my life? I mean there's not much to it, you know."[99] The successful Mahmood to which Dorothy refers runs a news stand in the middle of nowhere, with a wife whom he hates, selling to racist customers. Apart from his lack of urbanity, however, he is an archetypal figure of postcolonial migration, one whose narrative is defined by a masculine hardship that is overcome for the sake of a hybrid existence in the Global North.[100] Similarly, Gabriel, the young solider that escapes genocide and witnesses the trauma of war, endures a dangerous crossing and finally creates a new identity in a foreign land. Both men are thus associated with the difficulties and traumas of movement.

As opposed to this is Dorothy, whose narrative is characterized by stillness and passivity, consisting of the intricacies of relationships occurring within the relative safety and prosperity of the First World. The dual narratives of *A Distant Shore* are thus gendered along these lines: the masculine, "dominant narrative" of migration, on the one hand, and the provincial, personal narrative of English inaction on the other. Even if under compulsion, Gabriel abandons his world and identity; Dorothy is abandoned and defines her life by that term. All this leaves Dorothy in an awkward position, part of a dominant culture but also needing to defer to and be dependent on masculine narratives. This gap expresses itself as a lack of content: Her life is boring, nothing happened. What does happen, in turn, always happens mostly in relation to the male figures in her life and their continual disappearance. She is defined by abandonment, alienation, and her lack of solid, consistent connection with others, and as she is abandoned she slowly abandons the possibility of such connection, instead becoming radically alienated from the thought of connection and community, indeed from the idea of a shared reality. This alienation, however, is already prefigured in her structural inability to craft her own narrative, because such a construction is only "male." Her identity is constructed via negative absences that leave her without relation to place or community, yet these negative relationships themselves constitute a positive articulation of identity.

Tournay-Theodotou writes that Dorothy's "general mental instability aptly reflect the current 'disturbed' state of the British nation," with the "break up of [her] European mind" being "symptomatic of that of the entire nation."[101] For Di Maio, Dorothy is similarly an "an embodiment of England," and as such "healing still is a long way away for Dorothy as well as for her melancholic, postcolonial England."[102] However, if the Britain (or Europe or England) is unstable and melancholic, Dorothy's narration shows how the effects of this instability are not distributed evenly but are brought to bear most painfully on its excessive subjects: Dorothy is no longer needed by the state school system, Solomon/Gabriel is the byproduct of wars for the blood diamonds and minerals that fuel consumer modernity, and Weston is a postindustrial backwater subject to real estate speculation and development.

In this material context, Dorothy's psychological collapse provides a narratological device that reveals the multifaceted nature of marginalization in contemporary Britain. Ping Su suggests that for Dorothy "there is no escape but insanity—a determined dissociation from harsh reality to prevent further psychological damage and to fight depression and anxiety. In this sense, madness might function as a defensive strategy that actively contributes to the healing process."[103] In this way, Dorothy's abandonment of reality is the only logical and sane response to a reality that has always abandoned her. Phillips, by narrating Dorothy's withdrawal from her own perspective, records both her tentative grasp on reality and that reality's objective insanity.

The Opacity of Affect

Throughout *A Distant Shore*, Dorothy alternates between two modes of (non)relation: silence and shouting. These are forms of anticommunitarian communication, delivering affect without meaning, isolating her through opaque relationship. Her silences are a dissatisfaction with observed reality, as she looks away to something else: imagining what her absent friend Solomon is doing, looking through a window, convalescing with a flower.[104] These concrete-utopian moments open up and close down alternative modes of relating in the very same gesture, such that relation, as silence, exists as the absence of relation. Blanchot will argue that the absence of community is also community's condition of possibility: "A being is either alone or knows itself to be alone only when it is not."[105] Yet the other side of Dorothy's communitarian silence is a form of speech that is excessive, shouting, in which she both comes out of herself and at the same time closes off possibility for relating to a world marked by abandonment and disappearance.[106] In this way, *A Distant Shore* helps disclose the stakes for me of the speculative imaginary of development. The latter conceives of future places as realizable utopian enclaves that reconcile social tension and mediate local experiences of global modernity. It colonizes the frame that subjects might use to imagine otherwise and in so doing works concretely to reproduce the political economies and geographies of abandonment. The forms of communication—and community—that result are marked by absence and excess, unreadable except as silence and noise yet at the same time unmistakable enunciations of fracture and discontent.

An analysis that understands this fracture as only symptomatic of something latent, imperial residues perhaps, misses the way that fracture is reproduced through ongoing structures of violence and if anything correlates to an emergent structure of feeling. For example, Paul Gilroy diagnoses the condition of twenty-first-century Britain as a postcolonial melancholia, writing that in contemporary society one finds the "obsessive repetition of key themes—invasion, war, contamination, loss of identity" that together indicate that an "anxious, melancholic mood has become part of the cultural infrastructure of the place, an immovable ontological counterpart to the nation-defining ramparts of the white cliffs of Dover."[107] Britain is unable to come to terms with its colonial history, and so "racist violence provides an easy means to 'purify' and rehomogenize the nation."[108] This formulation relies upon a familiar postcolonial depth of field, in which the jouissance and precarity of the migrant operates against a static background of British national identity, found in a particularly ossified form in nonurban areas. Instead, Gilroy privileges the ordinary "conviviality" and multiculturalism of the postcolonial metropolis. This is indicative, John McLeod writes, of a sentimentally admirable but ultimately myopic "theoretical commitment to post-national and post-racial modus operandi—where itinerancy, temporariness, and plurality are ethically unquestionable."[109]

Gilroy reads British nativism as the result of a lack of change, a survival from an earlier, more homogenous, more reliably imperial past. Expressed geographically, this position not only fetishizes mobility and transience as inherently resistant but also links spatial and social immobility to static identities. The limitation of this position is not, as nationalists like David Goodhart might argue, that it is insufficiently sympathetic to the "white working class" or to British or English identity.[110] Rather, it misreads what is actually the active production of nativist sentiment as only in reference to a prior homogenization, without thinking through how fantasies of empire and homogeneity not only reference a lost past but are reproduced toward the construction of a speculative future. In essence, it reads into contemporary social relations survivals that should have been determined out of existence.[111] Turning his sense of melancholy in contemporary society into a social pathology, Gilroy contends that Britain can be both postnational and still cohere into a convivial structure by attending to its "painful obligations to work through the grim details of imperial and colonial history and to transform paralyzing guilt into a more productive shame that would be . . . no longer phobic about the prospect of exposure to either strangers or otherness."[112]

Putting aside the fact that nativists have no interest in such a working through, this formulation problematically relies upon a metaphor of individual development and health to describe the social. Thus he argues that "healthier patterns in which Britain renounces its pursuit of greatness" will "reap[] immediate benefits in civil society" and thus represent a "psychological and ethical maturity" for Britain.[113] Just like a mentally unhealthy adult who regresses into childish immaturity, so Britain has failed to develop a positive postimperial identity. In such a formulation, violence in the present moment is only understood as an echo of a homogenous imperial past. Rather than follow our scripts of how gender, race, and class are articulated against a postimperial landscape, we might follow Stuart Hall in considering the ways that they are *continually rearticulated* through concrete social formations in the present. In doing so, we see the "noninevitable—yet nonarbitrary—nature of social formations."[114] Here we see the "lived experience" of social formations—the different modes of abandonment in *A Distant Shore*, for example—as shaped by long histories of patriarchy, empire, and capitalism without being determined by them in a singular and static fashion.

However, this also raises the question about what aspects of these social formations remain unarticulated, perhaps constitutively. A gesture repeated throughout *Topothesia* has been to register the social affects of the contemporary and trace their genealogy while not attempting to completely resolve moments and facets of indiscernibility and opacity. For example, if we query the affects of the Brexit vote, we might perceive a vague sense of being left behind, abandoned, insignificant, or not mattering. The vote has been seen as indicative of an anxiety over change and a desire, per the slogan of the leave campaign, of "taking back control."[115] The tone of the exhaustive and excessive discourse around Brexit since 2016 has accordingly veered between absolute confidence and persistent confusion: confidence in any given explanatory model to locate the determinant cause of the above affects and confusion that the situation fails to resolve itself.[116] That is, there is something about the spatial dislocation and alienation produced by the eras of deindustrialization and ostensible regeneration that resists demystification, instead resolving into a series of affective responses. This is not to say that different interpretations of the politics of Brexit are all equally contingent. For example, as noted, it is not difficult to see how the leave campaign was motivated by and made use of xenophobia and nationalism; so empowered, racial animosity and white resentment in the United Kingdom has led to an increase in attacks on minorities and people of color. Rather, I am arguing that the confusion and excessiveness of contemporary political discourse indicate an inability to locate structural, determinant causes for concrete social phenomena. That is, the entanglement of interrelating structures of neoliberalism, histories of empire and ongoing colonization, intractable racism, geographical dislocation, emerging political divisions, global politics, and much else produces not just theoretical complexity but rather opacity.

In this sense, the turn to affect and sensibility to characterize phenomena related to Brexit do not make these phenomena any less opaque. For example, the leave vote has been characterized as stemming from an "anxiety about change." Somehow, this seems both particularly true and overgeneralized: Even if anxiety is distributed unevenly, ultimately what politics and what historical moments are free from such anxiety? As applied to the labor market or changing demographics, anxiety in this usage subtly introduces a kind of affective determinism that is as one-dimensional as economic determinism. Instead, Brexit—not "itself" but as a discursive category—is overdetermined to the point of incapacitation. To the extent this is a populist discourse, it functions, per Ernesto Laclau, not through "finding an abstract common feature underlying all social grievances, but with a performative operation."[117] Laclau argues that such populist signifiers, rather than containing positive contents, operate as a performative abstraction that calls attention to a gap in the "fullness of communitarian being."[118] In this formulation, rather than being composed of affects that attempt to name structures that are not yet namable, political discourse consists in empty signifiers (such as "white working class") with variable meanings, filled in by processes of cathexis.

Laclau defends the possibility of such empty signification as a political apparatus for the disenfranchised in general. Yet overdetermination is an open process: As Louis Althusser writes in his foundational text on the subject, "From the first moment to the last, the lonely hour of the 'last instance' never comes."[119] That is, the way history is concretely realized also means that there is no determination in the last instance. Here Althusser contrasts what he sees as Marx's complex, multidirectional dialectic with Hegel's more idealistic understanding of history that operates by way of supersession. He sarcastically describes the Hegelian mode of historical progress: "In each instant of Time the past survives in the form of a memory of what has been; that is, as the whispered promise of its present."[120] Conversely, for Marx, "his past was no shade, not even an 'objective' shade—it is a terribly positive and active structured reality, just as cold, hunger, and the night are for his poor worker."[121] That is, history, instead being a metaphysical palimpsest of determinate negations and supersessions, operates by way of a more complex, multidirectional set of contradictions and oppositions that are always mutable.

It seems, however, that Althusser opens a problem that undermines, both theoretically and practically, the notion that overdetermination can still resolve itself to a sort of Marxist contradiction of classes, even if "complexly." At what point does complexity become the chaos and opacity of empty signification? As Etienne Balibar writes, Althusser is struggling with the tension between opposition and reconciliation in Marxist thought itself.[122] Balibar shifts the problem somewhat by trying to think of the negativity of the dialectic without a subject, or with a subject that neither precedes nor succeeds its determination.[123] At this point, it would seem that empty signification, far from being a container for political heterogeneity, is a vexed and hostile place for the discursive subject to both encounter and displace its own formation. Only through a kind of violence, one that contingently and even arbitrarily curtails signification's excess and its opacity, does such signification cohere into identity as such. The resultant political sphere could be characterized both as a "terribly positive and active structured reality" and as a series of shades—ghosts of histories, landscapes, modes of being that are almost imperceptibly imprinted onto the subject.[124] Not only do these shades linger, but they are both, as Balibar suggests, overdetermined and underdetermined.[125] That is, the overwhelming density of past specters is also and equally a blindness to this past's ongoing presence. Here, ghosts only manifest as an opaque absence of meaning and of the possibility of forming a relationship to a world.[126]

Coda
Colonization by Design

In 2017, I saw an exhibit at the Stedelijk Museum in Amsterdam entitled "Solution or Utopia: Design for Refugees." Part of the "refugee challenge" by the international organization What Design Can Do, the exhibit featured various design-oriented "solutions" to the continuous and increasing arrival of refugees from the Global South to Western Europe. In addition to the Stedelijk Museum, this exhibition would be on display at Loka Lik, "a creative hub situated near the asylum seekers' centre in the former Bijlmerbajes prison in Amsterdam."[1] Exhibitions were various—for example, a display of "refugee emojis" that claimed to "raise awareness and spark dialogue around the daily struggles faced by the Syrian refugees," and "Exchanging Room," a set of instructions for constructing temporary, easily dismantled shelters for refugees.[2] One exhibit that caught my eye in particular was "Europe in Africa" (EIA), a proposal to build an island in the Mediterranean Sea off the coast of Tunisia to house refugees departing North Africa and seeking asylum in Europe, designed by the Dutch architecture firm TD (Theo Deutinger and Stefanos Filippas). EIA is a planned city that promises to be "a new country with its own constitution, economic and social system under the protection of the states of the European Union," and its construction, we are told, is a direct response to the drowning deaths of migrants attempting to cross the Mediterranean (Figure 23).

EIA is a legacy of many elements of the ideology and epistemology of planning that I have traced throughout this book. It is an attempt, yet again, to design away the problem. That is, it considers the phenomenon of migration and asylum-seeking from the Global South, including the extreme precarity

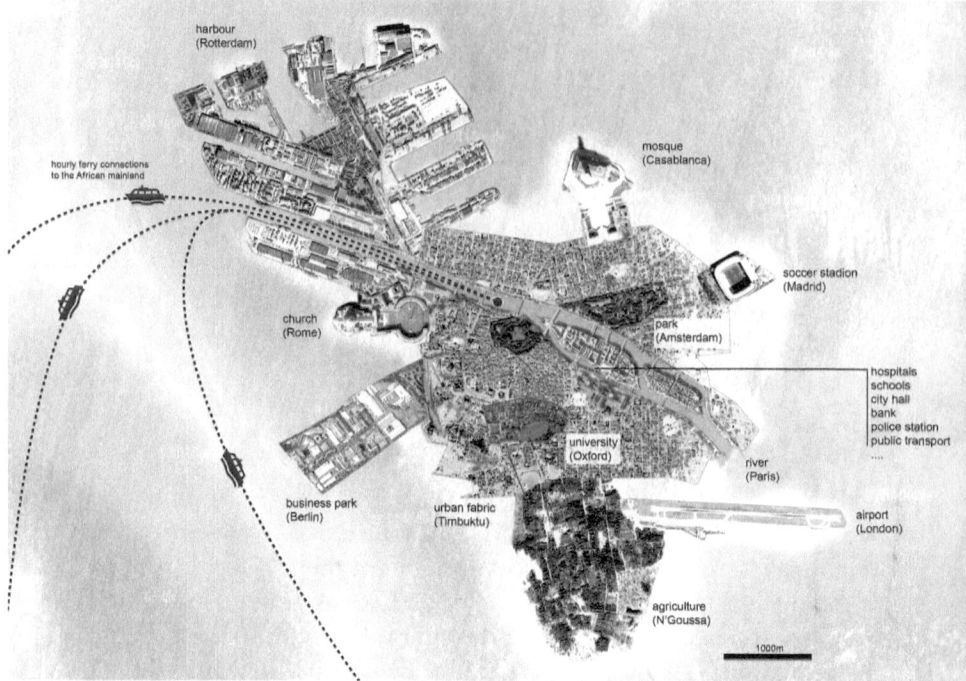

Figure 23. Plan for *Europe in Africa*.

of those refugees in making the journey and the hostility and racism they face if they arrive in European countries, and proposes a technological fix, as if these legacies of past and ongoing colonialism were simply matters of material and legal infrastructure. As such, it features a specifically bourgeois development aesthetic that often simply classes itself as "good design." For example, to address the historical legacy of European capitalism on the Global South's climate and of European extractive imperialism on the Global South's polities, it aims to be powered by a sustainable "mix of tidal, sun and wind power plants" only. Similarly, it stresses that it "will focus on pedestrian and public transport and its building construction will meet European standards."

Through such references, EIA leverages the utopian aesthetics of green sustainability to create a planned city on an artificial island that would be, in effect, yet another concentration camp subtended by the legal and ideological articulation of apartheid. Ferries would run regularly between Tunisia and EIA (but not to Europe). The designers claim that since "residents are granted at arrival with an EIA citizenship (EIA passport), there are no refugees." It would be "ruled by the European Union" for twenty-five years and then adopt

CODA   217

the European Constitution and an already-determined governing structure. It is, in so many words, a colony "by design":

> EIA is a compromise, but a legal and human compromise; it is not Europe but also not Africa; it is not 100% without crime but for sure not criminal; it is not ideal but better than any other option. Everybody is welcome in EIA; nobody would be sent away. EIA is all what the European Union wants to be. This city has the potential to experiment with new forms of nationhood or introduce an intercontinental cityness. It has the potential to blur borders and to build bridges where at the moment just fences and barbwire exists. EIA will not become a Ceuta or Melilla since it does not belong to any nation, EIA will not be colonial since it belongs to its inhabitants and not to any European nation, EIA will not be a ghetto since it will not be fenced. EIA will be the first truly European city, yet would be run and populated by people from Africa and Asia that had to flee their countries and want to enjoy European living standards.

This rhetoric echoes that of globalization projects in which people (or perhaps just the elite) could live the liberal cosmopolitan dream of global, frictionless life with no constraints on either movement or capital. In the context of a European Union that is collapsing under the weight of financial predation, xenophobia, and renewed (did it ever go away?) nationalism, the designers displace their cosmopolitan hopes upon this island, a humanitarian gesture that yet aims to keep the Global South in its place. In that, it bears all the traces of More's insular Utopia or the less theoretical schemes of Edward Gibbon Wakefield and all the other utopian colonialists. Or, like Howard's garden city, EIA is a place that, once designed and implemented, starts to run itself:

> The island will establish its own economy, starting with building construction and its adjacent businesses, yet additionally existing European businesses would be invited to set up branches in EIA, in order to give a boost to the island's welfare. EIA city is an accumulation of everything desirable from both worlds. It is a full blown city built according to European standards filled with African styles of living and working. . . . EIA city will not be clean like Zurich nor will it be chaotic like Lagos but a perfect merger of these two worlds. It will be chaotically organised, formally informal and colourful black and white.[3]

The essentialism in this project is not subtle. Africa is one place: a topos that stands for everything premodern, that is inherently chaotic, informal, lacking

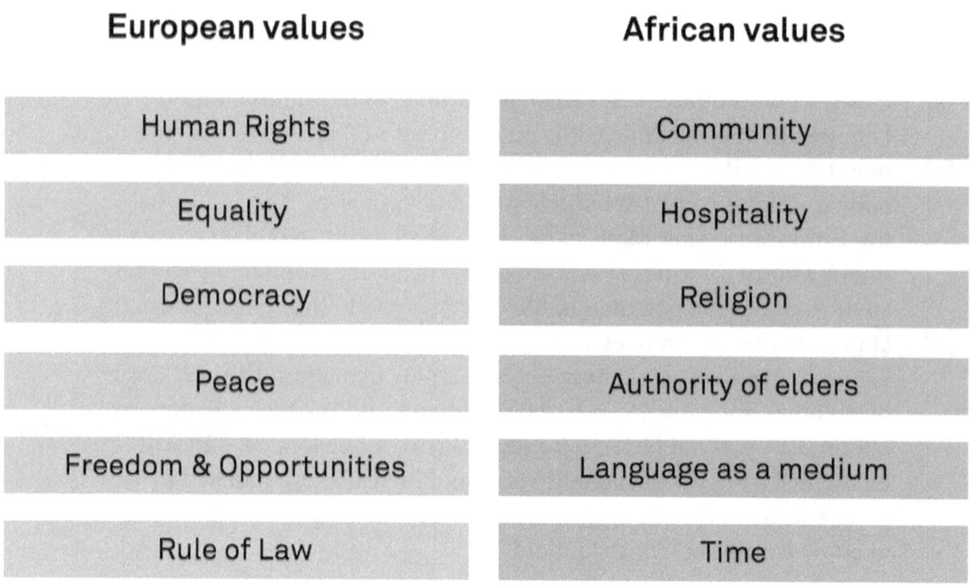

European values	African values
Human Rights	Community
Equality	Hospitality
Democracy	Religion
Peace	Authority of elders
Freedom & Opportunities	Language as a medium
Rule of Law	Time

Figure 24. *Europe in Africa*'s "values."

in "standards" and not "clean." This "Africa" brings an element of criminality, but one that can be tempered through its slow association with Europe (see Figure 24). The scheme has proponents including the Oxford scholars Robin Cohen and Nicholas Van Hear, who add elements like a biometric identity card specifically for such refugees that would not only be a passport (even granting movement between different "camps and detention centers") but would also serve as a bank (holding internet/phone credits, for example) and a citizenship registry, to keep track of possible held "entitlements" like "first aid kits, education, health care, food, clothing."[4] The topothesia of this imagined city works to present a colonial surveillance dystopia as a sustainable, green, and humanitarian project.

Different, if also familiar, kinds of apartheid are being established by "sustainable" planning and intentional design in the Global South, for example in Narendra Modi's India. His 2014 program for one hundred "smart" cities shares so many of the hallmarks of "regeneration" projects in the UK: development corporations who handle planning authority, the creation of special enterprise zones, the idea that public investment can draw private capital, the reality of gated communities. It is ambiguous what makes these cities "smart," but it appears to be some combination of "good design," vague gestures of digital infrastructure, and no small amount of performative nationalism meant to convince citizens that their cities are "world class." Of these smart-city plans, Antarin Chakrabarty writes:

> Famous and highly reputed architectural firms were hired for the design of these townships, as much to ensure architectural merit as for marketing purposes. Serious studies of social and cultural issues, post-occupancy realities and relationships with the surrounding environment were conspicuous by their absence. The architectural firms, often from other cities and sometimes from other countries, had neither the opportunity nor any apparent inclination to harmonize the projects with the urban context in which they were situated. While observing the design process of these projects, I could not help describing them as projects of Gated New Urbanism. Within their privately guarded boundary walls, these projects contained all the elements of the New Urbanism movement, albeit of a rather alien and ridiculous type. . . . Apparently ample (but in reality carefully constrained and often cosmetic) green spaces lined the pedestrian walkways and bicycle lanes. However, the townships, with their own private security, were totally isolated from the surrounding urban environment and drew on architectural styles that bore no resemblance to the buildings outside.[5]

As such, Indian smart cities adopt the aesthetics and idiom of their northern counterparts: These cities are exercises in place making and sustainability, informed, supposedly, by ground-up consultation of the local community, and existing not just as discrete places in their own right but as *models* for future cities.[6] What is produced, however, is "Gated New Urbanism," a township for the elite. A similar, if scaled-up, dynamic is on display in Modi's much-criticized Central Vista development in Delhi. Under the guise of fulfilling elements of Lutyens and Baker's original design for the capital's central parliamentary buildings but now with a more nationalist sentiment, Central Vista will feature sustainable transportation, "world-class" architecture that reconciles tradition and modernity, and a large arboretum.[7]

I have mentioned throughout *Topothesia* that the forms of knowledge I am tracking—from garden cities to the Olympics, colonization at "home" or abroad or post-, between riots, ruins, and trees, among the affects of abandonment that follow the logics of social reproduction—can be understood as *metonymic* and thus in relation to the global politics and aesthetics of development. These are a couple examples of what I mean, though there are countless others. A speculative project like Europe in Africa emplaces a structure of precarity within its pretentions of design; Smart Cities propose to expel the specter of that precarity to outside its always-expanding walls. In both cases, the subaltern subject posed in relation to "good design" remains noisy but without speech.[8] As Denise da Silva writes, the racial subaltern is the "negative but interior ground on which the force of law stands" and inhabits what she calls "affectable territory."[9] This territory is legal, ideological, and epistemological but is also the concrete space of development. Development takes as its object those spaces cast as anachronisms, that are out of time, disjunctive with the ever-receding horizon of a technological modernity. The aesthetics of this development are not incidental to but constitutive of the state's law-preserving violence even if, through its green aesthetics, development can appear as immediate and therefore as natural, self-evident, unrelated to political processes. In different ways, these are spaces of the not-yet, wherein the fulfillment of development leads to demolition, gentrification, or displacement, or, not fulfilled, they remain as the other to progress.

If there is one gesture I have resisted here, it is to adhere to a script that says a critique of power ought necessarily to make space for forms of resistance. If anything, this book is a small attempt at "denying oneself the ideological misuse of one's own existence"[10] and also a project of "making room for the affective abilities that forestall premature reconciliations, forgivenesses, and optimisms on someone else's time."[11] In these gestures, the ambivalence and indiscernibility of the not-yet, the way it discloses itself in unreadable genres of excess and absence, begrudgingly makes way for the being-with of thought, which finds itself most committed to the world when it is by itself, questioning all attachments, lost in daydream or dream.

Acknowledgments

Portions of this book have been published in *Environment and Planning D: Society and Space*, *Postcolonial Text*, *Open Cultural Studies*, and *The Global South*.

Academic works are the end result of a process involving and made possible through life in so many different places and institutions, and especially through so many important people. It's not only that this book would not exist without that support but also that the process of being-with is as meaningful and essential as the end product, if not more so.

Rei Terada has been a constant source of support and intellectual engagement and encouragement from the moment I entered graduate school at UC Irvine. The kinds of interdisciplinary work I try to do in this book would not have been possible without an academic advisor who was supportive and interested in all my research non sequiturs and the constellated ephemera that I brought to her. She always challenged me to go further and be more intellectually ambitious and curious. Likewise, I learned so much from my graduate committee: Étienne Balibar, David Lloyd, Adriana Johnson, and Lilith Mahmud, all generous, incisive, caring, and deeply knowledgeable interlocutors. I have been lucky to learn from many others at UCI, including Jane Newman and Rajagopalan Radhakrishnan. The UC Humanities Research Institute has given me the opportunity to continue conversations with my faculty mentors formally, both in inviting me to respond to David Lloyd's *Under Representation* and by providing support for the Reading for Infrastructure seminar, organized by Adriana Johnson and Susan Zieger. Thanks to Asma Abbas for inviting me to what turned out to be an extremely generative workshop, "Materialism and the Colony." Finally, I would have never made it to graduate school without the help of Elliott Colla, who mentored me as an undergraduate at Brown University.

I benefited immensely from the truly brilliant and kind individuals that I met during my time in graduate school. I would not have completed my dissertation without the joy and commiseration shared with Sarah Kessler in our perambulations around Los Angeles. Usually, these would be joined by Karen Tongson, who has been an unofficial faculty mentor and dear friend. Rachel Mykkanen has similarly been a writing buddy, a sharer of urban adventures, and a dear friend. Tamara Beauchamp and Ben Garceau have been a consistent source of encouragement and support. So many other valued friends and colleagues have engaged with my work at its most formative, helped me figure out academia (to the extent that I have), and been a source of comfort and aid: Ana Baginski, Michelle Cho, Trudi Connolly, J. Daniel Elam, Emma Heaney, Vicki Hsieh, Deanna Kashani, Alexandra Lippman, Chris Malcolm, Nasser Mufti, Joanne Nucho, Julia Obert, Sam Solomon, Robin Stewart, and Jacqueline Way. There are many others who provided much-needed perspective and friendship throughout the years writing this book: Allison Carter, Andrea Chen, Winston Groman, Victoria Hsieh, Clare Johnson, Michael Klein, Brett Lockspeiser, Nina Mamikunian, Ryan Mosley, Kim Samek, Harry Siple, Joy Tehero, Cassie Tharinger, Phillip Trevett, Phimy Truong, Aly Two Eagles, and many more. Finally, I should not neglect to thank Peeky, my gentle, calming, and somewhat aristocratic animal companion.

The School of Humanities and Graduate Division at the University of California, Irvine provided me with support and funding, including to make the visit to London in 2011 that would prove foundational for my subsequent research. Conversations with Andrea Luka Zimmerman, Gareth Evans, and Lasse Johansson have been tremendously influential and helpful, and I have admired and learned so much from their creative and professional work. Likewise, Devorah Baum has read and generously engaged with portions of this book. There are many other people that I have been able to meet to talk about London, architecture, Olympics, gardens, riots, Brexits, and the like during my times spent in the United Kingdom.

Istanbul and the wonderful students of Boğaziçi University—resilient, resistant, and kind toward animals—will always have a place in my heart. I learned so much from the students and colleagues there and stand with them in their continued struggles. It was a joy to explore the city with Jennifer Brittan and Kerry Hunt during what was a tumultuous time both personally and politically.

The Department of Literature at UC San Diego has provided me time and stability, crucial elements for any academic work. This has been bolstered by the university in the form of an award from the Faculty Career Development Program and by grants from the Institute of Arts and Humanities that provided me with two manuscript support awards. I was also fortunate enough to receive a Junior Faculty Manuscript Workshop grant from the UCHRI. The ensuing conversation with Neetu Khanna, John Marx, Poulomi Saha, and Rei Terada was extraordinarily useful as I revised my manuscript. I cannot thank them enough for their deep engagement with this book in its "penultimate" form.

UC San Diego has been an exceptionally welcoming and generative community. Andrea Mendoza, Sal Nicolazzo, Brandon Som, Erin Suzuki, and Katie Walkiewicz, in addition to being amazing scholars and dedicated teachers, have become dear friends. I learn from them constantly and am excited at the community that we are producing together. I have also been fortunate to befriend, learn from, and write with Mati Cordoba Azcarate, Lilly Irani, Wendy Matsumura, Roy Perez, and Fernando Dominguez Rubio. Many others here and elsewhere have provided guidance and encouragement: Kazim Ali, Kathleen Frederickson, Amelia Glaser, Lily Hoang, Janelle Iglesias, Stephanie Jed, Sara Johnson, Nancy Kwak, Jin-kyung Lee, Hoang Nguyen, Nancy Postero, Babak Rahimi, Dan Vitkus, Meg Wesling, and Elana Zilberg. It has been amazing to think with the graduate students in my seminars on "Absence and Excess" and "Concrete Utopia" and through engaging with their work on committees and other fora. Special thanks to Marina Vlahaki and Yaprak Yıldırım for helping assemble the images for this book. Thanks to the Sir Patrick Geddes Memorial Trust for their permission for several images, especially in Chapter 2.

All of us who work in public universities continually confront its stark inequities and thus all of the thought, teaching, research, and learning that is not happening because of lack of access and lack of support. I have been appreciative to join many of the individuals named above to stand with our many union allies—UAW, AFSME, UPTE, and AFT—and to participate in protests against budget cuts and austerity, against racism on campus, and for security and a sustainable cost of living for undergraduate and graduate students, lecturers, staff, and everyone in the university community.

Finally, nothing would be possible without family. This project has been punctuated by regular visits to see my sister, Anupama, and brother-in-law, John, and later my nephew, Kiran, and niece, Maya. My parents, Nampalli and Rekha Vijay, are a source of inspiration, wisdom, and kindness and have supported me at every turn. This book is dedicated to them.

Notes

Introduction. Topothesia: Planning, Colonialism, and Places in Excess

1. Itself on the centennial of the Crystal Palace exhibition.

2. Southbank Centre, "Festival of Neighbourhood" (London, 2013), http://www.southbankcentre.co.uk/whatson/festivals-series/festival-of-neighbourhood/about-festival-of-neighbourhood-0.

3. These pop-up installations were scattered between the Southbank Centre, Queen Elizabeth Hall, and the Hayward Gallery.

4. Southbank Centre, "Festival of Neighbourhood."

5. "The Edible Bus Stop Presents . . . Roll out the Barrows," Semble, https://semble.org/blog/the-edible-bus-stop-presents-roll-out-the-barrows/. The artists write: "'Roll out the Barrows' TM (RotB) is a playful collective of small wheelbarrow gardens, all lined up and ready for action. Inspired by the forms of roller coasters, the plants flow round the space inhabiting it, animating it & creating a place for interaction and engagement. . . . We are working with London based community groups to come and help plant, tend and nurture the installation throughout the 3-month 'Festival of Neighbourhood'. Each community involved with helping to do so will be awarded a barrow to take back to their plot at the end of the summer to green up their own part of London."

6. This aesthetic of juxtaposition recalls the way that late-Victorian social reformers like Hill and Henrietta Barnett used to juxtapose images of slum squalor with pictures of quaint houses on tree-lined streets to encourage support for their movement. What If: Projects, "Octavia's Orchard" (London: What If: Projects, 2013), http://www.what-if.info/octavias-orchard/.

7. According to their website, these trees were adopted in "Trewlaney Estate (Hackney), Pembury Estate (Hackney), Albert Barnes House (Elephant & Castle), Phipps Bridge Estate (Morden)."

8. What If: Projects, "Octavia's Orchard."

9. This was displayed by another installation at the Festival of Neighborhood, "The Sweepers," which features hedge-like figures sweeping up after the 2011 riots. A different project by the Edible Bus Stop articulates the role the garden plays in such a reconciliation: "Our 'Riot of Colour' installation is a post-apocalyptic interpretation of the after effects of the 2011 London riots. A red telephone box and London taxi have been rioted and left in neglect, but are now reclaimed by nature. The double yellow lines rise up from the street around the tree to form a bench. The wild plants and trees, fruit and vegetables represent re-growth in the community." "Riot of Colour," *The Edible Bus Stop* (blog), https://theediblebusstop.com/riot-of-colour/.

10. "Blair's Speech : Single Mothers Won't Be Forced to Take Work," BBC, 1997, http://www.bbc.co.uk/news/special/politics97/news/06/0602/blair.shtml.

11. Stephen Adams, "General Election 2010: For David Cameron, Battersea Power Station Is a Place Called Hope," *Telegraph*, April 14, 2010.

12. Topothesia is introduced to English from Latin in Henry Peacham's 1577 *The Garden of Eloquence*: "Topothesia, a fained description of a place, that is, when the Orator describeth a place, and yet no such place: As is the house of envy, in the 6. booke of Metamorphosis, the house of sleepe in the eleventh booke, or else when the place is not such a one as is fained to be, as is heaven and hell. In the fourth booke of Aeneidos. This figure is proper to Poets, and is seldom used of Orators: and because the use hereof is rare and of small utilitie in Rhetorike, I do omit both the observation of the use, and Caution." Henry Peacham, *The Garden of Eloquence (1593): A Facsimile Reproduction, with an Introd. by William G. Crane* (Gainesville, FL: Scholars' Facsimiles & Reprints, 1954); Grant Williams, Rory Loughnane, and William E. Engel, eds., "Henry Peacham, The Garden of Eloquence (1593)," in *The Memory Arts in Renaissance England: A Critical Anthology* (Cambridge: Cambridge University Press, 2016), 120–23; "Henry Peachum, The Garden of Eloquence (1593): Schemas, SCHEMATES RHETORICAL, The Third Order, Amplification What It Is, Topothesia," Perseus Digital Library.

13. Ebenezer Howard's *Garden Cities of To-morrow* (1902) is often credited with marking the beginnings of modern urban planning. Ebenezer Howard, *Garden Cities of To-Morrow* (London: Faber and Faber, 1960).

14. John Rieder, *Colonialism and the Emergence of Science Fiction*, illustrated ed. (Middletown, CT: Wesleyan University Press, 2008); Mark C. Jerng, *Racial Worldmaking: The Power of Popular Fiction*, 1st ed. (New York: Fordham University Press, 2017).

15. H. Rider Haggard, *King Solomon's Mines* (New York: Penguin, 2007).

16. Morris's novel was of course a response to Edward Bellamy's socialist speculative novel *Looking Backward*. William Morris, *News from Nowhere and Other Writings*, new ed. (London: Penguin, 1994); Edward Bellamy, *Looking Backward: From 2000 to 1887* (Applewood, 2000).

17. Sami Schalk, for example, argues for a capacious use of *speculative fiction*

to "reference any creative writing in which the rules of reality do not fully apply, including magical realism, utopian and dystopian literature, fantasy, science fiction, voodoo, ghost stories, and hybrid genres." Sami Schalk, *Bodyminds Reimagined: (Dis)Ability, Race, and Gender in Black Women's Speculative Fiction* (Durham, NC: Duke University Press, 2018), 17.

18. Shelley Streeby, "Speculative Writing, Art, and World-Making in the Wake of Octavia E. Butler as Feminist Theory," *Feminist Studies* 46, no. 2 (2020): 4.

19. José Esteban Muñoz, *Cruising Utopia: The Then and There of Queer Futurity* (New York: New York University Press, 2009), 1, 3.

20. As Bloch writes, concrete utopias inhere in imagined perception: "Anticipatory illumination provides this aesthetic significance of happiness at a distance, concentrated into a frame." Qtd. in Ernst Bloch, Jack Zipes, and Frank Mecklenberg, *The Utopian Function of Art and Literature* (1990), 63:xxxix.

21. Fredric Jameson, *Archaeologies of the Future: The Desire Called Utopia and Other Science Fictions* (London: Verso, 2005).

22. Michel Foucault, "Of Other Spaces: Utopias and Heterotopias," in *Architecture Culture 1943–1968*, ed. Joan Ockman (New York: Rizzoli, 1967), 419–26.

23. Terada classifies this as "phenomenophilia," a "bearable and nontragic, yet relentless" dissatisfaction with reality as social fact (24). This dissatisfaction is with the Kantian distinction between appearance (*Erscheinung*) and illusion (*Schein*): "As *Erscheinung*, appearance is replete, lawful, and connotes no attenuation of the intensity of reality of what appears. . . . Unlike *Erscheinung*, *Schein* designates a sensory or cognitive aberrance, a wayward experience that really is an epistemological dead end" (19). Phenomenophilia bears with appearance so as to linger in "illusion." Bloch's conception of *Vor-Schein* (anticipatory illumination) is optimistic in that he claims that *Schein*, as illusion, can still serve as a corrective to what is currently lacking in reality by pointing to a realizable future. Terada and Muñoz, by contrast, focus on the potential inherent in ephemeral perception. Rei Terada, *Looking Away: Phenomenality and Dissatisfaction, Kant to Adorno*, 1st ed. (Cambridge, MA: Harvard University Press, 2009), 19, 24. Qtd. in Bloch, Zipes, and Mecklenberg, *The Utopian Function of Art and Literature*, 63:xxiv.

24. Kara Keeling cites Édouard Glissant's claim of a "right to opacity" that still yields forms of relation but outside the scope of measurement, scale, and the circuits of exchange.

25. Kara Keeling, *Queer Times, Black Futures* (New York: New York University Press, 2019), 36, 86.

26. These investments would only seem to go against the de Certeauian grain of treating the skyscraper as a site of disaffiliation and top-down dominance if one does not take into account its potential as a speculative enclave. Adrienne Brown, *The Black Skyscraper: Architecture and the Perception of Race* (Baltimore, MD: Johns Hopkins University Press, 2017), 144.

27. Walter Benjamin, *The Origin of German Tragic Drama* (London: Verso, 2003); Ann Laura Stoler, *Imperial Debris: On Ruins and Ruination* (Durham, NC:

Duke University Press, 2013); David Lloyd, *Irish Times: Temporalities of Modernity* (Field Day, 2008); Gastón R. Gordillo, *Rubble: The Afterlife of Destruction* (Durham, NC: Duke University Press, 2014).

28. Aimee Bahng, *Migrant Futures: Decolonizing Speculation in Financial Times*, illustrated ed. (Durham, NC: Duke University Press, 2018), 7.

29. Dipesh Chakrabarty, *Provincializing Europe: Postcolonial Thought and Historical Difference, new ed.* (Princeton, NJ: Princeton University Press, 2009).

30. The future is "always-already occupied." Bahng, *Migrant Futures*, 12. She observes that corporate speculative futures congeal into financial products—literal futures, creating knowledge of the not yet by means of extrapolation and projection. Keeling takes note of how Royal Dutch Shell articulates its interventions as an interdisciplinary mode of the speculative. This, she writes, "calls attention to the convergence of the knowledge-production apparatus of a controversial transnational corporation with current academic discourse and practices . . . as a way to engage with the world that might direct attention to what Capital has not (yet) taken into account, interdisciplinary and collaborative scholarship emerges in accordance with the needs of finance capital." Keeling, *Queer Times, Black Futures*, 9–10.

31. Carse and Kneas identify this as the function of the "unbuilt." As they write, "the prefix 'un-' implies absence, but unbuilt and unfinished infrastructures can be surprisingly consequential. Whereas shadow histories recover the past's forgotten possibilities, the present absences heuristic draws attention to what unbuilt and unfinished projects leave behind, including institutional forms, knowledges, altered landscapes, social movements, and new subjectivities." Ashley Carse and David Kneas, "Unbuilt and Unfinished," *Environment and Society* 10, no. 1 (September 1, 2019): 17.

32. Jameson notes that these sorts of practices also create "utopian" enclaves: "To see traces of the Utopian impulse everywhere, as Bloch did, is to naturalize it and to imply that it is somehow rooted in human nature. Attempts to realize Utopia, however, have been historically more intermittent, and we need to limit them even further by now insisting on everything peculiar and eccentric about the fantasy production that gives rise to them. Daydreams, in which whole cities are laid out in the mind, in which constitutions are enthusiastically composed and legal systems endlessly drafted and emended, in which the seating arrangements for festivals and banquets are meditated in detail, and even garbage disposal is as attentively organized as administrative hierarchy, and family and child-care problems are resolved with ingenious new proposals—such fantasies seem distinct enough from erotic daydreams and to warrant special attention in their own right." Jameson, *Archaeologies of the Future*, 10.

33. Similarly, Keeling uses the "term 'futures,' with all of its economic valences intact, in order to underscore that even the imagination might be rendered complicit with Capital." Keeling, *Queer Times, Black Futures*, 85.

34. Matilde Córdoba Azcárate, *Stuck with Tourism: Space, Power, and Labor in Contemporary Yucatan* (Berkeley: University of California Press, 2020), 17.

35. Ross Adams, "Longing for a Greener Present: Neoliberalism and the Eco-City," *Radical Philosophy* 163 (2010).

36. Ann Laura Stoler, *Race and the Education of Desire: Foucault's History of Sexuality and the Colonial Order of Things* (Durham, NC: Duke University Press, 1995); Paul Rabinow, *French Modern: Norms and Forms of the Social Environment* (Cambridge, MA: MIT Press, 1991).

37. Étienne Balibar, *We, the People of Europe? Reflections on Transnational Citizenship* (Princeton, NJ: Princeton University Press, 2009).

38. Leela Gandhi expertly tracks an intellectual genealogy of critical thought on community in relation to both excess and absence. Specifically on utopia, she writes, "Although indispensable, however, the very idea of community (found or elective) presupposes closure: a circular return, ad nauseam, to the tedious logic of the Same. Now what? The arrival, to put it simply, of utopianism; the reappearance of a long forgotten ghost from 1892. For if the very idea of community is, notwithstanding its necessity, from a postmodern perspective inevitably unworkable, inoperative, negative, then we can only speak, under erasure, of an impossible community: perpetually deferred, 'indefinitely perfectible,' yet-to-come. In what remains of this discussion I propose to describe this ingenious compromise as a project of anti-communitarian communitarianism." Chapters 1 and 2 explore the modes of community and anticommunity at stake in late-nineteenth- and early-twentieth-century planning and literature. Leela Gandhi, *Affective Communities: Anticolonial Thought, Fin-de-Siècle Radicalism, and the Politics of Friendship* (Durham, NC: Duke University Press, 2006), 26; Georges Bataille, *The Absence of Myth: Writings on Surrealism* (London: Verso, 2006); Jean-Luc Nancy, *The Inoperative Community* (Minneapolis: University of Minnesota Press, 1991); Maurice Blanchot and Pierre Joris, *The Unavowable Community* (Barrytown, NY: Station Hill, 1983); Benedict Anderson, *Imagined Communities: Reflections on the Origin and Spread of Nationalism* (London: Verso, 2006); Jacques Derrida, *The Politics of Friendship* (London: Verso, 2020); Jacques Rancière, *Disagreement*, trans. Julie Rose, 1st ed. (Minneapolis: University of Minnesota Press, 2005).

39. Lauren Berlant, *Cruel Optimism* (Durham, NC: Duke University Press Books, 2011).

40. Here I follow Neetu Khanna, who is interested in understanding the "conditions of racialization and colonialism through the lens of affect." Neetu Khanna, *The Visceral Logics of Decolonization* (Durham, NC: Duke University Press, 2020), 9.

41. Raymond Williams, *The Country and the City* (New York: Random House, 2013).

42. David Matless, *Landscape and Englishness* (London: Reaktion, 2005).

43. David Lloyd and Paul Thomas, *Culture and the State* (London: Routledge,

2014); David Lloyd, *Under Representation: The Racial Regime of Aesthetics*, 1st ed. (New York: Fordham University Press, 2018).

44. Brenna Bhandar, *Colonial Lives of Property: Law, Land, and Racial Regimes of Ownership* (Durham, NC: Duke University Press Books, 2018), 8.

45. Tania Murray Li, *The Will to Improve: Governmentality, Development, and the Practice of Politics* (Durham, NC: Duke University Press, 2007), 5.

46. Hill and others were specifically influenced by John Ruskin in their work. See Peter Mandler and Susan Pedersen, *After the Victorians: Private Conscience and Public Duty in Modern Britain* (London: Taylor & Francis, 2005); Judith R. Walkowitz, *City of Dreadful Delight: Narratives of Sexual Danger in Late-Victorian London* (Chicago: University of Chicago Press, 2008); James Winter, *Secure from Rash Assault: Sustaining the Victorian Environment* (Berkeley: University of California Press, 2002).

47. Walter L. Creese, *The Search for Environment: The Garden City, Before and After* (Baltimore, MD: Johns Hopkins University Press, n.d.); Standish Meacham, *Regaining Paradise: Englishness and the Early Garden City Movement* (New Haven, CT: Yale University Press, 1999).

48. On this point, Gramscian understandings of hegemony and consent overlap with Rancière's conceptualization of politics as such as calling attention to the "incommensurable at the heart of the distribution of speaking bodies [which] breaks not only with the quality of profits and losses, [but] also ruins in advance the project of the city ordered according to the proportion of the *cosmos* and based on the *arkhê* of the community." This concern is present throughout *Topothesia*. Rancière, *Disagreement*, 19.

49. Uday Singh Mehta, *Liberalism and Empire: A Study in Nineteenth-Century British Liberal Thought* (Chicago: University of Chicago Press, 2018); Bhikhu C. Parekh, "Liberalism and Colonialism: A Critique of Locke and Mill," in *The Decolonization of Imagination: Culture, Knowledge, and Power*, ed. Jan P. Nederveen Pieterse and Bhikhu C. Parekh (Oxford: Oxford University Press, 1997); Jennifer Pitts, *A Turn to Empire: The Rise of Imperial Liberalism in Britain and France* (Princeton, NJ: Princeton University Press, 2009).

50. See Edward W. Said, *Culture and Imperialism* (New York: Vintage, 1994), 48–51; Frederick Cooper and Ann Laura Stoler, *Tensions of Empire: Colonial Cultures in a Bourgeois World* (Berkeley: University of California Press, 1997).

51. Thomas R. Metcalf, *An Imperial Vision: Indian Architecture and Britain's Raj* (Berkeley: University of California Press, 1989).

52. These assessments can be found in Foucauldian accounts of planning, for example Paul Rabinow, who understands planners as "social technicians [who] were articulating a normative . . . modernism." Rabinow, *French Modern*, 13.

53. James C. Scott, *Seeing Like a State: How Certain Schemes to Improve the Human Condition Have Failed* (New Haven, CT: Yale University Press, 1999), 88.

54. Scott, *Seeing Like a State*, 53–57, 93–94.

55. Jane Jacobs, *The Death and Life of Great American Cities*, reissue ed. (New

York: Vintage, 1992); Michel de Certeau, *Practice of Everyday Life*, 1st ed. (Berkeley: University of California Press, 2011).

56. These critiques are more recent echoes of well-known midcentury criticisms of high-modernist planning. Elleke Boehmer and Dominic Davies, eds., *Planned Violence: Post/Colonial Urban Infrastructure, Literature, and Culture* (Cham: Springer, 2018), 3.

57. Chakrabarty, *Provincializing Europe*, 66, 69.

58. Scott notes explicitly that his critique of modernization is not to be read as a valorization of the local. Still, I argue that the wider critique of high modernism positions it against an undertheorized notion of the from-below local.

59. Appel writes that infrastructural time is "haunted by abandonment," as we will see in Part II. Hannah Appel, "Infrastructural Time," in *The Promise of Infrastructure*, ed. Nikhil Anand, Akhil Gupta, and Hannah Appel (Durham, NC: Duke University Press, 2018), 50, 45.

60. Karen Tongson, *Relocations: Queer Suburban Imaginaries* (New York: New York University Press, 2011), 10.

61. Henri Lefebvre, *The Production of Space*, trans. Donald Nicholson-Smith, 1st ed. (Malden, MA: Wiley-Blackwell, 1992); Tim Cresswell, *Place: An Introduction*, 2nd ed. (Malden, MA: Wiley-Blackwell, 2014); Yi-Fu Tuan, *Space and Place: The Perspective of Experience*, reprint ed. (Minneapolis: University of Minnesota Press, 2001).

62. Jaqueline Nassy Brown, *Dropping Anchor, Setting Sail: Geographies of Race in Black Liverpool* (Princeton, NJ: Princeton University Press, 2005); Doreen Massey, *Space, Place, and Gender* (Minneapolis: University of Minnesota Press, 1994); Doreen Massey, *World City* (Cambridge: Polity, 2007).

63. In considering "topothesic" planning in this way, this book differs from work that would like to use an association between particularity and place to ground resistances to the hegemony of capital and colonialism. This hegemony can also employ notions of locality and particularity, even in the service of advancing a particular vision of modernity. *Topothesic* is the adjectival form of *topothesia*, of my own fabrication, that I'll use throughout this book.

64. Much of it formalized by the 1948 Town and Country Planning Act. The creation of social housing predated this act, owing much of its impetus to groups like the London County Council (LCC), who were in general disciples of the garden-city movement. We see this also in the Geddesian plan for London of Patrick Abercrombie.

65. Raymond Unwin, *Nothing Gained by Overcrowding: How the Garden City Type of Development May Benefit Both Owner and Occupier* (Westminster: P. S. King & Son, 1912; Forgotten Books, 2018).

66. Alison Ravetz marks the ways that the drive to build council housing was in part an extension of Victorian social philanthropic attitudes. "To planners, with their core faith that better environments would bring about better societies, it seemed obvious that the necessary ingredients of community life could not flourish—indeed

could not even exist—in slums or obsolescent working-class neighbourhoods." Alison Ravetz, *Council Housing and Culture: The History of a Social Experiment* (London: Taylor & Francis, 2001), 138.

67. Ashley Maher, *Reconstructing Modernism: British Literature, Modern Architecture, and the State* (New York: Oxford University Press, 2020), 90–91; Paula Derdiger, *Reconstruction Fiction: Housing and Realist Literature in Postwar Britain*, 1st ed. (Columbus: Ohio State University Press, 2020), 180. See also Leo Mellor, *Reading the Ruins: Modernism, Bombsites and British Culture* (Cambridge: Cambridge University Press, 2011)

68. An interesting example of this is Jane and Maxwell Fry. The latter would declare in a 1941 *Picture Post* article that "the new Britain must be planned," before both joined Le Corbusier in planning Chandigarh in postindependence India. The Frys were also involved in planning in postcolonial Ghana.

69. As Nancy Kwak documents, this context shaped the politics of housing both in the United States and the United Kingdom. Nancy H. Kwak, *A World of Homeowners: American Power and the Politics of Housing Aid*, Historical Studies of Urban America (Chicago: University of Chicago Press, 2018), 27–35.

70. Within its own corporate idiom, these might be described as "actors," "stakeholders," "users," etc.

71. Paul Gilroy, *Postcolonial Melancholia* (New York: Columbia University Press, 2005).

72. Ranajit Guha, ed., *A Subaltern Studies Reader, 1986–1995*, 1st ed. (Minneapolis: University of Minnesota Press, 1997).

73. Ian Baucom, *Out of Place: Englishness, Empire, and the Locations of Identity* (Princeton, NJ: Princeton University Press, 1999); Jed Esty, *A Shrinking Island: Modernism and National Culture in England* (Princeton, NJ: Princeton University Press, 2003); Paul Gilroy, *The Black Atlantic: Modernity and Double-Consciousness*, reissue ed. (Cambridge, MA: Harvard University Press, 1993); Homi K. Bhabha, *The Location of Culture*, 2nd ed. (London: Routledge, 2004).

74. Robert J. C. Young, *Colonial Desire: Hybridity in Theory, Culture, and Race*, 1st ed. (Abingdon: Routledge, 1995).

75. Jodi A. Byrd, *The Transit of Empire: Indigenous Critiques of Colonialism* (Minneapolis: University of Minnesota Press, 2011); Lisa Lowe, *The Intimacies of Four Continents*, illustrated ed. (Durham, NC: Duke University Press, 2015).

76. AbdouMaliq Simone, *For the City Yet to Come: Changing African Life in Four Cities*, illustrated ed. (Durham, NC: Duke University Press, 2004).

77. Aamir R. Mufti, *Forget English! Orientalisms and World Literatures*, reprint ed. (Cambridge, MA: Harvard University Press, 2018); Emily Apter, *Against World Literature: On the Politics of Untranslatability*, 1st ed. (London: Verso, 2013).

78. Saskia Sassen, *The Global City: New York, London, Tokyo* (Princeton, NJ: Princeton University Press, 2013).

79. As with all periodizations, this is a topic of considerable debate given, for example, the work of British and continental architects in remaking the nineteenth-

century city. Less considered, as I will argue, is the influence of town planning in British colonies. Nevertheless, Howard's garden-city ideal becomes a common reference point organizing professional planning in the twentieth century.

80. As Marxist historians have noted, Morris struggled with the political possibilities and limitations of design. E. P. Thompson and Peter Linebaugh, *William Morris: Romantic to Revolutionary*, 1st ed. (Oakland, CA: PM, 2011).

81. Here I examine not only his prolific writing, including his planning reports and documents for towns in India, but also his extensive correspondence with the poet Rabindranath Tagore, particularly regarding their ideas about education and the planning of Santiniketan and other universities.

82. Rob Imrie, Loretta Lees, and Mike Raco, *Regenerating London: Governance, Sustainability, and Community in a Global City* (London: Routledge, 2009).

83. Loretta Lees, Tom Slater, and Elvin Wyly, *Gentrification* (London: Routledge, 2008); Neil Smith, "Gentrification, the Frontier, and the Restructuring of Urban Space," in *Gentrification of the City*, ed. Neil Smith and Peter Williams (Winchester Place: Allen & Unwin, 1986); Neil Smith, "New Globalism, New Urbanism: Gentrification as Global Urban Strategy," *Antipode* 34, no. 3 (2002); Kenneth A. Gould and Tammy L. Lewis, *Green Gentrification: Urban Sustainability and the Struggle for Environmental Justice*, Routledge Equity, Justice, and the Sustainable City (London: Routledge, 2016); Noah Quastel, "Political Ecologies of Gentrification," *Urban Geography* 30, no. 7 (2013): 694–725.

84. Richard H. Grove, *Green Imperialism: Colonial Expansion, Tropical Island Edens, and the Origins of Environmentalism, 1600–1860* (Cambridge: Cambridge University Press, 1996).

85. Cindy Isenhour, Gary McDonogh, and Melissa Checker, eds., *Sustainability in the Global City*, New Directions in Sustainability and Society (Cambridge: Cambridge University Press, 2014); Gavin Poynter, "The 2012 Olympic Games and the Reshaping of East London"; and Paul Watt, "Social Housing and Regeneration in London," both in *Regenerating London: Governance, Sustainability, and Community in a Global City*, ed. R. Imrie, L. Lees, and M. Raco (London: Taylor & Francis, 2008).

86. For a critique of the "metronormativity" of this figuration, see Tongson, *Relocations*.

87. Lilly Irani, *Chasing Innovation: Making Entrepreneurial Citizens in Modern India* (Princeton, NJ: Princeton University Press, 2019).

88. Brown, *The Black Skyscraper*, 125.

1. Garden Cities: The Art and Craft of Making Place in Edwardian Britain

1. Nick Clegg and Eric Pickles, "Locally-Led Garden Cities," Department for Communities and Local Government, March 2016.

2. Earmarked in a time of government austerity.

3. As the planners write, "Where London meets the Garden of England, on

the banks of the River Thames, Ebbsfleet exploits its strategic location to continue the tradition of great placemaking in the UK; combining the best of urban and rural living and building on the ethos and pioneering spirit of Georgian, Victorian and Edwardian planned communities to deliver a new benchmark for 21st century development including up to 15,000 high quality new homes." Ebbsfleet Development Corporation, "The Vision," https://ebbsfleetdc.org.uk/the-vision/.

4. Patrick Barkham, "Britain's Housing Crisis: Are Garden Cities the Answer?," *Guardian*, October 1, 2014, https://www.theguardian.com/politics/2014/oct/01/britains-housing-crisis-are-gaden-cities-the-answer-ebbsfleet-kent-green-belt.

5. Jonathan Glancey, "Do We All Dream of Life in a Garden City?," *Telegraph*, November 22, 2012.

6. Planning thus attempts to foreclose the possibility of dissensus. Jacques Rancière, *Disagreement*, trans. Julie Rose, 1st ed. (Minneapolis: University of Minnesota Press, 2005).

7. For example, the epigram of Zadie Smith's NW (see Chapter 5) makes reference to Morris's political fable *A Dream of John Ball*. For her (postcolonial) characters, the political ideals of English radicalism persist even as paths to its realization are closed down or co-opted by liberalism and its ideologies.

8. Marie Kondo, *The Life-Changing Magic of Tidying Up: The Japanese Art of Decluttering and Organizing* (Clarkson Potter/Ten Speed, 2014).

9. A later note by F. J. Osborn makes clear Wakefield is actually favorably quoting Dr. Hind (Dean of Carlisle) from his work *Thoughts on Secondary Punishment*. Ebenezer Howard, *Garden Cities of To-morrow* (London: Faber and Faber, 1960), 119–20.

10. "Rank," suggesting an obscene excess, *OED Online*, https://www.oed.com/view/Entry/158048.

11. Wakefield was not only an advocate of "planned colonization for the poor" but also a supporter of some of the first master-planned colonies, Adelaide and Christchurch in Australia, designed by William Light. William Beinart and Lotte Hughes, *Environment and Empire* (Oxford: Oxford University Press, 2007).

12. Howard, *Garden Cities of To-morrow*, 119–20.

13. From J. A. Hobson's discussion of both farm and penal colonies in *Problem of the Unemployed*: "An establishment in which persons who are otherwise unemployed or unemployable are engaged to work or are trained for some occupation or trade." "Colony, n.," *OED Online*, https://www.oed.com/view/Entry/36547.

14. They note that "in nineteenth-century South Africa or turn-of-the-century East Africa, the British used a vocabulary to describe Africans remarkably like that used at home to describe the lowest elements of the class order, 'the residuum,' the degraded class of criminals and casual laborers of Victorian cities." The mobility of these discourses complicates any distinction between an inward-facing national identity and an outward-facing imperial identity. Frederick Cooper and Ann Laura Stoler, *Tensions of Empire: Colonial Cultures in a Bourgeois World* (Berkeley: University of

California Press, 1997), 9, 27; David Armitage, *The Ideological Origins of the British Empire* (Cambridge: Cambridge University Press, 2000), 19.

15. This is perhaps best epitomized by J. S. Mill, the impassioned leader of the Jamaica committee who nonetheless advocated for a benevolent, preferably privately run empire and worked toward its construction, like his father, as an employee of the East India Company. It is in fact through Mill's discussion of a "vent for surplus population" that Howard favorably encounters Wakefield. John Stuart Mill, *The Collected Works of John Stuart Mill*, vol. 3: *Principles of Political Economy Part II* (Online Library of Liberty, 1848), 967; Bhikhu C. Parekh, "Liberalism and Colonialism: A Critique of Locke and Mill," in *The Decolonization of Imagination: Culture, Knowledge, and Power*, ed. Jan P. Nederveen Pieterse and Bhikhu C. Parekh (Oxford: Oxford University Press, 1997), 95; Jennifer Pitts, *A Turn to Empire: The Rise of Imperial Liberalism in Britain and France* (Princeton, NJ: Princeton University Press, 2009), 136; Andrew Sartori, "The British Empire and Its Liberal Mission," *Journal of Modern History* 78, no. 3 (September 1, 2006): 642.

16. Specifically, "Victorian liberals looked to three values in particular when measuring moral progress—the values of competition, cultivation and domesticity. Or to put it another way, they sought to make mutually supportive the market economy, the education of the people, and the bourgeois family." Peter Mandler and Susan Pedersen, *After the Victorians: Private Conscience and Public Duty in Modern Britain* (London: Taylor & Francis, 2005), 4.

17. For Mill, "Liberal colonialism thus constitutes citizens and civil society in explicit opposition to the idle, irrational, custom-bound 'Indian' who may be transformed into a citizen but only if he/she gives up his/her 'customs' or 'ways' and instead becomes industrious and rational" (492). Uday Singh Mehta points out that liberals were generally absorbed with empire. Barbara Arneil, "Liberal Colonialism, Domestic Colonies, and Citizenship," *History of Political Thought* 33 (2012): 492; Uday Singh Mehta, *Liberalism and Empire: A Study in Nineteenth-Century British Liberal Thought* (Chicago: University of Chicago Press, 2018), 6.

18. It was believed that the "growing concentration of the population in congested, unhealthy cities was leading to dangerous social unrest and physical and social degeneration of the nation," adding that "after visiting the slum areas of east London in 1895, Cecil Rhodes proclaimed that 'if you want to avoid civil war you must become imperialists.'" Frederick Aalen, "English Origins," in *Garden City: Past, Present, and Future*, ed. Stephen Ward (London: Taylor & Francis, 1992), 37.

19. Both liberal land reform within Britain and colonial land logic in India advocated for the cultivation, improvement, and "utilization of land," which had "an economic and moral purpose." Jeremy Burchardt, *Paradise Lost: Rural Idyll and Social Change in England since 1800* (London: I. B. Tauris, 2002), 80–84; Beinart and Hughes, *Environment and Empire*, 13.

20. Kalliney notes that "no one in a position of authority, however, questioned the fundamental promise that the urban poor constituted a cancerous, foreign body in the heart of the metropole." Peter J. Kalliney, *Cities of Affluence and Anger: A*

Literary Geography of Modern Englishness (Charlottesville: University of Virginia Press, 2007), 43; Stuart Hall et al., *Policing the Crisis: Mugging, the State, and Law and Order* (Basingstoke: Macmillan, 1978), 189.

21. A play on Henry Morton Stanley's *In Darkest Africa*, also published in 1890. William Booth, *In Darkest England and the Way Out* (Cambridge: Cambridge University Press, 2014); Henry Morton Stanley, *In Darkest Africa* (LULU, 2010).

22. *In Darkest England* makes substantial rhetorical use of the extended simile: "Darkest England, like Darkest Africa . . ."; "Just as in Darkest Africa . . ."; etc. Booth, *In Darkest England and the Way Out*, 14; Cooper and Stoler, *Tensions of Empire*, 247.

23. The figure of the prostitute was the "central spectacle in a set of urban encounters and fantasies." Judith R. Walkowitz, *City of Dreadful Delight: Narratives of Sexual Danger in Late-Victorian London* (Chicago: University of Chicago Press, 2008), 21; Seth Koven, *Slumming* (Princeton, NJ: Princeton University Press, 2004), 59, 185.

24. Kalliney, *Cities of Affluence and Anger*, 42–43.

25. James Winter, *Secure from Rash Assault: Sustaining the Victorian Environment* (Berkeley: University of California Press, 2002), 19.

26. "The causes of a degraded lifestyle were assumed to originate in the physical decay of the slums. Provide a healthier home, and spiritual and moral improvement would be secure; without this, any amelioration would be temporary, with backsliding inevitable." Mervyn Miller, *Hampstead Garden Suburb: Arts and Crafts Utopia?* (History Press, 2006), 15; Standish Meacham, *Toynbee Hall and Social Reform, 1880–1914: The Search for Community* (New Haven, CT: Yale University Press, 1987), 23.

27. Those most involved in this endeavor were Henry Lever, George Cadbury, and Joseph Rowntree. Model villages like Thornton Manor, Port Sunlight, Bournville, and New Earswick were all built in a "rural idiom . . . replete with medieval symbolism and an idealized version of the rural vernacular (visible for example in the half-timbered cottages and the thatched shelter on the village green)." Later, Lever, Cadbury, and Rowntree were all members of the Garden City Association. Burchardt, *Paradise Lost*, 62; Standish Meacham, *Regaining Paradise: Englishness and the Early Garden City Movement* (New Haven, CT: Yale University Press, 1999).

28. "Environmentalism by century's end had superseded the 'time honored doctrines of original sin, grace, election and reprobation' as an explanation for behavior and character." Stanley Buder, *Visionaries and Planners: The Garden City Movement and the Modern Community* (Oxford: Oxford University Press, 1990), 70.

29. Many social reformers were women, and charity work reflected both increasing roles for women and a class-inflected investment in their motherly and domestic qualities for the sake of cultivating the poor. Walkowitz, *City of Dreadful Delight*, 63.

30. Meacham, *Toynbee Hall and Social Reform*, 40, 84.

31. "A settlement in a new country; a body of people who settle in a new locality, forming a community subject to or connected with their parent state; the community so formed, consisting of the original settlers and their descendants and successors, as long as the connection with the parent state is kept up." "Colony, n.," *OED Online*, http://www.oed.com/view/Entry/36547.

32. "Plantation, n.," *OED Onli e*, http://www.oed.com/view/Entry/145169; Robert K. Home, *Of Planting and Planning: The Making of British Colonial Cities* (London: Taylor & Francis, 1996), 2.

33. Peter Gould writes: "The 'surplus labor' in the cities would be reduced and would relieve the demands for employment and accommodation." Moreover, poor law would shift from punishment to education and training. This led to the creation of the Home Colonization Society in 1887 by H. W. Mills. Arneil, "Liberal Colonialism, Domestic Colonies, and Citizenship," 497; Peter C. Gould, *Early Green Politics: Back to Nature, Back to the Land, and Socialism in Britain, 1880–1900* (Harvester, 1988), 124–28.

34. To this end, Barnett organized trips to the countryside for East End children. In 1903, 34,000 children were given countryside holidays through the Children's Country Holiday Fund. Micky Watkins, *Henrietta Barnett in Whitechapel: Her First Fifty Years* (London: Hampstead Garden Suburb Archive Trust, 2005), 58, 61.

35. This included everything from large-scale projects like public parks to small constructions like window flower boxes. Winter writes that George Godwin, editor of *The Builder*, thought that "love of flowers was building bridges across the class divides." Other architects thought similarly. Sydney Smirke "was of the opinion that working-class horticulturalists stayed out of pubs and were never lazy," while Samuel Broome advocated the planting of chrysanthemums, which he called "essentially a working man's plant . . . ideally suited to London's climate." Qtd. in Winter, *Secure from Rash Assault*, 196–202.

36. For example, Maltz draws attention to figures like "Margaret Harkness [cousin of Beatrice Webb, who] celebrated the unencumbered female middle-class slum-worker through a fictional figure who lives in an all-women residence in a room 'furnished with Japanese ware, art muslin, and the various nick-knacks that lady students and their consoeurie gather.'" Diana Maltz, *British Aestheticism and the Urban Working Classes, 1870–1900: Beauty for the People* (Springer, 2005), 1, 11.

37. These include many land- and architecture-preservation groups, including the Society for the Protection of Ancient Buildings, founded by William Morris and others in 1877, which claimed that "the England that we love is the England of old towns, tilled fields, little river towns, farms, churches and cottages." Qtd. in Michael H. Lang, *Designing Utopia: John Ruskin's Urban Vision for Britain and America* (Black Rose, 1999), 108; David Matless, *Landscape and Englishness* (London: Reaktion, 2005).

38. Howard first published his vision in *To-morrow: A Peaceful Path to Real Reform* in 1898 before publishing *Garden Cities of To-morrow* as a revised manuscript in 1902.

39. Howard, *Garden Cities of To-morrow*, 42.

40. Similarly, "the true remedy for capitalist oppression where it exists, is not the strike of no work but the strike of true work, and against this last blow the oppressor has no weapon," "nor is the scheme to be regarded as a socialistic experiment." Howard, *Garden Cities of To-morrow*, 90, 108, 114.

41. See Paul Rabinow, *French Modern: Norms and Forms of the Social Environment* (Cambridge, MA: MIT Press, 1991), 257; Peter Hall and Colin Ward, *Sociable Cities: The 21st-Century Reinvention of the Garden City* (London: Routledge, 2014); John Simonds, *Garden Cities 21: Creating a Livable Urban Environment* (New York: McGraw-Hill, 1994).

42. Peter Bailey, *Leisure and Class in Victorian England: Rational Recreation and the Contest for Control, 1830–1885* (London: Routledge, 2014), 14–15.

43. All strong proponents of the garden-city movement.

44. Howard, *Garden Cities of To-morrow*, 2.

45. Jameson identifies the "small-scale model" as a limited means to represent the social totality within this enclave. Fredric Jameson, *Archaeologies of the Future: The Desire Called Utopia and Other Science Fictions* (London: Verso, 2005), 16, 14.

46. Howard, *Garden Cities of To-morrow*, 44.

47. Thus, for example, chapter epigrams juxtapose quotations from Blake and Goethe with reports from contemporary news articles.

48. The "archaic charm" of these images is similar to the ways that gentrification aesthetics forms through a kind of kitsch appreciation and reuse of previously in-vogue styles (late-Victorian iconography, for example). See Chapters 4 and 5. Hall and Ward, *Sociable Cities*, 17.

49. The image of the key appears in the earlier 1898 version of the text.

50. Howard writes, "I have shown how it can be achieved . . . in a manner which need cause no ill-will, strife, or bitterness; is constitutional; requires no revolutionary legislation; and involves no direct attack upon vested interests." Howard, *Garden Cities of To-morrow*, 131. Garden-city planners and reformers "believed that the great political debate between capitalist and socialist, whatever the outcome, was irrelevant to thinking creatively about urban living." Hellen Meller, *The Ideal City* (Leicester: Leicester University Press, 1979), 21.

51. The image also includes the final stanza from "The Present Crisis," an abolitionist poem by the American James Russell Lowell. Howard does not elaborate on how this poem is related; implicitly, he seems to be comparing the garden city to the abolition of slavery.

52. What Lloyd and Thomas call an "ethical habit of generalization of particular experiences." David Lloyd and Paul Thomas, *Culture and the State* (London: Routledge, 2014), 77.

53. Howard, *Garden Cities of To-morrow*, 48. This image is accompanied by text in the center of these three magnets reading "The People, Where Will They Go." The magnet thus replaces the metaphor of the safety valve, in which the excess

population is simply dissipated into the colonies. Howard, *Garden Cities of To-morrow*, 57.

54. Howard, *Garden Cities of To-morrow*, 48.

55. Similar to the figure of the female reformer "as a social mother caring for all the strays and waifs who crossed her path." Mandler and Pedersen, *After the Victorians*, 40; Howard, *Garden Cities of To-morrow*, 47.

56. Elizabeth Outka, *Consuming Traditions: Modernity, Modernism, and the Commodified Authentic* (Oxford: Oxford University Press, 2009), 7.

57. The garden-city architect Raymond Unwin wrote that "we shall find that modern suburbs specially offend in coming between." Qtd. in Miller, *Hampstead Garden Suburb*, 51. More strongly, Thomas Sharpe would later write that "the strong, masculine virility of the town; the softer beauty, the richness, the fruitfulness of that mother of men, the countryside, will be debased into one sterile, hermaphroditic beastliness. The crying need of the moment is the re-establishment of the ancient antithesis. The town is town: the country is country: black and white: male and female." Qtd. in Matless, *Landscape and Englishness*, 56.

58. By contrast, in Letchworth, Meacham writes, "Factory works experience the tensions of industrial relations that were not markedly different at Letchworth than those in any other English town or city. . . . A member of the militant Church Socialist Union, who visited Letchworth in 1913, declared with some truth that it was 'no more than Leeds whitewashed. In Letchworth, the same system obtained, but it happens to be painted in more beautiful colours. There is the same division of classes, the same separation of members of the human race into masters and men." Mandler and Pedersen, *After the Victorians*, 95.

59. Indeed the diagram of the garden city was much more influential than the plan for the first garden city, at Letchworth in 1903, that was produced by the architects Raymond Unwin and Barry Parker. That being said, the gap between the plan and the city can clearly never be closed, such that plans also have an expressive function.

60. Howard, *Garden Cities of To-morrow*, 76.

61. Phillip Steadman has a detailed account of the ways in which biological analogy informed the aesthetics and morality of nineteenth-century architecture. Philip Steadman, *The Evolution of Designs: Biological Analogy in Architecture and the Applied Arts* (London: Routledge, 1979).

62. "Homes for waifs," "home for inebriates," etc.

63. The aim being to "change the nature of society itself by demonstrating an alternative example within it." Hall and Ward, *Sociable Cities*, 42.

64. Howard, *Garden Cities of To-morrow*, 125.

65. "Howard intended to steer a middle course not only between town and country but also between reform and revolution . . . idealism and realism were to be reconciled, as were socialism and capitalism." Gould, *Early Green Politics*, 84.

66. "Howard's plans were also part of an early effort to imagine England as a

postimperial nation. . . . No longer assured of the relatively peaceful dispersal of surplus people and capital through the imperial system, the English were beginning to turn inward, concentrating on self-sufficiency and national ingenuity." Kalliney, *Cities of Affluence and Anger*, 39–47.

67. Mehta, *Liberalism and Empire*, 12.

68. John Freeman-Moir, "Crafting Experience: William Morris, John Dewey, and Utopia," *Utopian Studies* 22, no. 2 (2011): 203.

69. Ashbee was active in the East End reform movement, for example in organizing educational events in Samuel Barnett's Whitechapel Art Gallery or in proposing the creation of a "temple of arts and crafts" for such purposes. He would later work in interwar Palestine alongside figures like Patrick Geddes (see Chapter 2). Lang, *Designing Utopia*, 177; Volker M. Welter, *Biopolis: Patrick Geddes and the City of Life* (Cambridge, MA: MIT Press, 2002), 165–66.

70. Welter, *Biopolis*, 140.

71. Michelle Weinroth, *Reclaiming William Morris: Englishness, Sublimity, and the Rhetoric of Dissent* (Montreal: McGill-Queen's University Press, 1996), 8.

72. Garden cities were a way of using "commerce and advertising" to help fund the "utopian vision," though it remains questionable what is still utopian about that vision except for the prevalence of trees. Outka, *Consuming Traditions*, 30.

73. William Morris, *News from Nowhere and Other Writings* (London: Penguin, 1994), 105, emphasis added.

74. Morris, *News from Nowhere*, 106.

75. Raymond Williams, *The Country and the City* (New York: Random House, 2013), 43.

76. David Rodgers, qtd. in Regenia Gagnier, "Morris's Ethics, Cosmopolitanism, and Globalisation," *Journal of William Morris Studies* (Summer/Winter 2005): 11. See also Anna Vaninskaya, *William Morris and the Idea of Community: Romance, History and Propaganda, 1880–1914* (Edinburgh: Edinburgh University Press, 2010), 47.

77. Vaninskaya, *William Morris and the Idea of Community*, 45.

78. Qtd. in Elizabeth Carolyn Miller, "William Morris, Print Culture, and the Politics of Aestheticism," *Modernism/Modernity* 15, no. 3 (December 3, 2008): 488.

79. Boos contends that the aesthetics of a place like Letchworth could sway the minds of philanthropic capitalists. George Orwell was much less sanguine, noting while in Letchworth that for the majority "a crank meant socialist and socialist meant a crank": "every fruit-juice drinker, nudist, sandal-wearer, sex-maniac, Quaker, 'Nature Cure' quack, pacifist and feminist in England." George Orwell, *The Road to Wigan Pier* (New York: Harcourt, 1958), 174; Florence S. Boos, "'News from Nowhere' and Garden Cities: Morris's Utopia and Nineteenth-Century Town-Design," *Journal of Pre-Raphaelite Studies* 7, no. 2 (1998): 12–13.

80. Leela Gandhi, *Affective Communities: Anticolonial Thought, Fin-de-Siècle Radicalism, and the Politics of Friendship* (Durham, NC: Duke University Press Books, 2006), 6.

81. Gandhi, *Affective Communities*, 21–26.

82. Gandhi, *Affective Communities*, 26.
83. Butler, qtd. in Gandhi, *Affective Communities*, 31.
84. Jacques Derrida, *The Politics of Friendship* (London: Verso, 2020), 34, 63.
85. David Latham reads *Nowhere* as a "reclamation of the home colony from imperialist appropriation." However, the home colony was a key part of an imperial apparatus that sought to modernize itself through aesthetic planning. David Latham, "*News from Nowhere* as Autoethnography: A Future History of 'Home Colonization,'" in *Writing on the Image: Reading William Morris* (Toronto: University of Toronto Press, 2007), 87.
86. As such, he writes that "what is at stake in the concept of a community and whether the community, no matter if it has existed or not, does not in the end always posit the absence of community." Maurice Blanchot and Pierre Joris, *The Unavowable Community* (Barrytown, NY: Station Hill, 1983), 17, 7, 3.
87. Morris, *News from Nowhere and Other Writings*, 204.
88. Morris, *News from Nowhere and Other Writings*, 57.
89. Morris, *News from Nowhere and Other Writings*, 161–62.
90. Morris, *News from Nowhere and Other Writings*, 159.
91. Morris, *News from Nowhere and Other Writings*, 53.
92. Morris, *News from Nowhere and Other Writings*, 57.
93. Morris, *News from Nowhere and Other Writings*, 169.
94. Qtd. in Rob Breton, "WorkPerfect: William Morris and the Gospel of Work," *Utopian Studies* 13, no. 1 (2002): 50.
95. Qtd. in Ruth Kinna, "William Morris: Art, Work, and Leisure," *Journal of the History of Ideas* 61, no. 3 (2000): 505.
96. Kinna, "William Morris," 495.
97. However, see Patrick Parrinder, "Eugenics and Utopia: Sexual Selection from Galton to Morris," *Utopian Studies* 8, no. 2 (1997): 8.
98. E. P. Thompson and Peter Linebaugh, *William Morris: Romantic to Revolutionary*, 1st ed. (Oakland, CA: PM, 2011); Martin Delveaux, "'O Me! O Me! How I Love the Earth': William Morris's *News from Nowhere* and the Birth of Sustainable Society," *Contemporary Justice Review* 8, no. 2 (June 1, 2005): 131–46.
99. See Miller, "William Morris, Print Culture, and the Politics of Aestheticism," 492.
100. Including through comic dystopia, as in the 2013 film *The World's End*, about a horrific garden-city pub crawl. Edgar Wright, dir., *The World's End* (Universal Pictures, Focus Features, Relativity Media, 2013).

2. Planning as Imperial Cultivation in the Work of Patrick Geddes

1. Amelia Dorothy Defries, *The Interpreter Geddes: The Man and His Gospel* (London: Boni & Liveright, 1928), 168.
2. Patrick Geddes, "Civics as Applied Sociology, Part I," in *The Ideal City*, ed. Helen E. Meller (Leicester: Leicester University Press, 1979), 79.

3. Martin Beattie, "Sir Patrick Geddes and Barra Bazaar: Competing Visions, Ambivalence, and Contradiction," *Journal of Architecture* 9, no. 2 (2004): 133.

4. Qtd. in Jaqueline Tyrwhitt, *Patrick Geddes in India* (London: Lund Humphries, 1947), 22.

5. Noah Hysler-Rubin, *Patrick Geddes and Town Planning: A Critical View* (London: Routledge, 2011), 109.

6. Hysler-Rubin, *Patrick Geddes and Town Planning*, 36.

7. Patrick Geddes, *Cities in Evolution* (London: Williams & Norgate, 1915), 88.

8. And later writes, "When they asked Dante, 'Where didst thou see Hell?' he answered, 'In the city around me,' as indeed the whole structure and story of the Inferno shows." Geddes, *Cities in Evolution*, 91, 92, 87.

9. Geddes, *Cities in Evolution*, 404.

10. Patrick Geddes's son, Arthur, was a frequent visitor to Shantiniketan and translated some of Tagore's songs for the Edinburgh Festival in 1961. Murdo J. S. Macdonald, "Education, Visual Art and Cultural Revival: Tagore, Geddes, Nivedita, and Coomaraswamy," *Gitanjali & Beyond* 1, no. 1 (November 9, 2016): 52. There are in fact several similarities between Geddes's worldview and Tagore's universal humanism in general. "The humanism that Tagore admired so much in Geddes . . . is evident in these endeavours to bring about communal and racial harmony through educational institutions with universal programmes." Bashabi Fraser, ed., *A Meeting of Two Minds* (Edinburgh: Word Power, 2008), 43, 21.

11. William Beinart and Lotte Hughes, *Environment and Empire* (Oxford: Oxford University Press, 2007), 166.

12. Planners wanted "not only England but all parts of the Empire to be covered with Garden Cities." "Geddes got many commissions of this type [In India], and earned more money from them than he had in his life before, writing between 1915 and 1919 a total of fifty reports on Indian cities." Robert K. Home, "Town Planning and Garden Cities in the British Colonial Empire, 1910–1940," *Planning Perspectives* 5, no. 1 (January 1, 1990): 32; Robert K. Home, *Of Planting and Planning: The Making of British Colonial Cities* (Taylor & Francis, 1996), 150.

13. On the planning of New Delhi, see Thomas R. Metcalf, *An Imperial Vision: Indian Architecture and Britain's Raj* (Berkeley: University of California Press, 1989); Jane Ridley, "Edwin Lutyens, New Delhi, and the Architecture of Imperialism," *Journal of Imperial and Commonwealth History* 26, no. 2 (May 1998): 67–83.

14. "Only in Mandatory Palestine did Ashbee get the chance to realize [utopia] in full. Ashbee was the second British planner working in Jerusalem after its occupation by the British in 1917." Noah Hysler-Rubin, "Arts & Crafts and the Great City: Charles Robert Ashbee in Jerusalem," *Planning Perspectives* 21, no. 4 (2006): 348.

15. Liora Bigon and Yossi Katz, eds., *Garden Cities and Colonial Planning: Transnationality and Urban Ideas in Africa and Palestine* (Manchester: Manchester University Press, 2014), 15–16.

16. This influence extended beyond the United Kingdom to "those who converged in London and Paris to re-establish pre-war ties in the context of the new

UN organizations then being established" and included figures like Albert Mayor, the American architect advisor to Jawaharlal Nehru. Ellen Shoshkes, "Jaqueline Tyrwhitt Translates Patrick Geddes for Post World War Two Planning," *Landscape and Urban Planning* 166 (2017): 17.

17. Particularly around two figures: the social reformer as caretaker and the prostitute as object of reform. Judith R. Walkowitz, *City of Dreadful Delight: Narratives of Sexual Danger in Late-Victorian London* (Chicago: University of Chicago Press, 2008), 55; Seth Koven, *Slumming* (Princeton, NJ: Princeton University Press, 2004), 40.

18. Similarly influential for Geddes in *Cities* are "Mr Cadbury's successful village of Bournville, with its generously designed Trust, and Sir William Lever's striking achievement at Port Sunlight." Further, "Eutopian" suggests the "good place," rather than the unrealizable "no place" of utopia, as he describes in report for Indore. Geddes, *Cities in Evolution*, 154; Patrick Geddes, "Town Planning towards City Development. A Report to the Durbar of Indore. By Patrick Geddes" (Indore: Holkar state printing press, 1918), 14.

19. Geddes, *Cities in Evolution*, 60.

20. Geddes, *Cities in Evolution*, 117.

21. Geddes, *Cities in Evolution*, 122, 124.

22. Geddes, *Cities in Evolution*, 295.

23. "Geddes habitually considers his subject matters as a collection of classifiable types. Each single plant represents not only itself but also its species and the evolution of that species; knowledge about a specific plant is at the same time a reference to the species." Similarly, in his exhibitions of city planning, "each artifact or exhibit derived from the local survey refers not only to its own source or locality but to all similar things elsewhere." Volker M. Welter, *Biopolis: Patrick Geddes and the City of Life* (Cambridge, MA: MIT Press, 2002), 130, 131.

24. Geddes, *Cities in Evolution*, 396–97, 254.

25. Naveeda Khan, "Geddes in India: Town Planning, Plant Sentience, and Cooperative Evolution," *Environment and Planning D: Society and Space* 29, no. 5 (2011): 843.

26. Home, *Of Planting and Planning*, 150.

27. Influenced by Henri Bergson's idea of the *élan vital*.

28. Frederick Cooper and Ann Laura Stoler, *Tensions of Empire: Colonial Cultures in a Bourgeois World* (Berkeley: University of California Press, 1997), 31.

29. Khan, "Geddes in India," 848.

30. There were certainly examples of imperial top-down planning, particularly Edwin Lutyens's work in Delhi in 1911. Lutyens was more interested in creating garden-city apartheids for Anglo-Indian officials. Ridley, "Edwin Lutyens, New Delhi, and the Architecture of Imperialism," 69; Metcalf, *An Imperial Vision*; A. D. King, *The Bungalow: The Production of a Global Culture* (Oxford: Oxford University Press, 1984).

31. Geddes was himself "more aware of the relationship between Indian social

practices and the urban landscape than British colonial officials had ever been. He wanted to encourage the revival of customs and traditions which prompted a clean environment." Home, *Of Planting and Planning*, 150. Geddes, *Cities in Evolution*, 240; Garth Andrew Myers and Makame Ali Muhajir, "The Afterlife of the Lanchester Plan: Zanzibar as the Garden City of Tomorrow," in *Garden Cities and Colonial Planning: Transnationality and Urban Ideas in Africa and Palestine*, ed. Liora Bigon (Manchester: Manchester University Press, 2014), 103.

32. Geddes, "Town Planning towards City Development," 3.

33. The goal of Geddes's reimagined Diwali in Indore was to "attack was the condition of neurasthenia, or depression, amongst the people which was caused by hostile urban and industrial conditions." Meller, *Patrick Geddes*, 256; see also Khan, "Geddes in India," 844.

34. Geddes's philosophy of localism was heavily inspired by the French sociologist Frédéric le Play. Qtd in Home, *Of Planting and Planning*, 144; Paul Rabinow, *French Modern: Norms and Forms of the Social Environment* (Cambridge, MA: MIT Press, 1991), 88.

35. In one instance, Geddes was hired to produce a report for the industrial city of Jamshedpur after a series of labor strikes and riots. Meller notes that "the Indian workers, however, wanted more money, not English-style suburbs to lie in." Meller, *Patrick Geddes*, 226.

36. Pierre Clavel and Robert Young, "'Civics': Patrick Geddes's Theory of City Development," *Landscape and Urban Planning* 166 (2017): 37, 38; see also in the same issue Robert F. Young and Pierre Clavel, "Planning Living Cities: Patrick Geddes' Legacy in the New Millennium," *Landscape and Urban Planning* 166 (2017): 1–3.

37. Volker Welter explains at length the theoretical meaning of his thinking-machine diagrams. The point here, however, is that these diagrams are numerous, holistic in intention, yet exceedingly complex and idiosyncratic. In particular, Geddes was fond of symmetrical forms for many of these diagrams: squares, hexagons, octagons. Welter, *Biopolis*.

38. Philip Steadman details the history of biological analogy in architecture and design. Philip Steadman, *The Evolution of Designs: Biological Analogy in Architecture and the Applied Arts* (London: Routledge, 1979).

39. Geddes, *Cities in Evolution*, v–vi.

40. Geddes, *Cities in Evolution*, 401.

41. Geddes, *Cities in Evolution*, 400, 392.

42. Welter, *Biopolis*, 189.

43. From Voltaire's "Il faut cultiver son jardin." Geddes, *Cities in Evolution*, 19.

44. Patrick Geddes, *The World Without and the World Within: Sunday Talks with My Children* (Bournville: The Saint George Press LD, 1905), 8, 9.

45. Geddes makes a more specific connection between the dreaming/planning of the garden and various figures of literary travel, perhaps most importantly in a reading of Keats's "On First Looking into Chapman's Homer." Geddes repeats

Keats's emphasis on the visual as the primary means of perceiving, knowing, and dreaming. There is an obvious colonial undertone in this reference. Keats: "Or like stout Cortez when with eagle eyes / He star'd at the Pacific—and all his men / Look'd at each other with a wild surmise— / Silent, upon a peak in Darien." Other literary figures mentioned are Shakespeare, Tennyson, Emerson, and Stevenson. Geddes, *The World Without and the World Within*, 4.

46. Geddes, *The World Without and the World Within*, 7–8.

47. Hysler-Rubin is specifically referring to Geddes's plan for Tel Aviv, which specified the creation of urban allotments, a horticultural society, and a tree-planting holiday, all of which had significance beyond a simple greening of the city. Hysler-Rubin, *Patrick Geddes and Town Planning*, 91.

48. Geddes, "Town Planning towards City Development," 52.

49. Philip Boardman, *The Worlds of Patrick Geddes: Biologist, Town Planner, Re-Educator, Peace-Warrior* (London: Routledge and Kegan Paul, 1978), 294.

50. Geddes, "Town Planning towards City Development," xxvi.

51. Boardman, *The Worlds of Patrick Geddes*, 1978, 294.

52. *The World Without and the World Within* not only figures the planner as a gardener but does so through a dramatized dialogue between a Geddes, as the adult educator, and his children as imaginative pupils; the cultivation of the garden becomes a means to the cultivation of the child.

53. Ola Söderström, "Paper Cities: Visual Thinking in Urban Planning," *Ecumene* 3, no. 3 (1996): 250.

54. "These techniques created the possibility of new means of gazing at the city." Söderström, "Paper Cities," 252, 267.

55. The Outlook Tower museum consisted in an "extensive array of globes, maps, atlases, photographs, oil paintings, charts, relief models, etchings and books in various rooms dedicated to Edinburgh, Scotland, Europe. This mainly geographical material rubbed shoulders with scientific equipment . . . through a collection of very diverse photographs, survey material and maps, the driving rationale was the belief in its potential to foment a new kind of urban citizen empowered through information." Geddes, *Cities in Evolution*, 325; Marco Amati, Robert Freestone, and Sarah Robertson, "'Learning the City': Patrick Geddes, Exhibitions, and Communicating Planning Ideas," *Landscape and Urban Planning* 166 (2017): 100, 102.

56. What Susan Stewart calls an "empire of sight." Qtd. in Constance Classen and David Howes, "The Museum as Sensescape: Western Sensibilities and Indigenous Artifacts," in *Sensible Objects: Colonialism, Museums, and Material Culture*, ed. Elizabeth Edwards, Chris Gosden, and Ruth B. Phillips (Oxford: Berg, 2006), 200; Sally Price, *Primitive Art in Civilized Places*, 2nd ed. (Chicago: University of Chicago Press, 2002).

57. This ethos of collection, preservation, and display was highly influenced by Ruskin and continued by figures like Henry Cole, George Birdwood, John Kipling, and many others. Metcalf, *An Imperial Vision*, 145, 142; see also Ian Baucom, *Out of*

Place: Englishness, Empire, and the Locations of Identity (Princeton, NJ: Princeton University Press, 1999).

58. "In 1922 Ashbee displayed craft objects he had collected from across the country in an exhibition entitled 'Palestine Crafts and Industries.'" Hysler-Rubin, "Arts & Crafts and the Great City," 357.

59. Welter also mentions Robert Pemberton's *Happy Colony* (1854), in which the plan for a potential settlement in New Zealand includes large-scale maps on the ground for settlers. Welter, *Biopolis*, 176, 177.

60. For example, the Pitt Rivers museum at Oxford, which organized tools and implements from a multitude of cultures along an explicitly evolutionary scale, from most primitive to most "advanced." See Annie E. Coombes, *Reinventing Africa: Museums, Material Culture, and Popular Imagination in Late Victorian and Edwardian England*, rev. ed. (New Haven, CT: Yale University Press, 1997).

61. His plan for Tel Aviv, for example, was not "merely to be a new town built upon progressive urban planning techniques, it was also to be a living and working model for the rest of the world; one that would attract support from and instill pride within the Jewish community in the Diaspora." Neal I. Payton, "The Machine in the Garden City: Patrick Geddes' Plan for Tel Aviv," *Planning Perspectives* 10, no. 4 (October 1995): 363.

62. James Clifford, *The Predicament of Culture: Twentieth-Century Ethnography, Literature, and Art*, 1st ed. (Cambridge, MA: Harvard University Press, 1988), 218.

63. Geddes, *Cities in Evolution*, 255.

64. Bernard S. Cohn and David Scott, *Colonialism and Its Forms of Knowledge: The British in India* (Princeton, NJ: Princeton University Press, 1996), 10.

65. Beattie, "Sir Patrick Geddes and Barra Bazaar," 146.

66. Michiel Dehaene, "Survey and the Assimilation of a Modernist Narrative in Urbanism," *Journal of Architecture* 7, no. 1 (January 1, 2002): 42–43.

67. Hysler-Rubin, *Patrick Geddes and Town Planning*, 111.

68. David Harvey, *The Condition of Postmodernity: An Enquiry into the Origins of Cultural Change* (Oxford: Wiley, 1992), 35.

69. James C. Scott, *Seeing Like a State: How Certain Schemes to Improve the Human Condition Have Failed* (New Haven, CT: Yale University Press, 1999), 88–90.

70. Geddes, *Cities in Evolution*, 325.

71. Geddes, *Cities in Evolution*, 325.

72. Geddes, *Cities in Evolution*, 321.

73. Geddes, "Town Planning towards City Development," 29.

74. In writing this text, he consulted with the Indian intellectual Ananda Coomaraswamy. Macdonald, "Education, Visual Art, and Cultural Revival," 48.

75. Patrick Geddes, *The Masque of Learning and Its Many Meanings; a Pageant of Education through the Ages; Devised and Interpreted by Patrick Geddes.*, n.d., vi.

76. Geddes, *The Masque of Learning and Its Many Meanings*, 2.

77. Michael Batty and Stephen Marshall, "Thinking Organic, Acting Civic: The

Paradox of Planning for Cities in Evolution," *Landscape and Urban Planning* 166 (2017): 6.

78. See Frances Fowle and Belinda Thomson, *Patrick Geddes: The French Connection* (White Cockade, 2004).

79. Donna V. Jones, *The Racial Discourses of Life Philosophy: Négritude, Vitalism, and Modernity* (New York: Columbia University Press, 2010), 6, 110.

80. Geddes, *The Masque of Learning and Its Many Meanings*, 12.

81. Geddes, *The Masque of Learning and Its Many Meanings*, 19.

82. Geddes, *The Masque of Learning and Its Many Meanings*, 78.

83. Geddes and Ernst Haekel were in contact in the 1880s while the former was at the University of Edinburgh. For Geddes, recapitulation was a biological version of the core ideas of Plato's *Meno*. Welter, *Biopolis*, 131–33, 198.

84. Geddes, "Civics as Applied Sociology, Part I," 77.

85. Geddes, "Civics as Applied Sociology, Part I," 77.

86. This invitation came through an introduction by Geddes's friend David Eder, a pioneering British psychoanalyst. To the Zionist Commission about Geddes, Eder states that "Prof. Geddes knows how to maintain what is traditional and beautiful of the past whilst combining it with all the necessary requirements in a way of sanitation and hygiene and modern requirements. Welter, "The 1925 Master Plan for Tel-Aviv by Patrick Geddes," 96–98.

87. Miki Zaidman and Ruth Kark, "Garden Cities in the Jewish Yishuv of Palestine: Zionist Ideology and Practice, 1905–1945," *Planning Perspectives* 5433 (January 2015): 57.

88. Payton, "The Machine in the Garden City," 372.

89. Welter, "The 1925 Master Plan for Tel-Aviv by Patrick Geddes," 115.

90. Geddes involved himself in planning colonial universities, most notably Ousmania University in Hyderabad and Hebrew University in Jerusalem's new city. These were both connected to the Collège des Écossais, which he founded in Montpellier, France, in 1924.

91. Geddes, "Town Planning towards City Development," 56–57.

92. See Joshua F. Cerra, Brook Weld Muller, and Robert F. Young, "A Transformative Outlook on the Twenty-First Century City: Patrick Geddes' Outlook Tower Revisited," *Landscape and Urban Planning* 166 (2017): 92. On Geddes's sociological approach to evolution, see Theodore S. Eisenman and Tom Murray, "An Integral Lens on Patrick Geddes," *Landscape and Urban Planning* 166 (2017): 43–54.

93. Poulomi Saha, "Singing Bengal into a Nation: Tagore the Colonial Cosmopolitan?," *Journal of Modern Literature* 36, no. 2 (2013): 3, 15.

94. Samir Dayal, "Repositioning India: Tagore's Passionate Politics of Love," *Positions: East Asia Cultures Critique* 15, no. 1 (2007): 166; Dilip Parameshwar Gaonkar, "On Alternative Modernities," *Public Culture* 11, no. 1 (January 1, 1999): 1–18.

95. Dayal, "Repositioning India," 170.

96. Dayal, "Repositioning India," 177.

97. Tagore thought that the "system of British colonial rule had certain progressive, meta-historical functions" and that his concern was for "both coloniser and colonised. The great failure of the British in India, Tagore felt, was to misunderstand, and thus fail to learn from, Indian culture . . . in this respect [empire] degraded the British, just as it degraded India." Fraser, *A Meeting of Two Minds*, 63; Michael Collins, *Empire, Nationalism, and the Postcolonial World: Rabindranath Tagore's Writings on History, Politics and Society*, 1st ed. (New York: Routledge, 2011), 13.

98. Elise Coquereau, "Modernism and Modernity in Rabindranath Tagore," *Planeta Literatur, Journal of Global Literary Studies* 3 (2014): 98.

99. Coquereau, "Modernism and Modernity in Rabindranath Tagore," 86.

100. He writes of the need of "some shelter into which to gather the best seed of past flowerings and in which to raise and tend the seedlings of coming summers. We need definitely to acquire such a centre of survey and service in each and every city—in a word, a Civicentre for sociologist and citizen." This is one of the earliest uses of the term "civic center." Geddes, "Civics as Applied Sociology, Part II," 157–58; "Civic, Adj.," OED.

101. Qtd. in Nezar AlSayyad, *Hybrid Urbanism: On the Identity Discourse and the Built Environment* (Greenwood, 2001), 100.

102. Fraser, *A Meeting of Two Minds*, 109.

103. This took the form of utopian literature like Theodor Herzl's novel *Altneuland*. Brenna Bhandar, *Colonial Lives of Property: Law, Land, and Racial Regimes of Ownership* (Durham, NC: Duke University Press, 2018), 121.

104. Bhandar, *Colonial Lives of Property*, 121.

105. Qtd. in Ines Sonder, "'May Be Solved by the Construction of Garden Cities': German-Jewish Literary Proposals on Garden Cities in Eretz Israel," in *Garden Cities and Colonial Planning: Transnationality and Urban Ideas in Africa and Palestine*, ed. Liora Bigon and Yossi Katz (Manchester: Manchester University Press, 2014), 140.

106. Sonder, "'May Be Solved by the Construction of Garden Cities,'" 135.

107. LeVine, "Conquest through Town Planning," 37.

108. Zaidman and Kark write that Zionists were very "aware of the fact that they were building an urban model for a new nation. Therefore, they deliberately planned an environment that stood out against the existing city and separated it from the city of Jaffa, by building it at some distance from the city." Zaidman and Kark, "Garden Cities in the Jewish Yishuv of Palestine," 57. Sonder, "'May Be Solved by the Construction of Garden Cities,'" 126.

109. Prominent architect/planners include Geddes, Austen St. Barbe Harrison, Clifford Holliday, Charles Robert Ashbee, Frank Mears, John Burnet, Henry Edward Kendall, and Benjamin Chaikin. Ashbee was influenced by Arts and Crafts design, which he brought to Palestine through the "Palestine Crafts and Industries"

exhibition. Ron Fuchs and Gilbert Herbert, "A Colonial Portrait of Jerusalem: British Architecture in Mandate-Era Palestine," in *Hybrid Urbanism: On the Identity Discourse and the Built Environment*, ed. Nezar AlSayyad (Westport, CT: Praeger, 2001), 85; Hysler-Rubin, "Arts & Crafts and the Great City," 356–57.

110. Nicholas E. Roberts, "Dividing Jerusalem: British Urban Planning in the Holy City," *Journal of Palestine Studies* 42, no. 4 (2013): 9.

111. Roberts, "Dividing Jerusalem," 9, 16, 19.

112. See Roberts, "Dividing Jerusalem," 18.

113. Welter, *Biopolis*, 230.

114. "By the mid-1930s, Nehru had already dropped his insistence on politicizing civic matters, and was beginning to prefer an apolitical mode of planning. New towns and garden suburbs were reimagined as pedagogical interventions to teach residents the practices of citizenship afresh. When Master planning for Delhi was taken up in the 1950s, unplanned neighborhoods continued to be treated with a mix of apathy, paternalism, and distrust, though now hidden beneath the rhetoric of socialist town planning." Karthik Rao-Cavale, "Patrick Geddes in India: Anti-Colonial Nationalism and the Historical Time of 'Cities in Evolution,'" *Landscape and Urban Planning* 166 (2017): 79; Tridib Banerjee, "U.S. Planning Expeditions to Postcolonial India: From Ideology to Innovation in Technical Assistance," *Journal of the American Planning Association* 75, no. 2 (March 27, 2009): 193–208.

3. Capturing the City: Regeneration, Policing, and the Ghosts of Postcolonial Britain

1. Barry Newman, "British Tinderbox: A Year after the Riots, Toxteth Is Still Racked by Anger and Despair," *Wall Street Journal*, 1982.

2. Tom Cordell et al., *Utopia London*, documentary, 2010, http://www.utopia london.com/.

3. Jaqueline Nassy Brown, *Dropping Anchor, Setting Sail: Geographies of Race in Black Liverpool* (Princeton, NJ: Princeton University Press, 2005), 69.

4. Paul Coslett, "International Garden Festival," BBC, http://www.bbc.co.uk /liverpool/content/articles/2009/04/28/local_history_garden_festival_feature.shtml.

5. SevenStreets, "Bloom and Bust: Liverpool's Garden Festival Site," http://www .sevenstreets.com/bloom-and-bust-liverpools-garden-festival-site/.

6. The site was virtually abandoned after six months, became derelict again, was closed in 1997, and has recently been "restored" again by private developers into condominiums.

7. Groundwork UK, "Our History | Groundwork," https://www.groundwork.org .uk/about-groundwork/our-history/.

8. Leslie Scarman, *The Scarman Report* (Middlesex: Penguin, 1981).

9. For a fuller account, see Alison Ravetz, *Council Housing and Culture: The History of a Social Experiment* (London: Taylor & Francis, 2001).

10. In which residents of social housing could opt to purchase their flat at a discounted rate, thus transferring ownership from the state (specifically local councils) to private hands.

11. I'm thinking specifically of the way political debates unfold after different kinds of riots and disturbances in the United Kingdom, the United States, and France.

12. Butler similarly writes about how the neighborhood of Toxteth in Liverpool was created by the *Daily Mail*. Visiting the area after the 1981 riots, a photographer captured a sign reading "Toxteth," and term became associated with the neighborhood through its aural resonance with an area already characterized as deprived, bleak, and ruined. Jeff Rodrigues, "The Riots of '81," *Marxism Today*, 1981, http://banmarchive.org.uk/collections/mt/pdf/81_10_18.pdf; Alice Butler, "Toxic Toxteth: Understanding Press Stigmatization of Toxteth during the 1981 Uprising," *Journalism* 21, no. 4 (April 1, 2020): 546; see also Zana Vathi and Kathy Burrell, "The Making and Unmaking of an Urban Diaspora: The Role of the Physical Environment and Materialities in Belongingness, Displacement, and Mobilisation in Toxteth, Liverpool," *Urban Studies* 58, no. 6 (May 1, 2021): 1213.

13. Rodrigues, "The Riots of '81," 18. Similarly, speaking of the Handsworth riots in 1985, Connell writes, "The *Daily Mail*, latching on to Dear's comments, ran the front-page headline 'BLOODLUST,' while an article in the *Daily Express* asserted that it was '400 young blacks,' 'driven on by bloodlust' '[who] started the riot.'" Kieran Connell, *Black Handsworth: Race in 1980s Britain* (Berkeley: University of California Press, 2019), 132.

14. "Television scenes of burning streets and kids looting shops have left the public and media with a picture of the Inner City as a problem caused by its inhabitants: unemployed youth tending to crime and drugs, decaying, uncared-for buildings and bad environments driving out business. This has been handily backed up by the prevalent social theory of 'cultures of deprivation,' in which the poor are seen as inadequate and apathetic, passing on their weaknesses to their children, the cause of their own wretchedness. An insidious racism is characteristic of this approach." Michael Jacobs, "Margaret Thatcher and the Inner Cities," *Economic and Political Weekly* 23, no. 38 (1988): 1942.

15. These are intertwined: "If we read the riot only as a protest against more restrictive immigration policies and unofficial, tacitly condoned harassment . . . we understate the degree to which racial exclusion depends on and mobilizes class affect . . . connections between race, gentrification, and the crisis in public housing." Peter J. Kalliney, *Cities of Affluence and Anger: A Literary Geography of Modern Englishness* (Charlottesville: University of Virginia Press, 2007), 200.

16. Simon Parker and Rowland Atkinson, "Disorderly Cities and the Policy-Making Field: The 1981 English Riots and the Management of Urban Decline," *British Politics*, September 11, 2018, 15.

17. This view held enough purchase at the time that it was "widely acceptable in English society for landlords to discriminate against potential tenants based on race

even when it was unacceptable to do so in the sphere of employment." Jonathan Foreman, "Race, Englishness, and the Media: Depictions of Urban Rioting in England, 1980–81," Lakehead University, 2014, 19–21.

18. Parker and Atkinson, "Disorderly Cities and the Policy-Making Field," 15.

19. He further downplays a sensationalist appraisal of the riots: "To keep a perspective, Liverpool 8 is an area of barely a square mile; and at the height of the riots only 200–300 local people were involved." Michael Heseltine, "It Took a Riot," n.d., 6, 4, https://www.margaretthatcher.org/document/127058.

20. John Lea and Simon Hallsworth, "Understanding the Riots: John Lea and Simon Hallsworth Put the Riots into Political and Historic Perspective," *Criminal Justice Matters* 87, no. 1 (March 2012): 30.

21. The available copy of this text in the national archives features underlines made by hand, though it is unclear by whom. They are repeated here because they indicate what aspects of his report were seen to be noteworthy and thus have a paratextual function. In this instance, one can imagine a reader shaking their heads at these single, unemployed parents.

22. Heseltine, "It Took a Riot," 5.

23. The urban scholar Loïc Wacquant would want to read urban riots as a symptom of a "dissolution of place" in deterritorialized hyperghettos." However, UK state policy under Thatcher (and beyond) responded to the riots precisely through place creation. Loïc Wacquant, *Urban Outcasts: A Comparative Sociology of Advanced Marginality* (Cambridge: Polity, 2007), 241.

24. Heseltine, "It Took a Riot," 11.

25. Michael Heseltine, *Life in the Jungle: My Autobiography* (London: Hodder & Stoughton, 2000), 228.

26. Heseltine, *Life in the Jungle*, 216.

27. Heseltine, *Life in the Jungle*, 219.

28. See Erik Bleich, Carolina Caeiro, and Sarah Luehrman, "State Responses to 'Ethnic Riots' in Liberal Democracies: Evidence from Western Europe," *European Political Science Review* 2, no. 2 (July 2010): 280.

29. Features such as "'quality design,' 'sustainable living,' 'urban amenity,' and 'heritage and culture' become central to urban policies as a means of stimulating investment in the inner city." Libby Porter and Austin Barber, "The Meaning of Place and State–Led Gentrification in Birmingham's Eastside," *City* 10, no. 2 (July 1, 2006): 8.

30. There has been ongoing debate about what kinds of development can be considered gentrification, given Glass's original discussion of the term. Speaking specifically of Birmingham, Porter and Barber, "The Meaning of Place and State–led Gentrification in Birmingham's Eastside," 7, define gentrification as "this redifferentiation of place [that] requires, for its policy rationale, the definition of an inner-city 'problem' caused by the lack of middle class presence (resident population, investment or visitation), leaving it to become marked by deprivation and disadvantage." In this sense, Dillon and Fanning have argued that "gentrification

has emerged as a global urban strategy, something to be levered by combinations of regulation and deregulation and state facilitation of developer interests, rather than to be left to the gradual takeover of once deprived localities by more affluent residents." Denis Dillon and Bryan Fanning, "Tottenham after the Riots: The Chimera of Community and the Property-Led Regeneration of 'Broken Britain,'" *Critical Social Policy* 35, no. 2 (May 2015): 193; Denis Dillon and Bryan Fanning, "Developer-Led Gentrification and Legacies of Urban Policy Failure in Post-Riot Tottenham," *Community Development Journal* 54, no. 4 (October 1, 2019): 605.

31. Heseltine, *Life in the Jungle*, 213.

32. Heseltine, *Life in the Jungle*, 201.

33. He uses similar language elsewhere: "Within a mile of Liverpool's city centre were a thousand acres of decaying, toxic waste, dumped over the decades to fester as a monument to the pollution of a bygone day and occupying a great waterfront site with no prospect of regeneration. It was, incidentally, within a mile of Toxteth, with its alienated population and high unemployment." Heseltine, *Life in the Jungle*, 211.

34. Neoliberal regeneration "is just the latest instalment on a representational continuum: as notions of the 'dead' inner city serve to grease the wheels of regeneration today, so too . . . did Victorian slum stereotypes translate into 'disruptive programmes of inner-city revitalization.'" Michael Romyn, "'London Badlands': The Inner City Represented, Regenerated," *London Journal* 44, no. 2 (May 4, 2019): 136.

35. Sal Nicolazzo, *Vagrant Figures: Law, Literature, and the Origins of the Police* (New Haven, CT: Yale University Press, 2020), 144.

36. Nicolazzo, *Vagrant Figures*, 138.

37. Roy Coleman and Joe Sim, "From the Dockyards to the Disney Store: Surveillance, Risk, and Security in Liverpool City Centre," *International Review of Law, Computers & Technology* 12, no. 1 (March 1, 1998): 30.

38. Neil Smith, "Toward a Theory of Gentrification: A Back to the City Movement by Capital, Not People," *Journal of the American Planning Association* 45, no. 4 (1979): 538–48.

39. Neil Smith, "Gentrification, the Frontier, and the Restructuring of Urban Space," in *Gentrification of the City*, ed. Neil Smith and Peter Williams (Winchester Place: Allen & Unwin, 1986); Loretta Lees, Tom Slater, and Elvin Wyly, *Gentrification* (London: Routledge, 2008); Rob Imrie, Loretta Lees, and Mike Raco, *Regenerating London: Governance, Sustainability, and Community in a Global City* (London: Routledge, 2009).

40. Vathi and Burrell, "The Making and Unmaking of an Urban Diaspora," 1221.

41. "The membership of the UDC boards had been carefully chosen to balance the need for private, entrepreneurial experience with the legitimate interests of local government. It had taken a Tory government to begin to tackle the worst areas of urban decay. The council tenants were buying their homes, the Volume Housebuilders were starting to build private sector homes in the inner cities," Heseltine writes (*Life in the Jungle*, 215). Mickey Lauria elaborates that "MDC's decision-making style follows a corporate model: decisions are made by a small

number of elites within the corporation, by large private developers and financial institutions based principally on their particular market criteria." Mickey Lauria, "Waterfront Development, Urban Regeneration and Local Politics in New Orleans and Liverpool," University of New Orleans, College of Urban and Public Affairs Working Papers, 1994, 6.

42. See Murray Stewart, "Between Whitehall and Town Hall: The Realignment of Urban Regeneration Policy in England," *Policy & Politics* 22, no. 2 (1994): 133–46.

43. Heseltine, *Life in the Jungle*, 210.

44. Coleman and Sim, "From the Dockyards to the Disney Store," 31.

45. Jacobs, "Margaret Thatcher and the Inner Cities," 1943.

46. The results of this state-led gentrification were indeed transformative, as east London has become a space of bourgeois consumption. In fact, after the 2011 riots in Tottenham, the same solution of urban renewal was suggested in a report, taking after Heseltine, entitled "It Took Another Riot." GLA, "It Took Another Riot," 2012, https://www.london.gov.uk/sites/default/files/it_took_another_riot.pdf; Dillon and Fanning, "Developer-Led Gentrification and Legacies of Urban Policy Failure in Post-Riot Tottenham," 611.

47. Heseltine, *Life in the Jungle*, 217.

48. He writes similarly of the brownfield sites along the Thames Estuary, specifically the docklands: "Later, as Minister for Aerospace with responsibility for the third London airport project on the Foulness mudflats off the Essex coast, I had found myself in a small plane, heading in that direction by way of London's East End. My indignation at what was happening on the South Bank was as nothing compared to my reaction to the immense tracts of dereliction I now observed." As in the scene in Liverpool, Heseltine occupies a surveying position, viewing the dereliction from a plane. Heseltine, *Life in the Jungle*, 211.

49. Heseltine, *Life in the Jungle*, 227.

50. Lauria, "Waterfront Development, Urban Regeneration, and Local Politics," 12.

51. Patrick Loftman and Brendan Nevin, "Prestige Projects and Urban Regeneration in the 1980s and 1990s: A Review of Benefits and Limitations," *Planning Practice & Research* 10, nos. 3–4 (August 1995): 303.

52. Heseltine, *Life in the Jungle*, 210.

53. Robert Holden, "British Garden Festivals: The First Eight Years," *Landscape and Urban Planning* 18, no. 1 (September 1989): 17.

54. See Lauria, "Waterfront Development, Urban Regeneration and Local Politics," 10.

55. The Scarman inquiry, conducted in the aftermath of the Brixton riots, focused in particular on policing tactics and criticized the police for failing to "consult locally" and work with the communities they were policing. Peplow notes that Leslie Scarman was "criticised from both sides, being simultaneously too left-wing" for law-and-order conservatives and "not radical enough" for communities who wanted change more substantive than could be provided by a localized government

inquiry. The report's turn to "local consultation" was seen even at the time as "the establishment of a whole array of community participation projects and systems which were eventually to buy many activists off the streets." Qtd. in Simon Peplow, *Race and Riots in Thatcher's Britain* (Manchester: Manchester University Press, 2019), 35, 128. Anandi Ramamurthy, *Black Star: Britain's Asian Youth Movements* (London: Pluto, 2013), 147; Peplow, *Race and Riots in Thatcher's Britain*, 142; see also Michael Keith, *Race, Riots and Policing: Lore and Disorder in a Multi-Racist Society* (London: UCL Press, 1993).

56. Bernard E. Harcourt, *Illusion of Order: The False Promise of Broken Windows Policing* (Cambridge, MA: Harvard University Press, 2005), 7–8.

57. George L. Kelling and James Q. Wilson, "Broken Windows," *Atlantic*, March 1, 1982, https://www.theatlantic.com/magazine/archive/1982/03/broken-windows/304465/; Harcourt, *Illusion of Order*, 17–18.

58. This famous article is written in a familiar speculative mode, with consequences for urban spaces that move quickly from litter to serious crimes and social decay. Large parts of the article are thus written in the future tense. Kelling and Wilson, "Broken Windows."

59. David Thacher, "Order Maintenance Policing," in *The Oxford Handbook of Police and Policing*, ed. Michael D. Reisig and Robert J. Kane (Oxford: Oxford University Press, 2014), 129.

60. Stuart Hall et al., *Policing the Crisis: Mugging, the State, and Law and Order* (Basingstoke: Macmillan, 1978), 184.

61. Mark Neocleous, "Social Police and the Mechanism of Prevention: Patrick Colquhoun and the Condition of Poverty," *British Journal of Criminology* 40, no. 4 (n.d.): 18.

62. Similarly, broken-windows policing requires an extensive infrastructure to "process" individuals cited and/or arrested for petty "crimes." Hall et al., *Policing the Crisis*, 185.

63. Nicole M. Jackson, "Imperial Suspect: Policing Colonies within 'Post'-Imperial England," *Callaloo* 39, no. 1 (2016): 205; Cecil Gutzmore, "'Carnival, the State, and the Black Masses in the United Kingdom," in *Inside Babylon: The Caribbean Diaspora in Britain*, ed. Winston James and Clive Harris (London: Verso, 1993), 208.

64. "Sus" has become contemporary slang for "suspicious," but apparently as the result of the videogame *Among Us* and not from nineteenth-century British vagrancy law. Peplow, *Race and Riots in Thatcher's Britain*, 36; Jackson, "Imperial Suspect," 205, 207, 211.

65. Alice Coleman, King's College (University of London) Staff Design Disadvantagement Team, and Sarah Brown, *Utopia on Trial: Vision and Reality in Planned Housing* (H. Shipman, 1985), 6.

66. Jane Jacobs, *The Death and Life of Great American Cities*, reissue ed. (New York: Vintage, 1992).

67. Coleman et al., *Utopia on Trial*, 23; see Romyn, "'London Badlands,'" 142.

68. Coleman et al., *Utopia on Trial*, 45–46.

69. Coleman et al., *Utopia on Trial*, 181.

70. Coleman et al., *Utopia on Trial*, 31.

71. This method and others like it tend not to take into account how "perceptions of neighborhood disorder have a social meaning independent from objective physical conditions," namely, that "neighborhood racial composition was more strongly related to perceptions of disorder than systematic observations of disorder." Sophie M. Aiyer et al., "From Broken Windows to Busy Streets: A Community Empowerment Perspective," *Health Education & Behavior* 42, no. 2 (April 1, 2015): 137; Robert J. Sampson and Stephen W. Raudenbush, "Seeing Disorder: Neighborhood Stigma and the Social Construction of 'Broken Windows,'" *Social Psychology Quarterly* 67, no. 4 (December 1, 2004): 319–42.

72. Coleman et al., *Utopia on Trial*, 44.

73. Coleman et al., *Utopia on Trial*, 25–26.

74. Coleman et al., *Utopia on Trial*, 20.

75. Coleman et al., *Utopia on Trial*, 87.

76. Coleman's logic on which kinds of space provide more or less surveillance are highly speculative and often beg the question, in that they assume that suburban-style space will maximize the right kind of communal self-policing.

77. Coleman et al., *Utopia on Trial*, 25.

78. Coleman's concern for the supposed instability or urban, flat-dwelling families is repeated by Scarman in his reports on the riots, specifically as related to the Black family, as detailed by Paul Gilroy, *"There Ain't No Black in the Union Jack": The Cultural Politics of Race and Nation* (Chicago: University of Chicago Press, 1991), 105. Meanwhile, the rhetoric on protecting children echoes that used to implement closed-circuit television—the technology of order maintenance par excellence—in the more "confused" public spaces, for example shopping malls; Coleman and Sim, "From the Dockyards to the Disney Store," 35.

79. Coleman et al., *Utopia on Trial*, 18.

80. Stuart Hall, "Assembling the 1980s: The Deluge—and After," in *Shades of Black: Assembling Black Arts in 1980s Britain*, ed. Sonia Boyce, Ian Baucom, and David A. Bailey (Durham, NC: Duke University Press, in collaboration with the Institute of International Visual Arts and the African and Asian Visual Artists' Archive, 2005), 14.

81. We see the tension between expression and surveillance in a piece like Denzil Forrester's 1985 painting *Police in Blues Club*, for example.

82. The founding members of BAFC were John Akomfrah, Reece Auguiste, Edward George, Lina Gopaul, Avril Johnson, Claire Joseph, and Trevor Mathison. "Along with other African and Caribbean diasporic filmmaking workshops such as Ceddo and Sankofa, The Black Audio Film Collective (BAFC) were representatives of a growing, grant-funded cultural film sector in London. The Ethnic Minorities Committee was created in 1981 as a response to riots and increasing racial tension within Thatcher-era England. The Black Arts Division, a subsidiary of the EMC,

was subsequently created in order to fund black cultural projects." Josh Romphf, "'Invention in the Name of Community': Workshops, the Avant-Garde, and the Black Audio Film Collective," *Kino: The Western Undergraduate Film Studies Journal* 1, no. 1 (June 10, 2010): 1, https://ojs.lib.uwo.ca/index.php/kino/article/view/6249.

83. Lehin notes: "Segregated production practices are reproduced in the films' depiction of a rather divided British society. The financing and the making of these films is evidence of the government's policy of multiculturalism." Barbara Lehin, "Giving a Voice to the Ethnic Minorities in 1980s French and British Cinemas," *Studies in European Cinema* 2, no. 3 (January 2005): 214; Sophia Phoca, "Filming the Alternative," *Art Monthly*, no. 342 (2010): 7–10; Gargi Bhattacharyya and John Gabriel, "Gurinder Chadha and the *Apna* Generation: Black British Film in the 1990s," *Third Text* 8, no. 27 (June 1994): 55–63.

84. "Prior to the 1970s, the majority of British residents answering the description of 'black' were immigrants from the Caribbean and Africa and their descendants. However, by the mid-1970s immigrants from the Indian sub-continent formed the largest ethnic group of color, and became targets of forms of racist violence and oppression that African and Afro-Caribbean immigrants had experienced previously upon their arrival in England. This shared experience of racism and racial violence formed the basis of a coalition between communities of color. Consequently, from the late 1970s onwards, 'Black British' came increasingly to suggest an identity inclusive of all minority ethnicities of color, which in turn became, as Hall states, 'hegemonic.'" Ifeona Fulani, "Celluloid Documents: Migrant Women in Black Audio Film Collective's *Handsworth Songs* and *Twilight City* and Sankofa Film and Video Collective's *Dreaming Rivers*," *Atlantic Studies* 15, no. 1 (2018): 3.

85. Sophie Orlando, *British Black Art: Debates on Western Art History* (Paris: Dis Voir, 2016), 19.

86. This is a point made throughout the gallery book for the seminal 1989 exhibition *The Other Story*, in which its curator Rasheed Araeen notes how being particularized and otherized also worked to separate the work of minority artists from "modern" Euro-American art. Eddie Chambers, *Black Artists in British Art: A History since the 1950s* (London: Bloomsbury Academic, 2014), 1, 6; Rasheed Araeen, *The Other Story: Afro-Asian Artists in Post-War Britain : Hayward Gallery, London [10.3.–22.4.1990]: Art Gallery Wolverhampton [10.3.–22.4.1990]: Manchester City Art Gallery and Cornerhouse, Manchester [5.5.–10.6.1990]* (Hayward Gallery, 1989), 13.

87. Araeen, *The Other Story*, 72–77; see also Stuart Hall, "Black Diaspora Artists in Britain: Three 'Moments' in Post-War History," *History Workshop Journal*, no. 61 (2006): 17.

88. See Gilane Tawadros, "Beyond the Boundary: The Work of Three Black Women Artists in Britain," *Third Text* 3, no. 8–9 (September 1989): 121–50.

89. Kodwo Eshun and Anjalika Sagar, eds., *The Ghosts of Songs: The Film Art*

of the Black Audio Film Collective, 1st ed. (Liverpool: Liverpool University Press, 2007), 15.

90. Mercer is responding in part to Paul Gilroy's criticism of *Handsworth Songs* appealing to an elite white audience; Gilroy asks, "Is there a non-literate, black, working- or non-working-class audience eagerly anticipating these particular cultural products?" Conversely, Mercer finds that this leads to the risible position that "black artists who choose to work in vernacular or popular forms, and who address their work to a black working class audience, are the only artists who produce anything worth talking about." Kobena Mercer, "Black Art and the Burden of Representation," *Third Text* 4, no. 10 (March 1990): 67; Paul Gilroy, "Cruciality and the Frog's Perspective*: An Agenda of Difficulties for the Black Arts Movement in Britain," *Third Text* 2, no. 5 (December 1988): 35–36; see also Kodwo Eshun, "Untimely Meditations: Reflections on the Black Audio Film Collective," *Nka: Journal of Contemporary African Art* 19, no. 1 (2004): 42.

91. Eshun and Sagar, *The Ghosts of Songs*, 75.

92. "For BAFC, then, intervention at the level of form, genre, memory, and technology exceeded questions of access or representation and declared nothing less than a new formulation of what counted as sound and image." Eshun and Sagar, *The Ghosts of Songs*, 94. Rancière, *Disagreement*, xii.

93. Problems that are intrinsic to the structure of subalterity and the question of voice are famously posed by Gayatri Chakravorty Spivak, *A Critique of Postcolonial Reason: Toward a History of the Vanishing Present*, 1st ed. (Cambridge, MA: Harvard University Press, 1999).

94. Eshun and Sagar, *The Ghosts of Songs*, 89.

95. Romphf, "'Invention in the Name of Community,'" 4; J. Williamson, "Two Kinds of Otherness: Black Film and the Avant-Garde," *Screen* 29, no. 4 (December 1, 1988): 106–13.

96. Patrick Williams, "Imaged Communities: Black British Film in the Eighties and Nineties," *Critical Survey* 8, no. 1 (1996): 5.

97. The slogan belonged to the successful 1964 general election campaign of Smethwick MP Peter Griffiths.

98. Les Back and John Solomos, "Black Politics and Social Change in Birmingham, UK: An Analysis of Recent Trends," *Ethnic and Racial Studies* 15, no. 3 (July 1, 1992): 329–30.

99. Salman Rushdie, *Imaginary Homelands: Essays and Criticism, 1981–1991* (Penguin, 1992), 115–17.

100. John Akomfrah responds: "What Rushdie and other critics found really objectionable about the film, and some audiences found problematic, is precisely that anti-ethnographic bias—that you can't use the film to construct other knowledges about Handsworth, other than what you already know. . . . It seems to me that the missionary zeal with which black life is chased in this anthropological way, is precisely what is missing from *Handsworth Songs*." John Akomfrah, Paul

Gilroy, et al., "Audiences/Aesthetics/Independence: Interview with the Black Audio Collective," *Framework: The Journal of Cinema and Media*, no. 35 (1988): 14.

101. Nina Power, "Counter-Media, Migration, Poetry: Interview with John Akomfrah," *Film Quarterly* 65, no. 2 (December 1, 2011): 59.

102. Auguiste, in Eshun and Sagar, *The Ghosts of Songs*, 157.

103. Like many, Sessolo seems to view the project of subaltern studies to represent those who cannot represent themselves. One recalls, especially reading figures like Wacquant, Spivak's claim that "the ventriloquism of the speaking subaltern is the left intellectual's stock-in-trade." Simone Sessolo, "An Epic of Riots: The Multitude as Hero in Handsworth Songs," *Journal of Popular Culture* 47, no. 4 (2014): 747; Spivak, *A Critique of Postcolonial Reason*, 255; see also Alison Donnell, "Nation and Contestation: Black British Writing," *Wasafiri* 17, no. 36 (June 2002): 14.

104. John Akomfrah, dir., *Handsworth Songs*, documentary (Black Audio Film Collective, n.d.), 3:35, 51:08.

105. See Dara Waldron, "The Utopian Promise: John Akomfrah's Poetics of the Archive," *Open Library of Humanities* 3, no. 1 (February 21, 2017): 9.

106. Akomfrah, *Handsworth Songs*, 26:42, 54:52.

107. Eric Williams writes: "In the primeval forests of America the Birmingham axes struck down the old trees; the cattle pastures of Australia rang with the sound of Birmingham bells; in East India and the West they tended the fields of sugar cane with Birmingham hoes." Qtd. in Kevin Myers and Ian Grosvenor, "Birmingham Stories: Local Histories of Migration and Settlement and the Practice of History," *Midland History* 36, no. 2 (2011): 151.

108. David Marriott, *Haunted Life: Visual Culture and Black Modernity* (New Brunswick, NJ: Rutgers University Press, 2007), xiv.

109. Roy Coleman, "Reclaiming the Streets: Closed Circuit Television, Neoliberalism, and the Mystification of Social Divisions in Liverpool, UK," *Surveillance & Society* 2, no. 2/3 (2004): 298.

110. It is not a project, that is, of accounting for "imperial debris." Ann Laura Stoler, *Imperial Debris: On Ruins and Ruination* (Durham, NC: Duke University Press, 2013).

111. Mercer, in Eshun and Sagar, *The Ghosts of Songs*, 44.

112. Akomfrah, *Handsworth Songs*, 8:13.

113. Williams, "Imaged Communities," 8.

114. Stoffel Debuysere, "Signs of Struggle, Songs of Sorrow: Notes on the Politics of Uncertainty in the Films of John Akomfrah," *Black Camera* 6, no. 2 (2015): 75–76.

115. Akomfrah, *Handsworth Songs*, 29:37.

116. Given the cadence of the voiceover, I have chosen to render it here in verse. There is nothing in the film or in any commentary on the film that suggests this voiceover should be presented in this way.

117. Lara Cahill-Booth, "Walcott's Sea and Caribbean Geomythography," *Journal of Postcolonial Writing* 49, no. 3 (July 1, 2013): 357.

118. I use Gilroy's term here as a geographical and historical indicator, without necessarily subscribing to the full resonances of his theory.

119. Eshun, "Untimely Meditations," 41.

120. Debuysere, "Signs of Struggle, Songs of Sorrow," 72, 66.

121. Akomfrah, in Eshun and Sagar, *The Ghosts of Songs*, 130.

122. For example, in Akomfrah's OBE (Order of the British Empire) award.

123. Eddie Chambers, *Things Done Change: The Cultural Politics of Recent Black Artists in Britain* (Amsterdam: Rodopi, 2012), 93.

124. Hall, "Assembling the 1980s," 2.

125. Keeling provides a fuller reading of *The Last Angel of History*. Kara Keeling, *Queer Times, Black Futures* (New York: New York University Press, 2019), 117.

126. Ian Baucom, *Out of Place: Englishness, Empire, and the Locations of Identity* (Princeton, NJ: Princeton University Press, 1999).

127. GLA, "It Took Another Riot"; "Riots: Theresa May's Speech on 11 August 2011," https://www.gov.uk/government/speeches/riots-theresa-mays-speech-on-11-august-2011; *The Guardian* and the London School of Economics, "Reading the Riots: Investigating England's Summer of Disorder," vol. 1 (London: *The Guardian* and the London School of Economics, 2011).

128. Jacques Derrida, *Specters of Marx: The State of the Debt, the Work of Mourning, and the New International* (New York: Routledge, 2012).

4. The End of London: Temporalities of the Gentrified City

1. John Gold and Margaret Gold, *Olympic Cities: City Agendas, Planning, and the World's Games, 1896–2016* (London: Routledge, 2011), 388.

2. Jack Shenker, "Privatised London: The Thames Path Walk That Resembles a Prison Corridor," *Guardian*, July 24, 2015.

3. Guy Debord, *Society of the Spectacle* (Detroit, MI: Black & Red, 2002).

4. Among innumerable other reference points. *The Last London* displays a particular interest in W. G. Sebald, especially *Austerliz* (2001).

5. As will be discussed in what follows, this perspective on the city, like the immersed-but-distant gaze of the flâneur, is predominantly male and white. Patrick Wright, *A Journey through Ruins: The Last Days of London* (Oxford: Oxford University Press, 2009); Owen Hatherley, *A Guide to the New Ruins of Great Britain* (London: Verso, 2011); Owen Hatherley, *A New Kind of Bleak: Journeys through Urban Britain* (London: Verso, 2012); Patrick Keiller, dir., *London* (1994); Patrick Keiller, dir., *Robinson in Space* (1997); Patrick Keiller, dir., *Robinson in Ruins* (2010); Will Self, *Psychogeography* (London: A&C Black, 2013).

6. In London, these unused facilities included the White City's "huge and largely unwanted" stadium built for the 1908 games.

7. This is a critical reframing of the invocation of ruin in popular political discourse and sensationalist media.

8. Walter Benjamin, *The Origin of German Tragic Drama* (London: Verso, 2003), 223.

9. Famously, "the storm irresistibly propels him into the future to which his back is turned, while the pile of debris before him grows skyward. The storm is what we call progress." Walter Benjamin, *Illuminations: Essays and Reflections* (New York: Houghton Mifflin Harcourt, 1968), 257.

10. Ann Laura Stoler, *Imperial Debris: On Ruins and Ruination* (Durham, NC: Duke University Press, 2013); Gastón R. Gordillo, *Rubble: The Afterlife of Destruction* (Durham, NC: Duke University Press, 2014).

11. For example, one rhetoric of ruin is the conservative discourse, prompted by the likes of Iain Duncan Smith, of there being a "broken Britain." At the other end, left criticism, for example as found in Hatherley's *A New Kind of Bleak*, employs similar affects but for the sake of excoriating neoliberal ruination.

12. Ruth Glass, *London: Aspects of Change* (London: MacGibbon & Kee, 1964).

13. Neil Smith, "Gentrification, the Frontier, and the Restructuring of Urban Space," in *Gentrification of the City*, ed. Neil Smith and Peter Williams (Winchester Place: Allen & Unwin, 1986); Noah Quastel, "Political Ecologies of Gentrification," *Urban Geography* 30, no. 7 (2013): 694–725; Mark Davidson and Loretta Lees, "New-Build Gentrification: Its Histories, Trajectories, and Critical Geographies," *Population, Space, and Place* 16, no. 5 (2010): 395–411; Tim Butler and Chris Hamnett, "Walking Backwards to the Future—Waking Up to Class and Gentrification in London," *Urban Policy and Research* 27, no. 3 (2009): 217–28; David Harvey, "The Right to the City," *New Left Review* 53 (September/October 2008): 1–16.

14. Iain Sinclair, *The Last London: True Fictions from an Unreal City* (London: Oneworld, 2017).

15. Sinclair, *The Last London*, 5.

16. Sinclair, *The Last London*, 13.

17. Lauren Berlant, *Cruel Optimism* (Durham, NC: Duke University Press, 2011), 6.

18. Sinclair, *The Last London*, 6.

19. Sinclair, *The Last London*, 10.

20. Sinclair, *The Last London*, 70.

21. Sinclair, *The Last London*, 70–71.

22. Sinclair, *The Last London*, 164.

23. As in a volume edited by Sinclair, *London: City of Disappearances*, a book more optimistic that London could be a "city [that] would begin to write itself." Iain Sinclair, *London: City of Disappearances* (London: Penguin, 2007).

24. Neil Smith and Peter Williams, eds., *Gentrification of the City* (Winchester Place: Allen & Unwin, 1986).

25. Sinclair, *The Last London*, 70.

26. Sinclair, *The Last London*, 6–7; On the notion of "edgelands," see Marion Shoard, *A Right to Roam* (Oxford: Oxford University Press, 1999).

27. Even in validating this criticism, Sinclair implies that it is simplistic and unoriginal: "Sometimes from a visiting American researcher, brandishing Rebecca Solnit or Lauren Elkin, sometimes from a native-born academic, a practitioner suddenly struck by the originality of her challenge: 'Why are there no women on your walks?'" Sinclair, *The Last London*, 264; also see Rebecca Solnit, *Wanderlust: A History of Walking* (New York: Granta, 2014); Lauren Elkin, *Flaneuse: Women Walk the City in Paris, New York, Tokyo, Venice, and London* (New York: Random House, 2016).

28. Sinclair, *The Last London*, 9.

29. Sinclair, *The Last London*, 11.

30. Sinclair, *The Last London*, 190.

31. Sinclair, *The Last London*, 191, 197.

32. Sinclair, *The Last London*, 259.

33. Iain Sinclair, *London Orbital* (London: Penguin, 2003).

34. LOCOG, *A Vision for the Olympic Games and Paralympic Games* (London: LOCOG, 2004).

35. Coe was the chairman for the London Organizing Committee for the Olympic Games (LOCOG). Josh Ryan-Collins and Paul Sander-Jackson, "Fool's Gold: How the 2012 Olympics Is Selling East London Short, and a 10 Point Plan for a More Positive Local Legacy" (London: New Economics Foundation, 2008), 2.

36. Sinclair, *The Last London*, 291.

37. In the words of then-IOC president Jacques Rogge, "Each [Olympics] has a once-in-a-lifetime chance to showcase the celebration of the human spirit. And each creates a unique set of environmental, social and economic legacies that can change a community, a region, and a nation forever." IOC, "Final Report of the IOC Coordination Commission: Games of the XXX Olympiad, London 2012" (Lausanne: International Olympic Committee, 2013), 11, 6.

38. Many pop-ups were created with corporate funding preceding the Olympic Games, for example, a pop-up cinema next to the Olympic site named "Folly for a Flyover," funded by Bank of America Merrill Lynch. Assemble, "Assemble," https://assemblestudio.co.uk.

39. Katherine Faulkner, "Ten to a Room and One Shower for 75 People: Inside the 'Slum' Camp for Olympic Cleaners," *Daily Mail*, July 15, 2012; Matthew Sanders, "The Changing Face of the Labour Market: Temporary Versus Permanent," *International Business Times*, May 22, 2013.

40. Chartered Institute of Personnel and Development, "Zero Hours Contracts More Widespread Than Thought—but Only Minority of Zero Hours Workers Want to Work More Hours" (London, 2013).

41. Tony Blair, "Speech to Greater London Authority," April 4, 2006.

42. LOCOG, "London 2012 Olympic Games Final Report" (London: London Organising Committee of the Olympic Games and Paralympic Games Ltd., 2013), 58.

43. Hayes and Horne point out that it is "symptomatic of the nature of social

participation imagined by London 2012 that the recruitment and training of the 70,000 volunteers required for the staging of the Games is to be managed by McDonald's; in other words, to be subsumed within the IOC's corporate branding and sponsorship rights agenda, and run by a transnational corporation synonymous with standardization, top-down control, employee deskilling, job insecurity, environmental exploitation, de-unionization, and poor nutritional quality." Graeme Hayes and John Horne, "Sustainable Development, Shock and Awe? London 2012 and Civil Society," *Sociology* 45, no. 5 (2011): 760.

44. The number of entities involved is a "reflection of the fragmented governance and delivery structure and the stop-go regeneration regimes imposed over a fifty year period." These included the London Organizing Committee for the Olympic Games (LOCOG), the Olympic Delivery Authority (ODA), London Development Agency (LDA), the London Thames Gateway Development Corporation (LTGDC), and other no-longer-existing entities, along with the Greater London Authority (GLA), the local councils, and numerous nonprofit groups who served as consultants. Gold and Gold, *Olympic Cities*, 387.

45. Gold and Gold, *Olympic Cities*, 360.

46. The "Olympic" boroughs "are characterized by above national average numbers of young people as well as concentrated poverty and deprivation." For example, over one-third of children growing up in households across the Olympic boroughs are officially classified as poor; amongst the 1.25 million people living within the boroughs, about 290,000 are workless, i.e. 40 per cent of the working-age population." Jacqueline Kennelly and Paul Watt, "Sanitizing Public Space in Olympic Host Cities: The Spatial Experiences of Marginalized Youth in 2010 Vancouver and 2012 London," *Sociology* 45, no. 5 (2011): 765–81.

47. IOC, "Final Report of the IOC Coordination Commission," 48; DCMS, "Plans for the Legacy from the 2012 Olympic and Paralympic Games" (London: Department for Culture, Media and Sport, 2010), 11.

48. The host boroughs had, pre-Olympics, "some of the lowest per capita carbon emissions in the country; to be expected given their relative deprivation . . . a corollary of this is that they also have a starting infrastructure that will not be up to the job of delivering low carbon economic growth and development." The developers here seem not to notice the irony of stating that the low carbon emissions make the boroughs poorly situated to produce a low-carbon Olympics. DCMS, "Plans for the Legacy from the 2012 Olympic and Paralympic Games," 11; London—2012, "Towards a One Planet 2012" (London: London 2012, 2009), 13; Hayes and Horne, "Sustainable Development, Shock and Awe?," 759; Maarten A. Hajer, "Ecological Modernisation as Cultural Politics," in *Risk, Environment, and Modernity: Towards a New Ecology*, ed. Scott Lash, Bronislaw Szerszynski, and Brian Wynne (London: SAGE, 1996), 248.

49. ODA, "Demolish, Dig, Design" (London: Olympic Delivery Authority, 2007).

50. Davis and Thornley write that compulsory purchase was used not only to relocate both individuals and many small businesses from the relatively central area

of Stratford to more distant suburbs. Gold notes that by the time of the opening ceremonies there had already been a 190 percent increase in Newham housing prices since 1999 (compared with the national average of 117 percent). John Horne and Garry Whannel, *Understanding the Olympics* (London: Taylor & Francis, 2012); Juliet Davis and Andy Thornley, "Urban Regeneration for the London 2012 Olympics: Issues of Land Acquisition and Legacy," *City, Culture, and Society*, no. 1 (2010): 94; Gold and Gold, *Olympic Cities*, 382.

51. Doreen Massey, *World City* (London: Polity, 2007), 48.

52. The "254 highly diverse industries and businesses on the site" were included in the category "remnants," thus lumping together substances deposited into the ground in the early twentieth century and people who still occupied the site. Davis and Thornley, "Urban Regeneration for the London 2012 Olympics," 92.

53. Mike Raco and Emma Tunney, "Visibilities and Invisibilities in Urban Development: Small Business Communities and the London Olympics 2012," *Urban Studies* 47, no. 10 (2010): 2072; Richard Florida, *The Rise of the Creative Class and How It's Transforming Work, Leisure, Community, and Everyday Life* (Turtleback, 2003).

54. Ryan-Collins and Sander-Jackson, "Fool's Gold," 42.

55. Battersea Power Station, built from 1929 to 1955, served as a large generator of coal power and was part of the standardization of London's electrical grid. It featured an Art Deco design commissioned to make the existence of a large plant in central London more appealing. Half of it was closed in 1975 and declared an English Heritage Grade II site in 1980; the other half closed in 1983, seven years before Margaret Thatcher's government would privatize electricity.

56. BPS was the site of the 2010 Tory manifesto launch party. David Cameron called it a "building in need of regeneration in a country in need of regeneration." Owen Hatherley observed that this launch party was "on an industrial site where nothing is produced, upon a swathe of dereliction at the heart of a great capital, on a locus of highly dubious real-estate dealings." Ross Adams, "Longing for a Greener Present: Neoliberalism and the Eco-City," *Radical Philosophy* 163 (2010); Owen Hatherley, "Battersea Power Station," *Icon*, 2012.

57. Mark Davidson and Loretta Lees, "New-Build 'Gentrification' and London's Riverside Renaissance," *Environment and Planning A* 37 (2005): 1166–67.

58. The development of BPS involves a complex array of groups, from Malaysian financial groups (S P Setia Berhad, Sime Darby Property, and the Employees Provident Fund), the city of London and Wandsworth council, the BPS Development Corporation, and an unwieldy assortment of high-profile architecture and consulting firms. As such, unless otherwise specified, references in this chapter to the "developers," "planners," or "designers" refer to discursively produced subject positions.

59. BPSDC, *The Placebook* (London: Battersea Power Station Development Company and JTP Press, 2014), 56.

60. Only a few years ago, it was common to read stories of unbuilt million-

pound studios in BPS being resold for £1.5 million. Julia Kollewe and Hilary Osborne, "Battersea Power Station Home Prices 'Defying All Logic,'" *Guardian*, November 28, 2014.

61. Rockwell is the founder of the Rockwell Group, an architecture firm responsible for the "public areas" of the BPS development. BPSDC, "An Englishman in New York," *Powerhouse* 4 (2015): 4.

62. BPSDC, *The Placebook*, 44.

63. BPSDC, *The Placebook*, 47.

64. This includes "real festivals," which are "intimate, non-corporate and fan-friendly." Andrew Harris argues that such events, coded as spontaneous and local, are a means by which middle-class gentrifiers selectively appropriate the "practices of the archetypal British country fair or village fete . . . [and a] working-class tradition for street parties." BPSDC, *The Placebook*, 65–66, 68; Andrew Harris, "Art and Gentrification: Pursuing the Urban Pastoral in Hoxton, London," *Transactions of the Institute of British Geographers* 37, no. 2 (2012): 226–41.

65. BPSDC, *The Placebook*, 45.

66. BPSDC, *The Placebook*, 47.

67. Accordingly, retail must "genuinely enhance the experience of being in a particular place" and be attentive to the "drama involved in the physical realities of shopping" and the "texture and tactility" of consumption. The well-read designers cite Benjamin on this point, though in their gloss his work becomes about the colonial sensuality of "vivid shop windows of imported foreign goods and the Parisian 'flaneurs' who strolled along to see what he called the 'phantasmagoria.'" BPSDC, *The Placebook*, 192, 84, 89, 94.

68. To wit, the design critic Stephen Bayley's description of his own settlement practice in Battersea: "To a young, poor, newly-married house-hunter, the area south of Chelsea and Westminster appealed because, in 1983, it was the unlikely, but welcome, combination of 'central' and 'cheap.' These were the positive attributes. More negative were the terrible traffic, an ugly sense of being an outcast and a generalised miasma of failure and neglect." BPSDC, "Living Architecture," *Powerhouse* 3 (2014): 5.

69. Smith, "Gentrification, the Frontier and the Restructuring of Urban Space."

70. BPSDC, *The Placebook*, 47.

71. BPSDC, *The Placebook*, 45.

72. Already in 2005, Davidson and Lees, "New-Build 'Gentrification' and London's Riverside Renaissance," 1172–74, point to rapidly increasing prices of one-bedroom flat rentals in Battersea.

73. BPSDC, *The Placebook*, 171–72.

74. Definitions of the prefix "re-" include "back to the original place or position, again, anew, implying an undoing of some previous action." BPSDC, "Living Architecture," 7, 43; "Re-, Prefix," *OED Online*.

75. Ross Adams, "Longing for a Greener Present: Neoliberalism and the Eco-City," *Radical Philosophy* 163 (2010): 6.

76. Adams, "Longing for a Greener Present," 4.
77. BPSDC, "Living Architecture," 56.
78. BPSDC, *The Placebook*, 44.
79. Nik Heynen, Maria Kaika, and Erik Swyngedouw, *In the Nature of Cities: Urban Political Ecology and the Politics of Urban Metabolism* (London: Taylor & Francis, 2006), 64.
80. Melissa Checker, "Wiped Out by the 'Greenwave': Environmental Gentrification and the Paradoxical Politics of Urban Sustainability," *City & Society* 23, no. 2 (2011): 212; Quastel, "Political Ecologies of Gentrification," 696.
81. This includes the embassy gardens at the new US embassy, the Battersea Roof Gardens by the High Line's designers James Corner Field Operations, a new park by LDA designs, the BPS rooftop by Andy Sturgeon Landscape and Garden Design, and others. BPSDC, "Wild at Heart," *Powerhouse* 5 (2016): 12. BPSDC, *The Placebook*, 50.
82. Including, somewhat darkly, tree species that "have been selected [to] thrive in the increasingly warm and wet conditions London enjoys." BPSDC, *The Placebook*, 33.
83. BPSDC, *The Placebook*, 50.
84. "The relentless pressure on land in the capital, the need to build at high densities, and, in some cases, neglect and disuse, mean that allotments are slowly but surely being eroded." London Assembly Environment Committee, "A Lot to Lose: London's Disappearing Allotments," 2006, 1.
85. BPSDC, *The Placebook*, 43–44.
86. BPSDC, *The Placebook*, 130.
87. Again, elided with the literal: "We are playing our part to ensure wildlife that has colonised the brownfield site retain as much of their habitat as possible once development of the site begins. New habitats are being provided for a wide range of insects, black redstarts and peregrine falcons as part of a series of wildlife management strategies." BPSDC, "Positive Energy," in-house publication, 2014, 33.
88. BPSDC, *The Placebook*, 130.
89. Harvey, "The Right to the City."
90. BPSDC, "Living Architecture," 25.
91. What is produced are "gated ecologies in which wealthier residents . . . selectively reap the advantages of clean water, adequate sanitation, beautiful parks, and environmentally friendly buildings and products." Those in social housing adjacent to these amenities are sometimes segregated by separate entrances. Hilary Cunningham, "Gated Ecologies and 'Possible Urban Worlds': From the Global City to the Natural City," in *The Natural City: Re-Envisioning the Built Environment*, ed. Ingrid Leman Stefanovic and Stephen Bede Scharper (Toronto: University of Toronto Press, 2012), 153; Hilary Osborne, "Poor Doors: The Segregation of London's Inner-City Flat Dwellers," *Guardian*, July 25, 2014.
92. Guardian Cities, "Revealed: The Insidious Creep of Pseudo-Public Space in London," *Guardian*, July 24, 2017.

93. Isabelle Anguelovski, "Healthy Food Stores, Greenlining and Food Gentrification: Contesting New Forms of Privilege, Displacement and Locally Unwanted Land Uses in Racially Mixed Neighborhoods," *International Journal of Urban and Regional Research* 39, no. 6 (2015): 24.

94. Kenneth A. Gould and Tammy L. Lewis, *Green Gentrification: Urban Sustainability and the Struggle for Environmental Justice* (London: Routledge, 2016); Hamil Pearsall, "Moving Out or Moving In? Resilience to Environmental Gentrification in New York City," *Local Environment* 17, no. 9 (2012): 1013–26.

95. Sarah Dooling, "Ecological Gentrification: A Research Agenda Exploring Justice in the City," *International Journal of Urban and Regional Research* 33, no. 3 (2009): 621–39.

96. Aware of this suspicion of private development, BPSDC must both present its intervention as a genuine public good even while advertising the development to those who most benefit from and reproduce class inequality. In the process, potential residents can be assured that there will be "all manner of winter gardens, roof terraces and communal courtyard spaces exclusively for residents" and that "like the shared gardens at the Barbican, or the private squares of Bloomsbury, these spaces offer inhabitants a private alternative for relaxation between the balconies or winter gardens of their home and from the lively public spaces of The Power Station Park." Attaching itself to the modernist cultural capital of both Bloomsbury and the Barbican, BPS developers offer the park/garden spaces as both a public and private environmental good, the former lively and the latter relaxing and exclusive but still communal. BPSDC, "Community Charter," 2014, 40; BPSDC, *The Placebook*, 83.

97. BPSDC, *The Placebook*, 131.

98. BPSDC, *The Placebook*, 148.

99. BPSDC, *The Placebook*, 149.

100. BPSDC, *The Placebook*, 149.

101. BPSDC, *The Placebook*, 131.

102. Quastel, "Political Ecologies of Gentrification," 703.

103. BPSDC, *The Placebook*, 65.

104. Leslie Kern, "From Toxic Wreck to Crunchy Chic: Environmental Gentrification through the Body," *Environment and Planning D: Society and Space* 33, no. 1 (2015): 74.

105. One might add that in the imaginary of planning and the reality of gentrification, these women are often white. Kern, "From Toxic Wreck to Crunchy Chic," 74.

106. BPSDC, *The Placebook*, 80.

107. To aid in this activity, engineers conducted light studies to maximize light in each apartment. In a crowded, rainy city, access to the sun itself is a privatized environmental good. BPSDC, "Foster + Partners Design Book," 2014, 19.

108. BPSDC, "Living Architecture," 6.

109. BPSDC, *The Placebook*, 103.

110. BPSDC, "An Englishman in New York," 34.

111. The focus on aesthetic revival naturalizes the structural shifts in Britain's economy. Smith and Williams, eds., *Gentrification of the City*.

112. David Ley, "Artists, Aestheticisation and the Field of Gentrification," *Urban Studies* 40, no. 12 (2003): 2530.

113. Ley, "Artists, Aestheticisation and the Field of Gentrification," 2533.

114. BPSDC, "Living Architecture," 29.

115. Michael Jager, "Class Definition and the Esthetics of Gentrification," in *Gentrification of the City*, ed. Neil Smith and Peter Williams (Winchester Place: Allen & Unwin, 1986), 81.

116. Smith, "Gentrification, the Frontier and the Restructuring of Urban Space," 83.

117. BPSDC, "The Icon Book," 2014, 7; Davidson and Lees, "New-Build 'Gentrification' and London's Riverside Renaissance."

118. BPSDC, *The Placebook*, 14.

119. BPSDC, "Wild at Heart," 7.

120. BPSDC, *The Placebook*, 217.

121. BPSDC, "Living Architecture," 18.

122. BPSDC, "Living Architecture," 18.

123. Sharon Zukin, *Loft Living: Culture and Capital in Urban Change* (New Brunswick, NJ: Rutgers University Press, 1982), 59.

124. Zukin, *Loft Living*, 67.

125. BPSDC, "An Englishman in New York," 43; BPSDC, *The Placebook*, 217.

126. BPSDC, "The Cranes," 2017, https://batterseapowerstation.co.uk/about/heritage-cranes.

127. "It is great these iconic cranes will be as much a part of Battersea's future as its illustrious past," said one architect. BPSDC, "Wild at Heart," 48.

128. BPSDC, "An Englishman in New York," 21.

129. Resulting in a "rough yet refined look." BPSDC, "An Englishman in New York," 4; BPSDC, "Wild at Heart," 21.

130. BPSDC, *The Placebook*, 199.

131. As such, "mindful of those converted barns, our designers are being asked to put in split levels, high ceilings, double height spaces with galleries, even winter gardens you can use throughout the year." BPSDC, *The Placebook*, 135.

132. BPSDC, *The Placebook*, 135.

133. BPSDC, "An Englishman in New York," 20.

134. BPSDC, "Wild at Heart," 10.

135. BPSDC, *The Placebook*, 35.

136. BPSDC, *The Placebook*, 76.

137. David Lloyd and Paul Thomas, *Culture and the State* (London: Routledge, 2014), 2.

138. Lloyd and Thomas, *Culture and the State*, 7.

139. Lloyd and Thomas, *Culture and the State*, 19.

140. BPSDC, *The Placebook*, 63.

141. BPSDC, *The Placebook*, 52.

142. "Hegemony, or ideology, is the process by which certain paradigms become so self-evident as to relegate alternatives to spaces of the nonsensical and the unthinkable." Lloyd and Thomas, *Culture and the State*, 21.

143. BPSDC, *The Placebook*, 87.

144. BPSDC, *The Placebook*, 52.

145. BPSDC, *The Placebook*, 111.

146. As in the hope that "in ten years' time, Battersea has the highest number of innovative collectives, creative mavericks and entrepreneurs per capita of any other part of London. . . . That would be a real marker of success." BPSDC, *The Placebook*, 112, 52.

147. Harris, "Art and Gentrification," 226–41.

148. BPSDC, *The Placebook*, 59.

149. BPSDC, *The Placebook*, 103.

5. Level Up: Zadie Smith's NW and the Promise of Progression

1. Centre for Cities, "Cities Outlook 2021," London, January 2021, http://www.centreforcities.org. The report cites the dispersal of labor caused by people working from home, a dynamic that does not take into consideration the fate of service workers in the city.

2. David Marcus, "Post-Hysterics: Zadie Smith and the Fiction of Austerity," *Dissent* 60, no. 2 (Spring 2013): 70.

3. Leah is white; the rest of the major characters are not. Natalie is born Keisha Blake and changes her name as an adult.

4. Lauren Elkin, "'Anyone over the Age of Thirty Catching a Bus Can Consider Himself a Failure': Class Mobility and Public Transport in Zadie Smith's NW," *Études Britanniques Contemporaines. Revue de la Société d'Études Anglaises Contemporaines* 49 (October 16, 2015).

5. Zadie Smith, NW (New York: Penguin, 2012), 180–81.

6. Insofar as video games are typically associated with children and teenagers in popular culture.

7. Smith, NW, 360.

8. Iain Sinclair, *The Last London: True Fictions from an Unreal City* (London: Oneworld, 2017), 56.

9. Smith, NW, 372.

10. Lauren Berlant, *Cruel Optimism* (Durham, NC: Duke University Press, 2011), 2, 3.

11. Berlant calls this impasse, writing that "the holding pattern implied in 'impasse' suggests a temporary housing." That is, a relation of cruel optimism can be likened to an inhabitance that is temporary and that awaits the next, inevitable dislocation, while understandingly desiring the permanence and stability suggested not by "housing" but by "home." Berlant, *Cruel Optimism*, 5.

12. Insufficient, and thus, per Bataille, capable of ecstatic relation. Georges Bataille, *The Tears of Eros*, trans. Peter Connor (San Francisco: City Lights, 2001).

13. Wendy Knepper, "Revisionary Modernism and Postmillennial Experimentation in Zadie Smith's NW," in *Reading Zadie Smith: The First Decade and Beyond*, ed. Philip Tew (London: A&C Black, 2013), 118.

14. Smith, NW, 31.
15. Smith, NW, 116.
16. Smith, NW, 87.
17. Smith, NW, 31.
18. Smith, NW, 48.
19. Smith, NW, 48.
20. Smith, NW, 44.
21. Smith, NW, 86.
22. Smith, NW, 3.
23. Smith, NW, 28.
24. "She is ashamed before an imagined nobody who isn't real and yet monitors our thoughts."
25. Smith, NW, 31.
26. Lynn Wells, "The Right to a Secret: Zadie Smith's NW," in *Reading Zadie Smith: The First Decade and Beyond*, ed. Philip Tew (London: A&C Black, 2013), 104.

27. To escape a conversation between Pauline and Michel, Leah goes to the garden to find that "Ned from upstairs is in her hammock, which is communal and so not her hammock." Smith, NW, 21.

28. Smith, NW, 32.

29. This phrase is often apocryphally attributed to Thatcher. However, as Lauren Elkin writes, "It almost doesn't matter if she actually said it or not: what matters is that people believe she could have said it," because it encapsulates Thatcher's vision of self and the welfare state. Elkin appropriately reads figures of transport in the novel as indexing the paradoxes of liberalism, that is, ideology based around upward mobility and forward progress that, in its will to privatization, stunts that very mobility. Smith, NW, 48; Elkin, "'Anyone over the Age of Thirty Catching a Bus Can Consider Himself a Failure,'" 3.

30. Smith, NW, 80–81.
31. Smith, NW, 83.
32. Molly Slavin, "Nowhere and Northwest, Brent and Britain: Geographies of Elsewhere in Zadie Smith's NW," *Journal of the Midwest Modern Language Association* 48, no. 1 (2015): 113.
33. Knepper, "Revisionary Modernism and Postmillennial Experimentation," 121.
34. Smith, NW, 83.
35. Smith, NW, 67.
36. Smith, NW, 75.

37. Smith, NW, 74.
38. Smith, NW, 69.
39. Smith, NW, 73.
40. This echoes, in a more personal and modern context, Lisa Lowe's discussion of how "freedom" in liberal ideology works to conceal the continuation of its opposite. Lisa Lowe, *The Intimacies of Four Continents*, illustrated ed. (Durham: Duke University Press, 2015), 15–16.
41. Smith, NW, 90.
42. Smith, NW, 90.
43. Smith, NW, 96, 98.
44. Smith, NW, 99.
45. Lourdes López-Ropero, "Searching for a 'Different Kind of Freedom': Postcoloniality and Postfeminist Subjecthood in Zadie Smith's NW," *Atlantis* 38, no. 2 (December 2016): 132.
46. Smith, NW, 300.
47. Natalie's portion of the novel tracks her development from child to adult through vignettes that trace both the construction and eventual destruction of a self. Many sections are also ironically and allusively titled, references ranging from popular song titles to literary texts and philosophical ideas. The theme of alienated marriage perhaps recalls Godard's *Le mepris*.
48. Smith, NW, 298.
49. Smith, NW, 298.
50. Smith, NW, 299.
51. Smith, NW, 300.
52. Elsewhere, Felix tells his former partner Annie that his new girlfriend, Grace, "knows what she's about. She's conscious," to which Annie sardonically responds, "That's setting the bar rather low, don't you think? I mean, bully for you she's not in a coma." Political consciousness (which, incidentally, Grace does not seem to possess in any way) becomes another attribute of self to be advertised. "Consciousness" can be joined to similar metaphors for political engagement, such as awareness and being woke. Smith, NW, 179.
53. Smith, NW, 319.
54. This phrase is ironically repeated near the end of the novel, as Natalie escapes this house to find herself "in the center of Caldwell's basin. Five blocks connected by walkways and bridges and staircases, and lifts that were to be avoided almost as soon as they were built. Smith, Hobbes, Bentham, Locke, Russell. Here is the door, here is the window. And repeat, and repeat." This prototypical estate architecture, classical appellations and all, was also turned into a kind of advertisement for Cameron's "Broken Britain "and Blair's "forgotten people." In this way architecture becomes—is made into—destiny, not only for individuals but for the nation as a whole. Smith, NW, 320.
55. Smith, NW, 304.
56. Smith, NW, 325–26.

57. Smith, NW, 346.
58. Smith, NW, 346–47.
59. By inference, a Nike Air circa 1988. Smith, NW, 211.
60. Smith, NW, 207–8.
61. Smith, NW, 360–61.
62. Smith, NW, 220–21.
63. Smith, NW, 221.
64. Beatriz Pérez Zapata reads this as a "Lacanian moment of (mis)recognition [that] will deepen Keisha's internal divisions and precipitate further 'forgeries.'" Beatriz Pérez Zapata, "'In Drag': Performativity and Authenticity in Zadie Smith's NW," *International Studies: Interdisciplinary Political and Cultural Journal* 16, no. 1 (September 1, 2014): 91.
65. This scene is revisited later when, as an adult, Natalie and Layla meet over lunch. Natalie uses the lunch to detail the various bourgeois spaces she can access while simultaneously dismissing them as pretentious, which strikes Layla as disingenuous. Layla calls Natalie out: As Natalie is "struck with dread," Layla says, "You're exactly the same . . . you always wanted to make it clear you weren't like the rest of us. You're still doing it . . . even when we used to do those songs you'd be with me but also totally not with me. Showing off. False. Fake. Signaling to the boys in the audience, or whatever." This affirms Natalie's own perception of her personality, and she responds not with offense or self-reflection but with dread. This suggests that, if she is fake, she is also unable to locate any real self beyond its performance. Smith, NW, 332–33.
66. Smith, NW, 344.
67. Smith, NW, 316.
68. Smith, NW, 321.
69. Smith, NW, 328.
70. Smith, NW, 323.
71. These images had already been arriving for Leah and Natalie, taking the familiar form of "stunned-looking women with hospital tags round their wrists, babies lying on their breast, hair inexplicably soaked through. They seemed to have stepped across a chasm into another world . . . they were the new arrivals in the neighborhood . . . mother and baby doing well, exhausted. It was as if no-one had ever had a baby before, in human history." Smith, NW, 312.
72. Natalie suggests an alternative: Instead of breaking the image system open, an African mythos "drawn from the natural world and the collective imagination of the people" could offer "something beautiful in the alignment between the one and the many." This idealization, however, is interrupted by a parenthetical from the narration that notes, "When Natalie Blake said 'In Africa' what she meant was 'at an earlier point in time.'" The modern invocation of the mythical as such, as Johannes Fabian and others have detailed, relied upon a progressivist understanding of history. The result was either a dismissal of the other as historically and evolutionarily distant or the primitivist fetishization and appropriation of this

difference. Natalie, the "bearer" of this colonial history, internalizes and reproduces its terms. Smith, NW, 322. Johannes Fabian, *Time and the Other: How Anthropology Makes Its Object* (New York: Columbia University Press, 2014).

73. Smith, NW, 324.
74. Smith, NW, 333.
75. Zapata, "'In Drag,'" 91.
76. James Arnett (among others) identifies this thematic affect as the point that distinguishes the sobriety of NW from Smith's "hysterical" *White Teeth*: "What all of this drag covers is still a hysterical, poststructuralist fear: that underneath all of the chosen identities we parade is an essential emptiness. That is, the novel questions the politics of the deconstructed self, multiple, shifting, and engaged in liberating performance, while, at the same time, not returning to a notion of the sovereign self or to social realist pretentions." Zapata, "'In Drag,'" 94; James Arnett, "Neoliberalism and False Consciousness before and after Brexit in Zadie Smith's NW," *Explicator* 76, no. 1 (January 2, 2018): 4; Nick Bentley, "Trailing Postmodernism: David Mitchell's *Cloud Atlas*, Zadie Smith's NW, and the Metamodern," *English Studies* 99, no. 7 (October 3, 2018): 723–43; Marcus, "Post-Hysterics."
77. Smith, NW, 251.
78. Smith, NW, 251–52.
79. Smith, NW, 316.
80. Smith, NW, 316.
81. Smith, NW, 353.
82. The one time she manages to have sex (in a section entitled "Love in the ruins"), a mostly comical affair with a young man, motherly and organizational instincts kick in: "On top of the wardrobe there was a lot of boxed-up stuff . . . there was something terribly sad about the whole place. She wished she could take the boxes down and sift through them and save whatever needed to be saved." Smith, NW, 350.
83. She finds that "on the website she was what everybody was looking for." Smith, NW, 312.
84. Smith, NW, 270.
85. Smith, NW, 354.
86. Smith, NW, 360, 355.
87. Along with his friends, who are earlier described as "two girls and a boy. Two women and a man. But they were dressed as kids. Natalie Blake was dressed as a successful lawyer in her early thirties." Smith, NW, 314.
88. Smith, NW, 362.
89. Smith, NW, 360.
90. Smith, NW, 364.
91. As the novel thinks through her, "There is a connection between boredom and the desire for chaos. Despite many disguises and bluffs perhaps she had never stopped wanting chaos." The notion of Natalie as the bored housewife is unconvincing not only because of the tentative "perhaps" in this statement

but because absolutely nothing in Keisha/Natalie's past and her fundamental tendencies toward completion and organization suggests a desire for chaos. Smith, NW, 365.

92. Smith, NW, 372.

93. "All attachment is optimistic, if we describe optimism as the force that moves you out of yourself and into the world." Berlant, *Cruel Optimism*, 1.

94. Smith, NW, 372.

95. Berlant, *Cruel Optimism*, 10.

96. Berlant, *Cruel Optimism*, 4.

97. To say nothing of the attachments that "people" and their institutions have toward the project of segregating and/or eliminating minority subjects.

98. Asma Abbas, *Another Love: A Politics of the Unrequited* (London: Rowman & Littlefield, 2018), 31.

99. Smith, NW, 376–77.

100. As Alexander Beaumont writes, however, "The development of the pastoral . . . mirrors the development of culture as a civilisational discourse." Alexander Beaumont, *Contemporary British Fiction and the Cultural Politics of Disenfranchisement* (London: Palgrave Macmillan, 2015), 209.

101. Alice Coleman, King's College (University of London) Staff Design Disadvantagement Team, and Sarah Brown, *Utopia on Trial: Vision and Reality in Planned Housing* (H. Shipman, 1985).

102. Smith, NW, 132.

103. Raymond Williams, *The Country and the City* (New York: Random House, 2013).

104. At the same time, this imaginary becomes momentarily concrete in reference to history; for example, they stop briefly under the awning of a pub called Jack Straw's Castle to take refuge from the rain. Wendy Knepper points out that Jack Straw was a figure in the 1381 peasant revolt, the same revolt that gives the novel its epigram. Knepper, "Revisionary Modernism and Postmillennial Experimentation," 122–23. Within the novel, this space is a fiction, as it has been converted to luxury flats and a gym. That it's referenced speaks to the novel's central concern, whether a nonironic utopia is possible, whether, before the fall, there was no hierarchy of development and thus no selves to construct and destroy. Straw was memorialized by Chaucer: "Out of the hyve cam the swarm of bees. / So hydous was the noyse — a, benedicitee! / Certes, he Jakke Straw and his meynee / Ne made nevere shoutes half so shrille / Whan that they wolden any Flemyng kille." Daan Deol, "7 Secrets of Hampstead Heath," *Londonist*, 2017, https://londonist.com/london/secret/7-secrets-of-hampstead-heath.

105. Smith, NW, 372.

106. Smith, NW, 378.

107. Smith, NW, 378.

108. Smith, NW, 382.

109. Smith, NW, 383–84.

110. Including, now, the new Olympic stadium and Anish Kapoor's *ArcelorMittal Orbit*.

111. Smith, NW, 384.

112. Slavin, "Nowhere and Northwest, Brent and Britain," 111.

113. Both Alberto Fernández Carbajal and Vanessa Guignery call attention to the similarities to Clarissa's contemplation of suicide in Mrs. Dalloway. Smith, NW, 385; Alberto Fernández Carbajal, "On Being Queer and Postcolonial: Reading Zadie Smith's NW through Virginia Woolf's *Mrs Dalloway*," *Journal of Commonwealth Literature* 51, no. 1 (March 1, 2016): 85; Vanessa Guignery, "Zadie Smith's NW, or the Art of Line-Crossing," *E-Rea. Revue Électronique d'Études Sur le Monde Anglophone* 11, no. 2 (July 15, 2014).

114. Slavin has a much more optimistic reading of this scene, writing that "when Natalie pauses and articulates her geography, she turns the NW space of nowhere into the place of northwest." Slavin, "Nowhere and Northwest, Brent and Britain," 111.

115. Smith, NW, 361.

116. Smith, NW, 362.

117. Smith, NW, 362.

118. Felix is stabbed on Albert Road. There is an Albert Road in Kilburn (where the Brent Housing Partnership is located), but this location does not make sense in the context of the novel's plot. Instead, "Albert Road" in the novel may correspond to Aldershot Road, near a salon formerly called "Grace and Beauty."

119. The men are not explicitly identified as people of color, but this is rather tellingly implied through context: their clothing, manner of physical comportment, colloquial form of expression, and ability to make the white woman extremely frightened. Smith, NW, 194.

120. Tammy Amiel Houser, "Zadie Smith's NW: Unsettling the Promise of Empathy," *Contemporary Literature* 58, no. 1 (Spring 2017): 136–37.

121. Nathan, in a contextless aside, says to Natalie: "This is on him. Always taking shit too far. How can I stop Tyler though? . . . I shouldn't even be chatting with you, I should be in Dalston, cos this isn't even on me, it's on him. But I'm looking at myself asking myself Nathan why you still here? Why you still here? And I don't even know why. I ain't even joking. I should just run from myself." Here it is implied that Tyler took the robbery of Felix, revenge for being expelled from humanity, "too far" in stabbing him. Like Natalie, Nathan is perplexed by his own reproduction of self, the way he falls into patterns and situations. As such, he needs to escape not just from Caldwell and Kilburn but from himself. Smith, NW, 370.

122. Smith, NW, 397, 399.

123. Smith, NW, 400.

124. This perhaps complements Berlant's observation that, through evoking an atmospheric affect, the novel form "points to something barely apprehensible in ordinary life and consciousness." In this sense, Natalie reverts to the tropes of liberal individualism because she cannot imagine what comes after. However, what is less

pronounced in Berlant's theory is the possibility that the emergent is also a lastness, that nothing comes after the end of capitalism except more capitalism. Arnett, "Neoliberalism and False Consciousness," 4; Berlant, *Cruel Optimism*.

125. Smith, NW, 401.

126. López-Ropero, "Searching for a 'Different Kind of Freedom,'" 137; Wells, "The Right to a Secret," 109.

127. Jesse van Amelsvoort, "Between Forster and Gilroy: Race and (Re) Connection in Zadie Smith's NW," *Tulsa Studies in Women's Literature* 37, no. 2 (2018): 430.

128. Houser, "Zadie Smith's NW," 141; Marcus, "Post-Hysterics," 73.

129. Guignery, "Zadie Smith's NW, or the Art of Line-Crossing"; Annalisa Pes, "Post-Postcolonial Issues and Identities in Zadie Smith's NW," *European English Messenger* 23, no. 2 (Winter 2014): 26; Wells, "The Right to a Secret," 98.

130. Stuart Hall et al., *Policing the Crisis: Mugging, the State, and Law and Order* (Basingstoke: Macmillan, 1978).

131. As discussed in Chapter 3, this is a category legally introduced by the 1824 vagrancy act and used to police predominantly Black urban neighborhoods in the 1970s and 1980s.

6. Geographies of Discontent: Brexit and the Politics of Abandonment

1. Likewise, the term "postcolonial" does familiar double work here, referring both to a historical situation (i.e., the dynamics of immigration, settlement, and race after the end of formal empire) and a mode of critique, one that is in fact attentive to forms of *ongoing colonialism*.

2. "PM Economy Speech: 30 June 2020," https://www.gov.uk/government/speeches/pm-economy-speech-30-june-2020.

3. "Boris Johnson: First Speech as PM in Full," *BBC News*, July 24, 2019, https://www.bbc.com/news/uk-politics-49102495.

4. My emphasis. José Javier Olivas Osuna et al., "Understanding Brexit at the Local Level: Causes of Discontent and Asymmetric Impacts" (London: London School of Economics and Political Science, 2019), 17, 8.

5. Osuna et al., "Understanding Brexit at the Local Level," 4.

6. Christine Berberich et al., eds., *Affective Landscapes in Literature, Art, and Everyday Life: Memory, Place, and the Senses*. Ashgate, 2015.

7. For example, Dagenham—a short train ride away from the regenerated Olympic site—voted leave by a similar or greater margins to many areas of Yorkshire. "EU Referendum: The Result in Maps and Charts," *BBC News*, June 24, 2016, https://www.bbc.com/news/uk-politics-36616028.

8. It was also thought that places that voted leave were particularly affected by increased immigration.

9. Migration Observatory, "UK Public Opinion toward Immigration: Overall Attitudes," https://migrationobservatory.ox.ac.uk/resources/briefings/uk-public

-opinion-toward-immigration-overall-attitudes-and-level-of-concern/; Zack Beauchamp, "Brexit Was Fueled by Irrational Xenophobia, Not Real Economic Grievances," *Vox*, June 25, 2016, https://www.vox.com/2016/6/25/12029786/brexit-uk-eu-immigration-xenophobia; "Positive Economic Impact of UK Immigration from the European Union: New Evidence," *UCL News*, November 5, 2014, https://www.ucl.ac.uk/news/2014/nov/positive-economic-impact-uk-immigration-european-union-new-evidence.

10. The former leader of the Liberal Democrats, Vince Cable, phrased it thus: "Nostalgia for a world where passports were blue, faces were white and the map was coloured imperial pink." "Cable Says Nostalgia for 'White' UK Helped Leave Vote," *BBC News*, March 11, 2018, https://www.bbc.com/news/uk-politics-43364331. Among innumerable other examples, see Gurminder K. Bhambra, "The Imperial Nostalgia of a 'Small Island,'" *UK in a Changing Europe*, June 4, 2018, https://ukandeu.ac.uk/the-imperial-nostalgia-of-a-small-island/; Tony Barber, "Nostalgia and the Promise of Brexit," *Financial Times*, July 19, 2018.

11. See, for example, JRF, "Brexit Vote Explained: Poverty, Low Skills and Lack of Opportunities," August 26, 2016, https://www.jrf.org.uk/report/brexit-vote-explained-poverty-low-skills-and-lack-opportunities; Robert Ford, *Revolt on the Right: Explaining Support for the Radical Right in Britain*, 1st ed. (Abingdon: Routledge, 2014); Rosie Carter, "Understanding the Drivers of HOPE and Hate" (London: Hope not Hate, September 2018). Bhambra, however, claims that at least some of these articles are clouded by a "methodological whiteness." Gurminder K. Bhambra, "Brexit, Trump, and 'Methodological Whiteness': On the Misrecognition of Race and Class," *British Journal of Sociology* 68, no. S1 (2017): S214–32.

12. David Goodhart, *The Road to Somewhere: The Populist Revolt and the Future of Politics*, 1st ed. (London: Hurst, 2017).

13. Goodhart assumes that the culture of somewheres is homogeneous throughout Britain (despite being attached to locality) and, further, preexisted its encounter with postcolonial migration. Qtd. in Jonathan Freedland, "*The Road to Somewhere* by David Goodhart—a Liberal's Rightwing Turn on Immigration," *Guardian*, March 22, 2017, https://www.theguardian.com/books/2017/mar/22/the-road-to-somewhere-david-goodhart-populist-revolt-future-politics; see David Goodhart, "Too Diverse?," *Prospect*, 2004, https://www.prospectmagazine.co.uk/magazine/too-diverse-david-goodhart-multiculturalism-britain-immigration-globalisation. This can be read as a mirror to Richard Florida's fetishization of the creative class. Richard Florida, *The Rise of the Creative Class: And How It's Transforming Work, Leisure, Community, and Everyday Life* (Turtleback, 2003).

14. This has been described more recently by Andrés Rodríguez-Pose as the "revenge of places that don't matter." The LSE report referenced here frames this more neutrally as the "geography of discontent." My emphasis. Torsten Bell, "The Referendum, Living Standards and Inequality," *Resolution Foundation* (blog), June 24, 2016, https://www.resolutionfoundation.org/media/blog/the-referendum-living-standards-and-inequality/; Andrés Rodríguez-Pose, "The Revenge of the

Places That Don't Matter (and What to Do about It)," *Cambridge Journal of Regions, Economy and Society* 11, no. 1 (March 10, 2018): 189–209; Osuna et al., "Understanding Brexit at the Local Level," 4.

15. For example, Frank Gehry, speaking of his mutually beneficial relationship with Boris Johnson: "I liked the Mayor, he was cute and sassy. He was so young, I thought, and had a lot of energy. He seemed very happy with the scheme—with its direction and how many affordable units we're creating." BPSDC, "Living Architecture," *Powerhouse* 3 (2014): 22.

16. This shift has been described in terms of a hollowing out of the planning apparatus. Rhys Jones et al., "'Filling in' the State: Economic Governance and the Evolution of Devolution in Wales," *Environment and Planning C: Government and Policy* 23, no. 3 (2005): 337.

17. Jesse Heley, "Soft Spaces, Fuzzy Boundaries, and Spatial Governance in Post-Devolution Wales," *International Journal of Urban and Regional Research* 37, no. 4 (2013): 1336.

18. Philip Allmendinger and Graham Haughton, "The Fluid Scales and Scope of UK Spatial Planning," *Environment and Planning A* 39, no. 6 (2007): 1484.

19. Elizabeth A. Povinelli, *Economies of Abandonment: Social Belonging and Endurance in Late Liberalism* (Durham, NC: Duke University Press, 2011).

20. Abigail Gilmore, "Cold Spots, Crap Towns, and Cultural Deserts: The Role of Place and Geography in Cultural Participation and Creative Place-Making," *Cultural Trends* 22 (2013): 87.

21. Gilmore, "Cold Spots, Crap Towns, and Cultural Deserts," 89.

22. John Harris, "You Can't Just Catch a Bus to a Job That Doesn't Exist," *Guardian*, July 6, 2011, https://www.theguardian.com/commentisfree/2011/jul/06/job-south-wales-fantasy; see also Carole Cadwalladr, "View from Wales: Town Showered with EU Cash Votes to Leave EU," *Observer*, June 25, 2016, https://www.theguardian.com/uk-news/2016/jun/25/view-wales-town-showered-eu-cash-votes-leave-ebbw-vale.

23. Caryl Phillips, *A Distant Shore* (New York: Vintage, 2005), 179.

24. Jamaica Kincaid, *A Small Place* (New York: Farrar, Straus and Giroux, 2000).

25. Andrew Warnes, "Enemies Within: Diaspora and Democracy in *Crossing the River* and *A Distant Shore*," *Moving Worlds* 7, no. 1 (2007): 41.

26. Paola Della Valle, "Migration and Multiplicity of Belonging in Caryl Phillips," *Le Simplegadi* 18 (2018): 72.

27. Paul Gilroy, *Postcolonial Melancholia* (New York: Columbia University Press, 2005).

28. Petra Tournay-Theodotou, "Strange Encounters: Nationhood and the Stranger in Caryl Phillips's *A Distant Shore*," in *Caryl Phillips: Writing in the Key of Life*, ed. B. Ledent and D. Tunca (Amsterdam: Rodopi, 2012), 296, 297.

29. Alessandra Di Maio, "A New World Tribe in Caryl Phillips's *A Distant Shore*," in *Caryl Phillips: Writing in the Key of Life*, ed. B. Ledent and D. Tunca (Amsterdam: Rodopi, 2012), 257.

30. Bénédicte Ledent, "'Of, and Not of, This Place': Attachment and Detachment in Caryl Phillips' *A Distant Shore*," *Kunapipi* 26, no. 1 (2004): 152–60.

31. Phillips, *A Distant Shore*, 52.

32. Phillips, *A Distant Shore*, 3.

33. John McLeod, "Diaspora and Utopia: Reading the Recent Work of Paul Gilroy and Caryl Phillips," in *Diasporic Literature and Theory—Where Now?*, ed. Mark Shackleton (Newcastle upon Tyne: Cambridge Scholars, 2008), 10; Di Maio, "A New World Tribe in Caryl Phillips's *A Distant Shore*," 251.

34. David Ellis, "'They Are Us': Caryl Phillips' *A Distant Shore* and the British Transnation," *Journal of Commonwealth Literature* (2013): 6.

35. Qtd. in Jaqueline Nassy Brown, *Dropping Anchor, Setting Sail: Geographies of Race in Black Liverpool* (Princeton, NJ: Princeton University Press, 2005), 61.

36. Phillips, *A Distant Shore*, 3.

37. "The Great Divide," *Economist*, September 15, 2012.

38. Cindy Gabrielle, "The Civilized Pretence: Caryl Phillips and *A Distant Shore*," in *Caryl Phillips: Writing in the Key of Life*, ed. B. Ledent and D. Tunca (Amsterdam: Rodopi, 2012), 311.

39. Doreen Massey, *World City* (London: Polity, 2007), 121.

40. Josiane Ranguin, "Borderland Strangers in Caryl Phillip's *A Distant Shore*," in *A Fluid Sense of Self: The Politics of Transnational Identity*, ed. Silvia Schultermandl and Şebnem Toplu (Vienna: Lit, 2010), 206–7.

41. Phillips, *A Distant Shore*, 4.

42. Tournay-Theodotou, "Strange Encounters," 196; Gabrielle, "The Civilized Pretence," 310.

43. Qtd. in M. Parker, *Thatcherism and the Fall of Coal*, ed. Oxford Institute for Energy Studies (Oxford: Oxford University Press for the Oxford Institute for Energy Studies, 2000), 8.

44. Mining and provincial industrial production occurred in many areas of Britain, of course, not just in northern England. Huw Beynon, *Digging Deeper: Issues in the Miners' Strike* (London: Verso, 1985), 5.

45. "'Mrs. Thatcher? She's not to be mentioned,' he said. 'Just don't mention the lady. She set people against each other, she broke up families, and it's still the same today. There are still people who won't talk to each other, who'll cross the road rather than run into somebody they worked with for 30 years.'" John F. Burns, "As Thatcher Goes to Rest, Miners Feel No Less Bitter," *New York Times*, April 16, 2013.

46. When this politics is ignored, xenophobia becomes naturalized into place, as in the epithetic spatial metaphor of "Little England." Tom Nairn, *Pariah: Misfortunes of the British Kingdom* (London: Verso, 2002), 110.

47. Beynon, *Digging Deeper*, 152, 153.

48. "Cafe Owner in Race 'Warning' Sign," *BBC News*, July 10, 2013, https://www.bbc.com/news/uk-england-leeds-23248503.

49. Gordon Cherry and Alan Rogers, *Rural Change and Planning: England and Wales in the Twentieth Century* (London: E & FN Spon, 1996), 110.

50. "While work has become more white collar and far less obviously dangerous, it has also become more short-term—call centres are already looking less secure as jobs move abroad." Mary Hennock, "Yorkshire: Slag Heaps to Ski Slopes," BBC News, 2004.

51. Phillips, *A Distant Shore*, 4.

52. Jeremy Burchardt, *Paradise Lost: Rural Idyll and Social Change in England since 1800* (London: I. B. Tauris, 2002), 188.

53. Phillips, *A Distant Shore*, 39.

54. Cherry and Rogers, *Rural Change and Planning*, 160.

55. Howard Newby, *Country Life: A Social History of Rural England* (London: Weidenfeld and Nicolson, 1987), 233.

56. Newby, *Country Life*, 227.

57. Cherry and Rogers, *Rural Change and Planning*, 160.

58. Sue Glyptis, *Countryside Recreation*, ed. Brian Duffield (Harlow: Longman, 1991), 12.

59. Glyptis, *Countryside Recreation*, 11.

60. Newby, *Country Life*, 232.

61. See Burchardt, *Paradise Lost*, 188.

62. Newby, *Country Life*, 233.

63. Rowena Mason, "Ukip's Godfrey Bloom Will Not Apologise over 'Bongo Bongo Land' Comments," *Guardian*, August 7, 2013, https://www.theguardian.com/politics/2013/aug/07/ukip-bongo-bongo-land-godfrey-bloom.

64. Phillips, *A Distant Shore*, 5.

65. Phillips, *A Distant Shore*, 4.

66. Phillips, *A Distant Shore*, 4.

67. Phillips, *A Distant Shore*, 18.

68. Phillips, *A Distant Shore*, 256.

69. McCarthy and Stone, "Retirement Homes in Yorkshire," 2014, https://www.mccarthyandstone.co.uk/retirement-properties-for-sale/locations/yorkshire/.

70. Phillips, *A Distant Shore*, 236.

71. Originally, "the bungalow was the peasant's hut of rural Bengal. Subsequently, when it came to mean a house for Europeans in India, the criteria were explicitly racial and cultural." Within England, it would also come to symbolize "getting away from it all" for bohemian back-to-the-landers, who were a "small, middle class minority in a society marked by vast conspicuous consumption of the upper class on the one hand and immense poverty on the other." Anthony King, *The Bungalow: The Production of a Global Culture* (Oxford: Oxford University Press, 1984), 1, 119.

72. Phillips, *A Distant Shore*, 6.

73. Phillips, *A Distant Shore*, 6.

74. Burchardt writes that "by the 1980s rural recreation had become one of the dominant uses of leisure time in rural England." McCarthy and Stone tout the "picturesque towns" and the many walking routes, including the "Malham Tarn Upland Farm Walk [which] is a good option for those that enjoy learning about the

local history." Burchardt, *Paradise Lost*, 181; McCarthy Stone, "Retirement Homes in Yorkshire."

75. Phillips, *A Distant Shore*, 5.
76. Ledent, "'Of, and Not of, This Place,'" 154.
77. Newby, *Country Life*, 224.
78. Warnes, "Enemies Within," 42.
79. Phillips, *A Distant Shore*, 44.
80. See Lauren Elkin, "'Anyone over the Age of Thirty Catching a Bus Can Consider Himself a Failure': Class Mobility and Public Transport in Zadie Smith's NW," *Études Britanniques Contemporaines. Revue de la Société d'Études Anglaises Contemporaines* 49 (October 16, 2015).
81. Peter Ambrose, "The Rural/Urban Fringe as Battleground," in *The English Rural Community: Image and Analysis*, ed. Brian Short (Cambridge: Cambridge University Press, 1992).
82. Stephen Clingman, "England Has Changed: Questions of National Form in *A Distant Shore*," *Moving Worlds* 7, no. 1 (2007): 51.
83. Francesco Cattani, "Songs and Verses of New Ethnicities: Resistance and Representation in Black British Culture," *Between* 5, no. 10 (November 30, 2015): 60.
84. Cattani, "Songs and Verses of New Ethnicities," 59.
85. "PM: Broken Society Tops My Agenda," *BBC News*, August 15, 2011, https://www.bbc.com/news/uk-politics-14524834.
86. "Not So Broken," *Economist*, October 25, 2012.
87. Phillips, *A Distant Shore*, 209.
88. Phillips, *A Distant Shore*, 180–81.
89. Referred to here by the pejorative "slattern." The *OED* defines "slattern" as "a woman or girl untidy and slovenly in person, habits, or surroundings; a slut."
90. Phillips, *A Distant Shore*, 213.
91. Rei Terada, *Looking Away: Phenomenality and Dissatisfaction, Kant to Adorno*, 1st ed. (Cambridge, MA: Harvard University Press, 2009).
92. Phillips, *A Distant Shore*, 213.
93. Phillips, *A Distant Shore*, 204.
94. "Yob" is "boy" spelled backward and is thus a specifically masculine figure. *OED*: "a boy, a youth; in mod. use, a lout, a hooligan." Phillips, *A Distant Shore*, 213.
95. Phillips, *A Distant Shore*, 6–7.
96. Phillips, *A Distant Shore*, 198.
97. Bénédicte Ledent notes that the family (and its garden) as a model of community implies both attachment and detachment to a monstrous and ruinous violence (in the figure of her father). Ledent, "'Of, and Not of, This Place,'" 70.
98. Phillips, *A Distant Shore*, 180.
99. Phillips, *A Distant Shore*, 181.
100. Phillips, *A Distant Shore*, 179.
101. She also remarks critically on the "traditional identification of the land/country/nation with the female body" in relation to a different character, Denise.

The problematic nature of this identification between the nation and the female body could be extended to Dorothy as well. Tournay-Theodotou, "Strange Encounters," 295, 303.

102. Courtman similarly employs allegories of health: "Dorothy and Solomon are both refugees in unhealthy societies which prevent them from finding peace with each other"; "The collective trauma of civil wars in Africa have brutalized and maimed what should have been a group of healthy young nations"; "The Britain and Africa depicted in *A Distant Shore* are profoundly unhealthy societies." Di Maio, "A New World Tribe," 258; Courtman, "Dorothy's Heart of Darkness," 271, 275.

103. Ping Su, "Madness and Silence in Caryl Phillips's *A Distant Shore* and *In the Falling Snow*," in *Madness in Anglophone Caribbean Literature: On the Edge*, ed. Bénédicte Ledent, Evelyn O'Callaghan, and Daria Tunca (Cham: Springer International, 2018), 68.

104. Reading Adorno, Terada finds in dissatisfaction a still-inherent right to relation. As Adorno writes, "The very rebuttal through which the general has exerted its influence appears to the individual as exclusion from the general; he who has lost love knows himself deserted by all, and this is why he scorns consolation." Quoted in Terada, *Looking Away*, 193.

105. Maurice Blanchot and Pierre Joris, *The Unavowable Community* (Barrytown, NY: Station Hill, 1983), 5.

106. Perhaps she is an "existence shattered through and through, composing itself only as it decomposes itself constantly, violently and in silence." Blanchot and Joris, *The Unavowable Community*, 6.

107. Gilroy, *Postcolonial Melancholia*, 15.

108. Gilroy, *Postcolonial Melancholia*, 111.

109. "The admirable utopian principles of his [Gilroy's] work—equality, democracy, and freedom beyond the illiberalism of race and nation—at times divert him from a consideration of the ways in which the realities of contemporary Britain simply do not fit his schema." McLeod, "Diaspora and Utopia," 5, 7.

110. Given the supposed stasis of nativist identity, differences between the connotations of Britishness and Englishness are often elided. This is ironic, as the Brexit vote took place in the under-recognized context of debates over English devolution (termed the West Lothian question). See Michael Kenny, *The Politics of English Nationhood* (Oxford: Oxford University Press, 2014).

111. In fact, it is the idealism of this position that leads Althusser to emphasize overdetermination: "What is a 'survival'? What is its theoretical status? Is it essentially social or 'psychological'?" Louis Althusser, *For Marx* (London: Verso, 2005), 77.

112. Gilroy, *Postcolonial Melancholia*, 108.

113. Gilroy, *Postcolonial Melancholia*, 108.

114. Brenna Bhandar, *Colonial Lives of Property: Law, Land, and Racial Regimes of Ownership* (Durham, NC: Duke University Press Books, 2018), 12; Stuart Hall, "Signification, Representation, Ideology: Althusser and the Post-structuralist Debates," *Critical Studies in Mass Communication* 2, no. 2 (June 1985): 91–114.

115. "Factors of class, generation, nationality and ethnicity . . . potentially contradict one another, and it is this contradiction that the 'sovereigntist' discourse manipulated by the partisans of Brexit overlays." Étienne Balibar, "Brexit, the Anti-Grexit," https://www.versobooks.com/blogs/2735-brexit-the-anti-grexit.

116. "It's an endless stream of anticlimax . . . almost every day promises to be a grand, important day in our country's history, but most of them come to nothing." Martha Gill, "Brexit: The Most Boring Important Story in the World," *New York Times*, December 14, 2018, https://www.nytimes.com/2018/12/14/opinion/sunday/theresa-may-brexit.html.

117. Ernesto Laclau, *On Populist Reason* (London: Verso, 2018), 97.

118. Laclau, *On Populist Reason*, 94.

119. Althusser, *For Marx*, 76.

120. Althusser, *For Marx*, 78.

121. Althusser, *For Marx*, 78.

122. Etienne Balibar, "Structural Causality, Overdetermination, and Antagonism," in *Postmodern Materialism and the Future of Marxist Theory: Essays in the Althusserian Tradition*, ed. David F. Ruccio and Antonio Callari (Hanover, NBH: University Press of New England [for] Wesleyan University Press, 1996), 117.

123. Balibar, "Structural Causality, Overdetermination, and Antagonism," 119.

124. Althusser, *For Marx*, 78.

125. Balibar, "Structural Causality, Overdetermination, and Antagonism," 115.

126. This absence may be a more unreadable form of the *abandonment* that has been cited in reference to Brexit's "geography of discontent." Frantz Fanon writes, "The abandonment-neurotic demands proof. He is no longer content with isolated statements. He has lost confidence. Before forming an objective relationship, he demands repeated proof from his partner." Su, "Madness and Silence," 66.

Coda

1. "Solution or Utopia? Design for Refugees," Stedelijk Museum, https://www.stedelijk.nl/en/exhibitions/solution-or-utopia-design-for-refugees.

2. "Refugee Emojis," *SuperHeroes* (blog), https://hellosuperheroes.com/work/refugee-emojis/.

3. "Europe in Africa—Home," europeinafrica, https://www.europeinafrica.com.

4. The authors, of course, dutifully cite theory while draining it of its critical capacity: "Our territorial/transnational distinction parallels Zygmunt Bauman's distinction between solid and liquid forms of sociality, while our archipelagic metaphor is influenced by Edouard Glissant's mise en relation (establishing a connection)." Robin Cohen and Nicholas Van Hear, "Visions of Refugia: Territorial and Transnational Solutions to Mass Displacement," *Planning Theory & Practice* 18, no. 3 (July 3, 2017): 495.

5. Antarin Chakrabarty, "Smart Mischief: An Attempt to Demystify the Smart

NOTES TO PAGES 219–20   283

Cities Craze in India," *Environment and Urbanization* 31, no. 1 (April 1, 2019): 198; see also Ayona Datta, "A 100 Smart Cities, a 100 Utopias," *Dialogues in Human Geography* 5, no. 1 (March 1, 2015): 49–53.

6. Like regeneration projects in the United Kingdom, smart cities are announced through extensive corporate documentation. For example, "Making a City Smart" features exhortations to always involve the local community accompanied by charts whose dizzying complexity would be appreciated by the likes of Patrick Geddes. Sometimes, designers must make do with generic illustrations that clearly reference US cities, as in the documentation for Pune Smart City. Smart Cities Mission, "Making a City Smart: Learnings from the Smart Cities Mission" (Delhi: Smart Cities Mission, Ministry of Housing and Urban Affairs, Government of India, March 2021), https://smartnet.niua.org/sites/default/files/resources/making_a_city_smart_mar2021.pdf; Pune Smart City Development Corporation, "Pune Smart City: Place-Making" (Pune Smart City Development Corporation, 2017), https://smartnet.niua.org/sites/default/files/resources/Pune%20Placemaking%20-%20Concept%20notes.pdf.

7. As its chief architect, Bimal Patel, says, "The overall objective of works planned on the Central Vista is to ensure environmental sustainability, restore the vista's architectural character, protect its heritage buildings, expand and improve public space, and to extend its axis. . . . It is also very difficult to work on because of India's unique diversity. We have people whose sensibilities, attitudes, or beliefs are avant-garde. We also have a vast section whose sensibilities are pre-modern. Our architecture has to speak to all of them." Alpana Kishore, "Looking at Central Vista through a Different Lens: How World Class Is 'World Class'?," *Newslaundry*, December 2, 2021, https://www.newslaundry.com/2021/12/02/looking-at-central-vista-through-a-different-lens-how-world-class-is-world-class; Niharika Sharma, "The Chief Architect of Central Vista Thinks Modi's Project Will Define 'New India,'" *Quartz*, https://qz.com/india/2032660/chief-architect-explains-why-modis-central-vista-is-important/.

8. Jacques Rancière, *Disagreement*, trans. Julie Rose (Minneapolis: University of Minnesota Press, 2005), 19, 27; Jean-François Lyotard and Georges Van Den Abbeele, *The Differend* (Minneapolis: University of Minnesota Press, 1988), 45.

9. Denise Ferreira da Silva, "No-Bodies: Law, Raciality, and Violence," *Griffith Law Review* 18, no. 2 (January 2009): 231.

10. This section, "Antithesis," is one that I keep returning to in thinking of my own positionality within academia. It is still the case, as Adorno writes, that intellectuals "are at once the last enemies of the bourgeois and the last bourgeois. In still permitting themselves to think at all in the face of the naked reproduction of existence, they act as a privileged group; in letting matters rest there, they declare the nullity of their privilege . . . there is no way out of entanglement." My distaste for this script of "resistance" in academic writing is related to my continual unease at the hierarchies, exclusions, and pretensions of the academy and the university, and our

participation in them, and of course at the many complicities with development—spatial, material, epistemological—that make a project like this possible. I was at the Stedelijk Museum, for example, as a tourist, after ACLA; then I returned to one of many gentrifying neighborhoods I've inhabited in Southern California. Theodor Adorno, *Minima Moralia: Reflections from Damaged Life* (London: Verso, 2020), 27.

11. Asma Abbas, *Another Love: A Politics of the Unrequited* (Lanham, MD: Rowman & Littlefield, 2018), 4.

Bibliography

Aalen, Frederick. "English Origins." In *Garden City: Past, Present and Future*, ed. Stephen Ward. London: Taylor & Francis, 1992.

Abbas, Asma. *Another Love: A Politics of the Unrequited*. London: Rowman & Littlefield, 2018.

Adams, Ross. "Longing for a Greener Present: Neoliberalism and the Eco-City." *Radical Philosophy* 163 (2010).

Adams, Stephen. "General Election 2010: For David Cameron, Battersea Power Station Is a Place Called Hope." *Telegraph*, April 14, 2010.

Adorno, Theodor. *Minima Moralia: Reflections from Damaged Life*. London: Verso, 2020.

Aiyer, Sophie M., Marc A. Zimmerman, Susan Morrel-Samuels, and Thomas M. Reischl. "From Broken Windows to Busy Streets: A Community Empowerment Perspective." *Health Education & Behavior* 42, no. 2 (April 1, 2015): 137–47.

Akomfrah, John, dir. *Handsworth Songs*. Documentary. Black Audio Film Collective, n.d.

Allmendinger, Philip, and Graham Haughton. "The Fluid Scales and Scope of UK Spatial Planning." *Environment and Planning A* 39, no. 6 (2007): 1478–96.

AlSayyad, Nezar. *Hybrid Urbanism: On the Identity Discourse and the Built Environment*. Westport, CT: Greenwood, 2001.

Althusser, Louis. *For Marx*. London: Verso, 2005.

Amati, Marco, Robert Freestone, and Sarah Robertson. "'Learning the City': Patrick Geddes, Exhibitions, and Communicating Planning Ideas." *Landscape and Urban Planning* 166 (2017): 97–105.

Ambrose, Peter. "The Rural/Urban Fringe as Battleground." In *The English Rural Community: Image and Analysis*, ed. Brian Short. Cambridge: Cambridge University Press, 1992.

Amelsvoort, Jesse van. "Between Forster and Gilroy: Race and (Re)Connection in Zadie Smith's NW." *Tulsa Studies in Women's Literature* 37, no. 2 (2018): 419–34.

Anderson, Benedict. *Imagined Communities: Reflections on the Origin and Spread of Nationalism*. London: Verso, 2006.

Anguelovski, Isabelle. "Healthy Food Stores, Greenlining and Food Gentrification: Contesting New Forms of Privilege, Displacement and Locally Unwanted Land Uses in Racially Mixed Neighborhoods." *International Journal of Urban and Regional Research* 39, no. 6 (2015): 1209–30.

Appel, Hannah. "Infrastructural Time." In *The Promise of Infrastructure*, ed. Nikhil Anand, Akhil Gupta, and Hannah Appel. Durham, NC: Duke University Press, 2018.

Apter, Emily. *Against World Literature: On the Politics of Untranslatability*. 1st ed. London: Verso, 2013.

Araeen, Rasheed. *The Other Story: Afro-Asian Artists in Post-War Britain : Hayward Gallery, London, [10.3.–22.4.1990] : Art Gallery Wolverhampton, [10.3.–22.4.1990] : Manchester City Art Gallery and Cornerhouse, Manchester, [5.5.–10.6.1990]*. London: Hayward Gallery, 1989.

Armitage, David. *The Ideological Origins of the British Empire*. Cambridge: Cambridge University Press, 2000.

Arneil, Barbara. "Liberal Colonialism, Domestic Colonies and Citizenship." *History of Political Thought* 33 (2012).

Arnett, James. "Neoliberalism and False Consciousness before and after Brexit in Zadie Smith's NW." *Explicator* 76, no. 1 (January 2, 2018): 1–7.

Assemble. "Assemble." https://assemblestudio.co.uk.

Azcárate, Matilde Córdoba. *Stuck with Tourism: Space, Power, and Labor in Contemporary Yucatan*. Berkeley: University of California Press, 2020.

Back, Les, and John Solomos. "Black Politics and Social Change in Birmingham, UK: An Analysis of Recent Trends." *Ethnic and Racial Studies* 15, no. 3 (July 1, 1992): 327–51.

Bahng, Aimee. *Migrant Futures: Decolonizing Speculation in Financial Times*. Illustrated ed. Durham, NC: London: Duke University Press, 2018.

Bailey, Peter. *Leisure and Class in Victorian England: Rational Recreation and the Contest for Control, 1830–1885*. London: Routledge, 2014.

Balibar, Étienne. "Brexit, the Anti-Grexit." Versobooks.com. https://www.versobooks.com/blogs/2735-brexit-the-anti-grexit.

———. "Structural Causality, Overdetermination, and Antagonism." In *Postmodern Materialism and the Future of Marxist Theory: Essays in the Althusserian Tradition*, ed. David F. Ruccio and Antonio Callari. Hanover, NH: University Press of New England [for] Wesleyan University Press, 1996.

———. *We, the People of Europe? Reflections on Transnational Citizenship*. Princeton, NJ: Princeton University Press, 2009.

Banerjee, Tridib. "US Planning Expeditions to Postcolonial India: From Ideology

to Innovation in Technical Assistance." *Journal of the American Planning Association* 75, no. 2 (March 27, 2009): 193–208.
Barber, Tony. "Nostalgia and the Promise of Brexit." Financial Times, July 19, 2018. https://www.ft.com/content/bf70b80e-8b39-11e8-bf9e-8771d5404543.
Barkham, Patrick. "Britain's Housing Crisis: Are Garden Cities the Answer?" *Guardian*, October 1, 2014. https://www.theguardian.com/politics/2014/oct/01/britains-housing-crisis-are-gaden-cities-the-answer-ebbsfleet-kent-green-belt.
Bataille, Georges. *The Absence of Myth: Writings on Surrealism*. London: Verso, 2006.
——— . *The Tears of Eros*. Trans. Peter Connor. San Francisco: City Lights, 2001.
Battersea Power Station Development Company (BPSDC). "An Englishman in New York." *Powerhouse* 4 (2015).
——— . "Community Charter." 2014.
——— . "Foster + Partners Design Book." 2014.
——— . "Living Architecture." *Powerhouse* 3 (2014).
——— . "Positive Energy." *Powerhouse* 1 (2014).
——— . "The Cranes." 2017. https://batterseapowerstation.co.uk/about/heritage-cranes.
——— . "The Icon Book." 2014.
——— . *The Placebook*. London: BPSDC and JTP Press, 2014.
——— . "Wild at Heart." *Powerhouse* 5 (2016).
Batty, Michael, and Stephen Marshall. "Thinking Organic, Acting Civic: The Paradox of Planning for Cities in Evolution." *Landscape and Urban Planning* 166 (2017): 4–14.
Baucom, Ian. *Out of Place: Englishness, Empire, and the Locations of Identity*. Princeton, NJ: Princeton University Press, 1999.
BBC. "Blair's Speech: Single Mothers Won't Be Forced to Take Work." 1997. http://www.bbc.co.uk/news/special/politics97/news/06/0602/blair.shtml.
BBC News. "Boris Johnson: First Speech as PM in Full." July 24, 2019. https://www.bbc.com/news/uk-politics-49102495.
——— . "EU Referendum: The Result in Maps and Charts." June 24, 2016. https://www.bbc.com/news/uk-politics-36616028.
——— . "PM: Broken Society Tops My Agenda." August 15, 2011. https://www.bbc.com/news/uk-politics-14524834.
——— . "Yorkshire: Slag Heaps to Ski Slopes." March 10, 2004. http://news.bbc.co.uk/2/hi/business/3545591.stm.
Beattie, Martin. "Sir Patrick Geddes and Barra Bazaar: Competing Visions, Ambivalence and Contradiction." *Journal of Architecture* 9, no. 2 (2004): 131–50.
Beauchamp, Zack. "Brexit Was Fueled by Irrational Xenophobia, Not Real Economic Grievances." Vox, June 25, 2016. https://www.vox.com/2016/6/25/12029786/brexit-uk-eu-immigration-xenophobia.
Beaumont, Alexander. *Contemporary British Fiction and the Cultural Politics of Disenfranchisement*. London: Palgrave Macmillan, 2015.

Beinart, William, and Lotte Hughes. *Environment and Empire*. Oxford: Oxford University Press, 2007.
Bell, Torsten. "The Referendum, Living Standards and Inequality." *Resolution Foundation* (blog), June 24, 2016. https://www.resolutionfoundation.org/media/blog/the-referendum-living-standards-and-inequality/.
Bellamy, Edward. *Looking Backward: From 2000 to 1887*. Applewood, 2000.
Benjamin, Walter. *Illuminations: Essays and Reflections*. New York: Harcourt, 1968.
———. *The Origin of German Tragic Drama*. London: Verso, 2003.
Bentley, Nick. "Trailing Postmodernism: David Mitchell's *Cloud Atlas*, Zadie Smith's NW, and the Metamodern." *English Studies* 99, no. 7 (October 3, 2018): 723–43.
Berberich, Christine, et al., eds. *Affective Landscapes in Literature, Art, and Everyday Life: Memory, Place and the Senses*. Ashgate, 2015.
Berlant, Lauren. *Cruel Optimism*. Durham, NC: Duke University Press, 2011.
Beynon, Huw. *Digging Deeper: Issues in the Miners' Strike*. London: Verso, 1985.
Bhabha, Homi K. *The Location of Culture*. 2nd ed. London: Routledge, 2004.
Bhambra, Gurminder K. "Brexit, Trump, and 'Methodological Whiteness': On the Misrecognition of Race and Class." *British Journal of Sociology* 68, no. S1 (2017): S214–32.
Bhambra, Gurminder K. "The Imperial Nostalgia of a 'Small Island.'" UK in a Changing Europe, June 4, 2018. https://ukandeu.ac.uk/the-imperial-nostalgia-of-a-small-island/.
Bhandar, Brenna. *Colonial Lives of Property: Law, Land, and Racial Regimes of Ownership*. Durham, NC: Duke University Press, 2018.
Bhattacharyya, Gargi, and John Gabriel. "Gurinder Chadha and the *Apna* Generation: Black British Film in the 1990s." *Third Text* 8, no. 27 (June 1994): 55–63.
Bigon, Liora, and Yossi Katz, eds. *Garden Cities and Colonial Planning: Transnationality and Urban Ideas in Africa and Palestine*. Manchester: Manchester University Press, 2014.
Blair, Tony. "Speech to Greater London Authority." April 4, 2006.
Blanchot, Maurice, and Pierre Joris. *The Unavowable Community*. Barrytown, NY: Station Hill, 1983.
Bleich, Erik, Carolina Caeiro, and Sarah Luehrman. "State Responses to 'Ethnic Riots' in Liberal Democracies: Evidence from Western Europe." *European Political Science Review* 2, no. 2 (July 2010): 269–95.
Bloch, Ernst, Jack Zipes, and Frank Mecklenburg. *The Utopian Function of Art and Literature*. Vol. 63. 1990.
Boardman, Philip. *The Worlds of Patrick Geddes: Biologist, Town Planner, Re-Educator, Peace-Warrior*. London: Routledge and Kegan Paul, 1978.
Boehmer, Elleke, and Dominic Davies, eds. *Planned Violence: Post/Colonial Urban Infrastructure, Literature and Culture*. Cham: Springer International, 2018.
Boos, Florence S. "'News from Nowhere and 'Garden Cities': Morris's Utopia and

Nineteenth-Century Town-Design." *Journal of Pre-Raphaelite Studies* 7, no. 2 (1998).
Booth, William. *In Darkest England and the Way Out.* Cambridge: Cambridge University Press, 2014.
Breton, Rob. "WorkPerfect: William Morris and the Gospel of Work." *Utopian Studies* 13, no. 1 (2002): 43–56.
Brown, Adrienne. *The Black Skyscraper: Architecture and the Perception of Race.* Baltimore, MD: Johns Hopkins University Press, 2017.
Brown, Jaqueline Nassy. *Dropping Anchor, Setting Sail: Geographies of Race in Black Liverpool.* Princeton, NJ: Princeton University Press, 2005.
Buder, Stanley. *Visionaries and Planners: The Garden City Movement and the Modern Community.* New York: Oxford University Press, 1990.
Burchardt, Jeremy. *Paradise Lost: Rural Idyll and Social Change in England since 1800.* London: I. B. Tauris, 2002.
Burns, John F. "As Thatcher Goes to Rest, Miners Feel No Less Bitter." *New York Times*, April 16, 2013.
Butler, Alice. "Toxic Toxteth: Understanding Press Stigmatization of Toxteth during the 1981 Uprising." *Journalism* 21, no. 4 (April 1, 2020): 541–56.
Butler, Tim, and Chris Hamnett. "Walking Backwards to the Future—Waking Up to Class and Gentrification in London." *Urban Policy and Research* 27, no. 3 (2009): 217–28.
Byrd, Jodi A. *The Transit of Empire: Indigenous Critiques of Colonialism.* Minneapolis: University of Minnesota Press, 2011.
BBC News. "Cable Says Nostalgia for 'White' UK Helped Leave Vote." BBC News, March 11, 2018. https://www.bbc.com/news/uk-politics-43364331.
———. "Cafe Owner in Race 'Warning' Sign." BBC News, July 10, 2013. https://www.bbc.com/news/uk-england-leeds-23248503.
Cadwalladr, Carole. "View from Wales: Town Showered with EU Cash Votes to Leave EU." *Observer*, June 25, 2016. https://www.theguardian.com/uk-news/2016/jun/25/view-wales-town-showered-eu-cash-votes-leave-ebbw-vale.
Cahill-Booth, Lara. "Walcott's Sea and Caribbean Geomythography." *Journal of Postcolonial Writing* 49, no. 3 (July 1, 2013): 347–58.
Carse, Ashley, and David Kneas. "Unbuilt and Unfinished." *Environment and Society* 10, no. 1 (September 1, 2019): 9–28.
Carter, Rosie. "Understanding the Drivers of HOPE and Hate." London: Hope Not Hate, September 2018.
Cattani, Francesco. "Songs and Verses of New Ethnicities: Resistance and Representation in Black British Culture." *Between* 5, no. 10 (November 30, 2015).
Centre for Cities. "Cities Outlook 2021." London, January 2021. http://www.centreforcities.org.
Cerra, Joshua F., Brook Weld Muller, and Robert F. Young. "A Transformative Outlook on the Twenty-First Century City: Patrick Geddes' Outlook Tower Revisited." *Landscape and Urban Planning* 166 (2017): 90–96.

Certeau, Michel de. *Practice of Everyday Life*. 1st ed. Berkeley: University of California Press, 2011.
Chakrabarty, Antarin. "Smart Mischief: An Attempt to Demystify the Smart Cities Craze in India." *Environment and Urbanization* 31, no. 1 (April 1, 2019): 193–208.
Chakrabarty, Dipesh. *Provincializing Europe: Postcolonial Thought and Historical Difference*. New ed. Princeton, NJ: Princeton University Press, 2009.
Chambers, Eddie. *Black Artists in British Art: A History since the 1950s*. London: Bloomsbury Academic, 2014.
———. *Things Done Change: The Cultural Politics of Recent Black Artists in Britain*. Amsterdam: Rodopi, 2012.
Chartered Institute of Personnel and Development. "Zero Hours Contracts More Widespread Than Thought—but Only Minority of Zero Hours Workers Want to Work More Hours." London, 2013.
Checker, Melissa. "Wiped Out by the 'Greenwave': Environmental Gentrification and the Paradoxical Politics of Urban Sustainability." *City & Society* 23, no. 2 (2011): 210–29.
Cherry, Gordon, and Alan Rogers. *Rural Change and Planning: England and Wales in the Twentieth Century*. London: E & FN Spon, 1996.
Classen, Constance, and David Howes. "The Museum as Sensescape: Western Sensibilities and Indigenous Artifacts." In *Sensible Objects: Colonialism, Museums, and Material Culture*, ed. Elizabeth Edwards, Chris Gosden, and Ruth B. Phillips. Oxford: Berg, 2006.
Clavel, Pierre, and Robert Young. "'Civics': Patrick Geddes's Theory of City Development." *Landscape and Urban Planning* 166 (2017).
Clegg, Nick, and Eric Pickles. "Locally-Led Garden Cities." Department for Communities and Local Government, March 2016.
Clifford, James. *The Predicament of Culture: Twentieth-Century Ethnography, Literature, and Art*. 1st ed. Cambridge, MA: Harvard University Press, 1988.
Clingman, Stephen. "England Has Changed: Questions of National Form in A Distant Shore." *Moving Worlds* 7, no. 1 (2007): 46–58.
Cohen, Robin, and Nicholas Van Hear. "Visions of Refugia: Territorial and Transnational Solutions to Mass Displacement." *Planning Theory & Practice* 18, no. 3 (July 3, 2017): 494–504.
Cohn, Bernard S., and David Scott. *Colonialism and Its Forms of Knowledge: The British in India*. Princeton, NJ: Princeton University Press, 1996.
Coleman, Alice, King's College (University of London) Staff Design Disadvantagement Team, and Sarah Brown. *Utopia on Trial: Vision and Reality in Planned Housing*. H. Shipman, 1985.
Coleman, Roy. "Reclaiming the Streets: Closed Circuit Television, Neoliberalism and the Mystification of Social Divisions in Liverpool, UK." *Surveillance & Society* 2, no. 2/3 (2004).
Coleman, Roy, and Joe Sim. "From the Dockyards to the Disney Store:

Surveillance, Risk and Security in Liverpool City Centre." *International Review of Law, Computers & Technology* 12, no. 1 (March 1, 1998): 27–45.

Collins, Michael. *Empire, Nationalism and the Postcolonial World: Rabindranath Tagore's Writings on History, Politics and Society*. 1st ed. Abingdon: Routledge, 2011.

Connell, Kieran. *Black Handsworth: Race in 1980s Britain*. Berkeley: University of California Press, 2019.

Coombes, Annie E. *Reinventing Africa: Museums, Material Culture and Popular Imagination in Late Victorian and Edwardian England*. Rev. ed. New Haven, CT: Yale University Press, 1997.

Cooper, Frederick, and Ann Laura Stoler. *Tensions of Empire: Colonial Cultures in a Bourgeois World*. Berkeley: University of California Press, 1997.

Coquereau, Elise. "Modernism and Modernity in Rabindranath Tagore." *Planeta Literatur, Journal of Global Literary Studies* 3 (2014).

Cordell, Tom, John Allan, Dickon Robinson, and Patrick Abercrombie, dir. *Utopia London*. Documentary, History, 2010.

Coslett, Paul. "International Garden Festival." BBC. http://www.bbc.co.uk/liverpool/content/articles/2009/04/28/local_history_garden_festival_feature.shtml.

Courtman, Sandra. "Dorothy's Heart of Darkness: How Europe Meets Africa in A Distant Shore." In *Caryl Phillips: Writing in the Key of Life*, ed. Bénédicte Ledent and Daria Tunca, 265–82. Amsterdam: Rodopi, 2012.

Creese, Walter L. *The Search for Environment: The Garden City, Before and After*. Baltimore, MD: Johns Hopkins University Press, n.d.

Cresswell, Tim. *Place: An Introduction*. 2nd ed. Chichester: Wiley-Blackwell, 2014.

Cunningham, Hilary. "Gated Ecologies and 'Possible Urban Worlds': From the Global City to the Natural City." In *The Natural City: Re-Envisioning the Built Environment*, ed. Ingrid Leman Stefanovic and Stephen Bede Scharper. Toronto: University of Toronto Press, 2012.

Deol, Daan. "7 Secrets of Hampstead Heath." *Londonist*, 2017. https://londonist.com/london/secret/7-secrets-of-hampstead-heath.

Datta, Ayona. "A 100 Smart Cities, a 100 Utopias." *Dialogues in Human Geography* 5, no. 1 (March 1, 2015): 49–53.

Davidson, Mark, and Loretta Lees. "New-Build 'Gentrification' and London's Riverside Renaissance." *Environment and Planning A* 37 (2005).

———. "New-Build Gentrification: Its Histories, Trajectories, and Critical Geographies." *Population, Space and Place* 16, no. 5 (2010): 395–411.

Davis, Juliet, and Andy Thornley. "Urban Regeneration for the London 2012 Olympics: Issues of Land Acquisition and Legacy." *City, Culture and Society*, no. 1 (2010): 89–98.

Dayal, Samir. "Repositioning India: Tagore's Passionate Politics of Love." *Positions: East Asia Cultures Critique* 15, no. 1 (2007): 165–208.

Debord, Guy. *Society of the Spectacle*. Detroit, MI: Black & Red, 2002.

Debuysere, Stoffel. "Signs of Struggle, Songs of Sorrow: Notes on the Politics of Uncertainty in the Films of John Akomfrah." *Black Camera* 6, no. 2 (2015): 61.

Defries, Amelia Dorothy. *The Interpreter Geddes: The Man and His Gospel*. London: Boni & Liveright, 1928.

Dehaene, Michiel. "Survey and the Assimilation of a Modernist Narrative in Urbanism." *Journal of Architecture* 7, no. 1 (January 1, 2002): 33–55.

Delveaux, Martin. "'O Me! O Me! How I Love the Earth': William Morris's *News from Nowhere* and the Birth of Sustainable Society." *Contemporary Justice Review* 8, no. 2 (June 1, 2005): 131–46.

Department for Culture, Media and Sport. "Plans for the Legacy from the 2012 Olympic and Paralympic Games." London: DCMS, 2010.

Derdiger, Paula. *Reconstruction Fiction: Housing and Realist Literature in Postwar Britain*. 1st ed. Columbus: Ohio State University Press, 2020.

Derrida, Jacques. *The Politics of Friendship*. London: Verso, 2020.

——— . *Specters of Marx: The State of the Debt, the Work of Mourning, and the New International*. New York: Routledge, 2012.

Di Maio, Alessandra. "A New World Tribe in Caryl Phillips's A Distant Shore." In *Caryl Phillips: Writing in the Key of Life*, ed. Bénédicte Ledent and Daria Tunca, 249–63. Amsterdam: Rodopi, 2012.

Dillon, Denis, and Bryan Fanning. "Developer-Led Gentrification and Legacies of Urban Policy Failure in Post-Riot Tottenham." *Community Development Journal* 54, no. 4 (October 1, 2019): 605–21.

——— . "Tottenham after the Riots: The Chimera of Community and the Property-Led Regeneration of 'Broken Britain.'" *Critical Social Policy* 35, no. 2 (May 2015): 188–206.

Donnell, Alison. "Nation and Contestation: Black British Writing." *Wasafiri* 17, no. 36 (June 2002): 11–17.

Dooling, Sarah. "Ecological Gentrification: A Research Agenda Exploring Justice in the City." *International Journal of Urban and Regional Research* 33, no. 3 (2009): 621–39.

Economist. "The Great Divide." *Economist*, September 15, 2012.

——— . "Not So Broken." *Economist*, October 4, 2012.

Edible Bus Stop. "Riot of Colour." https://theediblebusstop.com/riot-of-colour/.

Eisenman, Theodore S., and Tom Murray. "An Integral Lens on Patrick Geddes." *Landscape and Urban Planning* 166 (2017): 43–54.

Elkin, Lauren. "'Anyone over the Age of Thirty Catching a Bus Can Consider Himself a Failure': Class Mobility and Public Transport in Zadie Smith's NW." *Études Britanniques Contemporaines. Revue de la Société d'Études Anglaises Contemporaines* 49 (October 16, 2015).

——— . *Flaneuse: Women Walk the City in Paris, New York, Tokyo, Venice, and London*. New York: Random House, 2016.

Ellis, David. "'They Are Us': Caryl Phillips' A Distant Shore and the British Transnation." *Journal of Commonwealth Literature* (2013): 1–13.

Eshun, Kodwo. "Untimely Meditations: Reflections on the Black Audio Film Collective." *Nka: Journal of Contemporary African Art* 19, no. 1 (2004): 38–45.
Eshun, Kodwo, and Anjalika Sagar, eds. *The Ghosts of Songs: The Film Art of the Black Audio Film Collective*. 1st ed. Liverpool: Liverpool University Press, 2007.
Esty, Jed. *A Shrinking Island: Modernism and National Culture in England*. Princeton, NJ: Princeton University Press, 2003.
europeinafrica. "Europe in Africa — Home." https://www.europeinafrica.com.
Faulkner, Katherine. "Ten to a Room and One Shower for 75 People: Inside the 'Slum' Camp for Olympic Cleaners." *Daily Mail*, July 15, 2012.
Fernández Carbajal, Alberto. "On Being Queer and Postcolonial: Reading Zadie Smith's NW through Virginia Woolf's Mrs Dalloway." *Journal of Commonwealth Literature* 51, no. 1 (March 1, 2016): 76–91.
Ferreira da Silva, Denise. "No-Bodies: Law, Raciality and Violence." *Griffith Law Review* 18, no. 2 (January 2009): 212–36.
Florida, Richard. *The Rise of the Creative Class: And How It's Transforming Work, Leisure, Community, and Everyday Life*. Turtleback, 2003.
Ford, Robert. *Revolt on the Right: Explaining Support for the Radical Right in Britain*. 1st ed. Abingdon: Routledge, 2014.
Foreman, Jonathan. "Race, Englishness and the Media: Depictions of Urban Rioting in England, 1980–81." Lakehead University, 2014.
Foucault, Michel. "Of Other Spaces: Utopias and Heterotopias." In *Architecture Culture 1943–1968*, ed. Joan Ockman, 419–26. New York: Rizzoli, 1967.
Fowle, Frances, and Belinda Thomson. *Patrick Geddes: The French Connection*. White Cockade, 2004.
Fraser, Bashabi, ed. *A Meeting of Two Minds*. 3rd ed. Edinburgh: Word Power, 2008.
Freedland, Jonathan. "The Road to Somewhere by David Goodhart — a Liberal's Rightwing Turn on Immigration." *Guardian*, March 22, 2017. https://www.theguardian.com/books/2017/mar/22/the-road-to-somewhere-david-goodhart-populist-revolt-future-politics.
Freeman-Moir, John. "Crafting Experience: William Morris, John Dewey, and Utopia." *Utopian Studies* 22, no. 2 (2011): 202–32.
Fuchs, Ron, and Gilbert Herbert. "A Colonial Portrait of Jerusalem: British Architecture in Mandate-Era Palestine." In *Hybrid Urbanism: On the Identity Discourse and the Build Environment*, ed. Nezar AlSayyad. Westport, CT: Praeger, 2001.
Fulani, Ifeona. "Celluloid Documents: Migrant Women in Black Audio Film Collective's *Handsworth Songs* and *Twilight City*, and Sankofa Film and Video Collective's *Dreaming Rivers*." *Atlantic Studies* 15, no. 1 (2018): 1–15.
Gabrielle, Cindy. "The Civilized Pretence: Caryl Phillips and *A Distant Shore*." In *Caryl Phillips: Writing in the Key of Life*, ed. B. Ledent and D. Tunca, 309–18. Amsterdam: Rodopi, 2012.
Gagnier, Regenia. "Morris's Ethics, Cosmopolitanism, and Globalisation." *Journal of William Morris Studies*, 2005.

Gandhi, Leela. *Affective Communities: Anticolonial Thought, Fin-de-Siècle Radicalism, and the Politics of Friendship*. Durham, NC: Duke University Press, 2006.
Gaonkar, Dilip Parameshwar. "On Alternative Modernities." *Public Culture* 11, no. 1 (January 1, 1999): 1–18.
Geddes, Patrick. *Cities in Evolution*. London: Williams & Norgate, 1915.
———. "Civics as Applied Sociology, Part I." In *The Ideal City*, ed. Helen E. Meller. Leicester: Leicester University Press, 1979.
———. "Civics as Applied Sociology, Part II." In *The Ideal City*, ed. Helen E. Meller. Leicester: Leicester University Press, 1979.
———. *The Masque of Learning and Its Many Meanings; a Pageant of Education through the Ages; Devised and Interpreted by Patrick Geddes*. n.d.
———. "Town Planning towards City Development. A Report to the Durbar of Indore. By Patrick Geddes." Indore: Holkar state printing press, 1918.
———. *The World Without and the World Within: Sunday Talks with My Children*. Bournville: Saint George Press, 1905.
Gill, Martha. "Brexit: The Most Boring Important Story in the World." *New York Times*, December 14, 2018. https://www.nytimes.com/2018/12/14/opinion/sunday/theresa-may-brexit.html.
Gilmore, Abigail. "Cold Spots, Crap Towns and Cultural Deserts: The Role of Place and Geography in Cultural Participation and Creative Place-Making." *Cultural Trends* 22 (2013): 86–96.
Gilroy, Paul. *The Black Atlantic: Modernity and Double-Consciousness*. Reissue ed. Cambridge, MA: Harvard University Press, 1993.
———. "Cruciality and the Frog's Perspective: An Agenda of Difficulties for the Black Arts Movement in Britain." *Third Text* 2, no. 5 (December 1988): 33–44.
———. *Postcolonial Melancholia*. New York: Columbia University Press, 2005.
———. "There Ain't No Black in the Union Jack": *The Cultural Politics of Race and Nation*. Chicago: University of Chicago Press, 1991.
Gilroy, Paul, Jim Pines, Reece Auguiste, John Akomfrah, Lina Gopaul, and Eddie George. "Audiences/Aesthetics/Independence Interview with the Black Audio Collective." *Framework: The Journal of Cinema and Media*, no. 35 (1988): 9–18.
GLA. "It Took Another Riot," 2012. https://www.london.gov.uk/sites/default/files/it_took_another_riot.pdf.
Glancey, Jonathan. "Do We All Dream of Life in a Garden City?" *Telegraph*, November 22, 2012.
Glass, Ruth. *London: Aspects of Change*. London: MacGibbon & Kee, 1964.
Glyptis, Sue. *Countryside Recreation*. Ed. Brian Duffield. Harlow: Longman, 1991.
Gold, John, and Margaret Gold. *Olympic Cities: City Agendas, Planning, and the World's Games, 1896–2016*. Routledge, 2011.
Goodhart, David. *The Road to Somewhere: The Populist Revolt and the Future of Politics*. 1st ed. London: Hurst, 2017.

———. "Too Diverse?" *Prospect*, 2004. https://www.prospectmagazine.co.uk/magazine/too-diverse-david-goodhart-multiculturalism-britain-immigration-globalisation.

Gordillo, Gastón R. *Rubble: The Afterlife of Destruction*. Durham, NC: Duke University Press, 2014.

Gould, Kenneth A., and Tammy L. Lewis. *Green Gentrification: Urban Sustainability and the Struggle for Environmental Justice*. London: Routledge, 2016.

Gould, Peter C. *Early Green Politics: Back to Nature, Back to the Land, and Socialism in Britain, 1880–1900*. London: Harvester, 1988.

Groundwork. "Our History." https://www.groundwork.org.uk/about-groundwork/our-history/.

Grove, Richard H. *Green Imperialism: Colonial Expansion, Tropical Island Edens and the Origins of Environmentalism, 1600–1860*. Cambridge: Cambridge University Press, 1996.

Guardian. "Nick Clegg to Promise up to Three New Garden Cities with 15,000 Homes Each." *Guardian*, April 14, 2014. https://www.theguardian.com/society/2014/apr/14/nick-clegg-garden-cities-homes.

———. "Revealed: The Insidious Creep of Pseudo-Public Space in London." *Guardian*, July 24, 2017.

Guardian and the London School of Economics. "Reading the Riots: Investigating England's Summer of Disorder." Vol. 1. London, 2011.

Guha, Ranajit, ed. A *Subaltern Studies Reader, 1986–1995*. 1st ed. Minneapolis: University of Minnesota Press, 1997.

Guignery, Vanessa. "Zadie Smith's NW or the Art of Line-Crossing." *E-Rea. Revue Électronique d'Études Sur le Monde Anglophone* 11, no. 2 (July 15, 2014).

Gutzmore, Cecil. "Carnival, the State and the Black Masses in the United Kingdom." In *Inside Babylon: The Caribbean Diaspora in Britain*, ed. Winston James and Clive Harris. London: Verso, 1993.

Haggard, H. Rider. *King Solomon's Mines*. London: Penguin, 2007.

Hajer, Maarten A. "Ecological Modernisation as Cultural Politics." In *Risk, Environment and Modernity: Towards a New Ecology*, ed. Scott Lash, Bronislaw Szerszynski, and Brian Wynne. London: SAGE, 1996. http://books.google.com/books?id=Q2wsbOkprvIC.

Hall, Peter, and Colin Ward. *Sociable Cities: The 21st-Century Reinvention of the Garden City*. London: Routledge, 2014.

Hall, Stuart. "Assembling the 1980s: The Deluge—and After." In *Shades of Black: Assembling Black Arts in 1980s Britain*, ed. Sonia Boyce, Ian Baucom, and David A. Bailey. Durham, NC: Duke University Press, in collaboration with the Institute of International Visual Arts and the African and Asian Visual Artists' Archive, 2005.

———. "Black Diaspora Artists in Britain: Three 'Moments' in Post-War History." *History Workshop Journal* 61 (2006): 1–24.

———. "Signification, Representation, Ideology: Althusser and the Poststructuralist Debates." *Critical Studies in Mass Communication* 2, no. 2 (June 1985): 91–114.
Hall, Stuart, Chas Critcher, Tony Jefferson, John Clarke, and Brian Roberts. *Policing the Crisis: Mugging, the State, and Law and Order*. Basingstoke: Macmillan, 1978.
Harcourt, Bernard E. *Illusion of Order: The False Promise of Broken Windows Policing*. Cambridge, MA: Harvard University Press, 2005.
Harris, Andrew. "Art and Gentrification: Pursuing the Urban Pastoral in Hoxton, London." *Transactions of the Institute of British Geographers* 37, no. 2 (2012): 226–41.
Harris, John. "You Can't Just Catch a Bus to a Job That Doesn't Exist." *Guardian*, July 6, 2011. https://www.theguardian.com/commentisfree/2011/jul/06/job-south-wales-fantasy.
Harvey, David. *The Condition of Postmodernity: An Enquiry into the Origins of Cultural Change*. London: Wiley, 1992.
———. "The Right to the City." *New Left Review* 53 (2008): 1–16.
Hatherley, Owen. "Battersea Power Station." *Icon*. 2012.
———. *A Guide to the New Ruins of Great Britain*. London: Verso, 2011.
———. *A New Kind of Bleak: Journeys through Urban Britain*. London: Verso, 2012.
Hayes, Graeme, and John Horne. "Sustainable Development, Shock and Awe? London 2012 and Civil Society." *Sociology* 45, no. 5 (2011): 749–64.
Heley, Jesse. "Soft Spaces, Fuzzy Boundaries and Spatial Governance in Post-Devolution Wales." *International Journal of Urban and Regional Research* 37, no. 4 (2013): 1325–48.
Heseltine, Michael. "It Took a Riot," n.d.
———. *Life in the Jungle: My Autobiography*. London: Hodder & Stoughton, 2000.
Heynen, Nik, Maria Kaika, and Erik Swyngedouw. *In the Nature of Cities: Urban Political Ecology and the Politics of Urban Metabolism*. London: Taylor & Francis, 2006.
Holden, Robert. "British Garden Festivals: The First Eight Years." *Landscape and Urban Planning* 18, no. 1 (September 1989): 17–35.
Home, Robert K. *Of Planting and Planning: The Making of British Colonial Cities*. London: Taylor & Francis, 1996.
———. "Town Planning and Garden Cities in the British Colonial Empire, 1910–1940." *Planning Perspectives* 5, no. 1 (January 1, 1990): 23–37.
Horkheimer, Max, Theodor W. Adorno, and Gunzelin Noeri. *Dialectic of Enlightenment*. Stanford, CA: Stanford University Press, 2002.
Horne, John, and Garry Whannel. *Understanding the Olympics*. London: Taylor & Francis, 2012.
Houser, Tammy Amiel. "Zadie Smith's NW: Unsettling the Promise of Empathy." *Contemporary Literature* 58, no. 1 (Spring 2017): 116–49.
Howard, Ebenezer. *Garden Cities of To-morrow*. London: Faber and Faber, 1960.

Hysler-Rubin, Noah. "Arts & Crafts and the Great City: Charles Robert Ashbee in Jerusalem." *Planning Perspectives* 21, no. 4 (2006): 347–68.
———. *Patrick Geddes and Town Planning: A Critical View*. London: Routledge, 2011.
Imrie, Rob, Loretta Lees, and Mike Raco. *Regenerating London: Governance, Sustainability and Community in a Global City*. London: Routledge, 2009.
International Olympic Committee. "Final Report of the IOC Coordination Commission: Games of the XXX Olympiad, London 2012." Lausanne: IOC, 2013.
Irani, Lilly. *Chasing Innovation: Making Entrepreneurial Citizens in Modern India*. Princeton, NJ: Princeton University Press, 2019.
Isenhour, Cindy, Gary McDonogh, and Melissa Checker, eds. *Sustainability in the Global City*. Cambridge: Cambridge University Press, 2014.
Jackson, Nicole M. "Imperial Suspect: Policing Colonies within 'Post'-Imperial England." *Callaloo* 39, no. 1 (2016): 203–15.
Jacobs, Jane. *The Death and Life of Great American Cities*. Reissue ed. New York: Vintage, 1992.
Jacobs, Michael. "Margaret Thatcher and the Inner Cities" *Economic and Political Weekly* 23, no. 38 (1988): 4.
Jager, Michael. "Class Definition and the Esthetics of Gentrification." In *Gentrification of the City*, ed. Neil Smith and Peter Williams. Winchester Place: Allen & Unwin, 1986.
Jameson, Fredric. *Archaeologies of the Future: The Desire Called Utopia and Other Science Fictions*. London: Verso, 2005.
Jerng, Mark C. *Racial Worldmaking: The Power of Popular Fiction*. 1st ed. New York: Fordham University Press, 2017.
Jones, Donna V. *The Racial Discourses of Life Philosophy: Négritude, Vitalism, and Modernity*. New York: Columbia University Press, 2010.
Jones, Rhys, Mark Goodwin, Martin Jones, and Kevin Pett. "'Filling In' the State: Economic Governance and the Evolution of Devolution in Wales." *Environment and Planning C: Government and Policy* 23, no. 3 (2005): 337–60.
JRF. "Brexit Vote Explained: Poverty, Low Skills and Lack of Opportunities," August 26, 2016. https://www.jrf.org.uk/report/brexit-vote-explained-poverty-low-skills-and-lack-opportunities.
Kalliney, Peter J. *Cities of Affluence and Anger: A Literary Geography of Modern Englishness*. Charlottesville: University of Virginia Press, 2007.
Keeling, Kara. *Queer Times, Black Futures*. New York: New York University Press, 2019.
Keiller, Patrick, dir. *London*, 1994. http://www.imdb.com/title/tt0110377/.
———. *Robinson in Ruins*, 2010. http://www.imdb.com/title/tt1714893/.
———. *Robinson in Space*, 1997. http://www.imdb.com/title/tt0120028/.
Keith, Michael. *Race, Riots and Policing: Lore and Disorder in a Multi-Racist Society*. London: UCL Press, 1993.

Kelling, George L., and James Q. Wilson. "Broken Windows." *Atlantic*, March 1, 1982. https://www.theatlantic.com/magazine/archive/1982/03/broken-windows/304465/.

Kennelly, Jacqueline, and Paul Watt. "Sanitizing Public Space in Olympic Host Cities: The Spatial Experiences of Marginalized Youth in 2010 Vancouver and 2012 London." *Sociology* 45, no. 5 (2011): 765–81.

Kenny, Michael. *The Politics of English Nationhood*. Oxford: Oxford University Press, 2014.

Kern, Leslie. "From Toxic Wreck to Crunchy Chic: Environmental Gentrification through the Body." *Environment and Planning D: Society and Space* 33, no. 1 (2015): 67–83.

Khan, Naveeda. "Geddes in India: Town Planning, Plant Sentience, and Cooperative Evolution." *Environment and Planning D: Society and Space* 29, no. 5 (2011): 840–56.

Khanna, Neetu. *The Visceral Logics of Decolonization*. Durham, NC: Duke University Press, 2020.

Kincaid, Jamaica. *A Small Place*. New York: Farrar, Straus and Giroux, 2000.

King, A. D. *The Bungalow: The Production of a Global Culture*. Oxford: Oxford University Press, 1984.

Kinna, Ruth. "William Morris: Art, Work, and Leisure." *Journal of the History of Ideas* 61, no. 3 (2000): 493–512.

Kishore, Alpana. "Looking at Central Vista through a Different Lens: How World Class Is 'World Class'?" *Newslaundry*. https://www.newslaundry.com/2021/12/02/looking-at-central-vista-through-a-different-lens-how-world-class-is-world-class.

Knepper, Wendy. "Revisionary Modernism and Postmillennial Experimentation in Zadie Smith's NW." In *Reading Zadie Smith: The First Decade and Beyond*, ed. Philip Tew. London: A&C Black, 2013.

Kollewe, Julia, and Hilary Osborne. "Battersea Power Station Home Prices 'Defying All Logic.'" *Guardian*, November 28, 2014.

Kondo, Marie. *The Life-Changing Magic of Tidying Up: The Japanese Art of Decluttering and Organizing*. Clarkson Potter/Ten Speed, 2014.

Koven, Seth. *Slumming*. Princeton, NJ: Princeton University Press, 2004.

Kwak, Nancy H. *A World of Homeowners: American Power and the Politics of Housing Aid*. Chicago: University of Chicago Press, 2018.

Laclau, Ernesto. *On Populist Reason*. London: Verso, 2018.

Lang, Michael H. *Designing Utopia: John Ruskin's Urban Vision for Britain and America*. Black Rose, 1999.

"Langtree Festival Gardens, Liverpool." http://www.waterscapeslimited.com/projects/langtree-festival-gardens-liverpool-44.aspx.

Latham, David. "*News from Nowhere* as Autoethnography: A Future History of 'Home Colonization.'" In *Writing on the Image: Reading William Morris*. Toronto: University of Toronto Press, 2007.

Lauria, Mickey. "Waterfront Development, Urban Regeneration and Local Politics

in New Orleans and Liverpool." University of New Orleans, College of Urban and Public Affairs Working Papers, 1994.
Lea, John, and Simon Hallsworth. "Understanding the Riots: John Lea and Simon Hallsworth Put the Riots into Political and Historic Perspective." *Criminal Justice Matters* 87, no. 1 (March 2012): 30–31.
Ledent, Bénédicte. "'Of, and Not of, This Place': Attachment and Detachment in Caryl Phillips' A *Distant Shore*." *Kunapipi* 26, no. 1 (2004): 152–60.
Lees, Loretta, Tom Slater, and Elvin Wyly. *Gentrification*. London: Routledge, 2008.
Lefebvre, Henri. *The Production of Space*. Trans. Donald Nicholson-Smith. 1st ed. Malden, MA: Wiley-Blackwell, 1992.
Lehin, Barbara. "Giving a Voice to the Ethnic Minorities in 1980s French and British Cinemas." *Studies in European Cinema* 2, no. 3 (January 2005): 213–25.
LeVine, Mark. "Conquest through Town Planning: The Case of Tel Aviv, 1921–48." *Journal of Palestine Studies* 27, no. 4 (1998).
Ley, David. "Artists, Aestheticisation and the Field of Gentrification." *Urban Studies* 40, no. 12 (2003): 2527–44.
Li, Tania Murray. *The Will to Improve: Governmentality, Development, and the Practice of Politics*. Durham, NC: Duke University Press, 2007.
Lloyd, David. *Irish Times: Temporalities of Modernity*. Field Day, 2008.
———. *Under Representation: The Racial Regime of Aesthetics*. 1st ed. New York: Fordham University Press, 2018.
Lloyd, David, and Paul Thomas. *Culture and the State*. London: Routledge, 2014.
Loftman, Patrick, and Brendan Nevin. "Prestige Projects and Urban Regeneration in the 1980s and 1990s: A Review of Benefits and Limitations." *Planning Practice & Research* 10, no. 3–4 (August 1995): 299–316.
London—2012. "Towards a One Planet 2012." London: London 2012, 2009.
London Assembly Environment Committee. "A Lot to Lose: London's Disappearing Allotments." 2006.
London Organising Committee of the Olympic Games and Paralympic Games Ltd. *A Vision for the Olympic Games and Paralympic Games*. London: LOCOG, 2004.
———. "London 2012 Olympic Games Final Report." London: LOCOG, 2013.
López-Ropero, Lourdes. "Searching for a 'Different Kind of Freedom': Postcoloniality and Postfeminist Subjecthood in Zadie Smith's NW." *Atlantis* 38, no. 2 (December 2016): 123–39.
Lowe, Lisa. *The Intimacies of Four Continents*. Illustrated ed. Durham, NC: Duke University Press, 2015.
Lyotard, Jean-François, and Georges Van Den Abbeele. *The Differend*. Minneapolis: University of Minnesota Press, 1988.
Macdonald, Murdo J. S. "Education, Visual Art and Cultural Revival: Tagore, Geddes, Nivedita, and Coomaraswamy." *Gitanjali & Beyond* 1, no. 1 (November 9, 2016): 39–57.
Maher, Ashley. *Reconstructing Modernism: British Literature, Modern Architecture, and the State*. New York: Oxford University Press, 2020.

Maltz, Diana. *British Aestheticism and the Urban Working Classes, 1870–1900: Beauty for the People.* Springer, 2005.

Mandler, Peter, and Susan Pedersen. *After the Victorians: Private Conscience and Public Duty in Modern Britain.* London: Taylor & Francis, 2005.

Marcus, David. "Post-Hysterics: Zadie Smith and the Fiction of Austerity." *Dissent* 60, no. 2 (Spring 2013): 67–73.

Marriott, David. *Haunted Life: Visual Culture and Black Modernity.* New Brunswick, NJ: Rutgers University Press, 2007.

Marx, John. *The Modernist Novel and the Decline of Empire.* Cambridge: Cambridge University Press, 2005.

Mason, Rowena. "Ukip's Godfrey Bloom Will Not Apologise over 'Bongo Bongo Land' Comments." *Guardian*, August 7, 2013. https://www.theguardian.com/politics/2013/aug/07/ukip-bongo-bongo-land-godfrey-bloom.

Massey, Doreen. *Space, Place, and Gender.* Minneapolis: University of Minnesota Press, 1994.

——— . *World City.* London: Polity, 2007.

Matless, David. *Landscape and Englishness.* London: Reaktion, 2005.

McCarthy Stone. "Retirement Homes in Yorkshire." 2014. https://www.mccarthyandstone.co.uk/retirement-properties-for-sale/locations/yorkshire/.

McLeod, John. "Diaspora and Utopia: Reading the Recent Work of Paul Gilroy and Caryl Phillips." In *Diasporic Literature and Theory—Where Now?*, ed. Mark Shackleton. Newcastle upon Tyne: Cambridge Scholars Pub., 2008.

Meacham, Standish. *Regaining Paradise: Englishness and the Early Garden City Movement.* New Haven, CT: Yale University Press, 1999.

——— . *Toynbee Hall and Social Reform, 1880–1914: The Search for Community.* New Haven, CT: Yale University Press, 1987.

Mehta, Uday Singh. *Liberalism and Empire: A Study in Nineteenth-Century British Liberal Thought.* Chicago: University of Chicago Press, 2018.

Meller, Hellen. *The Ideal City.* Leicester: Leicester University Press, 1979.

——— . *Patrick Geddes: Social Evolutionist and City Planner.* New York: Routledge, 1990.

Mellor, Leo. Reading the Ruins: Modernism, Bombsites and British Culture. Cambridge: Cambridge University Press, 2011.

Mercer, Kobena. "Black Art and the Burden of Representation." *Third Text* 4, no. 10 (March 1990): 61–78.

Metcalf, Thomas R. *An Imperial Vision: Indian Architecture and Britain's Raj.* Berkeley: University of California Press, 1989.

Migration Observatory. "UK Public Opinion toward Immigration: Overall Attitudes." Migration Observatory, 2018. https://migrationobservatory.ox.ac.uk/resources/briefings/uk-public-opinion-toward-immigration-overall-attitudes-and-level-of-concern/.

Mill, John Stuart. *The Collected Works of John Stuart Mill. Vol. 3: Principles of Political Economy, Part II.* Online Library of Liberty, 1848.

Miller, Elizabeth Carolyn. "William Morris, Print Culture, and the Politics of Aestheticism." *Modernism/Modernity* 15, no. 3 (December 3, 2008): 477–502.
Miller, Mervyn. *Hampstead Garden Suburb: Arts and Crafts Utopia?* History Press, 2006.
Morris, William. *News from Nowhere and Other Writings.* New ed. London: Penguin, 1994.
Mufti, Aamir R. *Forget English! Orientalisms and World Literatures.* Reprint ed. Cambridge, MA: Harvard University Press, 2018.
Muñoz, José Esteban. *Cruising Utopia: The Then and There of Queer Futurity.* New York: New York University Press, 2009.
Myers, Garth Andrew, and Makame Ali Muhajir. "The Afterlife of the Lanchester Plan: Zanzibar as the Garden City of Tomorrow." In *Garden Cities and Colonial Planning: Transnationality and Urban Ideas in Africa and Palestine,* ed. Liora Bigon. Manchester: Manchester University Press, 2014.
Myers, Kevin, and Ian Grosvenor. "Birmingham Stories: Local Histories of Migration and Settlement and the Practice of History." *Midland History* 36, no. 2 (2011): 149–62.
Nairn, Tom. *Pariah: Misfortunes of the British Kingdom.* London: Verso, 2002.
Nancy, Jean-Luc. *The Inoperative Community.* Minneapolis: University of Minnesota Press, 1991.
Neocleous, Mark. "Social Police and the Mechanism of Prevention: Patrick Colquhoun and the Condition of Poverty." *British Journal of Criminology* 40, no. 4 (n.d.): 18.
Newby, Howard. *Country Life: A Social History of Rural England.* London: Weidenfeld and Nicolson, 1987.
Newman, Barry. "British Tinderbox: A Year after the Riots, Toxteth Is Still Racked by Anger and Despair." *Wall Street Journal,* July 2, 1982.
Nicolazzo, Sal. *Vagrant Figures: Law, Literature, and the Origins of the Police.* New Haven, CT: Yale University Press, 2020.
ODA. "Demolish, Dig, Design." London: Olympic Delivery Authority, 2007.
———. "A Summer to Remember." London: Olympic Delivery Authority, 2013.
Orlando, Sophie. *British Black Art: Debates on Western Art History.* Paris: Dis Voir, 2016.
Orwell, George. *The Road to Wigan Pier.* New York: Harcourt, 1958.
Osborne, Hilary. "Poor Doors: The Segregation of London's Inner-City Flat Dwellers." *Guardian,* July 25, 2014.
Osuna, José Javier Olivas, Josh de Lyon, Kira Gartzou-Katsouyanni, Alexandra Bulat, Max Kiefel, Diane Bolet, Kuba Jablonowski, and Mary Kaldor. "Understanding Brexit at the Local Level: Causes of Discontent and Asymmetric Impacts." London: London School of Economics and Political Science, 2019.
Outka, Elizabeth. *Consuming Traditions: Modernity, Modernism, and the Commodified Authentic.* New York: Oxford University Press, 2009.
Parekh, Bhikhu C. "Liberalism and Colonialism: A Critique of Locke and Mill."

In *The Decolonization of Imagination: Culture, Knowledge, and Power*, ed. Jan P. Nederveen Pieterse and Bhikhu C. Parekh. Oxford: Oxford University Press, 1997.
Parker, M. *Thatcherism and the Fall of Coal*. Ed. Oxford Institute for Energy Studies. Oxford: Oxford University Press for the Oxford Institute for Energy Studies, 2000.
Parker, Simon, and Rowland Atkinson. "Disorderly Cities and the Policy-Making Field: The 1981 English Riots and the Management of Urban Decline." *British Politics*, September 11, 2018.
Parrinder, Patrick. "Eugenics and Utopia: Sexual Selection from Galton to Morris." *Utopian Studies* 8, no. 2 (1997): 1–12.
Payton, Neal I. "The Machine in the Garden City: Patrick Geddes' Plan for Tel Aviv." *Planning Perspectives* 10, no. 4 (October 1995): 359–81.
Peacham, Henry. *The Garden of Eloquence (1593). A Facsimile Reproduction, with an Introd. by William G. Crane*. Gainesville, FL: Scholars' Facsimiles & Reprints, 1954.
Pearsall, Hamil. "Moving Out or Moving In? Resilience to Environmental Gentrification in New York City." *Local Environment* 17, no. 9 (2012): 1013–26.
Peplow, Simon. *Race and Riots in Thatcher's Britain*. Manchester: Manchester University Press, 2019.
Pes, Annalisa. "Post-Postcolonial Issues and Identities in Zadie Smith's NW." *European English Messenger* 23, no. 2 (Winter 2014): 21–27.
Phillips, Caryl. *A Distant Shore*. New York: Vintage, 2005.
Phoca, Sophia. "Filming the Alternative." *Art Monthly* 342 (2010): 7–10.
Pitts, Jennifer. *A Turn to Empire: The Rise of Imperial Liberalism in Britain and France*. Princeton, NJ: Princeton University Press, 2009.
"PM Economy Speech: 30 June 2020." Gov.UK. https://www.gov.uk/government/speeches/pm-economy-speech-30-june-2020.
Porter, Libby, and Austin Barber. "The Meaning of Place and State-Led Gentrification in Birmingham's Eastside." *City* 10, no. 2 (July 1, 2006): 215–34.
Povinelli, Elizabeth A. *Economies of Abandonment: Social Belonging and Endurance in Late Liberalism*. Durham, NC: Duke University Press, 2011.
Power, Nina. "Counter-Media, Migration, Poetry: Interview with John Akomfrah." *Film Quarterly* 65, no. 2 (December 1, 2011): 59–63.
Poynter, Gavin. "The 2012 Olympic Games and the Reshaping of East London." In *Regenerating London: Governance, Sustainability, and Community in a Global City*, ed. R. Imrie, L. Lees, and M. Raco. London: Taylor & Francis, 2008.
Price, Sally. *Primitive Art in Civilized Places*. 2nd ed. Chicago: University of Chicago Press, 2002.
Pune Smart City Development Corporation. "Pune Smart City: Place-Making." 2017. https://smartnet.niua.org/sites/default/files/resources/Pune%20Placemaking%20-%20Concept%20notes.pdf.
Quastel, Noah. "Political Ecologies of Gentrification." *Urban Geography* 30, no. 7 (2013): 694–725.

Rabinow, Paul. *French Modern: Norms and Forms of the Social Environment.* Cambridge, MA: MIT Press, 1991.
Raco, Mike, and Emma Tunney. "Visibilities and Invisibilities in Urban Development: Small Business Communities and the London Olympics 2012." *Urban Studies* 47, no. 10 (2010): 2069–91.
Ramamurthy, Anandi. *Black Star: Britain's Asian Youth Movements.* London: Pluto Press, 2013.
Rancière, Jacques. *Disagreement.* Trans. Julie Rose. Minneapolis: University of Minnesota Press, 2005.
Ranguin, Josiane. "Borderland Strangers in Caryl Phillip's A Distant Shore." In *A Fluid Sense of Self: The Politics of Transnational Identity*, ed. Silvia Schultermandl and Şebnem Toplu. Vienna: Lit, 2010.
Rao-Cavale, Karthik. "Patrick Geddes in India: Anti-Colonial Nationalism and the Historical Time of Cities in Evolution." *Landscape and Urban Planning* 166 (2017): 71–81.
Ravetz, Alison. *Council Housing and Culture: The History of a Social Experiment.* London: Taylor & Francis, 2001.
Ridley, Jane. "Edwin Lutyens, New Delhi, and the Architecture of Imperialism." *Journal of Imperial and Commonwealth History* 26, no. 2 (May 1998): 67–83.
Rieder, John. *Colonialism and the Emergence of Science Fiction.* Illustrated ed. Middletown, CT: Wesleyan University Press, 2008.
"Riots: Theresa May's Speech on 11 August 2011." Gov.UK. https://www.gov.uk/government/speeches/riots-theresa-mays-speech-on-11-august-2011.
Roberts, Nicholas E. "Dividing Jerusalem-British Urban Planning in the Holy City." *Journal of Palestine Studies* 42, no. 4 (2013).
Rodrigues, Jeff. "The Riots of '81." *Marxism Today*, 1981. http://banmarchive.org.uk/collections/mt/pdf/81_10_18.pdf.
Rodríguez-Pose, Andrés. "The Revenge of the Places That Don't Matter (and What to Do about It)." *Cambridge Journal of Regions, Economy, and Society* 11, no. 1 (March 10, 2018): 189–209.
Romphf, Josh. "'Invention in the Name of Community': Workshops, the Avant-Garde, and the Black Audio Film Collective." *Kino: The Western Undergraduate Film Studies Journal* 1, no. 1 (June 10, 2010). https://ojs.lib.uwo.ca/index.php/kino/article/view/6249.
Romyn, Michael. "'London Badlands': The Inner City Represented, Regenerated." *London Journal* 44, no. 2 (May 4, 2019): 133–50.
Rushdie, Salman. *Imaginary Homelands: Essays and Criticism, 1981–1991.* New York: Penguin, 1992.
Ryan-Collins, Josh, and Paul Sander-Jackson. "Fool's Gold: How the 2012 Olympics Is Selling East London Short, and a 10 Point Plan for a More Positive Local Legacy." London: New Economics Foundation, 2008.
Saha, Poulomi. "Singing Bengal into a Nation: Tagore the Colonial Cosmopolitan?" *Journal of Modern Literature* 36, no. 2 (2013): 1.

Said, Edward W. *Culture and Imperialism*. New York: Vintage, 1994.
Sampson, Robert J., and Stephen W. Raudenbush. "Seeing Disorder: Neighborhood Stigma and the Social Construction of 'Broken Windows.'" *Social Psychology Quarterly* 67, no. 4 (December 1, 2004): 319–42.
Sanders, Matthew. "The Changing Face of the Labour Market: Temporary Versus Permanent." *International Business Times*, May 22, 5.
Sartori, Andrew. "The British Empire and Its Liberal Mission." *Journal of Modern History* 78, no. 3 (September 1, 2006): 623–42.
Sassen, Saskia. *The Global City: New York, London, Tokyo*. Princeton, NJ: Princeton University Press, 2013.
Scarman, Leslie. *The Scarman Report*. Middlesex: Penguin, 1981.
Schalk, Sami. *Bodyminds Reimagined: (Dis)Ability, Race, and Gender in Black Women's Speculative Fiction*. Durham, NC: Duke University Press Books, 2018.
Scott, James C. *Seeing Like a State: How Certain Schemes to Improve the Human Condition Have Failed*. New Haven, CT: Yale University Press, 1999.
Self, Will. *Psychogeography*. London: A&C Black, 2013.
Semble. "The Edible Bus Stop Presents . . . Roll Out the Barrows." https://semble.org/blog/the-edible-bus-stop-presents-roll-out-the-barrows/.
Sessolo, Simone. "An Epic of Riots: The Multitude as Hero in Handsworth Songs." *Journal of Popular Culture* 47, no. 4 (2014): 742–59.
SevenStreets. "Bloom and Bust: Liverpool's Garden Festival Site." http://www.sevenstreets.com/bloom-and-bust-liverpools-garden-festival-site/.
Sharma, Niharika. "The Chief Architect of Central Vista Thinks Modi's Project Will Define 'New India.'" *Quartz*. https://qz.com/india/2032660/chief-architect-explains-why-modis-central-vista-is-important/.
Shenker, Jack. "Privatised London: The Thames Path Walk That Resembles a Prison Corridor." *Guardian*, February 24, 2015.
Shoard, Marion. *A Right to Roam*. Oxford: Oxford University Press, 1999.
Shoshkes, Ellen. "Jaqueline Tyrwhitt Translates Patrick Geddes for Post World War Two Planning." *Landscape and Urban Planning* 166 (2017): 15–24.
Simonds, John. *Garden Cities 21: Creating a Livable Urban Environment*. New York: McGraw-Hill, 1994.
Simone, AbdouMaliq. *For the City Yet to Come: Changing African Life in Four Cities*. Illustrated ed. Durham, NC: Duke University Press Books, 2004.
Sinclair, Iain. *Ghost Milk: Calling Time on the Grand Project*. 1st ed. London: Hamish Hamilton, 2011.
———. *The Last London: True Fictions from an Unreal City*. Oneworld, 2017.
———. *London: City of Disappearances*. London: Penguin, 2007.
———. *London Orbital*. London: Penguin, 2003.
Slavin, Molly. "Nowhere and Northwest, Brent and Britain: Geographies of Elsewhere in Zadie Smith's NW." *Journal of the Midwest Modern Language Association* 48, no. 1 (2015): 97–119.
Smart Cities Mission. "Making a City Smart: Learnings from the Smart Cities

Mission." Delhi: Ministry of Housing and Urban Affairs, Government of India, March 2021. https://smartnet.niua.org/sites/default/files/resources/making_a_city_smart_mar2021.pdf.

Smith, Neil. "Gentrification, the Frontier, and the Restructuring of Urban Space." In *Gentrification of the City*, ed. Neil Smith and Peter Williams. Winchester Place: Allen & Unwin, 1986.

———. "New Globalism, New Urbanism: Gentrification as Global Urban Strategy." *Antipode*, 2002.

———. "Toward a Theory of Gentrification: A Back to the City Movement by Capital, Not People." *Journal of the American Planning Association* 45, no. 4 (1979): 538–48.

Smith, Neil, and Peter Williams, eds. *Gentrification of the City*. Winchester Place: Allen & Unwin, 1986.

Smith, Zadie. NW. New York: Penguin, 2012.

Söderström, Ola. "Paper Cities: Visual Thinking in Urban Planning." *Ecumene* 3, no. 3 (1996).

Solnit, Rebecca. *Wanderlust: A History of Walking*. London: Granta, 2014.

Sonder, Ines. "'May Be Solved by the Construction of Garden Cities': German-Jewish Literary Proposals on Garden Cities in Eretz Israel." In *Garden Cities and Colonial Planning: Transnationality and Urban Ideas in Africa and Palestine*, ed. Liora Bigon and Yossi Katz. Manchester: Manchester University Press, 2014.

Southbank Centre. "Festival of Neighbourhood." London, 2013. http://www.southbankcentre.co.uk/whatson/festivals-series/festival-of-neighbourhood/about-festival-of-neighbourhood-0.

Spivak, Gayatri Chakravorty. *A Critique of Postcolonial Reason: Toward a History of the Vanishing Present*. 1st ed. Cambridge, MA: Harvard University Press, 1999.

Stanley, Henry Morton. *In Darkest Africa*. LULU, 2010.

Steadman, Philip. *The Evolution of Designs: Biological Analogy in Architecture and the Applied Arts*. London: Routledge, 1979.

Stedelijk Museum. "Solution or Utopia? Design for Refugees." https://www.stedelijk.nl/en/exhibitions/solution-or-utopia-design-for-refugees.

Stewart, Murray. "Between Whitehall and Town Hall: The Realignment of Urban Regeneration Policy in England." *Policy & Politics* 22, no. 2 (1994): 133–46.

Stoler, Ann Laura. *Imperial Debris: On Ruins and Ruination*. Durham, NC: Duke University Press, 2013.

———. *Race and the Education of Desire: Foucault's History of Sexuality and the Colonial Order of Things*. Durham, NC: Duke University Press, 1995.

Streeby, Shelley. "Speculative Writing, Art, and World-Making in the Wake of Octavia E. Butler as Feminist Theory." *Feminist Studies* 46, no. 2 (2020): 510.

Su, Ping. "Madness and Silence in Caryl Phillips's *A Distant Shore* and *In the Falling Snow*." In *Madness in Anglophone Caribbean Literature: On the Edge*, ed. Bénédicte Ledent, Evelyn O'Callaghan, and Daria Tunca, 63–80. Cham: Springer, 2018.

SuperHeroes. "Refugee Emojis." https://hellosuperheroes.com/work/refugee-emojis/.
Tawadros, Gilane. "Beyond the Boundary: The Work of Three Black Women Artists in Britain." *Third Text* 3, no. 8–9 (September 1989): 121–50.
Terada, Rei. *Looking Away: Phenomenality and Dissatisfaction, Kant to Adorno*. 1st ed. Cambridge, MA: Harvard University Press, 2009.
Thacher, David. "Order Maintenance Policing." In *The Oxford Handbook of Police and Policing*, ed. M. D. Reisig and R. J. Kane, 1st ed., 122–47. Oxford: Oxford University Press, 2014.
Thompson, E. P., and Peter Linebaugh. *William Morris: Romantic to Revolutionary*. 1st ed. Oakland: PM, 2011.
Tongson, Karen. *Relocations: Queer Suburban Imaginaries*. New York: New York University Press, 2011.
Tournay-Theodotou, Petra. "Strange Encounters: Nationhood and the Stranger in Caryl Phillips's *A Distant Shore*." In *Caryl Phillips: Writing in the Key of Life*, ed. B. Ledent and D. Tunca, 293–307. Amsterdam: Rodopi, 2012.
Tuan, Yi-Fu. *Space and Place: The Perspective of Experience*. Reprint ed. Minneapolis: University of Minnesota Press, 2001.
Tyrwhitt, Jaqueline. *Patrick Geddes in India*. London: Lund Humphries, 1947.
UCL. "Positive Economic Impact of UK Immigration from the European Union: New Evidence." *UCL News*, November 5, 2014. https://www.ucl.ac.uk/news/2014/nov/positive-economic-impact-uk-immigration-european-union-new-evidence.
Unwin, Raymond. *Nothing Gained by Overcrowding: How the Garden City Type of Development May Benefit Both Owner and Occupier*. Forgotten Books, 2018.
Valle, Paola Della. "Migration and Multiplicity of Belonging in Caryl Phillips." *Le Simplegadi* 18 (2018): 65–74.
Vaninskaya, Anna. *William Morris and the Idea of Community*. Edinburgh: Edinburgh University Press, 2010.
Vathi, Zana, and Kathy Burrell. "The Making and Unmaking of an Urban Diaspora: The Role of the Physical Environment and Materialities in Belongingness, Displacement, and Mobilisation in Toxteth, Liverpool." *Urban Studies* 58, no. 6 (May 1, 2021): 1211–28.
Wacquant, Loïc. *Urban Outcasts: A Comparative Sociology of Advanced Marginality*. 1st ed. Cambridge: Polity, 2007.
Waldron, Dara. "The Utopian Promise: John Akomfrah's Poetics of the Archive." *Open Library of Humanities* 3, no. 1 (February 21, 2017): 4.
Wales, Sir Robin. "Strategic Regeneration Framework: An Olympic Legacy for the Host Boroughs." London: Host Boroughs Joint Committee, 2009.
Walkowitz, Judith R. *City of Dreadful Delight: Narratives of Sexual Danger in Late-Victorian London*. Chicago: University of Chicago Press, 2008.
Warnes, Andrew. "Enemies Within: Diaspora and Democracy in *Crossing the River* and *A Distant Shore*." *Moving Worlds* 7, no. 1 (2007): 33–45.
Watkins, Micky. *Henrietta Barnett in Whitechapel: Her First Fifty Years*. London: Hampstead Garden Suburb Archive Trust, 2005.

Watt, Paul. "Social Housing and Regeneration in London." In *Regenerating London: Governance, Sustainability, and Community in a Global City*, ed. R. Imrie, L. Lees, and M. Raco. London: Taylor & Francis, 2008.
Weinroth, Michelle. *Reclaiming William Morris: Englishness, Sublimity, and the Rhetoric of Dissent*. Montreal: McGill-Queen's University Press, 1996.
Wells, Lynn. "The Right to a Secret: Zadie Smith's NW." In *Reading Zadie Smith: The First Decade and Beyond*, ed. Philip Tew. London: A&C Black, 2013.
Welter, Volker M. *Biopolis: Patrick Geddes and the City of Life*. Cambridge, MA: MIT Press, 2002.
——— . "The 1925 Master Plan for Tel-Aviv by Patrick Geddes." *Israel Studies* 14, no. 3 (2009): 94–119.
What If: projects. "Octavia's Orchard." London: What If: projects, 2013. http://www.what-if.info/Octavias_Orchard.html.
Williams, Grant, Rory Loughnane, and William E. Engel, eds. "Henry Peacham, The Garden of Eloquence (1593)." In *The Memory Arts in Renaissance England: A Critical Anthology*, 120–23. Cambridge: Cambridge University Press, 2016.
Williams, Patrick. "Imaged Communities: Black British Film in the Eighties and Nineties." *Critical Survey* 8, no. 1 (1996): 3–13.
Williams, Raymond. *The Country and the City*. New York: Random House, 2013.
Williamson, J. "Two Kinds of Otherness: Black Film and the Avant-Garde." *Screen* 29, no. 4 (December 1, 1988): 106–13.
Winter, James. *Secure from Rash Assault: Sustaining the Victorian Environment*. Berkeley: University of California Press, 2002.
Wright, Edgar, dir. *The World's End*. Universal Pictures, Focus Features, Relativity Media, 2013.
Wright, Patrick. *A Journey through Ruins: The Last Days of London*. Oxford: Oxford University Press, 2009.
Young, Robert F., and Pierre Clavel. "Planning Living Cities: Patrick Geddes' Legacy in the New Millennium." *Landscape and Urban Planning* 166 (2017): 1–3.
Young, Robert J. C. *Colonial Desire: Hybridity in Theory, Culture, and Race*. 1st ed. Abingdon: Routledge, 1995.
Zaidman, Miki, and Ruth Kark. "Garden Cities in the Jewish Yishuv of Palestine: Zionist Ideology and Practice 1905–1945." *Planning Perspectives* 5433 (January 2015).
Zapata, Beatriz Pérez. "'In Drag': Performativity and Authenticity in Zadie Smith's NW." *International Studies. Interdisciplinary Political and Cultural Journal* 16, no. 1 (September 1, 2014): 83–95.
Zukin, Sharon. *Loft Living: Culture and Capital in Urban Change*. New Brunswick, NJ: Rutgers University Press, 1982.

Index

Note: Illustrations are indicated by page numbers in *italics*.

Abercrombie, Patrick, 64, 231n64
absence, 13, 219–20; Brexit and, 282n126; community and, 53–56, 229n38, 241n86; in *A Distant Shore*, 209–10; in *Handsworth Songs*, 98, 117, 120–21, 123; in *Last London*, 132–33; in NW, 171, 177, 181; postcolonialism and, 21; ruin and, 124; "unbuilt" and, 228n31
Adams, Ross, 144
Adorno, Theodor, 10, 281n104, 283n10
Affective Communities (Gandhi), 53
Akomfrah, John, 92, 98, 114, 125, 255n82, 257n100. See also *Handsworth Songs* (Akomfrah)
Althusser, Louis, 213, 281n111
anticipatory policing, 107–12
Appel, Hannah, 17, 231n59
Araeen, Rasheed, 256n86
Arneil, Barbara, 37
Arnett, James, 272n76
Arts and Crafts movement, 22, 34, 50–51, 53, 58, 248n109
Ashbee, Charles, 51, 64, 75, 240n69, 242n14, 246n58, 248n109
Ashcroft, Bill, 192
Atkinson, Rowland, 100
Auguiste, Reece, 116, 255n82
Australia, 35–36, 234n11

Baerwald, Alex, 88
BAFC. *See* Black Audio Film Collective (BAFC)
Bahng, Aimee, 11, 228n30
Baker, Herbert, 64
Baldwin, Stanley, 51
Balibar, Etienne, 213
Ball, John, 164
Barker, Robert, 75
Barkham, Patrick, 31
Barnett, Henrietta, 39–40, 64, 179, 225n6, 237n34
Barnett, Samuel, 39, 240n69
Bataille, Georges, 54
Battersea Power Station (BPS), 5, 5, 25, 127, 138–56, 139–41, 143, 153, 189, 263n56, 263n58, 264n68, 265n87, 266n96
Baudelaire, Charles, 128, 156
Bauman, Zygmunt, 282n4
Bayley, Stephen, 264n68
Beattie, Martin, 76
Beaumont, Alexander, 273n100
Bellamy, Edward, 35, 51, 226n16
Benjamin, Walter, 128–29, 156, 264n67
Berger, John, 128
Bergson, Henri, 82
Berlant, Lauren, 130, 161, 268n11
Bhandar, Brenna, 14

Birdwood, George, 245n57
Birmingham, 115, 251n30
Black Arts Division, 255n82
Black Atlantic, 123
Black Audio Film Collective (BAFC), 98, 113–16, 255n82, 257n92
Blair, Tony, 4, 127, 134, 136, 187
Blanchot, Maurice, 54
Bloch, Ernst, 9–11, 13, 227n20
Boehmer, Elleke, 16
Boos, Florence S., 240n79
Booth, Charles, 35, 39
Booth, William, 38–40
Bournville, 236n27
Boyce, Sonia, 113
BPS. *See* Battersea Power Station (BPS)
Bratton, William, 107
Bréton, André, 128
Brexit, 26–27, 187–91, 281n110, 282n116
British National Party, 196
Brixton, 98, 109, 253n55
"Broken Britain" political campaign, 5
broken-windows policing, 97, 107–8, 110–11, 254n62
Brown, Adrienne, 10
Brown, Jacqueline Nassy, 95
brownfield sites, 25, 31, 101, 103, 127, 137, 187, 253n48, 265n87
Burchardt, Jeremy, 279n74
Burne-Jones, Edward, 164, 165
Burnet, John, 248n109
Butler, Alice, 250n12

Cable, Vince, 276n10
Cadbury, George, 48, 236n27, 243n18
Calbi, Maurizio, 204
Cameron, David, 4–5, 127, 137, 187, 204, 263n56
"Can the Subaltern Speak?" (Spivak), 116
capitalism, 6, 11, 15, 33, 104, 187; cultivation and, 90; development and, 156; disaster, 137; in *A Distant Shore*, 212; guilt and, 168; heteronormative, 161; Howard and, 37, 239n65; last, 130, 275n124; in *Last London*, 133; late, 149–56, 164; legacy of, 216; London Olympics and, 136; Morris and, 53
Carse, Ashley, 228n31
Chaikin, Benjamin, 248n109
Chakrabarty, Antarin, 219
Chakrabarty, Dipesh, 11, 16

Chambers, Eddie, 113, 124
Chicago, 35
Church Socialist Union, 239n58
Cities in Evolution (Geddes), 60, 62–63, 65, 70
City Beautiful movement, 35
Clavel, Pierre, 69
Clegg, Nick, 31
Clifford, James, 76
Clingman, Stephen, 204
Coe, Sebastian, 134
Cohen, Robin, 218
Cohn, Bernard, 76
Cole, Henry, 245n57
Coleman, Alice, 24, 95, 97, 109–12, 255n76, 255n78
Coleman, Roy, 120
colonialism, 5; in Australia, 35–36; garden-city movement and, 32; gentrification as, 146–47; governmentality and, 37; legacy of, 186; liberal, 5, 12, 15, 18–19, 22, 24, 37, 50–51, 66, 96; ongoing, 275n1; progress and, 11; utopian genre and, 9. *See also* postcolonialism
colonial knowledge, 76–84
Colquhoun, Patrick, 108
community, 13, 17; absence and, 53–56; aesthetics of, 56–57; Battersea Power Station and, 138–39; in Coleman, 109; in critical thought, 229n38; development and, 156; in *A Distant Shore*, 192, 194, 209–10; dream of, planning and, 57–59; environment and, 96; excess and, 53–56; garden-city movement and, 50–57; insufficiency and, 53–56; in NW, 175, 179–80; planning and, 57–59, 62; policing and, 101, 110; private property and, 112; restoration and, 152; vibrancy and, 105
concrete utopias, 9–10, 227n20
Conservative Party, 96–97, 100–101, 196
Cooper, Frederick, 37
Coquereau, Elise, 86
Cortonwood strike, 197, 197–99, 198
Courtman, Sandra, 281n102
COVID-19 pandemic, 158, 187
Creative Evolution (Bergson), 82
Crossing the River (Phillips), 193

Daguerre, Louis-Jacques-Mandé, 75
da Silva, Denise, 220

Davis, Dominic, 16
Davis, Juliet, 262n50
Dayal, Samir, 85
Debord, Guy, 128
Debuysere, Stoffel, 124
decay, 4–5, 66, 70, 96, 106–10, 156, 190, 225n6, 236n26
Dehaene, Michiel, 78–79
Della Valle, Paola, 192
Derrida, Jacques, 54–55
development: dead ends of, 156–57; discourse of, 127; legacy and, 185; rural, 196–99; temporal progression of, 144–45; as term, 127
development corporations, 96, 104. *See also* Urban Development Corporations (UDCs)
Dillon, Denis, 251n30
Di Maio, Allesandra, 192, 209
disorder, 97–98, 107–8, 110, 255n71
Distant Shore, A (Phillips), 26, 63, 185–86, 191–212, 281n102
Doyle, Arthur Conan, 9
dreaming, 71, 244n45
Dream of John Ball, A (Morris), 164, 165, 234n7
Drew, Jane, 91
Duggan, Mark, 125
dystopia, 9, 218, 227n17

East India Company, 235n15
Ebbsfleet, 31–32, 233n3
Eder, David, 247n86
Edgelands, 132
Edible Bus Stop, 1, 2, 225n5, 226n9
education, 73–76, 85–90
Elkin, Lauren, 159, 261n27, 269n29
Eshun, Kodwo, 114, 123, 125
Ethnic Minorities Committee, 255n82
"Europe in Africa" (EIA) (exhibit), 215–18, 216, 218
Evans, Graeme, 137
excess, 12–13, 53–56, 131; colonialism and, 49; ecologies of, 128–34; garden-city movement and, 34, 46–47; in Geddes, 62; in Howard, 42; riots and, 125; slums and, 38; in Wakefield, 36

Fabian, Johannes, 271n72
Fanning, Bryan, 251n30
Festival of Britain, 1

Festival of Neighborhood (London), 1–4, 2–3, 225n5, 226n9
fiction, speculative, 8–13, 33–34, 51, 226n17
Foucault, Michel, 10, 12, 79
Fry, Maxwell, 91
future-proofing, 139–41

Gabrielle, Cindy, 195
Galton, Francis, 57, 71
Gandhi, Leela, 53–54, 229n38
Gandy, Matthew, 145
Garden Cities of Tomorrow (Howard), 31, 34–37, 41–50, 43, 47–48, 49–50, 65, 237n38, 238n50
garden-city movement, 6, 6, 15, 18, 22–23; aesthetic of, 32–33; community and, 50–57; Ebbsfleet in, 31–32; Geddes and, 63–65; home colonies and, 32; imaginary of, 32, 40; Morris and, 50–57; nature in, 40; place creation and, 44–50; slums and, 38–40; social reconciliation and, 44–50; social-spatial integration and, 41–44
Garden of Eloquence, The (Peacham), 226n12
Geddes, Arthur, 242n10
Geddes, Patrick, 6, 7, 17, 23, 59, 76–78, 80, 83, 144, 186, 231n64, 240n69; Coleman vs., 112; education and, 73–76; garden-city movement and, 63–65; gardening and, 70–72; in India, 60; models and, 66–67; place and, 61–63; on planning, 61; politics and, 68–69; range and volume of work of, 61–62; slums and, 65–66; university and, 85–90; vitalism and, 82
Gehry, Frank, 277n15
gender, 159–60, 171, 174, 209, 211
gentrification, 25–26, 104, 251n30; aesthetic of, 130, 150; as colonialism, 146–47; ecological, 144–49; exclusivity and, 126; frontier and, 131; placemaking and, 142, 144–49; rural, 26–27; in Sinclair, 129–30
George, Edward, 255n82
Ghana, 91
Gilmore, Abigail, 190
Gilroy, Paul, 20, 210–11, 257n90, 281n109
Glancey, Jonathan, 32
Glass, Ruth, 129
globalization, 188, 217
Glyptis, Sue, 198
Godard, Jean-Luc, 128
Godwin, George, 237n35

Golden, Thelma, 114
Goodhart, David, 189, 211, 276n13
Gopaul, Lina, 255n82
Gordillo, Gastón R., 129
Gould, Peter, 237n33
Gramsci, Antonio, 230n48
greenfield sites, 103, 127
Griffin, Nicholas, 196
Guide to the New Ruins of Great Britain, A (Hatherley), 128
Guignery, Vanessa, 184

Haekel, Ernst, 247n83
Haggard, H. Rider, 9
Hall, Stuart, 112
Hampstead Garden Suburb, 39
Handsworth, 98
Handsworth Songs (Akomfrah), 92, 98, 112–25, 118, 120, 122, 184, 257n90, 257n100
Happy Colony (Pemberton), 246n59
Harcourt, Bernard, 108
Harkness, Margaret, 237n36
Harris, Andrew, 264n64
Harvey, David, 79
Hatherley, Owen, 128, 263n56
Hayes, Graeme, 137, 261n43
Hebrew University, 87, 89, 90, 247n90
Hegel, Georg, 54
Herzl, Theodor, 88
Heseltine, Michael, 24, 95–107, 112, 115, 125, 127, 251n19
heterotopia, 10
high modernism, 15–16, 231n56
Hill, Miranda, 39
Hill, Octavia, 4, 15, 35, 39, 64, 225n6, 230n46
Himid, Lubaina, 113
Hobson, J. A., 234n13
Holliday, Clifford, 248n109
Home, Robert, 40, 64
Home and the World, The (Tagore), 86
home colonies, 32–33, 37
home ownership, 161, 171–72
"Homes for Heroes" program, 91
Horne, John, 137, 261n43
Houser, Tammy, 183
Housing and Town Planning Acts, 91, 97, 233n79
Howard, Ebenezer, 6, 17–18, 22–23, 31, 34–37, 41–47, 47, 49–50, 144, 233n79, 237n38, 238n50, 239nn65–66
humanism, 18, 39, 183, 242n10
Hysler-Rubin, Noah, 62, 245n47

imaginaries, 5–6; garden-city movement and, 32, 40; of home ownership, 161
immigration, 115–17
In Darkest England (Booth), 38, 236n22
India, 60–65, 68–69, 73, 76–78, 81, 85–87, 218–19, 242n12, 243n31, 243n33, 243n35, 248n97, 249n114
innovation, 149–56
insufficiency, 53–56

Jacob, Michael, 105
Jacobs, Jane, 109
Jager, Michael, 150
Jameson, Fredric, 228n32, 238n45
Jarrett, Cynthia, 119
Job, Otto, 95
Johnson, Avril, 255n82
Johnson, Boris, 127, 187, 277n15
Jones, Donna, 82
Joseph, Claire, 255n82
Journey through Ruins, A: The Last Days of London (Wright), 128

Kalliney, Peter J., 235n20
Kark, Ruth, 84, 248n108
Keats, John, 245n45
Keeling, Kara, 10–11, 228n30, 228n32
Keiller, Patrick, 128
Kelling, George L., 107
Kendall, Henry Edward, 248n109
Kern, Leslie, 148–49
Kincaid, Jamaica, 192
King, Martin Luther, Jr., 117
Kinna, Ruth, 57
Kipling, John, 245n57
Klein, Naomi, 137
Kneas, David, 228n31
Knepper, Wendy, 166, 273n104
knowledge, colonial, 76–84
Kropotkin, Peter, 35, 41
Kunzman, Klaus, 126

Laclau, Ernesto, 213
Lanchester, Henry Vaughan, 64
Last Angel of History, The (Akomfrah), 125
Last London, The (Sinclair), 128–34
lastness, 23–25, 35, 130–32, 157–58, 161, 167, 178
Latham, David, 241n85
Lauria, Mickey, 252n41
Lea valley, 128
Le Corbusier, 91

INDEX

Ledent, Bénédicte, 280n97
Lehin, Barbara, 256n83
Lever, Henry, 48, 236n27
Lever, William, 243n18
Levine, Mark, 88
Levy, Alexander, 88
Ley, David, 150
Li, Tania, 14
Life in the Jungle (Heseltine), 101
Light, William, 234n11
Liverpool, 32, 95–96, 105–6, 252n33
Livingstone, Ken, 127
Lloyd, David, 14, 154, 238n52
localism, 190, 244n34
locality, 14–17, 22–23, 25, 79, 231n65, 276n13
London, 126–57, 135, 139–41, 143, 153. See also Battersea Power Station (BPS)
London (Keiller), 128
London 2012 Olympic project, 127–28, 134–38, 189, 261n37, 261n43, 262n46, 262n48
London: Aspects of Change (Glass), 129
London Thames Gateway Development Corporation, 125
Looking Backward (Bellamy), 51, 226n16
López-Ropero, Lourdes, 183
Lowe, Lisa, 270n40
Lutyens, Edwin, 64, 243n30

magical realism, 227n17
Maher, Ashley, 18
Maltz, Diana, 237n36
Manchester, 32
Marx, Karl, 213
Masque of Learning and Its Many Meanings, The (Geddes), 63, 81
Massey, Doreen, 196
Mathison, Trevor, 255n82
Matless, David, 14, 40
Mayor, Albert, 91
McLeod, John, 211
Meacham, Standish, 239n58
Mears, Frank, 248n109
Mehta, Uday, 50
Meller, Hellen, 243n35
Meno (Plato), 247n83
Mercer, Kobena, 114, 257n90
Merseyside, 98
Metcalf, Thomas, 75
metonyms, 17, 35, 80, 99–100, 104, 106
Mill, J. S., 235n15
Miller, Carolyn, 52
model-village movement, 39

modernism, high, 15–16, 231n56
Modi, Narendra, 218–19
More, Thomas, 8
Morris, William, 9, 22, 33–35, 41, 50–58, 126, 161, 164, 226n16, 233n80, 234n7, 237n37
Mrs. Dalloway, 158–59
Mumford, Lewis, 61
Muñoz, José, 9–10

Nancy, Jean-Luc, 54
nationalism, 20, 85–86, 107, 123, 192, 211–12, 217–19
Nature of Blood, The (Phillips), 193
Nehru, Jawaharlal, 91, 249n114
neoliberalism, 101, 112, 150, 179, 252n34
Newby, Howard, 198–99
New Earswick, 236n27
New Kind of Bleak, A (Hatherley), 128
New Labour, 96–97, 101, 196
Newman, Barry, 95
Newman, Oscar, 110
News from Nowhere (Morris), 9, 22, 33–34, 51–58, 126, 226n16, 241n85
New Urbanism, 19, 219
Nicolazzo, Sal, 103
normativity, 17, 26, 32, 34, 101, 152, 160–61, 163, 192–93
NW (Smith), 26, 158–84, 234n7, 270n47, 270n52, 270n54, 271n65, 271nn71–72, 272n91, 273n104, 274n114, 274nn118–19, 274n124

Octavia's Orchard (What If: Projects), 1–4, 2–3
Olympics. *See* London 2012 Olympic project
Operation Swamp 81, 109
Oppenheimer, Franz, 88
order-maintenance policing, 97, 107–8, 110–11
Orlando, Sophie, 113
Orwell, George, 240n79
Osborne, George, 31
Ousmania University, 247n90
Outka, Elizabeth, 46
Outlook Tower, 63, 74–75, 79, 80, 81, 245n55

Paleologou, Effie, 132
Palestine, 64–65, 84, 87–90, 240n69, 248n109
pandemic, 158, 187
Parker, Barry, 239n59

Parker, Simon, 100
Patel, Bimal, 283n7
paternalism, 33, 39, 249n114
Pathfinder project, 32
Payton, Neal, 84
Peacham, Henry, 226n12
Pemberton, Robert, 246n59
Peplow, Simon, 253n55
Pes, Annalisa, 184
phenomenophilia, 227n23
Phillips, Caryl, 26, 63, 185–86, 191–212, 281n102
Pickles, Eric, 31
Piper, Keith, 113
place: creation, 44–50; Geddes and, 61–63; gentrification and, 142, 144–49; improvement of, 98–107; naturalization of, 199–204; speculative fictions of, 8–13; valuation of, 17
Plato, 247n83
policing, 97, 107–12
pop-up culture, 24
Port Sunlight, 236n27
postcolonialism, 20–24, 27, 85, 91–92, 96, 98, 119, 123–24, 171, 183–86, 192, 194, 204, 208–11, 275n1. See also colonialism
Potter, Beatrice, 39
poverty, 38, 42, 98–99, 109, 198–99, 262n46, 279n71
Powell, Enoch, 115
Power, Nina, 116
Problem of the Unemployed (Hobson), 234n13

Quatermain, Allan, 9
Queen Elizabeth Olympic Park, 134, 135

race, 20, 95–96, 98, 109, 112–25, 118, 120, 122, 125, 186
racism, 20, 99, 193–94, 207, 250n14, 256n84
Rancière, Jacques, 230n48
Ranguin, Josiane, 195
Ravetz, Alison, 231n66
real estate speculation, 129–32
Reclus, Elisée, 75
representation, 112–25, 118, 120, 122
reuse, creative, 149–56
Rhodes, Cecil, 235n18
Ricard, Sebastian, 152
"Right to Buy," 97
Rimbaud, Arthur, 128

"Riot of Colour" (Edible Bus Stop), 226n9
Road to Somewhere, The (Goodhart), 189
Roberts, Nicholas, 89
Robinson in Ruins (Keiller), 128
Robinson in Space (Keiller), 128
Rockwell, David, 142
Rodrigues, Jeff, 99
Rodríguez-Pose, Andrés, 276n14
Rogge, Jacques, 261n37
"Roll Out the Barrows" (Edible Bus Stop), 2, 225n5
Rowntree, Joseph, 236n27
rural development, 196–99
rural gentrification, 26–27
Ruskin, John, 39, 230n46

Saha, Poulomi, 85
Salvation Army, 39–40
Scarman report, 96, 253n55
Schalk, Sami, 226n17
Scott, David C., 16, 231n58
Self, Will, 128
self-actualization, 154–55
Sessolo, Simone, 116, 123, 258n103
Shades of Black (Hall), 112
Sharpe, Thomas, 239n57
Shenker, James, 126
Shock Doctrine, The (Klein), 137
Shoshkes, Ellen, 64
Sinclair, Iain, 128–34, 261n27
Sitassny, Wilhelm, 88
Slavin, Molly, 166, 180–81, 274n114
Smart Cities, 219–20
Smirke, Sydney, 237n35
Smith, Duncan, 196
Smith, Neil, 104, 131, 142
Smith, Zadie, 26, 158–84, 234n7, 272n76, 273n104
social city, 48, 48–49
social reconciliation, 44–50
social reform, 39–40
social-spatial integration, 41–44
Society for the Protection of Ancient Buildings, 237n37
Söderström, Ola, 74
Solnit, Rebecca, 261n27
Solomos, John, 115
South Africa, 64, 234n14
speculative fiction, 8–13, 33–34, 51, 226n17
Spivak, Gayatri, 116
statism, 109

INDEX   315

St. Barbe Harrison, Austen, 248n109
Steadman, Phillip, 239n61, 244n38
Stevenson, Robert Louis, 9
Stoler, Ann Laura, 37, 129
Stratford, 127
Streeby, Shelley, 9
surveillance, 109–12
Swadeshi movement, 86
"Sweepers, The" (art installation), 226n9

Tagore, Rabindranath, 63, 85–87, 233n81, 242n10, 248n97
Tel Aviv, 7, 84, 88, 245n47, 246n61
temporalities, 18–22, 134–56
Terada, Rei, 227n23
Thames Estuary, 31–32
Thames Gateway, 31–32, 127
Thatcher, Margaret, 24, 33, 95, 97, 99–102, 109, 196, 200, 203, 269n29, 278n45
Thomas, Paul, 14, 154, 238n52
Thompson, E. P., 58
Thornley, Andy, 262n50
Thornton Manor, 236n27
To-morrow: A Peaceful Path to Real Reform (Howard), 237n38
Tongson, Karen, 17
topothesia: defined, 4–5; origin of term, 226n12
Tottenham, 98
Tournay-Theodotou, Petra, 192, 209
Town and Country Planning Acts, 102, 231n64
Toxteth riots, 95–96, 98–100, 105–6, 250n12, 250n14, 251n19
Toynbee Hall, 39, 64
Treatise on the Police in the Metropolis (Colquhoun), 108
Trietsch, Davis, 88
Trump, Donald, 187
Tyrwhitt, Jaqueline, 64

UDCs. *See* Urban Development Corporations (UDCs)
unbelonging, 204–8
university, 85–90
Unwin, Raymond, 239n57, 239n59

Urban Development Corporations (UDCs), 104, 112, 252n41
utopia, 9–10, 34–35, 50–51, 176–80, 228n32; concrete, 9–10, 227n20; in critical thought, 229n38
Utopia (More), 8
Utopia on Trial (Coleman), 97, 109–10

Vagrancy Act 1824, 109
Van Hear, Nicholas, 218
vitalism, 82, 87

Wacquant, Loïc, 251n23, 258n103
Wainwright, Hilary, 196
Wakefield, Edward Gibbon, 35–36, 217, 234n11
Walcott, Derek, 123
War of the World (Wells), 9
Wayward Plants, 1
Webb, Beatrice, 237n36
Webb, Sidney, 39
Weinroth, Michelle, 51
Welter, Volker, 51, 71, 90, 244n37
What If: Projects, 1–4, 2–3
White Teeth (Smith), 272n76
Williams, Eric, 258n107
Williams, Patrick, 121
Williams, Raymond, 14, 52
Wilson, James Q., 107
Winter, James, 39
Woolf, Virginia, 158
World Without and the World Within, The (Geddes), 63, 71, 245n52
Wright, Patrick, 128

Young, Robert, 69

Zaidman, Miki, 84, 248n108
Zapata, Beatriz Pérez, 271n64
Zionism, 84, 87–89, 247n86, 248n108
Zukin, Sharon, 151

Ameeth Vijay is Assistant Professor of Literature at the University of California, San Diego.

www.ingramcontent.com/pod-product-compliance
Lightning Source LLC
Chambersburg PA
CBHW020354080526
44584CB00014B/1012